A CENTURY OF
ORANGE AND BLUE

ISBN: 1-58261-793-7

Unless otherwise noted, interior and cover photos courtesy of the University of Illinois Sports Information Office, with special thanks to University Archives and Mark Jones of The Tintype Shoppe of Photography.

Publisher: Peter L. Bannon
Senior managing editor: Susan M. Moyer
Acquisitions editor: Scott Musgrave
Developmental editor: Doug Hoepker
Art director: K. Jeffrey Higgerson
Book design: Jennifer L. Polson
Dust jacket design: Dustin Hubbart
Book layout: InnerWorkings, L.L.C.
Imaging: Dustin Hubbart, Heidi Norsen, Kenny O'Brien, Kerri Baker
Photo editor: Erin Linden-Levy
Vice president of sales and marketing: Kevin King
Media and promotions managers: Cory Whitt (regional),
      Randy Fouts (national), Maurey Williamson (print)
Editorial review: Kent Brown, Derrick Burson

Sports Publishing L.L.C.
804 North Neil Street
Champaign, IL 61820

Phone: 1-877-424-2665
Fax: 217-363-2073
Web site: www.SportsPublishingLLC.com

For my parents, brother, and Jacqui. Without your love and support, none of this would have been possible.

—Jared Gelfond

CONTENTS

FOREWORD

BY JERRY COLANGELO

I am thrilled to write the foreword for this book celebrating 100 years of Illinois basketball. Great players, coaches and championship moments have created a rich tradition and heritage at the University of Illinois.

I am proud to be a Fighting Illini (1959-1962) and to have served as captain of the 1961-62 team. My years were highlighted by playing with teammates Mannie Jackson, Govoner Vaughn, Dave Downey, and many others, along with competing against Don Nelson (Iowa), Walt Bellamy (Indiana), Jerry Lucas and John Havlicek (Ohio State) and Terry Dischinger (Purdue).

I remember like it was yesterday playing my first home game in Huff Gym against Butler. It was a dream come true to suit up and play for the Illini.

I set a goal of making it into the starting line-up for the first Big Ten game of the season. What a thrill it was to achieve that goal when on January 4, 1960, Coach Harry Combes inserted me into the starting five against Ohio State. Just a few years later, in my senior year, my last game in Huff was a very sad milestone, because it signified the end of my time in an Illini uniform in a place that I had grown to know and love.

Huff Gymnasium brings back fond memories of great games, intimate seating and noisy fans. The Assembly Hall has witnessed a continuation of Illinois basketball lore and taken it to even greater heights. Our alumni, faculty, students and fans have all shared in this 100-year journey with great support along the way for our basketball program.

The University of Illinois holds a warm place in my heart for the educational, social and competitive experiences I enjoyed while on campus. I have been blessed with much success in my personal life, and I credit my years in Champaign-Urbana as the place where I developed a solid foundation for my future.

Most importantly, I met and married my wife, Joan, while attending the University of Illinois, and we are blessed with four children and 10 grandchildren.

I know you will enjoy strolling down memory lane as you flip through the pages. Go Illini! God bless you.

▲ *Jerry Colangelo was a member of the Illinois varsity squad for three seasons between 1959 and 1962. He captained the 15-8 squad of 1961-62 on which he was a starting guard.*

PREFACE

BY LOU HENSON

To many thousands of fans throughout the years, Illinois basketball has been regarded as a program with a certain marvelous mystique. As a youngster, I was mesmerized by reports of the fabulous feats of the Whiz Kids and their fine coach, Doug Mills. Dike Eddleman brought new meaning to the term "all-around athlete" as he amazed in "superman-like" fashion, excelling in almost every sport. When Harry Combes took the helm of the Illini, the mystique broadened as the victories piled up, including three Final Four appearances. The makings of many rich, storied traditions were well underway.

The University of Illinois head basketball position was coveted by many outstanding candidates in 1975. Against mountainous odds, a relatively unknown young coach from Okay, Oklahoma was named "Lou Who", and eventually evolved into "Lou Do" courtesy of my good buddy, Dick Vitale. My 21-year stint leading the Illini was, for the most part, very rewarding. I was privileged to coach some of the finest young men anywhere. I had excellent assistants who were essential to the success we attained.

Fans from all over the state and alumni everywhere—as well as Illini administrators, faculty and staff—showed keen interest in and support for the program. Community folks were exceptionally loyal as the Rebounders booster club was formed and the establishment of the Orange Krush helped get the students heavily involved.

Many fond memories flood my mind upon reflection of my more than two decades at Illinois. Of course, the 1989 trip to the Final Four proved to be the ultimate culmination of our efforts toward achieving success in this much-celebrated program. The Flyin' Illini captured the imagination and hearts of America. Perhaps no basketball team elicited the emotion and sustained the excitement that these Illinois native sons brought to the college scene that magical season. Although I am so proud of all the other teams I coached, to me the Flyin' Illini will always be "national champions."

As we enjoy reading *A Century of Orange and Blue*, let us pay homage to this great University of the Heartland, to all the courageous student-athletes who entertained us while competing, to the behind-the-scenes support staffs and to those talented media personalities who have ably recorded it all.

GO ILLINI!

Lou Henson

Jonathan Daniel/Getty Images

▲ *Coach Lou Henson watches his Illini take flight during the 1988-89 season.*

ACKNOWLEDGMENTS

BY JARED GELFOND

There are so many people to thank that I am bound to forget a few.

First off, I have to thank Dr. Michael Raycraft, who for years has not only been a mentor but a great friend as well. In late December we laid out a plan and followed it to a 'T'. Who would have ever thought it would work to perfection? Without your help and guidance, none of this would have been possible.

Next, I would remiss not to thank the people who took a big chance on me six months ago, especially Illinois Sports Information Director, Kent Brown. I realize that bringing me back to Champaign was out of the ordinary and I greatly appreciate your effort to make that happen.

I definitely need to thank Chris Tuttle of the Varsity I Association. About six years ago, he was the one who saw a little loud freshman in the Orange Krush and got me involved with UI sports. Now, he is a great friend and without his help, I would never have been considered for this project. There are few people, if any, who care about their job and UI sports more than Chris.

It was an honor and a pleasure to work with Loren Tate. His knowledge on the history of Illinois basketball is unmatched and just having his name attached to the book afforded me instant credibility with the guys I interviewed.

Over the last six months, I have had the opportunity to work with what I consider the best and certainly the hardest working Sports Information department in the country. I certainly appreciate all of you welcoming a stranger under unusual circumstances and making him feel comfortable. Thanks to Cassie Arner, Derrick Burson, Mike Koon, Dick Barnes, Marsha Goldenstein and Michelle Warner.

To the remaining un-named members of the Illinois Basketball Centennial Committee: Rod Cardinal, Warren Hood, Sue Johnson, Dave Johnson and Marty Kaufmann. Thanks for your faith in me and all of your help throughout the project. I have been extremely fortunate to be a part of such a hard working and dedicated committee and I am very excited for the Centennial Season.

I also extend a special thanks to the Sports Information interns and friends—Travis Steiner, Kevin Walsh, Jamie Hixson and Derek Neal. Whether it was scanning photos, looking something up for me, or just giving me a much-needed break, their help was certainly appreciated. I'm looking forward to a great year in Champaign.

I received a lot of help in reviewing old films, pictures and articles. So thanks to Bill Maher, Debbie Pfeiffer and Chris Prom at the University Archives for all of their help and time.

I can't forget John Livengood, who is a big Illinois fan that helped me out more than he will ever imagine in sending me old game tapes.

I also need to thank Jeff Johnson of Orange and Blue News who afforded me the opportunity to stay involved with Illinois sports after I graduated. Without his help, I wouldn't be in the position I am today.

Thanks also to my group of die-hard Illini fans—Kevin Connor, Alex Marks, Barry Marks, Ryan Manning and Manas Venepally. In celebrating wins and agaonzing over losses, we have traveled all over the country to watch the Illini play. There is no better group of guys to call friends.

I certainly owe a lot to my family and friends back home in New York because they sacrificed a lot during this project. My parents and brother have always been there for me when I needed support and the thanks for that probably goes unsaid most of the time. I love you guys—thanks for everything.

I especially want to thank my girlfriend Jacqui, who probably sacrificed more than anyone else. Thank you Jac, for all of your support and encouragement.

Lastly and most importantly, I would like to thank the hundreds of former players, coaches, managers and alumni who took the time out of their busy schedules to share their stories and memories for the book. I thoroughly enjoyed talking to each and every one of you and without you there wouldn't be a book. I only wish that all UI basketball fans could listen to your Illini tales, because it certainly gave me a greater appreciation of the history of the program. Every single one of you was important in laying the foundation on which Illinois basketball stands today. The only regret I have throughout this entire project is that I didn't get a chance to talk to everyone who has been a part of this school's rich history.

The UI basketball program is on the verge of something special. It's going to be a fun ride watching Coach Weber and company take this program to the next level. Let's all enjoy minute of it!

GO ILLINI!

GAME NIGHT

The Official Game Day Program of the University of Illinois $2.00

Illinois vs. Memphis
December 13, 2003
Assembly Hall

welcome to Champaign:
ILLINI HEAD COACH
BRUCE WEBER

making a splash:
FIGHTING ILLINI
SWIMMING
AND DIVING

JIMMY JOHN'S®
Since 1983
WORLD'S GREATEST
GOURMET SANDWICHES

www.fightingill...

GAME NIGHT

The Official Game Day Program of the University of Illinois

Illinois vs. Michigan State
February 10, 2004
Assembly Hall

all energy, all the time:
ILLINI SOPHOMORE
DEE BROWN

report from the links:
ILLINOIS GOLF

$2.00

verizon wireless

www.fightingillini.com

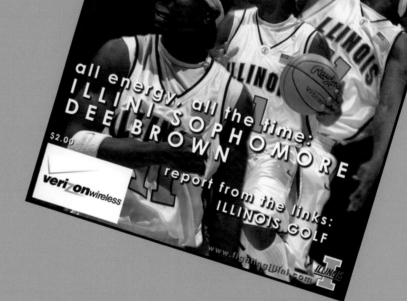

CHAPTER ONE

WE ARE THE CHAMPIONS, ONCE AGAIN 2003-04

Meet Bruce Weber, orchestra conductor, "A Rhapsody in Orange." One year in Illini Nation, and the longtime Purdue assistant basketball coach is as popular as a cherry-topped sundae on a hot summer evening.

Meet Dee and Deron, rock stars. Two years on campus and their shoulders are weak from back-slaps, their fingers cramped from autograph signings.

Weber and dual point guards Dee Brown and Deron Williams were the ringleaders as the Fighting Illini, shelving an old "sleeping giant" reputation, spread around bright orange coloring like a six-inch snowfall during the winter of 2003-04. They high-stepped over long-standing barriers and carried the UI pennant far afield.

Have you ever seen counter-coloring amid Carver-Hawkeye Arena's Black and Gold in Iowa City? Not until February 25, when 110 cleverly disguised Orange Krush members took advantage of waning Hawkeye fan interest and purchased tickets to make their presence felt.

Have Illinoisans ever invaded nearby Purdue? Not until Boilermaker followers fell off Gene Keady's wavering bandwagon, leaving spacious sections for Illini travelers on March 3.

A healthy expedition of cheering Illinoisans even trekked to Ohio State, convening with the team near courtside after a scary Big Ten clincher, the 64-63 triumph hinging on a last-second no-call as a hands-high James Augustine defended the lane.

It was unfortunate that more members of Illini Nation couldn't be present later at sold-out Nationwide Arena in Columbus, Ohio, when Williams scored 31 points and the torrid Illini destroyed all-talk, no-action Cincinnati, 92-68, with 63.6 percent shooting to reach the NCAA round of 16.

A disappointing 72-62 loss to Duke in Atlanta did not diminish expectations for the next two seasons as a 26-7 campaign sent researchers harking back a half-century or more.

Illinois defeated all 10 conference rivals, capturing the first outright Big Ten championship since 1952.

UI's 19-point win at Iowa City was the school's most decisive victory there since 1954. The victory for Weber's Orange Illini at Iowa was an elusive feat for World War II's Whiz Kids, the late-80s Flying Illini and two Bill Self products. (Fact is, UI teams won in Iowa City just twice from 1965 to 1990.)

Winning 12 straight down the stretch, the Illini went unbeaten in February for the first time since 1954, and posted the longest season-ending conference streak (10) since Andy Phillip, Gene Vance and the Whiz Kids went 12-0 in 1943.

The 2004 Illini posted road victories over arch-rivals Iowa, Indiana and Purdue for the first time in 67 seasons, dating to 1937 when Doug Mills was a rookie coach and the team featured senior Harry Combes and sophomore Lou Boudreau. The '37 Illini ended 14 years of failure in West Lafayette when sub center Hale Swanson's putback nipped Purdue 38-37, and they also ruled at Iowa, 40-29, and Indiana, 42-25.

The streak of six straight Big Ten road wins was the longest in a single season since 1943. The Illini also won six when the 1955 Illini captured their last two league games on the road, and the 1956 Illini won their first four.

◀ *The 2003-04 Illini overcame off-the-court adversity, injury, and a lengthy adjustment period to their new coach to eventually become a cohesive unit.*

The second-round NCAA rout of Cincinnati, in which the Illini drained eight consecutive three-pointers, was deemed Illinois's most outstanding NCAA tournament performance since the Flying Illini downed Louisville and Syracuse in Minneapolis in 1989. And Illinois, seeded No. 5, beat a higher seed (the Bearcats were No. 4) for the first time ever.

The 14-for-16 finish saw Illinois win 10 of those games in eight arenas in other states, a monumental accomplishment. The 13-3 Big Ten mark gave Illinois a 59-21 record (73.8 percentage) over the last five years, best in the conference.

ILLINI STAND 63-3 AT HOME

With Weber returning for his second season and the squad virtually intact, Illini basketball has never looked more promising. Sparkplugs Brown and Williams are moving to the forefront of the national consciousness. Luther Head and Roger Powell have persevered in the face of real and imagined obstacles to reach their senior campaign as firmly established standouts.

ESPN's Andy Katz tabs the Illini well up in the preseason Top 10. Various preseason projections label Illini guards "among the best in the nation."

This team has transformed the drab, conservative Assemby Hall into Planet Orange, crackling with electricity and defying those who say it is outmoded and doesn't provide home court advantage. Remarkably, under three coaches, the Illini possess the best five-year home-court record in the country (63-3), have captured four Big Ten championships since 1998, reached the NCAA's Elite Eight in 2001 and made the Sweet Sixteen in 2002 and 2004.

Much of this credit goes to athletic director Ron Guenther, the UI's "one-man search committee." Operating off his short list when Lou Henson retired in 1996, Guenther waded through local controversy when he rebuffed Henson's recommendation to promote assistant Jimmy Collins, being more influenced by Lon Kruger's performance in directing underdog Florida to the Final Four in 1994. In his second UI season, Kruger pieced together five seniors recruited by

Henson—Brian Johnson, Jerry Hester, Jarrod Gee, Matt Heldman and Kevin Turner—and directed a surprising 10-for-11 stretch run to finish 13-3 and share the Big Ten crown with powerhouse Michigan State.

When Kruger left to coach the Atlanta Hawks in 2000, Guenther again went into temporary seclusion—he always has "stealth" candidates—and came up with another winner, Tulsa's Bill Self. In three UI campaigns, Self produced nationally ranked clubs that finished No. 4 in 2001, No. 13 in 2002 and No. 11 in 2003. With the experienced duo of Frank Williams and Cory Bradford at the guards, and Lincoln's Brian Cook emerging as a front-line scorer, Self's Illini shared the Big Ten crown in his first two years. Then Brown, Williams and Augustine came aboard as Illinois took the 2003 Big Ten Tournament championship after missing the league title in the final second at Wisconsin.

Around Champaign-Urbana, the ground shook like a mighty earthquake when North Carolina's firing of Matt Doherty drew Roy Williams from Kansas, creating an opening too enticing and too close to Self's home for him to turn down.

A stunning success at Southern Illinois University, Weber was the choice after speculation revolved around Final Four finisher Tom Crean of Marquette, Missouri Valley perennial Dana Altman of Creighton, and Hoopeston native Thad Matta of Xavier, among others. Guenther's "stealth candidate" on this venture was Rice's Willis Wilson, but Weber was chosen for his work ethic, forthrightness, competitiveness and court sense. An 18-year assistant at Purdue, he drew Keady's support: "Some guys are born to coach. Bruce Weber is one of those guys."

Reflecting with *The News-Gazette's* Brett Dawson at season's end, Guenther said: "There was some struggle in the beginning (but) it really started to come around. We had two turning points, one against Providence (a 70-51 collapse) in New York, and one at Wisconsin (a 76-56 loss). Then we had the big win at Indiana (51-49). Against Michigan State, we did the 'Paint the Hall Orange' thing, which we'd done before, but this was the most significant orange I've seen. And then we had the Orange Krush kids, because tickets were available,

show up on the road, and we started to have an entourage. That's one of the most gratifying things that's ever happened for me because we saw people start to travel. For the first time, there were tickets at Iowa, there were tickets at Purdue. And people jumped on it.

"It's been something kind of magical that happened because they're magical kids," continued Guenther. "I think Bruce called them orphans at one time, and people rallied around them. We had the (off-court) problem that might have even accelerated the internal bonding, but for the most part, I've had no problems with these guys from a character standpoint, and they do the job in the classroom. So they're an easy group to pull for."

WEBER IN CHARGE

When Weber arrived, skeptics abounded. But some months later, when 22 midwestern media members selected Northwestern's Bill Carmody the Big Ten's "Coach of the Year," downstate Illinoisans were ready to form a necktie party, or at least a bloodless coup. Carmody upset Illinois and Wisconsin in Evanston during an 8-8 conference season, but a 14-15 NU club didn't qualify for the NIT, while Illinois won the outright championship and rattled off an unfathomable 12-game win streak that wasn't broken until the finals of the Big Ten tournament by Wisconsin. That vote, seemingly overlooking the distance Illinois traveled from early-season difficulties, brought even more of the orange brigade onto the Weber bandwagon.

Now, orange is the flavor of the day. The youth of Brown, Williams and Augustine is turning into maturity. An ever-blunt Weber is imposing his will over athletes who arrived on campus because of the Self staff, some of whom wavered about staying. Dee Brown went from considering a transfer to, "I love you, Coach. I love you!"

As he heads into Year No. 2, Weber is sinking his teeth into an operation that almost skittered out of his control early last season with the incidents of "the law and the jaw." Weber had great plans after going 28-8 and 24-7 as the Missouri Valley kingpin in his last two seasons at Southern Illinois University. He sought to bring the Illini team together with an overseas trip. Brown and Williams returned from Greece, where they starred on the U.S. Junior World team, and joined UI returnees for six August games (all wins) in Scandinavia.

But just when the season was starting, the trio of Head, Richard McBride and Aaron Spears received suspensions for off-court indiscretions. Obliged to attend daily meetings with Guenther and representatives of the chancellor's office, Weber acknowledged: "It was a bad situation. We're this new staff coming in, and we're trying to win people over and define roles, and then we had this happening. It was a major distraction, and mentally tiring. I just wanted to coach basketball."

Weber told beat writer Dawson: "I never got to the point where I was close to giving in or questioning what we were doing. But there were times where I was like, 'This is tougher than I thought it was going to be.'"

Reflecting months later, Weber told *Decatur Herald & Review* columnist Mark Tupper a revealing story.

"I'm half asleep and my daughter was yelling, 'There's a cat in the tree!' And I'm saying, 'So what? Who cares?'

"Then she says, 'Dad, it's hanging,' and I'm thinking, 'Oh, no, they used to hang Dean Smith in effigy. Now they've hung a cat and there's blood in the snow and, wow, they really do want me out of here.' That's how my mind was thinking at that point."

This was December, remember, when nothing was going smoothly. But, Tupper explained, it wasn't as it appeared. Members of the Orange Krush support group had strung up a Missouri Tiger in effigy and sprayed some orange paint in the Weber yard, all as an inspirational message to beat Missouri.

Still, from Weber's reaction, it's apparent he hadn't fully settled into his position. He was ready to think the worst. And it wasn't any easier when he was obliged to give Head, a standout in November practices, a suspension that carried through two exhibitions and the first two games. Head returned for an impressive 75-60 defeat of Temple in Philadelphia, but road losses to North Carolina (88-81) and Providence (70-51) created more uncertainties, particularly about the UI's ability to attack a zone defense.

Jamie Squire/Getty Images

▲ Coach Bruce Weber had his work cut out for him as the 2003-04 season got off to a rocky start. But he silenced his doubters when he righted the ship in early February and steered the Illini to their first outright Big Ten Championship since 1952.

Then, on December 11, a seemingly meaningless game against Maryland-Eastern Shore drew unexpected importance. First, in a defiant move, Weber arrived in black attire, later proclaiming it "a mock funeral ... marking the end of Bill Self" for all those fans making comparisons and for a media that wouldn't let it die. During the game, Williams ran into a stiff screen at midcourt, fracturing his jaw. Weeks of wiring were required. He missed three games, saw his weight drop by 26 pounds, and returned just in time to spark Illinois's nervous overtime defeat of Illinois State. He was barely regaining full strength when the Big Ten season opened.

And just as Ohio State arrived January 7 for the league opener, Head was dominating the news again. Acknowledging that he had become a serious distraction, Head offered to leave the team and transfer.

Weber elected to allow him to stay, again after weighty meetings with higher-ups, saying, "If we can save the young man, that's the most important thing."

Concerns for the program grew louder—again, everybody had an opinion—when Head absorbed another two-game suspension and Purdue, using delay tactics and shooting 60 percent in the second half, broke the UI's 23-game home win streak with a 58-54 victory. Illinois was dealt another blow when Weber, at this time not a candidate for Man of the Year, and his Fighting Illini were snookered at Northwestern, 70-60, and then fell to 3-3 in the conference with a 76-56 failure at Wisconsin.

TURNING THE CORNER

The Illini had reached the jumping-off point. It was sink or swim, fish or cut bait. Thankfully back home, they manhandled Michigan, 67-52, with Head scoring 18 and the defense holding the Wolverines to their lowest output of the season. The victory over Michigan at home was expected. But the road loomed large from that point. Heavy traveling was a feature of Illinois's late schedule, and Indiana was next in line. Mike Davis's Hoosiers were showing signs of recovering from a horrendous December, standing 5-2 in the conference after losing at Michigan State three days earlier.

Twice they led Illinois by 11 points while their fans grew increasingly loud and confident. The score held at 46-38 when Deron Williams went to the bench with 9:25 showing. If we could return and suspend that moment in time, with both clubs struggling offensively, there wasn't the slightest hint that the Illini were poised to pull this game out of the fire—let alone win all of their remaining conference games.

How could we have known? The Illini defense had been uncharacteristically porous in January. They even appeared helpless January 3 against a weak Illinois State club (which shot 54.5 percent). During that nailbiter, the Illini needed Nick Smith to earn a sharpshooter medal

◀ *Ask and ye shall receive: Coach Weber wanted guard Dee Brown to lead by example, and that's exactly what the heart and soul of the 2003-04 team did in directing the Illini to the Sweet Sixteen of the NCAA Tournament.*

in order to capture an overtime squeaker. Then Purdue checked in at 60 percent in the second half of a 58-54 win. Northwestern topped that with second-half accuracy of 61.9 in the surprise upset in Evanston. A weakened Iowa club came within 88-82 by shooting 55.3 percent, and Wisconsin drilled the Illini, 76-56, with 51.9 percent shooting accuracy.

But somehow, in that second half at Indiana, defense became the Illini forte, as it would be for the remainder of the season. The Hoosiers closed out making four of 26 field attempts, just two goals in the last 16 minutes, and none after A.J. Moye's 10-footer with 9:53 showing. Earning another medal was the enigmatic Smith. The seven-foot-two deadeye drilled 15-footers for the UI's last two baskets, and blocked Bracey Wright's late three-point attempt for a 51-49 victory.

"This was an unbelievably gutsy win," said Weber. "That's what you have to do on the road, hang in when things aren't going your way and, when your chance comes, take it. All that matters is that we got more points than Indiana."

It was a fork-in-the-road event for both clubs, Indiana falling off the charts to finish 14-15 overall, and Illinois surging to the outright title.

This was just one of several times that Weber's athletes sent researchers back for decades to complete the sentence, "Illinois, for the first time since ..." If February 3 in Bloomington, Indiana, was the turning point, the popular groundswell was ignited a week later when the 16,618-seat Assembly Hall was draped in orange for a showdown with Tom Izzo's Michigan State Spartans. Suddenly, the fans became a real-life part of it. Orange was in. Pride in Illini Nation swelled. And the team responded by donning their favorite orange uniforms.

"I always favored blue," said longtime Illini fan Joe Thompson. "I would never wear orange. I used to laugh at those who did. Now, I wouldn't think of entering the Assembly Hall wearing any other color. If I didn't have orange on, I'd buy something at the door.

"It's making a difference. We've always turned out strong for the big games, but with the players and fans in orange, we're all pulling together and it's 10 percent louder than ever before. There's a special feeling about it."

Williams (15), Augustine (16) and Luther Head (17) combined for 48 points in a 75-51 lashing of Michigan

State. It was a blowout, the worst loss suffered by the Spartans since they were routed 70-40 at Illinois the year before.

"This was amazing," said visiting Illini recruit Shaun Pruitt of West Aurora. "I didn't know it was like this."

No Illini fan had to remind his neighbor to wear orange for the follow-up February 18 clash with defending Big Ten champion Wisconsin. It had become the fashion of the day. Fair-weather fans became hoarse-throated fanatics. Septuagenarians ceased to complain about fans standing in front of them. One steal and breakaway by Dee Brown, and your typical Illini crazie turned purple, floated to the ceiling, and exploded in mid-air, never to be seen again. It was ear-popping wild, I-L-L, I-N-I reverberating from one side to the other, ordinary people taking a two-hour respite from their hum-drum lives, losing themselves in the excitement of the moment.

OK, so it wasn't pleasant to the television eye. Long camera shots couldn't distinguish Illini orange from Wisconsin red, although it was not difficult to separate Deron Williams and his 31-point outburst in a 65-57 UI triumph. The Big Ten office and associated television networks became interested in UI colors from that point on, the Illini needing clearance for their favored orange outfits in all remaining games (seven straight wins) until the Big Ten tournament in Indianapolis.

Tall hurdles remained in the UI's dash for the silver chalice. Penn State, an embarrassed 80-37 loser at Illinois and ending the season in a 0-11 tailspin, threatened in front of a partially filled Bryce Jordan Center by pulling within 47-43 with 7:21 showing. But Brown, who receives Jim Sheppard's reverberating "Dee for Threeeee" at home, went on a long-range spree without the verbal accompaniment. He nailed five extra-long second-half treys plus an eye-popping 15-foot fadeaway over seven-foot Jan Jagla to spark a 66-58 win. The "one-man fast break" was, at long last, free of his sophomore shooting slump as he assumed his anticipated share of production in the three-guard lineup with Williams and Head. With the three aces coming together as one, it was a case of spontaneous combustion. Illinois

entered the stretch run clicking on all cylinders.

ILLINI FINISH STRONG

A 78-59 blowout at Iowa drew "we're not leaving ... we're not leaving" chants from the Orange Krush as the Hawkeye fans departed with minutes remaining. This was an early version of what Cincinnati would see later, with four Illini starters reaching double figures as 38 points in the paint led to a 58.5 shooting percentage.

Northwestern was no match for the UI at home, 66-56, but struggling Purdue was waiting to produce its one special performance of the late season. It was the most stirring contest of the campaign as Smith pumped two huge treys in overtime and Head banked in a rebound to win it, 81-79, in the final second.

"When you're unselfish, when you give yourself to the team," said Weber, "good things happen."

Williams would be named first team All-Big Ten and Illini MVP, and Brown made the Big Ten's second team after a slow start. But they were equal in their contributions to a title team. That UI juggernaut wrapped it up at Ohio State, charging to a 55-41 lead, only to see the relaxed Buckeyes come storming back. Tony Stockman's three-pointer with six seconds remaining shaved the Illini's winning margin to 64-63. Brown and Williams combined for 32 points and nine assists, igniting a celebration that was cooled somewhat by the scary nature of the final seconds.

"We probably got on our heels a little bit," said Weber, "and the Ohio State crowd got into it. The Buckeyes isolated Terence Dials on the block and we didn't want to double-team him because, with our lead, we didn't want to open up three-point shots."

Orange-clad fans poured down from the upper reaches of the Schottenstein Center to form at court side as the team returned from the locker room to join them. And several hours later, a Flightstar hangar was cleared at UI-Willard Airport in Savoy to handle the hundreds of fans who greeted the team in a victory outpouring. A quest of more than a half-century for a Big Ten title had been fulfilled.

In Indianapolis for the Big Ten Tournament, the Illini set aside their orange uniforms. But they remained

Mark Jones

▲ *The moment: Luther Head's miraculous putback on an offensive rebound sealed the overtime victory against Purdue for the Fighting Illini on March 3 in West Lafayette, Indiana.*

the league's more dependable member as they became the only team to reach the semifinals all seven years of the event.

Head scored a career-high 29 and Williams broke a 54-54 tie with clutch plays as the Illini spanked Indiana, 71-59—the team's ninth win in the last 13 meetings with the Hoosiers. In the semifinal against Michigan, Brown broke loose for 21 points and the Illini had 22 assists on 27 baskets in a ninth consecutive defeat of the Wolverines, 76-60.

The 12-game streak ended in the tournament finale as Wisconsin dominated, 70-53, against a frigid UI club that shot a miserable 32.7 percent. Brown scored 15 in a hustling performance but the Illini were otherwise flat.

"We couldn't get shots, couldn't get a run, couldn't get momentum," said Weber.

Would the loss help the Illini in NCAA tournament? There was speculation to that end when the

Illini blistered Murray State (72-53) and Cincinnati (92-68) in the Nationwide Arena in Columbus. In an astounding two-game statistic, the Brown-Head-Williams trio produced 40 assists with five turnovers—an 8-1 ratio that is off the charts. In addition, they scored 88 points. At the same time, Augustine and Powell maintained what Weber called "a strong presence inside" in the shockingly easy rout of Cincinnati.

Thanks in part to Williams racking up 31 points, the Illini ripped the Bearcats with 63.6 percent field goal accuracy, producing the most overwhelming single-game shooting accuracy in the school's NCAA history, even more impressive than the back-to-back defeats of Louisville and Syracuse in 1989.

"We tried everything," said disgruntled Cincinnati coach Bob Huggins. "We tried a matchup, a zone and a man-to-man defense that have been good for us. Illinois just kept making shots."

The magical Illini run ended in Atlanta as foul troubles limited Augustine and Williams in a 72-62 loss to Duke. They couldn't convert the shots that felled Cincinnati, checking in at 40.6 percent despite the splendid, 15-point efforts of Augustine (in 22 minutes) and Powell.

Nor did Illinois have an answer for Duke's inside punch. Shelden Williams, the big Oklahoman who declined Self's strong overtures to choose Duke, expanded the Blue Devils' 31-30 halftime lead in going five for five, and Mike Krzyzewski's stars pulled away as their first eight baskets after intermission were layins and dunks.

Even with the Illini falling two games short of the Final Four, it was a stirring, captivating run, and an encouraging stage setter for the season in which all the key characters return.

And it will unfold in 2004-05 as the Big Ten appears poised to make a return to prominence. It is noteworthy that Illinois has maintained a high level of play while most other Big Ten members, with the notable exception of Wisconsin, allowed the conference to dip far below its long time standard.

There are skid marks all around. Even Michigan State, national champion in 2000 and still a preseason Top 10 pick prior to last season, tumbled out of the rankings and finished 18-12 in losing to Nevada in the NCAA tournament. Indiana, once the conference bellcow with 11 Big Ten titles during the Bob Knight era, didn't even qualify for the NIT in 2004, losing nine of its last 12 games. Minnesota shows a 29-51 conference record in five seasons since Clem Haskins was fired. The slippage at Iowa and Purdue has led to dramatic dips in attendance. Also, Ohio State, which rose from 2-16, 3-15, 5-13 and 1-15 campaigns to reach the Final Four in 1999, has tumbled again. Michigan, newly crowned NIT champion, hasn't fully recovered from sanctions that caused Fab Five accomplishments to be erased from the record books. Northwestern's improvement failed to reach .500, and Penn State has spent three straight years in the Big Ten basement.

Meanwhile, Illinois has rolled right along. With four Big Ten championships since 1998, with a developing position in the national consciousness, with a fan base that will again turn the big saucer bright orange with sellouts in the upcoming season, Weber is riding herd on a program that is just one good NCAA run from joining the elite in a new century.

After 100 years, Illini basketball is no longer a "sleeping giant," but rather an established winner challenging for the ultimate prize.

Streeter Lecka/Getty Images

▲ *James Augustine enthusiastically dunks the ball in the Illini's heartbreaking 72-62 loss to Duke in the Sweet Sixteen. Augustine and Roger Powell co-led the team in scoring with 15 points and rebounding with eight boards.*

Deron Williams proved to be a clutch shooter and a tough competitor during the 2003-04 season. After returning from a broken jaw to spearhead a come-from-behind overtime victory against Illinois State, Williams provided more than his share of critical plays down the stretch. His six three-point baskets against Cincinnati in the second round of the NCAA Tournament nearly single-handedly slayed the Bearcats. ►

POPKEN

POTTER

White	Yellow	ILLINOIS LINE UP		B	F.T.	P	T
No.	No.						
1	1	Carney (Capt)	F				
7	7	Popken	F				
9	13	Potter	F				
14	14	Danielson	F				
11	10	White	C				
5	4	Stillwell	G				
12	11	Neville	G				
3	6	Sabo	G				
2	5	Collins	G				
10	8	Tabor	G				
13	9	Hansen	G				
6	12	Vogel	G				

No.	Minnesota Line Up		B	F.T.	P	T
1	Kerney (Capt.)	C, G				
2	Hultkmas	G				
4	Severienson	F				
5	Swanson	F				
7	Hanson	G				
8	Doyle	F				
11	Bugshund	C				

CHAPTER TWO

THE EARLY YEARS
1890s—1930s

Long before the National Basketball Association was born, long before no-work scholarships eased the life of college athletes, long before it became a cultural mainstay for the black community, basketball served as a bridge to things better.

Charles Burdette "Bur" Harper competed for the University of Illinois in the bygone days of 1929-30-31. Basketball was his sport of choice in college, helped land him two jobs after graduation and served to ease 37 months in a Japanese prison camp during World War II.

At age 95, Harper told his story from his home in midstate Chandlerville this year.

"Basketball helped determine the direction of my life," said Harper. "My first job was coaching but money was scarce during the depression. Through a former teammate, Elbridge 'Horse' May, I was hired at Mandel Bros. in Chicago because I could contribute to their basketball team. Many companies fielded teams for the public-relations benefits. We won so many games that Lever Bros. wooed our team away by an offer of better jobs. Thus, I became a Lever Bros. employee and my business career began."

◄ *Interior pages from a 1921 Illini basketball program.*

Harper and wife Marion—wed more than six decades ago—went to the Philippines to set up a sales and marketing division for Unilever Co. in Manila. They were there on December 7, 1941, and were prisoners of war by the first of the year.

"We had separate living quarters," said Mrs. Harper, "but we saw each other every day. The entire American community was brought into the camp. There were 4,000 of us. The guards more or less left us alone."

That's when Harper's basketball background helped, in his words, "make our situation less intolerable."

As he explained: "I was appointed head of the recreation committee and organized baseball and basketball teams and other activities for the internees. Most rewarding was the mentoring and coaching of the teenagers who felt mightily the confines of a prison camp. These friendships remain to this day. We formed basketball leagues with bamboo cups for trophies."

▲ *Charles "Bur" Harper captained the 12-5 Illini team in 1930-31. He later used his skill as a player to organize basketball games and mentor youth in the Japanese prison camp he was forced into during World War II.*

This continued into the second year before food became scarce and the Japanese, seeing the war start to turn against them, had other priorities.

"The last year was really bad," said Mrs. Harper. "We were starving, with as many as 10 a day dying. Bur got down to 115 pounds."

"My conditioning as an athlete helped get me through," said Harper, acknowledging that he was skin and bones when liberated. "We were repatriated to the states to recover, and then we returned to Manila where we lived for a total of 35 years."

THE BALL BEGINS TO BOUNCE

That's just one story in 100 years of Fighting Illini basketball. There are hundreds more. We hark back to a time, the Gay '90s, when college men shunned the sport even though UI women were already playing ... privately with no spectators allowed.

But the idea of sports competition was growing. In 1894, Illinois began to assume a look that folks today would be familiar with, switching uniform colors from Dartmouth green to orange and navy blue. By 1896, Illinois was in the fold—along with Michigan, Minnesota, Chicago, Wisconsin, Purdue and Northwestern—when school representatives met at the Palmer House in Chicago to create the Western Conference and establish standards for administration.

One of their first rules was to require a year's residence for any athlete who changed institutions, a requirement still in effect for basketball and football. Shortly after the turn of the century, the conference passed a then-radical rule requiring athletes to complete a semester's work in residence before being eligible. As basketball became more prominent in the coming years, conference fathers passed legislation that only three years of competition would be allowed (no graduate students) and student and faculty basketball tickets could not cost more than 50 cents. They also decided to cut in half the two-man refereeing crews, deeming that one cage official was more than enough for a basketball game.

Indiana and Iowa joined the conference in 1899, and two years later the first conference outdoor track meet was held at the University of Chicago.

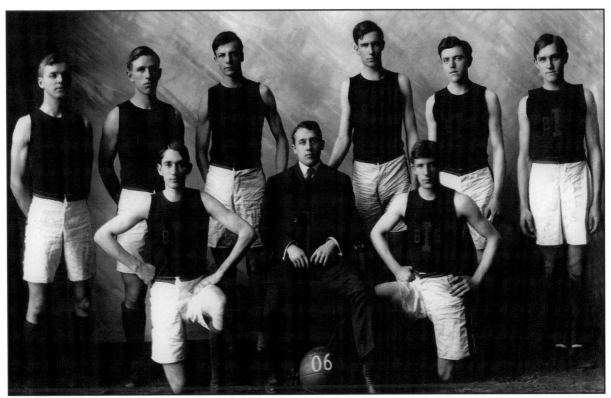

▲ *The inaugural Illini basketball team of 1905-06 went 5-8 after beating Champaign High School, 71-4, in their first ever game. Front row (left to right)—Charles Stewart, Coach Elwood Brown, Floyd Talmadge; back row (left to right)—Herbert Juul, Maurice Dadant, Albert Penn, Roy Riley, [unknown], Edward Ryan.*

On May 29, 1901, Illini baseball coach George Huff was named UI director of athletics. Chicagoan George Donoghue, a student from Chicago in the early 1900s, introduced the idea of men's basketball at the Men's Old Gym. Discussing it years later in 1953, when he was general superintendent of the Chicago Park District, Donoghue said it took a lot of selling.

"I went to George Huff and talked him into putting baskets and backboards in the gym, but they were removed several times before they were allowed to stand permanently," recalled Donoghue. "I was told they interfered with the physical education program.

"The boards were not re-established until 1904 or 1905. We had a basketball team the year I graduated (1906) but it was not recognized as a major sport where a man could earn a letter."

Following the lead of the women, UI men formed the first varsity basketball team in the autumn of 1905, the same year of the first commercial radio broadcast

in this country. Under the direction of Leo Hana and coached initially by center Roy Riley, the UI team defeated Champaign High School, 71-4, on January 6, 1906, before hosting its first two college rivals, Indiana and Purdue, later that month with Elwood Brown officially becoming head coach. The UI won both games, 27-24 over the Hoosiers and 25-19 over the Boilermakers, but both later avenged those setbacks on their home courts, Indiana winning 38-7 and Purdue ruling 48-22.

1905-6 was the first year for conference standings. The Illini finished last with a 3-6 record. This was considerably better than next year's squad, which started with a 38-19 victory over the Peoria YMCA and then lost their other 10 games, showing 0-8 in the league.

Illinois went 20-6 in 1907-08 with the benefit of a Christmastime southern trip that included 13 of the games against YMCA and athletic clubs, and finished 4-4 in the conference. During the first eight years, in

16

which the University of Chicago won four titles (going 12-0 in 1909), the Illini had six coaches and never finished their conference season more than one game over .500 until 1913-14, the year after all postseason games had been prohibited, when they were 7-3. Noteworthy in the season of 1912-13—which saw the Illini go 10-6 overall—was the fact that Illini player Homer Dahringer led conference scoring with 125 points, a miserly (by today's standards) 9.6 points per game.

The winning season of 1914-15 set the stage for the UI's first basketball championship. Coach Ralph Jones' team was named No. 1 in the country by the Helms Foundation. This was the first season in the Men's Old Gym Annex and the only perfect record in UI basketball

history, 16-0 overall and 12-0 in the Big Nine. The league stood at nine members in 1915 because, while Ohio State joined in 1912, Michigan had withdrawn in 1908 in a protest against "retroactive provisions," and didn't rejoin until 1917.

Ralf and Ray Woods, sophomore brothers from Evanston, spearheaded the UI title march that featured narrow escapes at Wisconsin (19-17) and Chicago (19-18). Ralf was a dead-eye shooter who attempted all the Illini free throws, and Ray was a stalwart defender and rebounder. The Illini continued their winning ways with a 13-3 record in 1916, finishing second to Wisconsin in the league.

▲ *Coach Fletcher Lane's only year at the helm produced a 20-6 record for the 1907-08 squad. Lane's .769 career winning percentage was the best career mark of any Illini coach until Bruce Webber's .788 mark nearly a century later in 2003-04. Front row (left to right)—[unknown], [unknown], Charles Stewart, Maurice Dadant (Captain), [unknown], [unknown], Albert Penn; back row (left to right)—Henry Popperfuss, [unknown], Thomas Thompson, Coach Lane, Avery Brundage, Edward Ryan, Roy Rennacker.*

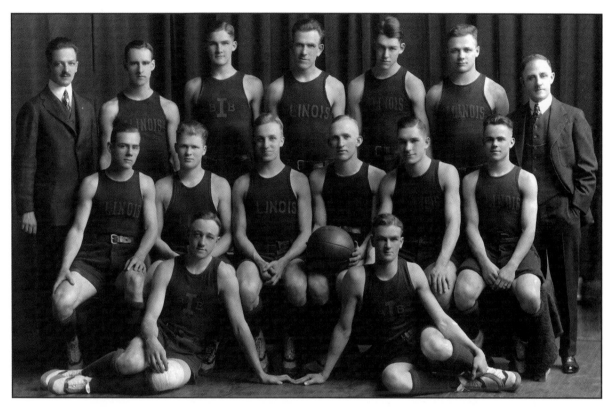

▲ *Coach Ralph Jones' 1914-15 club was deemed national champs by the Helms Foundation after going a perfect 16-0 on the season. Big wins of the year included a 20-4 spanking of Indiana, a 27-8 win over Purdue, and a 50-9 victory over Illinois Wesleyan. Front row (left to right)—Gordon Otto, [unknown]; middle row (left to right)—Ray Woods, Dudley Crane, Helmuth Kircher, Sven Duner (Captain), Edward Williford, Ralf Woods; back row (left to right)—[unknown] (Trainer), [unknown], Clarence Applegran, Frank Bane, Clyde Alwood, [unknown], Coach Jones.*

After a solid (13-3 overall, 9-3 conference) second-place season following the championship, Illinois added George Halas to a lineup still featuring the Woods brothers and Clinton's Clyde Alwood at center in 1916-17. The new lineup earned a share of the Big Nine title with Minnesota at 10-2. In their opener that season, the athletic department paid $29.70 for a 16-member entourage to take the interurban to Decatur for a game at Millikin, which Illinois won 38-18. Expanding rapidly from the minor-sport category, basketball took on a new look that February when, according to a reporter at the time, "special police were called to keep back the lines that struggled to get into Chicago's Bartlett Gym for the game with Chicago." Illinois salvaged a 19-16 victory as Ralf Woods scored 15 points.

In the final game of the Woods era, Illinois won at Northwestern, 21-12, with Ralf Woods' scoring 11 points. Ray Woods ended his career as a three-time Helms first-team All-American, and center Chuck Alwood joined him on the 1917 All-America team. Ralf Woods' prowess as the team's free throw shooter earned him lasting recognition with the Ralf Woods Trophy, which is presented to the UI's leading free throw shooter each year.

Halas, the founder of the Chicago Bears, was named co-captain of the 1917-18 team, which went 6-6 in conference play, but left for the armed services in January of that year. Along with him, two other UI football coaching names emerged in basketball during the World War I era. Burt Ingwersen, an All-Big Ten football lineman, was a three-year starter at guard ending in 1920, and Ralph

▲ *Coach Frank Winter's 1921-22 team—which featured standout senior Chuck Carney—went 14-5 and finished tied for fourth in the Big Ten. Front row (left to right)—Chuck Carney (Co-Captain), [unknown], Henry Reitsch, Charles Vail (Co-Captain), Walter Collins, W. W. Watts; back row (left to right)—John Sabo, Norton Hellstrom, Hubert Tabor, [unknown], Julian Mee, Matt Bullock (trainer), Lawrence Walquist, Coach Winters.*

Fletcher was a regular forward in 1919. Ingwersen was head football coach at Iowa from 1924 to 1931, and served as Illini line coach for two decades (1946-65). Fletcher was an Illini football assistant from 1942 to 1963.

The 1920s were marked by generally good UI teams with another Evanston product, Chuck Carney, emerging as the premier Illini player of that period. Carney, an all-star end in football, led the Big Ten in basketball scoring in 1920 (188 points) and 1922 (172), earning All-America honors in those two seasons. Carney's failure to receive recognition in 1921 was the result of a severe knee injury sustained in the final game of the football season, a 7-0 home loss to Ohio State on the nation's first official Dad's Day. Despite Carney's setback, new coach Frank Winters directed a team that finished 11-7 overall and 7-5 in the conference.

Coming down the stretch in his senior season in 1921-22, Carney scored 15 points on February 27 as Illinois rallied from a 35-31 deficit to nip Wisconsin 37-35 in Urbana. The Illini stood 14-3 overall with two games to go, but dropped both. An uphill climb against Chicago on March 3 resulted in a 26-25 overtime loss, with Carney scoring 19 points, including all 11 of the team's free throws. In the final game of the season at Purdue, the Illini fell 39-31 to leave them with a 7-5 mark in conference, 14-5 overall.

Illinois produced five conference scoring leaders in those early years—Dahringer in 1913, Ralf Woods in 1917, Earl Anderson in 1918 and Carney in 1920 and '22—and have had only four others in the ensuing eight decades. They are Bill Hapac in 1940, Andy Phillip in 1943, Kendall Gill in 1990 and Brian Cook in 2003. Noting the dramatic upswing in scoring, Hapac produced 164 points in 12 games (13.7 points per game) in 1940, and 12 years later Iowa's Chuck Darling had 364 points in 14 games (26.0 points per game).

In the fall of 1922, when most talk revolved around the new stadium going up on campus, noted tactician

continued on page 20

ILLINI ARENAS

KENNEY GYMNASIUM

1905-1925

▲ *The exterior of Kenney Gymnasium, circa the early 1900s.*

From the first bounce of the ball for Illinois basketball in 1905, the Men's Old Gymnasium, currently known as Kenney Gym, was its home. In 20 seasons of Illinois basketball, the gym held 154 Illinois basketball games with the Illini enjoying an incredible home court advantage by winning 74 percent of their games there, including two undefeated home seasons in 1915 and 1925.

The origin of Kenney Gymnasium stems from a fire on June 9, 1890, in the old Drill Hall and Machine Shop Building. The flames engulfed the building and rendered it useless. The administration decided that the school's growing population was best served by constructing several different buildings to house the numerous activities for which the Drill Hall was used. State Legislators agreed, and only one year later they appropriated new funds for a brand new gymnasium. In 1902, a $91,000 men's gym was designed by architect N.S. Spencer and constructed near the corner of Springfield and Wright.

The University of Illinois basketball squad tipped off their first game in the gym's annex—which also has been known as the Old Armory or Military Hall—on January 12, 1906, against Champaign High School. The Illini kicked the season off in style with a lopsided 71-4 victory

In its 20 seasons of Illinois basketball, Kenney Gym saw players like Ray and Ralf Woods, Chuck Carney, George Halas, Wally Roettger, Leland "Slim" Stilwell, and Bert Ingwersen take to its floor. It was home to three Big Ten championship teams

continued on page 20

▲ *Illinois prepares to battle Michigan in March of 1924 at the old Kenney Gymnasium, which the Illini vacated in late 1925 to move into their new home, Huff Gym. Illinois prevailed 23-20 in the contest.*

continued from page 19

including the national championship squad of 1914-15.

Originally called the "New Gymnasium," Kenney lost that name with the construction of a new building on Fourth and Armory in 1925, which today is known as Huff Gym. Between 1925-74, Kenney Gym was affectionately known as the Men's Old Gymnasium until it was officially named for H.E. Kenney, who was the Illinois wrestling coach from 1929-43.

The gym closed its doors to Illinois basketball March 6, 1925, with a resounding 37-27 victory over the Purdue Boilermakers. Over the course of its tenure as host to Illini basketball, Kenney Gymnasium wasn't the prettiest or the biggest, nor was it probably the loudest, but in the history of Illinois basketball it can claim one thing: it was the first.

▲ *Leland "Slim" Stilwell starred at center for new Illini head coach J. Craig Ruby's 1922-23 and 1923-24 teams, leading the team in scoring on the later squad. He later became the team doctor.*

continued from page 18

J. Craig Ruby arrived to take charge of the basketball team. Two of his inherited players were longtime UI institutions, Wally Roettger and Leland "Slim" Stilwell. Roettger, the leading scorer in 1923, went on to become the UI baseball coach. Stilwell, the top UI scorer in 1924, was later the team doctor.

The 1923-24 club shared the Big Ten title with Wisconsin and Chicago at 8-4 in a scramble that saw three other teams finish 7-5. Ruby's Illini rallied for their share. After dropping a 13-12 midseason game at Wisconsin, they won their last six. This included a 36-35 triple-overtime verdict over a Northwestern team that was 0-10 going in. Illinois rallied from a 20-10 deficit as booing became so loud at NU's Patten Gym that a formal warning had to be issued to the crowd by referee Fred "Brick" Young, a Bloomington sports writer who filed stories by Western Union on the games that he whistled.

Another late rally beat Michigan 23-20 with Johnny Mauer's go-ahead basket "raising the roof of Urbana's (Kenney) Gym Annex several inches." In the season finale, "Slim" Stilwell closed his collegiate career by converting 11 free throws in a 31-19 defeat of Minnesota.

Maurer, Jack Lipe and T.D. Karnes were key returnees ahead of the 1924-25 season, and sophomore Russell Daugherty earned the first of three team scoring crowns. The team finished 8-4 in conference again, earning third place. Unlike the 1924 edition, this team crumbled at the end, losing four of the last five games and bowing 24-9 at Wisconsin in the season ender.

MOVING INTO HUFF

The Illini moved into new Huff Gymnasium for a game on December 12, 1925, edging Butler 23-22 in the contest. The move was overseen by UI Professor James M. White, a member of various athletic committees that served as the supervising architect along with Charles A. Platt. Professor F.R. Watson consulted on acoustics. The main portion of Huff was completed that year, and a swimming pool was added on the south side. Total cost was $772,000, and it was officially named some 12 years later in 1937 shortly after Huff's death.

Offices of the Athletic Association and the school of physical education were located in the building. The gym

continued on page 23

ILLINI ARENAS
HUFF GYMNASIUM
1925-1963

▲ *Named for former UI director of athletics George Huff, Huff Gym hosted its first Illini game on December 12, 1925. Total cost to build Huff was $772,000.*

For 38 seasons, Illinois basketball players and fans called it home. It was the scene of countless unforgettable moments, great games, legendary names and outstanding performances. There was no place like Huff Gym.

The new "New Gymnasium"—which was renamed Huff Gym after George Huff some 12 years after its opening—greeted Illini fans for the first time on December 12, 1925. At 7:30 p.m., the Illini kicked off the 1925-26 basketball season against Butler and opened their new gym in grand style. A capacity crowd of 6,100 packed into the gym to watch the Illini hold off the Bulldogs, 23-22, and set the winning precedent at Huff that would last for almost four decades.

When opposing teams entered Huff, they were usually leaving with a loss. From 1925-63, Huff Gym was home to 460 Illinois basketball games with the Illini winning a remarkable 74 percent of them. For five of those seasons, Illinois went undefeated there.

Huff was a nightmare for the opposition, but for young kids growing up in the state, it was a place they dreamed of one day playing in.

"The state high school basketball tournament was played at Huff, so it was a shrine for everyone who played basketball in Illinois," said Jerry Colangelo, who played in the gym for Illinois from 1959-1962. "When I finally suited up in an Illinois uniform at Huff it was an incredible feeling."

It was the Mecca of Illinois basketball, and I loved the coziness of it," said Govoner Vaughn, who first stepped foot in the gym as a high school player for Edwardsville. "When people talked about the tradition of Illinois that gym was a big part of it."

For young men seeing Huff for the first time on their trip to the state tournament it was an awe-inspiring experience.

"When I walked into Huff to play in the Sweet Sixteen it was the biggest building I had ever seen," recalled Illinois guard Irv Bemoras. "I couldn't believe my eyes."

The first time stepping onto the hallowed court is something that no player ever forgot.

"One of the most exciting times of my college career was the first time I put on the Illinois uniform and walked onto the Huff Gym court to play the varsity," said Illinois guard Jim Wright. "It was something I had dreamed about for a long time."

When Huff Gym was packed to the rafters it was a sight to behold. Capacity was a little over 7,000 people and the fans were packed in very close quarters.

"I loved being in that building," said current Illinois athletic director Ron Guenther. "I don't know what the fire code was but I marvel at the fact that now they say we can only have 3,500 people in there, but when we look back at the records there was always about 7,000 people in the building for basketball games."

Due to its small size and the demand for Illinois basketball, tickets for a game in Huff Gym were very hard to obtain. Most students only got to see a handful of games and people were always looking for ways to get in.

"I remember getting tickets for two bucks that were quite valuable," laughed former Illinois manager Dennis Swanson.

The fans were right on top of the floor, sitting body to body and ready to erupt. As a player if you weren't careful, you would go out of bounds and fly right into the crowd.

"The fans were so close they could reach out and basically pinch you in the butt," said Illinois forward Mel Blackwell.

Across from the Illinois bench sat the I-Men. These football players would be in full force wearing their letterman jackets and making their presence felt.

"The I-Men were all over the other team," said Hiles Stout, a forward on the basketball team in the mid 1950s who also played quarterback on the football team. "They were trash talking and getting on the other team the entire game. It was just fantastic."

continued on page 22

continued from page 21

If the building itself coupled with the atmosphere weren't intimidating enough, staring you right in the face were the likes of Ray Nitschke and Dick Butkus.

"It was unmerciful for the visiting team coming in," recalled Bill McKeown. "It had to be very, very intimidating for the other team to take the abuse they did from the guys who were right on top of them."

On game day, the gym had a certain aura to it, and before tip-off the other team could certainly feel it.

"It was almost like going to a concert or something, because they used to turn the lights down right before the game," said Walt Kirk, who played in Huff in the mid-40s. "The only lights turned on when the game began were the ones that flooded the floor and it was then you really felt the Illinois tradition."

The names of opposing players to come through Huff read like a who's who of college basketball. Don Nelson of Iowa, George Mikan of DePaul, Don Schlundt of Indiana, John Wooden of Purdue, Jerry Lucas and John Havlicek of Ohio State, Whitey Skoog of Minnesota, and a guy named Bobby Knight.

"I remember interviewing Bobby [Knight] for a piece I was doing for CBS," said Bill Geist, who was an Illinois student in the mid 1960s and is now a journalist for CBS. "He said he used to love playing in Huff Gym, because all the football players would try to trip him as he came by."

Perhaps what people remember most about Huff is the noise level that became deafening on the day of a big game.

"The people who never had a chance to see a game there can't understand what the noise was like," said Skip Thoren. "It was thunderous in there when we were playing well."

Huff Gym closed its doors for the last time on Saturday, February 23, 1963, but not before it would go out with one last bang. The 6,192 fans that filled it to the brim made sure the sound would reverberate in the building for years to come.

"That game against Wisconsin to close the place was the most noise I have ever heard in my entire life," recalled Illinois guard Bill Small, who scored 19 points in the 12-point victory over the Badgers. "There was no other place we played in that was as loud as Huff Gym and that day was by far the loudest I ever heard it."

A week and a half later, the Illini moved into the 16,000 seat Assembly Hall, but the memories of quaint Huff Gymnasium always remained. Today, more than 40 years since Illinois basketball stopped playing there, people still smile when they recall the deafening noise, the intimidation of the I-Men, and the bleachers packed all the way to the top. For 38 seasons it was something special, but more than anything else it was "home."

▲ *The only time Huff Gym was kind on the ears was when it was empty. A sold-out Huff Gym—as it so often was—packed a mighty wallop and served as a definite home-court advantage.*

continued from page 20

area covered 14,900 feet, and was used extensively at a time when two years of physical education was required at the UI. The basement had 24 handball and squash courts, just across the street from a spacious armory.

Of 7,040 tickets printed for the opener, 875 went unsold due to some bleacher seats unready for use. Complimentary tickets included 28 for the media, and certainly one for UI president Dave Kinney. Police and gatemen numbered 100.

With Pug Daugherity and John Mauer leading the way, Illinois led 18-5 at halftime, after which Ruby's substitutions all but allowed the Bulldogs to catch up.

In what evolved as an up-and-down season, the 1925-26 Illini shocked Purdue 29-28 behind Jack Lipe's 10 points, and reached first place temporarily with a 5-2 record after a February 19 win at Indiana, 21-20. In handing the Hoosiers their first home loss, Illinois was never behind after streaking out in front, 10-2. The visitors stalled it out to seal the victory in front of a frenzied Indiana crowd. However, after an unimpressive win at Chicago, the Illini dropped their last four games to fall out of the chase and finish fifth. And if the 28-23 loss at Purdue on March 1 wasn't bad enough, they were to receive just $100 for the trip, less one-half of the officials' expenses. Cost of transportation for 14 men was $70, and a one-night hotel stay at $2 per came to $26.56. Meals cost an additional $44.20 plus a $5 tip. In the season finale, Minnesota used five players for a 28-21 verdict over a crippled and sagging UI club. Illinois had beaten Minnesota 17-8 earlier.

A series of "average" teams followed. The 1927-28 club—the exception to "average"—slipped to 2-10 in the conference when Elgin sophomore Doug Mills joined the lineup. While that team won just twice, a last-second shot by Johnny How served Wisconsin a stunning 34-33 upset that cost the Badgers a share of the title. Struck down by injuries and ineligibilities, the Illini lost their last seven games to hit the low point of the Ruby era. As difficult as the games of that era proved to be, traveling to road contests wasn't any easier. The Illini found Indiana roads too rain-softened for one particular bus trip to Purdue, forcing a late decision to take several automobiles on the short trip.

▲ *Guard Doug Mills captained the 1929-30 team. Six years later he became head coach of the Illini and put together some of the program's most historic clubs— most notably the Whiz Kids.*

Mills, who became head basketball coach six years after he graduated, captained the 1929-30 club that checked in at 8-8 overall and 7-5 in the league. That was the year Purdue's John Wooden earned the first of three All-America honors. Illinois was fortunate not to play Purdue's 10-0 Big Ten champions that season and managed to split with the Boilermakers the next two years, dropping two in West Lafayette and winning two in Urbana. Succeeding Mills as UI captain in 1931 was Chandlerville's Harper, now 95. He competed against Wooden, calling him in 2003 the "smartest player I ever played against ..."

Back in the early '30s, when Frank Froschauer was handling most of the scoring and Atwood's Kamm brothers, Albert and Alfred, were coming aboard, the Illini treaded just above the water line. They finished 7-5 in the conference in four of five seasons, but began looking forward with optimism to the members of freshman coach Slim Stilwell's class that would join three-time UI scoring leader Froschauer the next fall.

COMBES ARRIVES

The sophomore group in 1934-35 featured Monticelloan and future Illini coach Harry Combes, Pick Dehner, Wib Henry, Bud Riegel, Hale Swanson and Jim Vopicka. These newcomers helped the Illini win eight of their last nine games to share the Big Ten crown at 9-3 with Purdue and Wisconsin. This ended a stretch in which Ruby was 55-53 over the nine previous Big Ten seasons.

On the heels of a 37-36 win over Purdue at a time when Purdue's Ward "Piggy" Lambert was regarded the nation's No. 1 coach, *News-Gazette* writer Eddie Jacquin couldn't contain his enthusiasm. "Who said sophomores couldn't play basketball?" wrote Jacquin. "Who said Champaign County (Riegel) and the Okaw Valley (Combes) didn't turn out cage stars?" Citing the UI rally from a 27-19 deficit, Lambert said, "That kid Combes beat us with those two dizzy shots. Does he always hit 'em like that?"

Combes played every minute of the game and scored 12 points in a 44-23 win at Ohio State on January 12. The 1935 title run was full steam ahead. It was interrupted briefly at Purdue, where the Boilermakers gained revenge, 35-27. But the Illini stormed down the stretch, winning their last five games, four by double-figure margins. Froschauer and Tolono's Riegel shared the scoring lead on a balanced attack that saw no one average eight points.

Combes, Riegel & Co. started strong again as juniors in 1935-36, winning 26-24 at DePaul and going undefeated through December. But a 27-26 setback at Iowa on January 4 got the 1936 Big Ten race off to a bad start, and the Illini dropped two mid-January dates with Ohio State (18-13) and Northwestern (40-28) to fall out of the race. Oddly, Illinois did not play either of the 11-1 co-champions, Indiana and Purdue, and tied for third with a 7-5 league record.

The prospects were burning bright with the great Lou Boudreau on the freshman team and a youthful Mills primed to replace Ruby as head coach. As a rookie coach in 1936-37, Mills put together a flashy, undersized team that picked up steam after Combes recovered from a leg injury to earn All-Big Ten honors for the second time. Of a 42-28 rout of Iowa, *Urbana Courier*

columnist Bert Bertine wrote: "The lads from tall corn country were reputed to have a stout defensive club, but all their efforts availed them little (because of) the brilliant play of Louie Boudreau and Harry Combes."

Combes added 16 points against Indiana at Huff Gym, with a reported 7,000 packing the stands. Touted as the UI's most recognizable name since the Galloping Ghost, Harold "Red" Grange, who ran wild against Michigan in the inaugural game at Memorial Stadium in 1924.

Swanson's tip in at Purdue broke a 14-year losing streak in West Lafayette. The 38-37 result precipitated a riot in which Mills and Combes were knocked to the floor. Jacquin noted: "The attack on the (UI) team was inexcusable and added another black chapter to the long list of poor sportsmanship charges against Purdue followers." The attack had little long-term effect on Combes, who racked up 19 points in the next win against Chicago. But Purdue gained revenge with a 61-34 victory in Huff Gym. The Illini needed to win their last four games to share the Big Ten crown with Minnesota, and they motored through Indiana (42-25), Wisconsin (48-31), Iowa (40-29) and Northwestern (32-26) to complete the task.

Boudreau, the whirlwind sophomore from Thornton of Harvey, led another balanced attack with 8.7 points per game while Combes closed his career by receiving the Big Ten Medal of Honor for proficiency in scholarship and athletics. By accepting a position on the staff at Champaign High School, Combes began a coaching trek that would lead him back to the UI. He became head basketball coach at the high school in his second year and won 84.7 percent of his games (including the 1946 state title) in nine prep seasons. Combes was barely 32 and coming off 34-2, 38-1 and 34-4 seasons at CHS when he succeeded Mills as head coach of the Illini.

But while Combes was building his portfolio across town at CHS, Mills was putting together dashing, high-scoring teams that were stage-setters for the most famous group of that era, "The Whiz Kids."

GREATEST GAMES
ILLINOIS 28, PURDUE 21

JANUARY 9, 1932 • HUFF GYM, CHAMPAIGN, ILLINOIS

ILLINOIS HANDS PURDUE ITS ONLY LOSS OF THE SEASON

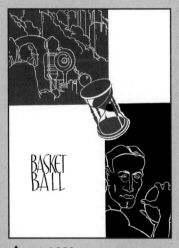

▲ *A 1932 game program.*

By the beginning of the 1931-32 basketball season, Purdue's Ward "Piggy" Lambert had established himself as one of the best coaches in all of college basketball. And he was about to add to his legend with his high-powered Boilermakers.

Led by captain and two-time All-American John Wooden, Purdue took off for Champaign with a 6-0 record and an average margin of victory of about 20 points. The Boilermakers were steamrolling their competition, and it looked like it would be an easy win waiting for them at Huff Gym. Wooden was one of the best players in the country at the time, and the guys on that Illinois team knew all about him.

"John Wooden was a better player than he ever was a coach," recalled Sidney Port, who is the second oldest living Illinois basketball player. "He was about 5-10, could jump real high, and if he was on, he could score all day."

The Illini were led by head coach J. Craig Ruby and were coming off a crushing 29-28 defeat at the hands of the Ohio State Buckeyes that pushed their record to 3-2. A capacity crowd of 6,859 people jammed into the New Gym (later to be named

Huff) to see the game, but little did they know the Boilers had their own trouble on the way to Champaign.

"I remember my senior year trip to Champaign very well," said Wooden from his home in Encino, California "We were driving in Champaign and got caught on a car track and when the driver tried to pull over our car flipped over. The glass on the car broke and I had quite a cut on my finger. I still played in the game, but I wasn't 100 percent."

The Illini, led by Red Owen, who had been slowed early in the season while recovering from a football injury, broke out early and never looked back. By the time the first half was over and the dust cleared, the Illini held Purdue to one basket—scored by Wooden—and led 19-5.

Illinois fell into foul trouble early in the second half, but held off a late Boilermaker run to hand Purdue its first defeat of the season, 28-21.

Covering the game for *The Daily Illini*, Joe Bumgarner - talked about the feat: "Unheralded and in the least propitious circumstances imaginable, the Illinois basketball team "arrived" last night to the last season form, which everyone had been waiting for."

The Boilermakers wouldn't lose another game that season, finishing 17-1. Lambert's group went on to win the 1932 national championship. As memorable a season as it was, co-captain John Wooden would never forget, "the only game I lost in my entire senior season."

It was a perfect season for the Boilermakers, except for that one night in the New Gym when Ruby's men stopped them right in their tracks.

CHAPTER THREE

THESE WHIZ KIDS

1939-40—1946-47

As the 1930s wound to a close, it was a world that would be unrecognizable today. The spread of information was so unsophisticated, so constrained and respectful, that few voters realized their multiterm president, Franklin Delano Roosevelt, was too crippled to stand on his own. In the popular culture, basketball took a deep back seat to Joe Louis' next heavyweight fight. George Halas' Bears were developing as the Monsters of the Midway, but professional football hadn't yet taken off. There were no cell phones, no World Wide Web, no television. When Chester Gould drew a futuristic picture-watch on Dick Tracy's wrist, it was as hard to comprehend as a trip to the moon.

On most farms, outhouses hadn't yet been replaced by indoor plumbing and rural electrification. In town, morning chores included shoveling coal to keep the furnace going. Split divided highways were unheard of. If federal funds cleared the way for "hard roads" to weave across the level plains of Illinois, it was a bumpy, curvy ride in southern Indiana or Kentucky. Just in case, youths with weak stomachs were provided brown bags on swooping hills that resembled Space Mountain ... the bags coming in handy if dad couldn't pull off the road in time.

This was the world Gene Vance grew up in. He learned about Illini basketball stars like Lou Boudreau and Bill Hapac from radio, usually a big console that allowed the imagination to run wild with The Shadow and The Lone Ranger.

On the hardwood, Illinois blacks would conduct their own high school tournament, not to be confused with the all-white event sanctioned by the Illinois High School Association. World War II would later serve as the impetus to integrate a nation, and would set the stage for Jackie Robinson breaking the color line in baseball.

Fans wouldn't see the UI's first African-American cager in an official game until Walt Moore, a teammate of Illini Max Hooper on Mt. Vernon's state champions, made a brief appearance during the Korean War period when freshmen were eligible at the outset of the 1951-52 season. After appearing in several warmup games (Combes had 17 men on the varsity), Moore played two minutes as the 13th man in an 86-66 defeat of North Carolina.

"A short debut," Moore was quoted in *The News-Gazette.*

It was also a short UI career as Moore became ineligible at the semester and, after a service tour, transferred to Western Illinois where he was a high-scoring star for the Leathernecks.

It was a different time, a different culture. Much of the nation wasn't ready for *To Kill a Mockingbird,* much less *Guess Who's Coming to Dinner?*

In basketball, the jump shot hadn't even been developed. Vance shot two-handers from the perimeter and went underhanded from the free throw line. To dribble between your legs would draw a "hotshot"

▲ *Bill Hapac starred for the Illini in the late 1930s and once scored a then-record 34 points in a 60-31 victory over Minnesota in 1940.*

tongue-lashing and a seat on the bench. The style of the time was conservative. If a team shot 30 percent from the field, it was a good day.

THE WHIZ KIDS ARRIVE

Out of those circumstances, in the pre-war period, four strapping, exquisite athletes would arrive at the university from four sections of the state: Vance from nearby Clinton, Andy Phillip from 1940 state champion Granite City near St. Louis, Ken Menke from suburban Dundee (state champs in 1938) and Jack Smiley from tiny Waterman, out west of Aurora.

Vance was Hollywood handsome with broad shoulders, sturdy legs and brown hair parted near the middle. If Paul Newman and Robert Redford hadn't yet reached the scene, he would do. Vance saw Illinois play once before he enrolled, attending the Minnesota game on February 10, 1940, with Chuck Farrington, a Clinton assistant coach.

"I had heard so much about [Huff Gym], and it was awfully impressive for a young athlete from Clinton," said Vance. "Two of my teammates, John Kent and Jim Corrington, came along."

In that game, a 60-31 conquest of Minnesota, Hapac scored a Western Conference record 34 points. This was just one of many offensive records that would be set by the Illini in the early 1940s. Another Illini who played in that game was Bill Hocking, who would be captain and sub when the spectacular sophomores emerged two years later.

This was a highlight in a 7-5 Big Ten season in which the Illini took fourth in the conference. When Clinton lost an overtime clash with Champaign High in the state playoffs, Vance had no thoughts about going anywhere but Illinois.

"It was the thing to do, to go to the state university," said Vance. "I remember meeting Menke and Phillip at *The News-Gazette* All-State banquet. But we didn't know what we were going to do at that point."

At Illinois, the future Whiz Kids would be greeted by a coach both versatile and accomplished, and barely in his 30s: Doug Mills. Mills was smart, easy-going and flexible, a calm motivater who gave the athletes room to

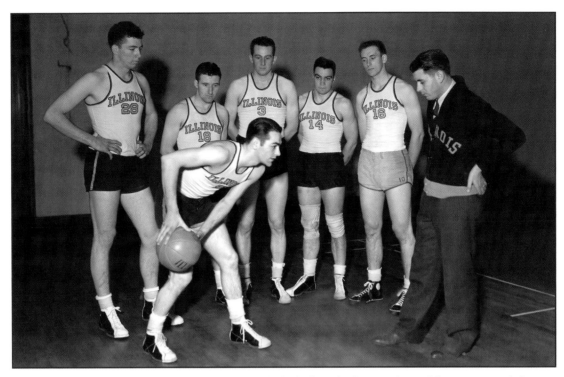

▲ Coach Mills (right) oversees Lou Boudreau, with the ball, and other members of the 1939 squad during a practice. Mills was an incredibly popular coach who in 1941—at the age of 33—would also become athletic director.

maneuver. He was unlike the ref-baiting and fiercely demanding coaches in vogue today. Operating on the bench with the cool confidence of a man whose skills and athleticism had been proven many times, Mills came to the Illini from Joliet High School, where he rejuvenated a dismal athletic program. During five seasons as basketball coach, he was called "the sanest person in the Joliet gymnasium."

Nicknamed "Gaga" in college, he was a sophomore starter in basketball and his leadership was recognized early as he became captain of Craig Ruby's cagers in 1930. Mills' summers were dedicated to baseball, a sport at which his father excelled on the Pacific Coast. Mills played briefly in the Western League in 1931 before giving it up. He also played some football, teaming with Frosty Peters and Judson Timm in a "pony backfield" that led the Illini to sterling records of 7-0-1, 7-1 and 6-1-1 on the heels of the Red Grange era.

By the early '30s, Mills was into a five-year stint coaching at Joliet. He led league champions in football and basketball, taking Joliet to the Sweet 16 before returning to the UI as a football and basketball assistant in the autumn of 1935. College coaches were poorly paid in the 1930s, and they were obliged to handle more than one sport. Illinois was blessed to have two of the headiest workmen in Leo Johnson, track coach of champions and chief football scout, and Wally Roettger, head baseball coach and basketball strategist.

"Mills was a polished, personable guy," said Fred Green, former Illini center from Urbana and a long-time judge. "Everyone liked and respected him. Roettger was the technician. Illinois was fortunate during that period, when assistants went on the road to scout games, to have two of the best minds in Wally and Leo."

Mills wasn't much older than some of his players when, after one season assisting Ruby, he became the Big Ten's youngest major sport head coach at the age of 28. Yet he became overwhelmingly popular after molding a 10-2 league co-champion in his debut season of 1937. Mills was the natural choice when an ongoing controversy caused the Athletic Association board to back the 62-year-old Zuppke, coming off his worst ever football season (1-7), over athletic director Wendell S. Wilson.

In August 1941, at the age of 33, Mills took on the dual responsibility of basketball coach and athletic director at a salary of $6,000. One newspaper called it "a harmonious action contrasting sharply with the month of bitter controversy."

This led directly into Mills' most successful period with the Whiz Kids. With all those players standing around 6-3, Mills was able to employ a switching man-to-man defense that smothered the opposition.

"All were good rebounders and shooters, and you could count the turnovers on one hand every game," said Mills.

He would never separate them in future evaluations. In 1981, 15 years after his resignation as athletic director, Mills reflected: "Lou Boudreau could handle the basketball at top speed, and that's why I say he could have played with the Whiz Kids."

But Boudreau's career was shortened because his mother signed a baseball contract for him with the Cleveland Indians, and the Big Ten faculty represen-

tatives declared him ineligible. Boudreau helped Mills as an assistant, became the "boy manager" of the Indians, led them to the World Championship and reached the Hall of Fame as a shortstop.

Vance's freshman year was spent washing dishes and competing on a regular basis in practice against another varsity team that went 7-5 in conference, this one featuring future teammates Art Mathisen and Vic Wukovits and future major league outfielder Hoot Evers.

"We had two freshman-varsity games," recalled Vance, "and we had them beat in one of them. But there was a power failure with us ahead. When we came back, they won."

Vance always believed Mills wanted it that way.

"We weren't cocky as freshmen," said Vance. "They wouldn't let us be. But we filled in well together. I have a clearer memory of washing dishes than some of the varsity games I watched that year."

The sophomore campaign started slowly, the first three games resulting in two-point thrillers with the Illini

▲ *The Whiz Kids weren't cocky as freshman, said member Gene Vance, but they sure were good. They finished 13-2 in the Big Ten to nab first place. Left to right—Jack Smiley, Art Mathisen, Ken Menke, Gene Vance, and Andy Phillip.*

▲   *Art Mathisen scores a bucket in the Illini's lopsided 48-29 win over Notre Dame at Huff Gym on December 23, 1941. Gene Vance (No. 25) and Ken Menke (No. 38) look on.*

winning twice. It was already apparent that the captain, Bill Hocking, wouldn't crack the lineup.

"He never complained even though he didn't play much," said Vance.

Coach Mills liked to experiment but settled quickly on the four sophomores in the starting lineup. Fellow sophomore Ed "Ace" Parker, who had served as fifth man on the freshman team, was used as a sixth man. UI's 48-29 defeat of Notre Dame before Christmas was the biggest winning margin in the series up to that time.

"All we worked on was getting the ball out and running," said Vance. It was a perfect unit in which everyone passed, everyone scored, everyone played defense and everyone ran. And they hit the Big Ten like an elephant flying into a whirlpool.

First on the league schedule was Wisconsin, defending NCAA champion, and the dashing Illini launched 80 shots and breezed to a 55-40 victory in Madison.

"More than anything, we played well together," said Vance. "It caught everybody by surprise. All of us shot two-handed set shots except on fast breaks."

A week later Illinois held off a Michigan rally, 44-40, with Vance and Phillip garnering six field goals apiece. The Illini won their first seven league games before traveling to Indiana, which halted the streak, 41-36, in registering the Hoosiers' 34th home win out of 35. Indiana's defense held Illinois scoreless for nine minutes in the second half.

"Mills didn't say much. He never did," said Vance. "He wasn't a coach to jump up and down. He was quiet and under control. We were down after the loss and it was a long bus ride home."

Illinois won the next five straight and clinched the first clear Big Ten title since 1915 at Northwestern, beating Otto Graham & Co., 63-49. On March 2, 1942, with the title tucked away, Mills started the second team at Iowa. The Whiz Kids, as they would be nicknamed the following year, scored just four points during brief appearances in a 46-32 loss, just the team's second conference loss on the year against 13 victories.

In 1942, the NCAA tournament was still in its embryo period. Staged around a collegiate basketball

coaches convention at Tulane in New Orleans, where the humidity was insufferable, the tournament proved to be a disappointment for the young UI squad, which finished 18-5 overall on the season. Ahead of Kentucky's Wildcats by four points with three minutes to go, the sophomore-laden Illini saw their tournament hopes evaporate as the legendary Adolph Rupp's men rallied to win 46-44. It was described at the time as an upset.

THE UNDEFEATED RUN

The 1943 season was difficult because of wartime travel restrictions. During one stretch, the Illini played two with Iowa at home, then two at Ohio State and two at Minnesota. It made no difference as the Illini went undefeated in the conference, acquiring the Whiz Kid

continued on page 34

▲ *The 1942-43 Illini team was nearly perfect—17-1 overall and 12-0 in conference. Their only loss came early in the season against Camp Grant, a game in which Coach Mills started the reserves. Front row (left to right)—Bill Hocking, Andy Phillip, Charles Fowler, Ken Menke; back row (left to right)—Assistant coach Wally Roettger, Jack Smiley, Art Mathisen, Gene Vance, Coach Mills.*

GREATEST GAMES
ILLINOIS 50, WISCONSIN 26
FEBRUARY 20, 1943 • HUFF GYM, CHAMPAIGN, ILLINOIS

THE WHIZ KIDS BEAT UP THE BADGERS

It was only fitting for the Whiz Kids that their last tough test before leaving for duty in World War II during the spring semester of 1943 would come against the Wisconsin Badgers. A little more than a year earlier, it was against those same Badgers that the Whiz Kids first arrived on the scene.

In early January of 1942, the Whiz Kids headed up to the Wisconsin Field House to face the defending national champion Badgers and their All-American, John Kotz. In the first Big Ten game of the season, the Illini delivered a statement to the rest of the conference that the power in the league was shifting. Behind 14 points from Andy Phillip and 12 from Art Mathisen, the Illini crushed the Badgers 55-40 on their way to their first Big Ten Championship.

"We had everything fall into place for us that year starting with that game," said guard Gene Vance. "Being able to beat Wisconsin really helped our confidence because they were the defending Big Ten champs."

By February of 1943, the Whiz Kids were rolling through the Big Ten on their way to a second straight league title. With three games left to go in the season they brought a 14-1 record into their final showdown with the Badgers and Kotz.

Kotz came into Champaign with a resume full of accomplishments. He was an All-Big Ten selection in 1941 and 1942 who was named the most outstanding player in the 1941 NCAA Championship game. His scoring prowess netted him an All-America selection in 1942, and he was averaging over 20 points a game in his senior season heading into the battle with the Illini.

A sell-out crowd of 7,102 fans packed into Huff Gym to see the Whiz Kids take on the Badgers.

"I remember with big games at Huff you had to fight to get into the place," recalled Larry Stewart, who later on became the voice of the Illini. "I didn't have a ticket for the game so I bribed a doorman to let me in. I was glad I did, because it was probably the most exciting game I ever saw."

The Whiz Kids controlled the game from the opening tip. Andy Phillip and Art Mathisen were scoring, Ken Menke and Gene Vance were all over the boards, and John Kotz was getting to know Jack Smiley.

Ray Grierson, an end on the Illinois football team and basketball reserve, had a good idea what Kotz was going to face that night.

"That week before the game I was imitating Johnny Kotz on the scout team," recalled Grierson.

"Jack Smiley was all over me that week and when he was guarding you on defense you could barely breathe. I don't know if I even got a shot off all week in practice."

"Jack was a really rough and aggressive defender," recalled reserve Cliff Fulton. "When he put his mind to stopping you it would be very difficult to even get the ball."

Jack Smiley completely shut down Kotz. By the time a frustrated Kotz was taken out late in the game, he had only taken two shots and scored zero points. It was the only scoreless game in his illustrious college career.

The Illini steamrolled the Badgers 50-26 in what Pat Harmon, the sports editor of The News-Gazette, called "without a doubt the best game the Whiz Kids ever played." Phillip scored 22, Mathisen added 19, but no one who was around will ever forget one of the greatest defensive performances in the history of Illinois basketball.

It was the night that Jack Smiley blanked a humbled Badger star.

continued from page 32

nickname in an early 57-53 defeat of Great Lakes in Chicago. The only loss in a 17-1 season came when Mills, as he had done against Iowa a year earlier, started the reserves against Camp Grant in Rockford.

On archrival Wisconsin's home floor, the Whiz Kids darted ahead 11-0 and, with Menke ailing, Phillip broke loose with 24 points in the 45-43 Illini victory. When Illinois rained 104 shot attempts in a 68-51 defeat of Northwestern, both the team and Phillip were dashing toward scoring records.

Along the way, *The News-Gazette's* Pat Harmon wrote: "Vance and Smiley long ago earned their spurs as the best pair of guards in the Big Ten."

Illinois peaked late against Wisconsin, 50-26, as Phillip scored 22, cracking two scoring records in the process. The rugged Smiley held the previous year's Big Ten scoring leader, John Kotz, to two attempts and no points. Afterwards, Harmon proclaimed the Illini "one of the great college teams in history playing its greatest game."

Next the Illini exploded at Northwestern in what Vance calls an even more dominant performance. The Illini beat Graham and NU, 86-44, before 19,848, then the largest midwest attendance in basketball history at the Chicago Stadium. In so doing, the Whiz Kids shattered the conference season scoring record, drilling 38 of 91 shots in an era without the three-point shot, one-and-one free throws or a shot clock to force action.

Finally, in bombarding Chicago 92-25, records fell like rain in the tropics.

"Andy started scoring and we just let him go," said Vance of Phillip's 40-point spree. He set five records in that game, running his season point total to 255.

But it was the team's final game. In his recap, Harmon described them as "Phillip of the U.S. Marines, Vance of the ROTC, and Mathisen, Menke and Smiley of the Army."

"Art, Kenny and Jack went in March, and Andy and I went in June," recalled Vance. "We didn't play in the NCAA that year because if we all couldn't play, none would. It became a bigger item later but, with the war going on, that was the main concern.

"We were shooting for the national championship and Uncle Sam changed all that. It's hard to imagine Illinois still hasn't won the national championship. We thought we were No. 1 but there were no rankings we were aware of."

DEEP INTO WARTIME

The war years were difficult for Mills and the Illini. On the heels of a 11-9 (5-7 in conference) season in 1943-44, Mills went with three solid returnees—Howard Judson, Walt Kirk and Don Delaney—in 1944-45. They played Great Lakes three times, nearby Chanute Field twice and DePaul twice, splitting with the Demons even as big George Mikan scored 26 and 28 points against them. Experimenting in a 77-39 rout of Nebraska, Mills used 19 players including flashy Taylorville freshman John Orr, playing his lone UI season before rejoining famous prep coach Dolph Stanley at Beloit.

It was a strange Big Ten season. The Illini dropped their opener to Michigan 43-38 (making 14 of 88 shots), captured the next seven, and lost their last four. The winning streak began with Kirk scoring 21 and Judson adding 14 in a turnaround 55-37 triumph over the same Wolverines in Ann Arbor. The streak gathered momentum with home triumphs over Northwestern (51-42) and Iowa (43-42). The latter game went to the final minute and teetered on three jump balls that the Illini gained possession of to hang onto a narrow lead.

With Kirk and Judson carrying the load, and freshmen Walt Kersulis, Jack Burmaster and Orr contributing, the Illini carried their victory surge through eight games (including a win over Chanute Field), peaking with another one-point victory, 49-48, against Minnesota at home. Burmaster scored 16 points including a one-hander that created a 49-44 Illini lead.

Then the tide suddenly turned as Mills' wartime club sank into a deep slump in which no member scored more than 11 points over the last four games. Against defending Big Ten champion Ohio State in Columbus, the Illini fell behind 27-16 at the half and never recovered in a 60-44 setback. Four days later, with 15,862 attending at the Chicago Stadium, Big Ten scoring leader Max Morris and the Northwestern Wildcats prevailed 57-45. The slump continued at Indiana, 65-55, as Kirk was held scoreless, missing all six free throw attempts. And finally, with Iowa clinching its first Western Conference title before 14,400

▲ While the Whiz Kids were serving their country instead of enjoying their senior year of ball, the Illini had to look elsewhere for help in 1944-45. This group defeated DePaul and the mighty George Mikan, but ultimately failed to find the consistency needed to win the Big Ten. Left to right—Howard Judson, Jack Burmaster, Don Delaney, Walt Kirk, John Orr, and Walt Kersulis.

screaming fans, the Illini gave way to Dick Ives & Co., 43-37.

The loss ended the UI's season in third place in Big Ten play with an overall mark of 13-7.

WAR ENDS, WHIZ KIDS RETURN

Orr and Kersulis were gone when the 1945-46 season rolled around. Decatur freshman Bob Doster stepped into a lineup captained by Kirk. Early-season foes included Wright Field, Great Lakes and Great Lakes Hospital, among others.

Most noteworthy of Mills' war-era victories was a freshman-laden 56-37 upset of veteran, No. 1-ranked DePaul and big George Mikan at Huff on December 29,

1945. The Illini had DePaul's number during that period. The Demons lost just eight games in three years, and three of the losses were to Illinois. Burmaster and Doster scored 14 apiece, and Wally Mroz tallied 11 in the second half while the Illini did a team job on Mikan, who fell three short of his 23-point average.

The three-day trip to Wisconsin for a January 1, 1946 game showed $225.50 for transportation, $247.41 for nine meals, $35.50 for tips and $112.50 for two overnight stays. It was money well spent, as Illinois won the game at the old Field House, 38-31, with Doster contributing 14 points.

In the second of four straight Big Ten road games, Mroz scored 21 points but Michigan won, 49-48. To seal the victory, the Wolverines elected to take

continued on page 37

GREATEST GAMES
ILLINOIS 56, DEPAUL 37

DECEMBER 29, 1945 • HUFF GYM, CHAMPAIGN, ILLINOIS

ILLINOIS BEATS BIG GEORGE MIKAN AND NO. 1 DEPAUL

The DePaul Blue Demons entered Huff Gym on December 29, 1945 as the top-ranked team in the country and on an incredible streak in which they lost only eight games over the three previous seasons. They carried an 8-0 record into the game, but more importantly, they brought with them the best post player in the first half-century of basketball.

He was a man who already was a two-time All-American and a player who defined dominating. That man was George Mikan. Mikan entered the contest as the nation's leading scorer and his legend was growing to epic proportions.

"Mikan was so big for his time, and I swear he had a wingspan that stretched from Champaign all the way to Chicago," remembered freshman Bob "Chick" Doster. "He would shoot a soft, true hook shot and if he got the ball in the lane he was virtually unstoppable."

The Illini were a depleted team. The Whiz Kids were still away fighting the war. Captain Walt Kirk had left for the service and nobody gave the undersized, young Illini any chance of winning the game. But what people didn't know is that Doug Mills and the Illini devised a plan to slow down Mikan.

"We dropped the weak side forward down every time and went for the ball," recalled Doster. "If we couldn't get a jump ball we would reach in immediately to foul and I know in that game he shot a lot of free throws."

"Our game plan was all about stopping Mikan," recalled Illinois reserve George Leddy. "We had a guy behind him, a guy in front of him, and then a third guy to come over to complete the triple team."

One of the guys assigned to stop Mikan and frustrate him was 5-9 guard Wallie Mroz.

"Doug Mills told me to back off and double on him every time he got the ball," said Mroz. "I knew all of the players from DePaul because they were from Chicago, and I knew the guy I was guarding, Chuck Allen, couldn't hit the broad side of a barn, so it was easy to drop back. I think I bottled him up about 10 times during the game and you can imagine that jump ball, because he was about a foot taller than me."

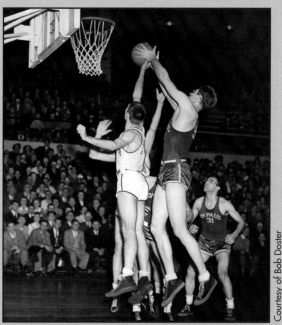

Courtesy of Bob Doster

▲ *Illinois player Bob Doster, in white, battles for a rebound with George Mikan of DePaul. Illinois triple-teamed Mikan throughout the game, often sending him to the free-throw line.*

The Illini held a 20-18 lead at the half, but blew the game wide open in the second half by scoring 36 points behind 11 points from Mroz. When the buzzer sounded, the unheralded Illini destroyed the Blue Demons, 56-37.

"We were thrilled to death with that win and to be able to beat DePaul and Mikan like that was just unbelievable," said Jack Burmaster, who along with Doster, led the Illini with 14 points that evening.

Mikan finished the game with 20 points, scoring only six baskets and shooting eight of 15 from the free-throw line.

DePaul went on to win the NIT in 1945, but in all of the "George Mikan" years the Blue Demons were never beaten as bad as they were that late December night in Huff Gym.

▲ *When the Whiz Kids returned from World War II, they found some new teammates awaiting them. Left photo (left to right)—Jack Burmaster, Dike Eddleman, and Gene Vance. Right photo (left to right)—Andy Phillip, Ken Menke, and Bob Doster.*

continued from page 35

the second of two free throws out of bounds to stall out the remaining seconds. A follow-up 41-35 loss at Ohio State dropped the 1946 Illini to 1-4 and out of the conference race. But the Illini rallied late as returnees Fred Green, Jack Smiley, Dike Eddleman and Jim Marks joined the club to put the finishing touches on a second straight 7-5 Big Ten record. Doster tallied 22 points in the finale, a 57-51 comeback from a 15-point deficit to knock Iowa out of first place. Doster led the Illini in scoring with 273 points in 20 games. Unbelievably, Mills used 31 players during the course of a 14-7 season, with Green and Smiley returning for four and Eddleman playing two.

The four Whiz Kids were reunited in the autumn of 1946."Three of us were married," said Vance. "Jack had two kids. It was an adjustment, going to class again and getting ready for the season. I enrolled that fall, and Doug had pretty much decided this would be his final season as coach."

Like all those who followed the Illini during World War II, Mills regretted that the Whiz Kids couldn't finish what they started. Smiley recalled the difficulty of

trying to attain their former athletic level.

"I was an artillery corporal, one of 16,000 in the 106th Division, and all but 800 were killed or captured in the Battle of the Bulge," said Smiley. "We were surrounded by the Germans, and I spent 90 consecutive hours without sleep at one point. I crossed the last bridge to safety five minutes before it was blown."

Smiley returned along with Green to play in the last few games of the 1946 season, and was MVP in 1947. But Phillip had been ill in the Pacific and didn't regain his scoring touch until later when he became a pro standout.

"Mills motivated us, and I feel he was one of the great college coaches of all time," said Smiley, "but we just weren't the same after the war."

The chemistry was gone. Mills would get Eddleman back from the 1946 Rose Bowl team in January of 1947, and tried to work in freshman Bill Erickson and the veteran Kirk, the UI's leading scorer in 1945, with tall Fred Green.

"We tried to blend in, but we never quite did," said Vance.

▲ *Guard Ken Menke drives to the basket in a 58-31 Illini victory over Pittsburgh in 1946. Despite finishing second in the Big Ten during the 1946-47 season, many felt the Whiz Kids struggled to regain their pre-War greatness.*

Ranked No. 2 after a 3-0 start, the Illini lost at Missouri 55-50 en route to California where the Illini split with Cal's Bears. In a 58-36 rout of Cal, Mills used four Whiz Kids and Urbana's Green for the first 15 minutes as the Illini raced to a 23-2 lead. But the second game was just the opposite as Cal toppled Illinois 53-35. All consistency was gone.

The Illini lost their Big Nine opener to Wisconsin, 53-47, and struggled throughout.

"Andy wasn't in good shape. He was ill. He never hit his form again until he turned pro," said Vance.

When the Illini lost again to Minnesota, the Courier's Bertine wrote: "The Whiz Kids had lost in Europe and the South Pacific the magic that made them the nation's outstanding collegiate cagers in 1942 and 1943. The heroes lost in the very cradle of their basketball, Huff Gym."

In the 34-31 loss to the Gophers, Mills started Erickson and Kirk instead of Vance and Menke and used Eddleman off the bench. The Whiz Kids later got revenge on Wisconsin, 63-37, with Smiley's defense again drawing accolades as he put a lid on Badger scoring machine Bob Cook. But the team had obviously lost its groove, despite finishing tied for second in the conference with an 8-4 mark and a 14-6 overall record.

"We could never quite get it together," related Vance. "We didn't qualify for the NCAA with a second-place finish and that was the end of the Whiz Kids."

Phillip would recover nicely, spending 11 seasons in the NBA with Chicago, Philadelphia, Fort Wayne and Boston. He averaged double figures through his first seven seasons and handed out five-plus assists in eight of those years. In 1952, he became the first NBA player to register more than 500 assists in a single season. Prior to the 1956-57 season, Red Auerbach talked him into joining the Celtics and he was a major player in Boston's championship run ... 17 years after he led Granite City to the state championship and 15 years after he broke in as an Illini sophomore.

Said NBA great Ed McCauley: "Phillip's great value was his ability to make everyone better. He always looked to pass."

The greatest Illini player through the first half-century, Phillip died on April 29, 2001 at age 79. He is the only Illini named to the Basketball Hall of Fame for his playing skills.

Guard Andy Phillip—an offensive force and the go-to guy for the Whiz Kids—drives to the bucket. ▶

Illini Coach Harry A. Combes (left) and Capt. Don Sunderlage, senior from Elgin

Basketball
Illinois
vs.
Washington State

GEORGE HUFF GYMNASIUM, CHAMPAIGN, ILL.

8:00 P.M.

(Doors Close at 7:58 P.M.)

Wednesday, December 20, 1950

Illini Coach Harry A. Combes (Left) and Capt. Bill Erickson, senior from Rockford

Basketball
Illinois
vs.
Indiana

GEORGE HUFF GYMNASIUM, CHAMPAIGN, ILL.

7:30 P.M.

(Doors Close at 7:28 P.M.)

Monday, February 13, 1950

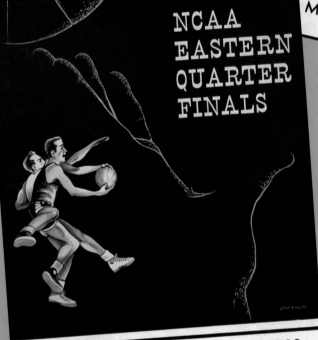

NCAA EASTERN QUARTER FINALS

COLUMBIA UNIV. vs. ILLINOIS
ST. JOHN'S U. vs. CONNECTICUT

MADISON SQUARE GARDEN

MARCH 20, 1951

25c

24c, N. Y. C. SALES TAX 1c

CHAPTER FOUR

THE RUNNIN' ILLINI
1947-48—1950-1951

Ted Beach didn't possess the speed and maneuverability of Bill Erickson or Don Sunderlage, the strength of Wally Osterkorn, the graceful athletic skills of Dike Eddleman or the rebounding prowess of Rod Fletcher. But the lean Champaign product had a pickpocket's hands and he could fill the basket, sneaking into holes in the defense like a possession receiver and drilling low-trajectory one-handers. During the coaching heyday of Combes, Beach was his constant companion ... riding from a 1946 state championship at CHS to two Final Four trips at Illinois.

"I played for the same coach for seven years in high school and college," said Beach. "That's pretty unusual."

Beach never considered attending any school other than Illinois. His father, Frank, was business manager of the old Athletic Association during the construction of Memorial Stadium in the early 1920s, and became a professor in the UI commerce department. Frank began running the scoreboard at UI basketball games in 1935 and Ted became backup timer in 1964-65 and concluded 40 years on the bench in 2004. His daughter, Becky, followed in his basketball footsteps, leading the UI in rebounding and scoring for three seasons and winning the Big Ten golf championship.

Ted was on the sideline as a freshman when Combes made his coaching debut in front of a packed house (6,905) as the UI defeated Coe, 67-27, on December 5, 1947. Illinoisans had never seen so intense a leader as Combes, nor a basketball coach willing to launch shots so quickly. His fast-break style broke the record for Big Ten points in his first season, a standard the Illini would break numerous times thereafter.

In the beginning, Combes had Roettger by his side (until 1949), as well as the heady, sharp-tongued Howard Braun, who served as an assistant for more than three decades. Just as Mills had been a "youthful sensation" as UI coach, Combes was still vigorous and athletic when he took charge.

"Harry was a straight shooter and a devoted student of the game ... an innovator in high school who brought his free-wheeling game to Illinois," said center Fred Green.

Combes inherited a rugged team. Erickson, Osterkorn, Burdette Thurlby and Jim Marks were

▲ *Ted Beach had the unique honor of playing for Coach Combes for seven straight years throughout high school and college.*

mature sophomores while Eddleman and Green were juniors back from the service. Jack Burmaster was the senior captain, having started in 1945 and 1946.

"Everyone looked up to Eddleman," said Beach. "He was a legend in high school at Centralia. In my eyes, he was on a pedestal, an all-around sports star. Playing against him in practice, he was very competitive, never stopped running, perpetual motion. And he had that Centralia kiss shot that was distinctive. In that era, only a few guys still shot two-handed from the outside. Most shot one-handed push shots."

Combes' first season in 1947-48 was highlighted by two stunning wins over Indiana, both one-pointers that vaulted Illinois to 15-5 overall and 7-5 in the league, which was dominated at 10-2 by Michigan and its MVP, Pete Elliott. Hosting the Hoosiers at home, Sullivan's Van Anderson, who had failed on his first six attempts, pushed back a missed shot by Thurlby for a 46-45 lead with :05 showing. But the thrills didn't stop there. Indiana coach Branch McCracken claimed an Illinois foul should have been called before the gun. This was overruled by timer R. Wayne Winters, who was put on the spot by refs Bill Haarlow and Gale Dickerson. After arguments resounded long and loud, the game was ruled over, and a stirring Illini comeback from an 11-point deficit was put in the books.

"It was the first such ruling I've had," Winters was quoted, "but sitting right by the gun, I heard it before the foul was called. That's all there is to it, except I'm glad we used a gun instead of a horn."

Unbelievably, Illinois took 100 shots (Combes' goal) while Indiana managed just 44, and yet the game wasn't decided until after the final gun had sounded.

The season-ender at Indiana was similar. Green helped to protect a narrow Illini lead with two clutch goals that made it 52-48. The game ended 52-51 with Eddleman, by now a 25-year-old junior, depositing 20 points to become the UI's second-highest scorer. Illinois finished the year with a 15-5 mark, 7-5 in league play.

Guard Bill Erickson goes up for a shot against Notre Dame in 1947. Fellow Illini Wally Osterkorn readies himself for the rebound. The Illini won the home game 40-38 en route to a 15-5 record in Coach Harry Combes' first season. ▶

FINAL FOUR FINISH

With only Burmaster gone and future All-American Don Sunderlage moving up as a sophomore in 1948-49, the Illini opened with a 67-62 triumph over Butler and Buckshot O'Brien.

"We didn't press all over the court like we did in high school," said Beach. "Harry thought it wouldn't work because college ballhandlers were better. It had been a surprise in high school."

A deep UI club, perhaps as strong on the bench as any that Combes fielded, marched straight to the Final Four. After edging Notre Dame a year earlier 40-38, they did it again in South Bend in the season's second game, 59-58, on Thurlby's basket in overtime.

This was a physical team, a rugged team, including veteran footballers Walter "Slip" Kersulis and Eddleman, the sturdy Van Anderson, and another multi-sport athlete in Thurlby, who bombed home runs onto Wright street at the old diamond on University avenue. Ken "Preacher" McBride of Centralia, who would have been the UI's first African-American basketball player, was a member of that Sunderlage-Beach class, but failed to meet academic standards in his freshman year.

In an upset, the Illini lost their next game to smaller DePaul before 17,189 in Chicago, 60-50. It was one of few times under Combes that his team was outshot. Harry's theory was the more a team shoots, the more it will score. The DePaul loss behind them, the Illini went on a six-

game win streak entering competition with old foe Wisconsin, the spoiler in Combes' Big Ten opener a year earlier. It turned out to be the UI's first Big Ten opening win since 1944. Rockford's Erickson racked up 17 points in a 62-50 triumph. Erickson was a flashy ballhandler with darting moves and clever passes. He was quick on his feet and determined to penetrate the lane, which made him particularly good at the scissors offense, whereby he and another guard would criss-cross and slice off the rugged Osterkorn. Ox, as Osterkorn was nicknamed, was a clever, six-foot-four postman who seemed to have eyes in the back of his head. Illinois has seldom had a better feeder off the post, and he was dangerous with a hook shot, more sweeping than Green's behind-the-ear release.

Just as he did the previous year, Urbana's Green made a baby hook to nip Indiana 44-42 in the final four seconds at Bloomington and get the Illini off to a 2-0 start in conference play.

"It was just as hard to win on the road as it is today," said Beach, "and it was rabid in Bloomington. They had more than 10,000 fans there."

Two days later, Combes' clutch kids nipped Ohio State 64-63 with centers Osterkorn and Green combining for 30 points and Osterkorn scoring the last four points of the game. Ox's game-deciding free throw

continued on page 46

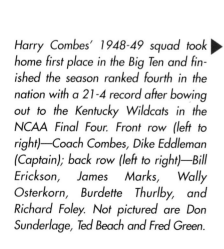

Harry Combes' 1948-49 squad took home first place in the Big Ten and finished the season ranked fourth in the nation with a 21-4 record after bowing out to the Kentucky Wildcats in the NCAA Final Four. Front row (left to right)—Coach Combes, Dike Eddleman (Captain); back row (left to right)—Bill Erickson, James Marks, Wally Osterkorn, Burdette Thurlby, and Richard Foley. Not pictured are Don Sunderlage, Ted Beach and Fred Green.

GREATEST GAMES
(NO. 7) ILLINOIS 45, (NO. 4) MINNESOTA 44
JANUARY 29, 1949 • HUFF GYM, CHAMPAIGN, ILLINOIS

ILLINOIS OVERCOMES 23-9 DEFICIT TO DEFEAT FOURTH-RANKED GOPHERS

▲ Forward Jim Marks tosses in a lay-up that put Illinois ahead 45-42. Marks was a key factor in the great Illini comeback against the Gophers.

This was going to be a showdown of epic proportions. The fourth-ranked Minnesota Gophers, 13-0 on the season and led by star forwards Whitey Skoog, Bud Grant and center Jim McIntyre, were heading to Huff Gym to take on the seventh-ranked, 12-1 Fighting Illini led by captain Dike Eddleman. It was a battle for the Big Ten Conference lead, but essentially it was more than that. This was going to be a battle for the Big Ten title and a trip to the NCAA Tournament.

"It was a game between semesters my freshman year and a bunch of us drove back to see it," remembered Illinois student and current CNN political commentator Bob Novak. "There was no way we were going to miss this game."

Fifteen minutes into the highly anticipated match-up, Novak and the rest of the 6,905 who packed Huff Gym might have wished they stayed home. Skoog, one of the first players in the Big Ten to shoot a jump shot, dominated the first portion of the game. He scored 10 of Minnesota's first 17 points and before long the Gophers held a 23-9 lead. In an era where there was no shot clock and stalling was customary, there wasn't one person in Huff Gym who didn't think the lead was insurmountable.

Except for Illini coach Harry Combes, who had a trick up his sleeve. The Illini enjoyed two weeks of preparation for the Minnesota game and they used much of that to work on Combes' old press defense, which was a throwback to his days at Champaign High School. They put the press on, and before long the lead had whittled down to 27-20 at the half.

"We started pressing and I remember we just kept hustling and hustling until we started to get to them," recalled reserve guard Dick Foley.

Heading into the locker room, the Illini received an inspirational message from their captain.

"That first half was a real grind, but I remember Dike walking in and saying, 'We are going to beat these guys,'" said Illinois center Wally "Ox" Osterkorn. "He told us to come out in the second half, play our game, and that we would have nothing to worry about."

The Illini listened to their captain's message and came out red-hot in the second half. They immediately went on an 8-0 run with baskets from Fred Green, Don Sunderlage, Jim Marks and Eddleman to take a 28-27 lead. Minnesota's Skoog got away from the Illinois defense on the next possession to hit a lay-up which gave the Gophers the lead. But that would be all for Skoog thanks to the defensive prowess of Illinois guard Bill Erickson, who was all over Skoog in the second half.

continued on page 46

continued from page 45

"That's where Bill Erickson got the nickname 'Rabbit,'" said Osterkorn. "He was on Skoog like a rabbit chasing a mouse. He just hung on him and shut him down completely."

Illinois reserve forward Benton Odum played the role of Skoog on the Illini scout team all week during practice and knew that Skoog would face a tough task in Erickson.

"The Gophers would move four guys to one side to isolate Skoog, but Erickson did an unbelievable job of shutting him down," remembered Odum. "He had quick hands and extremely quick feet, which took away the strengths of Skoog."

With about five minutes to play, the Gophers were clinging to a 42-41 lead. It was time for senior forward Jim Marks to step up. First he drove in, got fouled, and calmly sank two free throws. On the next possession he got into the lane and put in a short lay-up that made it 45-42.

After Minnesota got a basket on a Bud Grant put back, Illinois went into their stall and, while the Gophers fouled them continuously, the Illini refused to shoot free throws in favor of keeping the ball. When the buzzer sounded, Huff Gym erupted. The Illini, paced by ten points from seniors Fred Green and Jim Marks, had completed perhaps the greatest comeback in the history of the Illinois basketball program.

"I'll never forget that loss, because we were one point from the Big Ten Championship," said Skoog, reflecting on the game more than 50 years later.

Illinois went on to win the Big Ten title that season and advanced to the national semifinals in the NCAA Tournament in New York. All of which wouldn't have been possible if not for a miraculous comeback just a few months earlier at Huff Gym.

▲ *Members of the Illini celebrate with fans after their thrilling defeat of Minnesota at Huff Gym.*

continued from page 44

came when OSU all-star Dick Schnittker was whistled for charging him.

Next on the Big Ten docket was Minnesota with the fleet Whitey Skoog, future NFL coach Bud Grant and 6-9 Jim McIntyre. The Gophers were ranked fourth nationally. Erickson guarded Skoog, and held him to six for 18 from the field, while Marks and Green led a bench that scored 26 points in a 45-44 Illini win. The press defense, featuring Erickson and Sunderlage, sparked the rally from a 20-7 deficit.

The glittering Combes success story grew from those three straight league wins by a total margin of four points: 44-42, 64-63 and 45-44 with Urbana's longtime judge, Fred Green, in the middle of every late-game surge.

"If it's true that champions win the close ones, Illinois must be in," wrote Bert Bertine in the *Courier*. "The UI's deadly coolness at the free throw line (15 of 17) provided the victory margin as Minnesota scored three more field goals."

Two days later, in a disappointment at Purdue, the Illini fell 55-53, and their 11-game win streak was snapped. But they roared back to reel off six clearcut Big Ten victories to clinch the championship, only to lose at Michigan in a 70-53 final-game letdown. Eddleman fell six points shy of Phillip's season record of 305 points, but went on to be named Big Ten MVP. The team's final Big Ten mark was 10-2.

Playing in the NCAA for the first time since 1942, the Illini defeated Tony Lavelli and Yale 71-67 before 18,051 in New York's Madison Square Garden. Lavelli scored 27 points while Sunderlage and Osterkorn bagged 15 apiece for the winners. With Illinois trailing 67-65, Van Anderson and Kersulis drained consecutive 20-footers, and Dick Foley stole the ball and converted a clinching layup. Illinois refused three free throws in stalling out the final 1:10.

But Combes' Illini, competing in the Final Four, proved no match for powerhouse Adolph Rupp and his Kentucky team. The Wildcats featured Alex Groza and Ralph Beard, both Kentuckians who provided the nucleus for the 1948 U.S. Olympic team. The Illini had no one in double figures as the Wildcats ruled 76-47. Groza racked up 27 points in the win.

Illinois flew to Seattle for the third-place game, defeating Oregon State 57-53 with Osterkorn scoring 17 and Eddleman, in his final game, adding 11. The win left the Illini at 21-4 on the season, a mark that earned them a final AP ranking of fourth.

A STEP BACK

With Eddleman, Green and Foley gone, Champaign's Rod Fletcher (son of Ralph Fletcher, long-time football assistant) moved in to the starting lineup and Combes' Illini opened the 1949-50 season with a hard-fought 60-56 win over Butler as Beach, now a junior, knocked in a rebound to break a 56-56 tie. Osterkorn led scorers with 19.

In a home duel with UCLA during Christmas break, Roy Gatewood pulled Illinois even at 63-63 with 40 seconds left, but his late shot missed. Olympic high jumper George Stanich took the long rebound and drove the length of the court to score the Bruins' winning basket in the last five seconds.

The Illini were 7-2 going into the customary Big Ten opener at Wisconsin, and 33 UI fouls contributed to a 59-50 Badger triumph. Erickson sped around for 19 points but no other Illini had more than six. Lefty Don Rehfeldt sparked Wisconsin with 27. When the Illini lost the next game at Ohio State, 83-62, it was apparent that a repeat title wouldn't be a likely occurrence. As a consolation, the Illini avenged the OSU setback later at home, 66-50, with Sunderlage and Osterkorn combining for 44 points. But the Buckeyes were in charge and won the title.

The 1950 Illini dropped four of their last eight games, including a 62-42 collapse at St. Louis after January finals. Billiken coach Ed Hickey had stated following a 59-47 loss in Champaign that "We'll beat you in St. Louis, and that's a promise."

The Illini never got on track down the stretch—finishing 7-5 in conference and 14-8 overall—but the future was bright. Illinois entered the 1950-51 season with crack sophomores Irv Bemoras, Clive Follmer, Bob Peterson, Jimmy Bredar and Max Baumgardner joining the squad.

▲ *The 1948-49 Illini celebrate after defeating 11th-ranked Yale, 71-67, in the opening round of the NCAA Tournament in New York City. Coach Combes (center) is flanked by Dike Eddleman (No. 40) and Don Sunderlage (No. 11).*

BACK TO THE FINAL FOUR

Beach and Sunderlage, the captain, were the lone seniors, and Fletcher was the only junior earning significant playing time in 1950-51.

"Sunderlage was the best penetrator and had great body control," said Beach. "He had a good outside shot, but his strength was beating defenders off the dribble and drawing fouls. He was Big Ten MVP and an All-American. We didn't use the term 'point guard' in those days, but he was the one who put the offense in motion."

Beach was used primarily as sixth man, entering early for Follmer or Bemoras, and he wound up second in scoring, actually playing more minutes than the sophomores.

The Illini split with Ray Meyer's DePaul team, winning 69-68 when Irv Bemoras sank the winning free

▲ *Don Sunderlage played a key role on both the 1948-49 and 1950-51 Big Ten champion Illini. He would captain the 1950-51 team during a senior season in which he was named an All-American.*

throw in his first appearance in the Chicago Stadium since leading Marshall to the city championship in 1948. This capped a rally from a 59-54 deficit. However, the Illini fell to DePaul 68-65 in the first ever UI loss at Huff during the Christmas-New Year week. Down 57-41, the Illini rallied with Beach and Jim Bredar hawking the ball, and caught up at 65-all, but DePaul countered at the end.

As in 1949, the first three league games set the stage for the UI's 1951 title run. Wisconsin sub Jim Van Dien sank a free throw after the horn had sounded to throw the Big Ten opener into overtime, and the Illini hauled it out 71-69 with Beach breaking the last tie via one of his patented low-arch 20-footers. As was typical for that team, five Illini cashed double figures—Sunderlage (18), Peterson (17), Beach (12), and Bemoras and Fletcher (10).

Minnesota's Gophers still had the dynamic Skoog and were league co-favorites entering their only match with Illinois. Playing at home, the Illini prevailed 70-62 with Beach garnering 14 points in the first half and the hard-driving Follmer bagging 12 in the second half.

"This was one of my good games," said Beach. "Harry emphasized the importance of it because we wouldn't play them again. Minnesota got ahead early but we came back to lead 32-29 at half in front of a wild crowd at Huff. Typical for Sunderlage, he made 11 free throws."

NEXT WAS IOWA

"Like today, Wisconsin and Iowa were tough places to play," said Beach, "and the wild-eyed fans (13,732) were out at Iowa when we won our third straight. Illinois hadn't won in Iowa City since 1937."

Trailing the Hawkeyes 7-0, the Illini took their first lead at 22-21 and led the rest of the way. But it was a unique halftime. Combes was talking to Fletcher in rather strong terms about how he needed to get on the boards in the second half. Recalled Beach:

"He said, 'Rod, you've got to go up for the ball like you really want it ... like this!' Harry jumped high with his arms up to illustrate his point, completely forgetting about the low-hanging heat pipe in the dressing room at the old Iowa Fieldhouse. Combes' head hit the pipe hard and the pipe won. He tumbled to the floor, scrambled to his feet and said, 'And that's the way you've got to go up after the ball.' No player in that room dared to smile."

The Illini came back strong, making it 70-60 and hanging on for the 72-69 victory. Again, four Illini made double figures with the two Elgin products, Peterson and Sunderlage, getting 14 apiece.

Those three wins propelled the championship drive. The only loss came in the fifth game at Indiana where senior center Bill Garrett scored 21 and Collinsville guard Sammy Miranda tallied 19 for the Hoosiers.

On January 20, Iowa was late arriving in Champaign-Urbana due to inclement weather, and the game didn't start until nearly 11 p.m.

"Sunderlage and I played checkers in the dressing room for several hours, and Bob Hope, in town for a show, made an appearance before the waiting fans at Huff Gym. In the game, Sunderlage ran wild for 27 points and it was never close, 69-53," said Beach.

Illinois battles Pennsylvania at Huff Gym on December 22, 1950. The Illini were victorious 75-65. The Illini pictured, left to right, are Clive Follmer, Don Sunderlage, Rod Fletcher, and Mack Follmer.

In the return game with Indiana, Combes' Illini reached 10-1 in the league with a rousing rally from a 58-53 deficit. Sunderlage keyed the revival, tying the game at 60-60 as Garrett fouled out. Fletcher and Follmer followed with baskets as the Illini salted it away, 71-65.

"The atmosphere for that Indiana game was as chaotic as I ever saw it," said then-freshman Jim Wright. "Fans were jammed right down on the Huff Gym floor, and the I-Men were seated directly across from the Illini bench, and it was hard for anybody to take the ball out of bounds, especially Indiana.

"It was one of the best games I ever saw at Huff. The score went back and forth with Garrett leading the Hoosiers, and Sunderlage leading Illinois ... a shootout between two running coaches, Combes and McCracken."

The Illini assured themselves of a tie for the title in building a 71-50 lead and beating Northwestern 80-76, preventing what the Wildcat football team did in knocking the UI out of the Rose Bowl, 14-7, in the fall. Seniors Sunderlage and Beach scored 27 and 21, and Sunderlage broke Osterkorn's season scoring record on Combes' birthday.

A 49-43 win at Michigan State clinched the NCAA berth with a 13-1 conference mark. Illinois rallied from a 43-39 deficit as Fletcher twice stole the ball and scored to tie it. On fire, Fletcher added two more baskets as the Illini racked the last 10 points of the game.

"Indiana split with us, and we didn't have to go to Minnesota," said Beach. "Indiana lost at Minnesota and finished one game behind us."

After a tuneup with Kansas State (a 91-72 loss), Illinois headed into the NCAA tournament against undefeated Columbia, winning 79-71 as Sunderlage and Beach cashed 25 and 22. Beach hit seven of eight first-half shots after coming off the bench. No Columbia team had ever given up 79 points. In the quarterfinal game, Illinois rolled over North Carolina State 84-70 with Fletcher garnering a collegiate-high nine baskets, including a halftime heave from the far end that was believed to be the longest in UI history.

continued on page 51

GREATEST GAMES
(NO. 14) ILLINOIS 69, IOWA 53
JANUARY 20, 1951 • HUFF GYM, CHAMPAIGN, ILLINOIS

ILLINOIS BASKETBALL GAME LASTS TWO DAYS

There have been a lot of wild, crazy and lengthy games in the history of Illinois basketball. Illinois fans can vividly recall the four-overtime marathon at the Assembly Hall in 1984 against Michigan or the three-overtime thriller against Missouri in the 1993 Bragging Rights game.

But none of those games lasted longer or were as unbelievable as the January 20, 1951 contest between Illinois and Iowa.

The 14th-ranked, 10-3 Illini, were gearing up for a huge showdown with the Hawkeyes that was going to have major ramifications in the Big Ten race. Iowa—certainly a formidable opponent—was led by center Chuck Darling and forward Frank Calsbeek.

The night was set up perfectly. Game time was set for 8 p.m., comedian Bob Hope was scheduled to perform after the game and a capacity crowd of 6,905 fans jammed Huff Gym hours before the game to watch the junior varsity play in their usual warmup.

What those in attendance didn't know is that they would be watching that game for a long time.

Iowa couldn't get on their plane due to severe snowstorms throughout the Midwest and instead boarded a bus headed for Champaign. Due to the poor weather, Iowa's bus wasn't set to arrive at Huff Gym on time, and so the junior varsity teams were forced to keep playing.

"We played four quarters of the junior varsity game and Iowa hadn't arrived yet," recalled then-freshman John Kerr. "Just so we didn't have an empty gym we kept going, and I think I put up 100 points that night."

"The JV team just kept playing and playing and playing," laughed varsity center Mack Follmer. "I think the final score was like 178-90."

While the junior varsity attempted to keep the crowd entertained, Iowa was going through an absolutely disastrous trip.

"We used to travel by train to all the games, but it was such a big game that the University decided to charter a DC-3 plane into Illinois," remembered Darling, who was fighting the flu at the time. "Then the storm hit so we couldn't get out, but the weatherman predicted that the next morning—or the day of the game—was going to be much better."

When Iowa woke up to travel to Champaign that morning, the weather had gotten worse.

"We got in those limos from Iowa City and started our journey," said Darling. "We only stopped one time during that trip for a quick bite to eat, but it took us forever to get [to Champaign]."

The Illinois varsity was forced to deal with the unusual circumstances as they had no idea when the game was going to start.

"Ordinarily a game like that would have been cancelled or rescheduled, but Iowa stayed in touch with us throughout their trip and they kept thinking they were going to be there quicker than they were," recalled Clive Follmer. "We went back to the dressing room several times, warmed up a bunch and I think everyone was just ready to start the game."

During one of those trips to the locker room, the Illinois team had a choice to make.

"After we had been waiting for a while, Harry Combes called us all back to the dressing room and said, 'Well, they are two hours late and according to the rules we can take a forfeit,'" recalled Mack Follmer. "He told us we could play, but if we did that the result would count. We ended up taking a vote on whether we wanted to play the game or not, and we all wanted to play."

Iowa finally arrived in Huff at 10:30 p.m., and after a brief warm-up the game began two hours and 49 minutes late at 10:49. Amazingly, the Hawkeyes stormed out to an 8-3 lead, but after the Illini fought back to tie it up at eight, Illinois received 11 straight points from guard Don Sunderlage to take a 19-14 lead. The Illini took a 30-21 lead into the half and kept the pressure on throughout the entire second stanza. As the game progressed, the long trip eventually caught up to the Hawkeyes.

"We were beat and we weren't a very deep team," said Darling. "We were only playing seven guys that year and we just wore down."

Behind a career-high 27 points from Sunderlage, the Illini blew out the Hawkeyes 69-53 to move to 5-1 in the conference. By the time the final buzzer sounded, the clock in Huff Gym read 12:09 a.m.

For the only time in the 100-year history of Illinois basketball, the Illini had to fight for two days to come away with one big victory.

continued from page 49

Then came archenemy Kentucky, who handed the UI what Bertine called "one of the most heartbreaking losses in Illini history."

Shelby Linville, a 6-5 forward who replaced seven-foot Bill Spivey when he fouled out, made the final three field goals including the 74-74 tie-breaker. Thus did Illinois pay for a "dead spell" in the final nine minutes that gave Kentucky the opening to rally. Sunderlage, who became the UI's single-season scoring leader with 471 points, saw his contortionist, last-ditch shot to tie roll off the rim.

Other than 1989, when the Illini also lost by two to Michigan in the Final Four, this was the UI's closest bid for the elusive national title. Peterson, who fouled out,

and sub Max Baumgardner had been powerless to stop Spivey (28 points), causing Combes to wonder whether the UI might have pulled it off if he had elected to use sophomore Johnny "Red" Kerr, who became eligible at the semester. Kerr didn't want to lose a season for a half-season of play, and made good use of his upcoming three campaigns as he earned league MVP and second-team All-America honors in 1954.

Three days after the loss to Kentucky, Illinois ousted Oklahoma A&M, 61-46, in the third-place game in Minneapolis. The team's season-ending mark of 22-5 was good for fifth in the AP standings.

▲ The Illinois portion of the official scorecard from the team's season-opening victory over Marquette in 1950. Illinois won the game 66-47 on the strength of a double-double from Don Sunderlage, who scored 15 points and grabbed 13 rebounds.

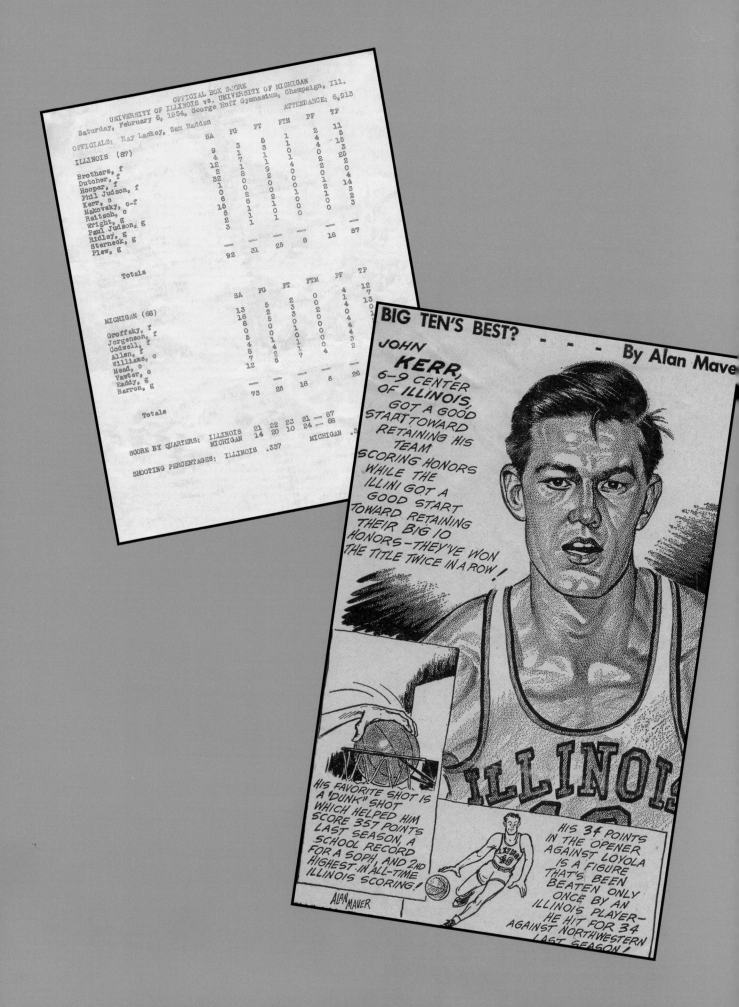

CHAPTER FIVE

ORANGE & BLUE & RED
1951-52—1953-54

In the last half of the 20th century, no Illini name was more closely linked to basketball, college and pro, than Johnny "Red" Kerr. He played on Tilden Tech's city champions, Illinois' Big Ten champions in 1952 and Syracuse's NBA champions in 1955. On the collegiate level, Kerr became the UI's career scoring leader on teams that finished 22-4, 18-4 and 17-5. In the pros, he was a three-time all-star as he produced 12,480 points and 10,092 rebounds in the NBA. Remarkably durable for so slender an athlete, the six-foot-nine Kerr played in 844 consecutive games from 1954-65, an NBA record that stood for nearly two decades.

After his playing days were through, Kerr coached the first Chicago Bulls team, earning Coach of the Year honors. He was then lured by old friend Jerry Colangelo to coach the fledgling Suns team in Phoenix. Kerr left coaching midway through his second season to begin a long broadcast career that is going strong to this day in Chicago.

Kerr shot up dramatically as a high school senior, the extra height drawing him from the soccer field to the hardwood. His mid-year enrollment at the UI raised a question as to when his collegiate career would begin.

◀ *Left, the official box score from the Illini's 87-68 trouncing of Michigan in 1954. Right, a cartoon from the era featuring Johnny "Red" Kerr.*

"Kerr had good scoring skills," said teammate Jim Wright. "It was a question all along between Combes and Braun whether or not he should play in the second semester of 1951. But they wanted to save his eligibility. Had he been on that team, I'm sure he and Bob Peterson would have split playing time, which they did the following year."

Combes had Kerr, Wright and Max Hooper on the 1951 freshman team, once again taking advantage of the UI's strong position with Illinois prep coaches.

"At that time and previously, the university's coaching school turned out a lot of men who became coaches around the state, and Harry and Howie knew them all," said Wright. "It was a great recruiting advantage. As I look back, I believe the elimination of that school hurt Illini basketball and football recruiting as much as any other factor."

Unlike today, Wright and other UI varsity athletes were on work-related scholarships. Wright recalled:

"A lot of the guys handed out towels or worked at Memorial Stadium," said Wright. "I had a choice and picked Illinois Power because I was in the business school. I reported over there two days a week. And I washed pots and pans for my meals. I don't ever want to look at a pot or pan again."

ON A STREAK

The 1951-52 Illini opened with 11-straight wins, in one 11-day stretch whipping a good Oklahoma team (69-51), North Carolina (86-66), DePaul (70-61) and UCLA (73-67). Little more than a half-century ago, Illinois was at the top of the nation's basketball elite. Balanced in the extreme, the Illini put six players in double figures with Kerr hitting 17 and Peterson 16 against the Sooners. Bemoras erupted with 21 to dump DePaul.

T.O. White of *The News-Gazette* wrote of the six-point defeat of UCLA: "A capacity crowd, with late

Coach Combes (left) couldn't have been more thrilled to have six-foot-nine Johnny "Red" Kerr (right) step into the team's lineup in 1951-52 after losing senior scoring sensation Don Sunderlage to graduation. Kerr went on to set the UI's career scoring mark before graduating in 1954.

comers turned away when the ticket supply was exhausted, saw the most exciting game of the holiday series."

Salem's Jim Bredar, taking over for the graduated Sunderlage, scored six quick points after UCLA forged ahead, and Kerr broke free to crack the final tie of 67-67.

"Bredar was a six-foot center in high school, and his conversion to guard at Illinois took time," recalled Wright, a prep rival at Lawrenceville.

"He was an average player as an Illini sophomore but, during the summer that followed, he worked on a jump shot with a friend from southern Illinois, Barney Oldfield. Bredar became one of the first to perfect the jump shot off the dribble, and had a rhythm to it where he'd fake and get a couple of bounces and create space so he could prevent it from being blocked. Other players hadn't seen it, and that's how he perfected one of the first jump shots ever used by players anywhere."

Neither Bemoras nor Follmer shot a true jump shot. Neither did Don Sunderlage. The jump shot was just coming into vogue.

Ranked No. 2 in the nation with a 7-0 record, Combes' 1951-52 team opened the Big Ten race before 17,862 shrieking fans at Minnesota. In a defensive gem, Kerr limited big Ed Kalafat while Rod Fletcher helped break down the Gopher zone with 14 points. Illinois won, 52-43. The Illini launched 85 shots with a .247 percentage in the next game against Wisconsin, winning 53-49 as Kerr broke the final tie at 43-43. It was an off night for Illinois, but it brought the Illini win streak to nine.

Rolling along at No. 2 in the nation, the Illini ripped Michigan in Ann Arbor, 67-51 behind 22 points from the talented but sometimes underrated Bemoras. The win streak reached 11 with a 78-66 blowout of No. 4-ranked Indiana as Kerr scored 17, Fletcher and Follmer chipped in 16 apiece and Bemoras added 15. As so often happened during that era, the duel between the superstitious Combes, with his red socks, and Indiana's "Sheriff," Branch McCracken, was the high-scoring highlight of the season. How those guys liked to run and gun!

Vaulting to No. 1 in the country during the semester break, the Illini came back on January 26 to meet

DePaul at Chicago Stadium in a non-conference game. Combes' kids built a 14-point lead before Ray Meyer's talented club rallied for a 69-65 decision. However, the Big Ten win streak continued until the Illini traveled to Iowa City where Chuck Darling (26 points) and the ninth-ranked Hawkeyes trimmed the Illini, 73-68, even as the Illini attempted 91 shots.

But the 1952 Illini regained their composure and won six straight to clinch the Big Ten title and start their march into the first official NCAA Final Four. Beating Dayton and DuQuesne in Chicago, Bredar emerged as a star with 19 and 16 points as the Illini qualified for Seattle's Final Four.

"That was one of the first trips we made by airplane," said Wright, "and we shared the plane with the players from St. John's. The weather was bad and the trip was rough; several players got sick on the plane.

▲ *Jim Bredar had to convert from a six-foot high school center to a scoring guard for the Illini. The transformation included Bredar developing a jump shot off the dribble. He was one of the first in the country to perfect that shot, which soon became fashionable.*

When we got to the West Coast, we had trouble getting into Seattle. When we came out of the clouds, Doug Mills was on the ground watching as the pilot overshot the runway. We were headed toward the top of the hangar when the pilot pulled the plane back up, and we flew on to Portland for the night's stay.

"A lot of the guys were sick. I firmly believe this had a lasting effect on how we played ... although the St. John's players were on the same plane and it was fair for both."

Bertine said the Illini "lacked zest" in a 61-59 loss, the second consecutive two-point loss in the national semifinals. Illinois was outrebounded by St. John's 52-35. Center Bob Zawoluk scored 24 points and tipped in a key rebound for St. John's to make it 60-55 with 1:40 remaining. Bredar and Fletcher led a weak Illini attack with 14 apiece.

Illinois took the consolation prize with a 67-64 victory over Santa Clara the following night. The season's disappointing finish didn't detract from what was still an amazing year as the team finished No. 2 in the AP rankings with a 22-4 record.

GOOD, BUT NOT GOOD ENOUGH

Next season, in the fall of 1952, Illinois was again ranked near the top. Fletcher had graduated and juniors Wright and Hooper stepped into key roles. Hooper, who led two Mt. Vernon teams to state titles, employed a unique set shot, taking the ball to the top of his head and releasing a two-handed push shot.

Kerr opened the 1952-53 season with 34 points in the 71-57 defeat of Chicago Loyola. Due to a new 18-game Big Ten schedule, Illinois opened the conference season on December 15 with a 96-66 rout of Michigan. The Illini launched 102 shots—making 38—and five players made double figures. Next up was a road game in Minnesota eight days later. Illinois took a No. 2 ranking into the game, then committed 34 fouls (to the Gophers' 10) and lost 77-73.

"I guarded Chuck Mencel," recalled Wright. "He was a heck of a player. During my last two years, I got to guard all those guys ... Robin Freeman, Bobby Leonard, guys like that. Harry asked who wanted to guard Julius McCoy at Michigan State, and I said, 'I'll try him.' By the

▲ The 1951-52 team, which finished the season ranked No. 2 in the nation, celebrates after toppling No. 4-ranked Duquesne, 74-68, in the second round of the NCAA Midwest Regional in Chicago. Front row (left to right)— Herb Gerecke, Jim Bredar, Irv Bemoras, Rod Fletcher; back row (left to right)—Bob Peterson, Johnny Kerr, Coach Combes, Max Hooper, Clive Follmer, Dick Christensen, Ed Makovsky, Jim Wright, and Cyrus Vaughn III.

time he scored three or four baskets, Howie (Braun) called out, 'Let somebody else take him.' McCoy was about 6-6, and could jump through the ceiling. I couldn't handle him.

"When we went to Indiana, we were ranked No. 4 and they were ranked No. 6," said Wright, "and we lost in double overtime 74-70."

The Illini sank 21 of 23 free throws in regulation, but Indiana used free throws in overtime to prevail.

"We had several good chances to win but we missed close-in opportunities," said Wright. "We held for the last shot with the score tied in the first overtime, but Bemoras' shot bounced off."

It was a two-team race with both clubs having national championship hopes, but Indiana set the stage

for its NCAA title by returning to Champaign and shattering the tradition of home court invincibility by beating Illinois 91-79. Big Don Schlundt scored 33 and Indiana led at one point, 56-38, before Follmer sparked a belated rally.

"The king is dead, long live the king," wrote Bertine.

Three more wins were not enough to win the Big Ten title, as the '53 Illini settled for second with a 14-4 conference record—18-4 overall—and the AP's No. 13 ranking. This ended Illinois' run of three undisputed Big Ten championships in four years. It would take over 50 years—until 2004—for the next.

The senior class of Follmer, Peterson, Bredar and Bemoras was 62-13 with two Final Four finishes. Kerr

▲ *Illini guard Jim Wright (left) and guard-forward Irv Bemoras (right) had plenty to cheer about during their time at Illinois. Wright provided steady play and solid defense for the Illini in the early 1950s. He later returned to his alma mater as an assistant coach under Harry Combes and Harv Schmidt. During Bemoras' stay on the varsity, the Illini won two Big Ten championships—finishing in second during his senior season—and went an astounding 62-13.*

became the big gun in 1954 for a 17-5 team that finished two games behind another Indiana powerhouse and second-place Iowa.

RED'S SENIOR SEASON

Kerr and Wright were the senior leaders in 1954. Quincy's Bruce Brothers moved in as a sophomore starter. So did Paul Judson, who along with twin brother Phil gained everlasting fame for leading tiny Hebron to the state championship.

A big early win came at Oklahoma when Kerr racked 34—converting 13 of 18 shots—and Wright added 14 in an 86-61 romp. In an 80-48 defeat of Butler four days later, Kerr set the Illini career scoring record in just the third game of his third season.

No. 6 Minnesota won the first Big Ten game, 84-72, with Dick Garmaker drilling 13 of 17 shots while Kerr needed 30 shots for his 31 points. Little Billy Ridley of

Taylorville made his first varsity splash with three late points to hold off Northwestern, 66-65, but the Illini lost a one-pointer at Michigan State five days later. That game was tied at 55-55, 57-57 and 59-59 before McCoy made the winning free throw after his basket was disallowed.

Kerr continued to roll up points, garnering a near-record 38 in a 90-76 thumping of Ohio State at home. Wright shadowed sensational sophomore Robin Freeman, holding him to two field goals (he totaled four in the game) directly after Freeman's 14-goal outburst against Purdue. Playing OSU again in Columbus, the Illini ruled 82-78 despite Freeman's 28 points.

Illinois also beat Wisconsin twice. The second game reached its climax in an uphill struggle as Wright nailed two free throws at :02 for the 66-64 win over the Badgers at Huff gym. Kerr's 18 points were low for him during the Big Ten season.

▲ *Both the rule book and the court looked quite different in the 1950s. Here, Illinois, in the dark jerseys, battles Wisconsin in a 70-64 win on the road in 1954.*

With a title tie in the balance, the Illini lost their finale, 67-64, at Indiana with Kerr scoring 20 and Wright 19. Leonard's four free throws at the end saved the Hoosiers. If the Illini had won, it would have created a three-way tie, requiring a blind draw between Indiana, Illinois and Iowa for the NCAA berth. It was the second year in a row that exceptional Indiana teams prevented Illinois from reaching the playoffs, despite a 17-5 mark (10-4 in conference) and a final AP ranking of 19th.

"That last Indiana game was terrific from start to finish," said Wright. "They were No. 2 in the nation

and they had 11,000 fans going wild. We lost on free throws. They had 33, we had 18.

"We were fortunate to have a lot of wins in that four-year period. It was a golden period. The team was 79-18 in my four college years."

Kerr averaged 25.3 points per game that season, the second highest total by an Illini in 100 years. Only Don Freeman's 27.8 average in 1966 was better.

Wright became an assistant coach in 1957 and served for 14 years under Combes and Harv Schmidt. Kerr headed on to greatness in the NBA as a player, coach, and broadcaster.

College Basketball

ILLINOIS
VS.
WISCONSIN

MONDAY, JAN. 9, 1956
8:00 P.M. (Doors Close at 7:58 P.M.)
GEORGE HUFF GYMNASIUM, CHAMPAIGN, ILLINOIS

Illini Coach
Harry Combes
and Captain
Harv Schmidt,
Senior Forward
from Kankakee

Basketball
Illinois vs. Minnesota
GEORGE HUFF GYMNASIUM, CHAMPAIGN, ILLINOIS
1:30 P.M. (Doors Close at 1:28 P.M.)
SATURDAY, MARCH 2, 1957

DON OHL
Guard

BILL ALTENBERGER
Forward

CHAPTER SIX

SECOND BEST
1954-55—1956-57

With Combes drawing almost unchallenged from the state's talent pool, and shocking adversaries with a new-style running game, Illini basketball was never consistently stronger than in the 1950s. Reaching the Final Four in 1949, his first season, Combes posted an 87-25 record in Big Ten play through 1956.

The misfortune for Illinois is that only the Big Ten champion advanced to the NCAA tournament in those days—that was the case until 1975. Indiana's Leonard-Schlundt-Kraak national champions edged out terrific Illini teams in 1953 and 1954, and Iowa's star-studded lineup of transplanted Illinoisans had the Illini's number in the big games in 1955 and 1956.

A central figure in those latter years was Harv Schmidt, an angular, six-foot-six forward from Kankakee. Like so many in-state stars before him, Schmidt never seriously considered any school but the UI.

"Harry never recruited anyone easier," said Schmidt from his Denver home this year. "My mother met with Harry and Doug. Then I went in, and Harry shook my hand and said, 'I'm glad to have you aboard.' That was it.

"Back then, the goal was just to be good enough to play for Illinois. You didn't negotiate. You just dove into the mix."

Schmidt was well known before he arrived. His Kays lost to LaGrange and Ted Caiazza in one of the legendary high school tournament games of the era. Both were undefeated at the time. With Kerr gone, the burr-headed Schmidt backed up George BonSalle, Bill Altenberger and Bruce Brothers in the UI's 1954-55 front line. The Taylorville flash, Billy Ridley, teamed with Paul Judson in a superb backcourt.

▲ Forward Harv Schmidt earned his stripes as a regular for Coach Combes before taking over coaching duties from Combes in 1967.

"That was a tough year for me, a learning experience," recalled Schmidt. "I couldn't quite get it going. I had never played outside (of the paint) exclusively like I had to do in college. That was a major adjustment.

"It was a real young team, and I don't know if Illinois ever had a better pair of guards than Ridley and Paul Judson."

Another early-season win streak consumed Missouri (77-49), Hank Iba's 11th-ranked Oklahoma A&M team (59-53) and No. 20 Notre Dame (66-57) with the Mutt & Jeff duo of BonSalle and Ridley dominating offensively. Ridley (21 points) was particularly destructive in rallying Illinois from a 42-34 deficit against the Irish.

"This was dog-eat-dog," wrote *The News-Gazette's* Jack Prowell of the Illini-Irish battle.

Said Schmidt: "For his size, Ridley was about as good as you get. The paper listed him at 5-9 but he wasn't that tall. He was quick and a great passer with peripheral vision, an exciting player who made flamboyant plays. And Paul Judson was a special player off that championship Hebron team. Those two were quick out front, and they were always knocking the ball away. They'd shake it loose and ping-pong it down the court."

Illinois hit a wall against Loyola of the South in New Orleans, falling 72-66 to a team packed with Catholic Leaguers out of Chicago.

Nor were they sharp in a 79-64 league-opening loss to Wisconsin at home.

"Illinois' basketball bubble burst early," wrote Prowell, noting that no Illini scored more than 11 points.

Intensified by the disappointment that saw them tumble to No. 12 in the AP poll, the Illini went on a high-scoring binge against Indiana. Launching 88 shots, they set a school and Huff Gym scoring record in a 99-75 romp that saw Ridley tally 20, Judson 19 and Brothers 18. They were never challenged after breaking to a 15-0 lead.

For his size, guard Bill Ridley was about as good as it got, said teammate Harv Schmidt. Here, Ridley—otherwise known as "The Taylorville Flash"—takes to the air for a shot in the lane. ▶

"We always seemed to play well against Indiana," said Schmidt.

But this was Iowa's year and the Illini season—in fact the rest of the 1950s—turned upside down in the last 16 minutes at Iowa. Illinois led 61-45 and seemingly had the Hawkeyes buffaloed. Then came the deluge!

"Iowa put rebounding strength in its lineup after BonSalle (fouled out in 12 minutes) had retired on fouls," wrote Prowell. "Iowa circled with 6-7 Bob George, 6-6 Bill Logan and springy 6-6 Carl Cain around the basket."

Ridley's 32 points could not prevent a devastating 92-80 setback.

"Iowa was really good," said Schmidt. "They had the Freeport guys, Carl Cain and Deacon Davis, and the only non-Illinoisan in the lineup was Logan. I got tangled up with Davis and he taught me a little basketball. He was tough."

Still, the Illini lost only to Minnesota in overtime before meeting Iowa again on February 21 at home. The same UI team that set a Wisconsin Fieldhouse field goal percentage record of .492 two days earlier fell to its lowest of the season, .287, in an 89-70 loss to the Hawkeyes. Three late-season wins left the Illini at 10-4, in a tie for second and just one game behind the Hawkeyes.

"We didn't beat those guys for two years," said Schmidt.

The team's overall 17-5 record placed them 18th in the final AP rankings.

IOWA RULES

Iowa was even better in 1956, going 13-1 in the league and chilling a red-hot Illini team that carried a 16-game win streak into late February. Schmidt moved into the lineup at forward that season, with Brothers earning team MVP honors as the most prominent sixth man since Beach.

"The starting lineup returned intact, and I consider that one of my great accomplishments to crack that lineup," recalled Schmidt. "Altenberger got sick to give me my first opening, and then I ultimately started ahead of Brothers. Practice was hard in those days.

Harry posted stats daily. He rewarded people who got things done on the court. We scrimmaged all the time."

Schmidt notched 24 points in an early 103-93 defeat of Notre Dame, the most ever points by a team against the Irish.

"The noise reverberated in Notre Dame's old place, and we just had an exceptional game, certainly my best game to date," said Schmidt.

Paul Judson peaked with 29 and 24 in early wins over DePaul and Oklahoma. Chopping through the Big Ten like a hot knife through warm butter, Illinois reached No. 2 in the nation and carried its 16-game streak to Ohio State.

This was a Saturday night Robin Freeman and big Frank Howard (of baseball fame) will never forget. Using long-range jumpers, Freeman outscored BonSalle 43-34 in an 87-84 upset. No individual had ever scored so many points against Illinois. Freeman's outburst avenged a 111-64 loss at Huff where he scored just 12 points.

"Our fans got on Freeman pretty good at Huff, and that created some animosity among the Buckeyes. They were waiting for us at their place," said Schmidt.

"[The] weather was terrible for that trip and we had to travel all night by train to Columbus. We made a stop and I was walking on an icy railroad track and accidentally slammed my foot into a spike inside the railing. It swelled up and I had ice treatment all night. I wasn't worth much, trying to play on that swollen foot.

"Howard was about 6-8 and 240 and, oh my, was he strong," Schmidt continued. "Howie Braun thought I should keep him off the boards and was after me pretty good. I had Howard pinned under the hoop before halftime but Judson deflected Freeman's shot and it fell a foot short, right to Howard who stuck it in. Howie made a bee-line toward me at halftime."

The championship was still within the UI's grasp when they traveled for their only meeting with Iowa. BonSalle responded with 32 points but this one was ugly. Iowa prevailed 96-72 as Logan led five Hawkeyes in double figures.

Illini forward Paul Judson (left) and center George BonSalle (right) battle for the ball with a Michigan State player. Ninth-ranked Illinois won the 1956 match up with 16th-ranked State, 73-65. ▶

"They just dominated us," said Schmidt. "If you look back, we were statistically blowing people out and they were winning close. The tough part was that we played them just once in 1956, and it was in Iowa City. The place was up for grabs. Nine of the starters on the court were Illinois guys, and to add to the psychological aspects of it, we tended to be the first-team all-staters, and they were the second-teamers. They put it to us."

It was the Illini's second consecutive second place finish, although this year they improved by a game to 11-3 in the league standings. Their 18-4 overall record was good for seventh place in the final AP rankings.

▲ Bill Altenberger was part of a senior-oriented attack for the 1956-57 Illini, who dropped five of their last eight games after center George BonSalle was declared ineligible. The downward spiral caused the team to fall out of the nation's polls and into seventh place in the conference.

1957 FALLS WITH BONSALLE

Having won 45 Big Ten games in four seasons, and failing to reach the NCAA each year, the Illini had high hopes for 1956-57. BonSalle, Schmidt, Altenberger and football quarterback Hiles Stout were seniors and long-time pro Don Ohl was a jump-shooting junior.

The Illini again started fast, winning their first five and steamrolling the defending national champion and No. 2-ranked San Francisco, 62-33. The Dons carried a 60-game win streak but had lost Bill Russell and K.C. Jones from two title teams.

"We really put them away, holding them to 33 points," said Schmidt. "It was a huge win."

Illlinois reached the Big Ten opener at Minnesota ranked No. 5, but fell 91-88. Jed Dommeyer scored 27 points in the second half for the Gophers.

"We were always ranked," said Schmidt. "We never gave much thought to that. It was the Big Ten that people paid attention to."

The Illini won the next three, finally beating Iowa 81-70, but trouble was just around the corner. Illinois had motored through the semester exam period with rocking wins over Indiana (112-91) and Notre Dame (99-81) when it was learned that BonSalle, a 20-point scorer and a dominant rebounder, might be in academic difficulty. He played two more games, scoring 27 in his final contest, a 96-89 defeat of Ohio State.

But BonSalle failed to complete his work in a sociology class and was deemed ineligible. The Illini would be found wanting at center for the rest of that season and several more. Combes' promising 1957 team finished 3-5 in BonSalle's absence as Indiana and Michigan State tied for the Big Ten title. Schmidt had his biggest game with 34 points in a 104-97 defeat of Northwestern, and the Illini knocked Ohio State out of a share of the Big Ten title, 79-72, in an otherwise disappointing finish.

"The disappointment was that we probably would have won it with BonSalle. Combes tried to go with Caiazza but he had chronic knee trouble and never quite came around," said Schmidt.

Michigan State advanced and reached the Final Four where North Carolina beat Kansas and Wilt Chamberlain in three overtimes in the championship game. Meanwhile, the Illini wrapped up their season at 14-8, 7-7 in the conference.

GREATEST GAMES

(NO. 7) ILLINOIS 62, (NO. 2) SAN FRANCISCO 33

DECEMBER 17, 1956• HUFF GYM, CHAMPAIGN, ILLINOIS

ILLINOIS HALTS DONS' 60-WIN STREAK

For two straight years the San Francisco Dons dominated college basketball. They became a college basketball dynasty, winning two national championships and 60 straight regular-season games by the time they arrived in Champaign in late December of 1956. Gone from their previous championship teams were Bill Russell and K.C. Jones, but back were three starters that included All-America center Mike Farmer.

The Dons were 5-0 on the young season and ranked number two in the country. But the guys in Champaign couldn't wait for them to get to Huff Gym.

"We circled that game from the day we saw it on our schedule," remembered junior guard Don Ohl, who was part of the Illini squads who had won 15 straight games in Huff. "We knew it would be a big feather in our cap if we could break that long winning streak."

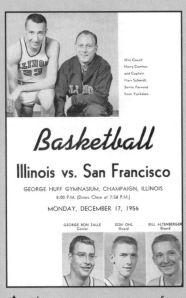

"We pointed to that game and talked about it for a long time," said captain Harv Schmidt. "It was extra motivation for that team to beat San Francisco because they had been so dominant and were so well known throughout college basketball."

When the week of the game rolled around the only thing that Illini team could think about was breaking the streak. Two days before the game, the Illini, with their minds focused on San Francisco, struggled to

▲ The game program from Illinois' 1956 win over No. 2 San Francisco.

beat lowly Loyola 83-72.

This match-up with the Dons wasn't your normal non-conference game.

"I remember Harry Combes and Howie Braun reminding us they were playing on our home court and they aren't going to get out of here with the streak alive," recalled senior center George BonSalle.

From the opening tip, it was all Illinois. They bolted out to an 8-0 lead just three minutes into the ball game and after the Dons cut the lead to 12-7, the Illini went on a 9-2 run capped by two Bill Altenberger jump shots to stretch the lead back to 13.

"It shocked me that Illinois took off so fast on them," said Mannie Jackson, a freshman guard watching the game from the stands. "They really ripped on them right from the start and after watching that game I thought they were destined to be Big Ten champs."

"After the game started we never looked back," said reserve forward Hiles Stout. "We were running up and down, hitting our shots, and it seemed like we could do nothing wrong."

On the defensive end of the floor, the Illini were just as dominating. They held the Dons to 15 first-half points on six field goals and only 22-percent shooting from the field for the game. They limited their big front line to one offensive rebound in the entire first half. In all, San Francisco shuffled 12 players in and out of the game and only six of them tallied any points. By the time Harry Combes cleared the bench late in the game, the Illini nearly doubled the Dons' score, winning 62-33.

For the first time since December. 11, 1954, San Francisco tasted defeat. It came at the hands of a red-hot Illini team who put on one of the greatest exhibitions in the history of Illinois basketball.

CHAPTER SEVEN

INTEGRATING
THE ILLINI
1957-58—1959-60

Mannie Jackson and Govoner Vaughn met in the second grade at Lincoln School in Edwardsville. They played, hiked in the woods and hung out together. They were childhood buddies. Today, four and a half decades after they performed side by side as the UI's first black basketball starters, they're living in Phoenix, headquarters of the internationally known Harlem Globetrotters.

"If it wasn't for Mannie, possibly the Globetrotters wouldn't be in existence today," said Vaughn, who came out of retirement four years ago after spending the previous 24 with Detroit Edison to become director of alumni relations for the Globetrotters. "He resurrected the team from near bankruptcy in 1993. The team has become one of the most admired and recognized sports entities in the world. Under Mannie's leadership, the Globetrotters have resurrected a series against the nation's top colleges in the fall."

Vaughn and Jackson saw their careers begin to take shape as sophomores at Edwardsville High School. They were instrumental in transforming the small town of Edwardsville into a basketball-crazed community, teaming with senior Don Ohl in marching to the 1954 Sweet 16 where they lost a stirring semifinal to Chicago DuSable. Two years later they reached the title game, losing to Rockford West, 67-65.

▲ *Mannie Jackson (left) and Govoner Vaughn (right) had been playing ball together since their younger years. The duo from Edwardsville High School became the first two African-American players to letter for the Illini when they teamed up from 1957-58— 1959-60.*

"Before and after graduation from high school, Mannie and I received offers from basically the same schools," Vaughn went on. "We received inquiries and offers from Maine to California. But practically right in our backyard, just across the river from Edwardsville, St. Louis University was highly interested in us. The St. Louis Billikens coach, Eddie Hickey, was consistently and constantly on our case to attend St. Louis U. An alumnus from St. Louis U. took us to a Cardinals baseball game during the summer of 1956. Mannie and I

spent an inning or two in the broadcast booth with the Cardinal announcers Harry Caray, Jack Buck and Joe Garagiola. That left quite an impression on two kids just one month out of high school.

Later that summer, the pair received their first airplane ride to Milwaukee to visit Marquette, who was also hot on the heels.

"Mannie and I began working at Richards Brickyard in Edwardsville after our junior year of high school. This would be our place of employment for the next four summers. During the summer of '56, basketball was the flavor of the day in Edwardsville after we left the brickyard for the day. We took to the outdoor courts and played until dark. Coach Hickey would be there watching more often than not. Braun was from Belleville, which is only 10 to 12 miles south of Edwardsville, and he came there several times during that summer and did an in-depth job of selling us on the benefits of attending Illinois."

The two prep stars were beginning to hear the positives of being the first blacks to play varsity basketball for the Illini.

"I always wondered why a black athlete never played for the UI," said Gov. "The Buddy Youngs, the J.C. Carolines and the Bobby Mitchells were standouts in football, and the Herb McKenleys, the Ron Mitchells and Bobby Mitchells had starred in track. Why not basketball?

"Almost simultaneously, Mannie and I agreed and committed to attend Illinois," Vaughn said. "I had several reasons. Ohl was already playing for the Illini. And my brother was attending Illinois State. I wanted to remain in my home state."

Freshmen were not eligible in those days, and the Edwardsville athletes were relegated to intrasquad games. In their first public scrimmage as varsity on November 26, 1957, the first blacks to start for Combes were on the "White" team. Six days later Vaughn bagged 11 field goals and Jackson seven in a 100-90 rout of Marquette as they joined forces with Ohl, a senior.

"Prior to the start of the game, my nerves were on end, my mouth was dry and my palms were sweaty. The first shot I took swished right through. Then the butterflies were gone," said Vaughn.

Roger Taylor, captain John Paul and Ohl were the primary scorers in a 75-70 defeat of DePaul on December 7, 1957. Ohl, with a marvelously smooth jump shot, erupted for 29 in an 85-82 defeat of 14th-ranked Rice. The win streak reached five, all at home, before a 68-60 loss at Iowa State. That's when it became evident that the Illini, minus the knee-injured Ted Caiazza, lacked size for defense and rebounding.

"I recall practice during the week before the first game. I was not a starter," said Vaughn. "Caiazza was at center. I was on the other end of the gym working out

with the second unit. Suddenly, there's this blood-curdling scream that echoed throughout the gym. Ted's knee locked and popped, and he collapsed to the floor. Our trainer and four players were needed to lift [the 240-pounder] off the floor. Coach Combes called me down to fill in for Caiazza, and I started every game except one in my three years."

After a Big Ten-opening win at Wisconsin, 64-59, which allowed the 1958 Illini to creep into the Top 20, they dropped four straight including an 89-82 setback at

▲ Senior guard Don Ohl and his smooth jump shot anchored the Illini offense in 1957-58. The problem for the 11-11 team wasn't scoring, however, it was defending. The team lacked the size to keep up in the Big Ten, where they fell to eighth place.

Indiana where the Edwardsville trio scored an incredible 76 points ... perhaps a Big Ten high for three players from the same high school.

"That was something to behold," said Vaughn. "The three of us couldn't miss. We scored all but six of our points. Archie Dees said at one point during a free throw: 'When are you guys going to miss?'"

Ohl had 97 points after four league games —these guys could shoot—but the problem was obvious: 6-8 Archie Dees had 20 rebounds and teammate Jerry Thompson 15 for the winning Hoosiers. Illinois was too small.

A return date with Wisconsin at home resulted in a 71-70 loss that dropped the UI from championship consideration. The outsized Illini trailed off to 5-9 in the conference. They couldn't handle the wide bodies outside their conference, either. Tom Hawkins, Mike Graney and Notre Dame had their way with the Illini in late January for the first time in eight Chicago trips. Ohl scored just three points in the Stadium for his lowest output as an Illini starter.

"If we would have had Caiazza or any other big man to clog the middle, we could have done much better," said Vaughn. "But my 6-3 1/2 height and 180-pound frame in the pivot did not intimidate those big guys. And players like Johnny Green of Michigan State could jump out of the gym."

Before a 78-70 loss at Ohio State on February 3, Combes became ill and was unable to coach, and Braun took over for that game.

"We were going up against the gentle giant, Frank Howard," recalled Vaughn. "I put a fake on him and he landed on me and flattened me. He scooped me up off the floor and apologized to me for the duration of the game."

A 99-84 upset of Purdue at Huff did not pull the Illini out of the league cellar, but lifted spirits in an underdog season. Combes used just six players against the Boilermakers. Ohl broke the last tie of 76-76 with three quick goals, and the Illini led 91-80 in the last three minutes. Taylor, a slick junior from Park Forest, led scoring with 29. But this was a lost season, and the offense crumbled at Michigan State in mid-February as Green and the Spartans shot ahead 21-1.

"That was the epitome of embarrassment, totally embarrassing," said Vaughn. "I don't know what happened. None of us knew what happened. We made two or three baskets in a row, and the Spartan fans cheered. Their cheers were strictly out of pity and sympathy. We did make a slight comeback, but we lost 69-56."

The 11-11 season audit was the worst under Combes, and the suffering finally ended at the hands of big Joe Ruklick as he tallied 40 points in Northwestern's 88-72 assault. Illinois finished in eighth place at 5-9 in the conference.

Ohl averaged 19.6, Vaughn 14.9 and Jackson 11.1 on the season. The trio from one high school accounted for more than 46 points per game.

THE 1958-59 SEASON

Don Ohl and John Paul were gone after the 1957-58 season, leaving Rockford sophomore John Wessels to take over the post. But matchup problems continued to plague a 12-10 Illini team that went 7-7 in conference play.

"I was happy to move to the forward position," said Vaughn.

"I sprained my ankle and missed my only game as an Illini against Marquette. For some reason, I favored the ankle for several games. When I jumped, I always wondered how I would land. The season never quite clicked as I thought it would. I just could not get on track. My junior year was the worst of the three."

The Illini made another fast start with a 103-79 win over Butler. But with Vaughn absent, they lost their game at Marquette, falling 69-53 as Gosnell led a weak effort with 11 points. Bill Lyon, longtime Philadelphia columnist then writing for *The News-Gazette*, said: "The Illini played a little too slow and a little too low." It was Marquette's first win in an eight-year series.

The Illini rebounded to mount a four-game win streak heading in to Lexington to face No. 1-ranked Kentucky. The game at Freedom Hall drew more than 18,000 the following night.

"That was the largest crowd to attend a game in the South," said Vaughn.

"With seconds to go in the game, Illinois [was] down one point. I took the last shot from about 25 feet as the buzzer sounded. The shot bounced off the rim, and I don't know whether or not it would have counted," recalled Vaughn, who remembers racial taunts from the Kentucky crowd directed at him and Jackson occurring throughout the game.

Reflecting on the 76-75 outcome, Combes said, "It was our best game against our best opponent."

Disappointment was shortlived as the Illini opened the 1959 Big Ten campaign with an 81-80 triumph over Ohio State. Illini reserve Lou Landt scored the winning basket as he replaced the injured Taylor. Jackson's 15-footer set up the winning play, which began when Landt stole the ball from Buckeye star Larry Siegfried.

▲ *The 1958-59 squad made a slight stride forward with the presence of John Wessels at center. Adding the larger Wessels to the lineup allowed the 6'3 ½" Govoner Vaughn to move from center to forward.*

"My dad and uncle drove up to the game in Champaign," said Vaughn. "It was ice cold in Huff Gym that day and I was equally as cold. I had one of the worst games in my career. My dad said, 'Maybe I shouldn't come to see you play anymore.' He preferred to watch on TV."

Only 3,618 showed up to support a weak Wisconsin team in game two, and the 1959 Illini coasted 77-51 with Vaughn and Wessels garnering 18 apiece. However, the third one-point game in four swung the wrong way as the Spartans' Johnny Green ran wild for 33 points, and No. 5 Michigan Sate prevailed at Huff, 97-96.

"We had to alter our strategy to try to stop Green," said Combes. "We couldn't stop him when he got the ball."

"We had them on the ropes in the last five seconds when they missed a free throw, and Green jumped up and tipped it in," Vaughn added. "I had never seen a guy

react and move as fast as Green did on that missed free throw. One of our players had the inside position but he never had a chance. That game psyched us out pretty good."

The Illini earned a brief share of first place as Jackson and Taylor scored 24 apiece in a 103-97 defeat of Iowa. But a five-game losing streak was kicked off by zoning Notre Dame, who beat Illinois 85-75 in Chicago. Purdue shot .554 to score 102 points two games later in a Boilermakers victory. Then, even as Wessels picked up his scoring, the Illini lost a tough 87-85 decision to Michigan at Huff.

Combes' 1959 team swung out of the five-game slump to win four in a row, knocking off No. 18 Indiana, 100-98, at home on February 21. Walt Bellamy (6-11) and Frank Radovich (6-8) were a load—combing for 48 points—but UI starters scored all 100 points with Taylor (26), Wessels (25) and Jackson (23) on fire.

Taylor was the hero again with "one of his greatest games," wrote Bertine, as the sparkling guard scored the winner and stole the ball at the end of a 72-70 triumph at Iowa. But the Illini dropped their last two games at Michigan and at home against Northwestern to finish in fifth place at 7-7 in the league, 12-10 overall.

OHIO STATE TOO TOUGH

Combes' teams almost always started fast. His first UI club in 1947-48 began 7-0, and subsequent records out of the gate were 13-1, 5-1, 10-2, 11-0, 8-1, 5-0, 6-0, 17-1, 5-0, 5-0, 5-1 and, again, 5-0, in 1959-60.

But optimism wasn't as high after consecutive 7-7, 5-9 and 7-7 records in the Big Ten. The Jerry Lucas-John Havlicek team at Ohio State was preparing to take over, the Hoosiers rode the tall shoulders of Walt Bellamy, and the Boilermakers were prominent with a sensational sophomore, Terry Dischinger, who would lead the conference in scoring for three years with averages of 27.4, 28.3 and 32.8.

It took everything the Illini had to share third place with an 8-6 league record in 1959-60. If a 5-0 start was

impressive, a 62-48 loss to third-ranked Cal in the opener of the Los Angeles Classic put the Combesmen in their place. Only Jackson, with 17 points, reached double figures while Cal's defending national champions ruled with large Darrell Imhoff collecting 23 points and 16 rebounds.

"It was our first trip to California," said Vaughn. "Jerry Colangelo had a fraternity brother who lived in the Los Angeles area. He came by our hotel and took several of us out to see Hollywood. I was impressed with the sights along Sunset Strip. Several players went for a walk one morning and they came across Burt Lancaster and Jean Simmons shooting scenes for the movie, *Elmer Gantry*.

"We lost to Cal but we recovered to beat Northwestern and Stanford to finish third out there."

Illinois was ranked No. 8 entering the Big Ten race at Ohio State, where 6-8 Jerry Lucas dominated the Illini with 30 points and 23 rebounds. The eventual national champions breezed past Illinois, 97-73.

"Lucas was a smooth, quiet, dominating player," said Vaughn. "He was a finesse player for that size, and the team around him was a buzz-saw.

continued on page 77

▲ *The 1958-59 team dropped one-point decisions to No. 1-ranked Kentucky and No. 5-ranked Michigan State. Left to right—Coach Combes, Mannie Jackson, Alan Gosnell, Govoner Vaughn, Roger Taylor, and John Wessels.*

GREATEST MOMENTS

GOVONER VAUGHN AND MANNIE JACKSON: ILLINOIS' FIRST TWO AFRICAN-AMERICAN LETTERMEN

Many people have said the 160-mile trip from Edwardsville, Illinois up to Champaign is an easy one—a straight shot up Interstate 55 and then 80 miles east on Interstate 72. But for Govoner Vaughn and Mannie Jackson, the Illini's first African-American lettermen on the basketball team, their road was one less traveled.

Gov and Mannie. Mannie and Gov. You can't talk about one without talking about the other.

"They were two peas in a pod," remembered teammate Jerry Colangelo.

By the time they got to Champaign they were inseparable best friends who had been that way for as long as either could remember.

"I don't even remember when I first met Gov," reflected Jackson, who today is the CEO of the Harlem Globetrotters. "I was probably about four years old and his family was kind of like my family. His mother was like my second mother, and she really took an active interest in looking out for me and caring for me."

Growing up together, the pair merged into a stellar basketball tandem. They got their first taste of Huff Gym as high school sophomores when they traveled up to Champaign on an Edwardsville squad that finished fourth in the state tournament. Two years later they returned as seniors to lead their team all the way to the championship game before falling to West Rockford. In that title game, Vaughn and Jackson combined for 49 of their team's 65 points.

"Right after the championship game and the presentation of the trophies, Coach Combes and Coach Braun ushered Mannie and I along with our former high school teammate Don Ohl, into his office," remembered Vaughn.

"They said they would like to offer us a four-year athletic scholarship to Illinois, and I was just amazed," recalled Vaughn.

Braun and Combes knew no black athlete had ever lettered in Illinois basketball, but they were willing to take a chance on Vaughn and Jackson.

"I have always appreciated Howie and Harry for being such pioneers," said Jackson. "They brought two guys of color into a very volatile situation not knowing if we were going to be good students or good citizens. I can't even put into words what kind of move that was for a white guy to make."

Walt Moore had been the first African-American player to play in a basketball game at Illinois when he made a brief appearance in a 1952 game against North Carolina. His stay in Champaign was short lived, however, as Moore left the university at semester break due to grade issues.

Vaughn and Jackson were going to be the trailblazers for Illinois basketball, but they sure didn't have an easy road ahead of them. They faced intense pressure to succeed and racial prejudice on the road—all of that in addition to trying to adjust to college both on and off the court. The one place their race was never an issue was with their teammates, and it didn't take long for the duo to blend right in.

"Mannie and Gov were the type of guys you wanted to have on your team," said guard Lou Landt. "They were really humble and always conducted themselves in a first-class way."

At only 6-3, Vaughn had to play most of his Illinois career at the center position, matched up with opposing big men like Indiana's Walt Bellamy and Ohio State's Jerry Lucas.

"Gov had a great touch and was a really good shooter," recalled Don Ohl.

Jackson was a quick 6-2 guard known for his leaping ability and shooting touch.

"Mannie Jackson was like Doctor J before there was Doctor J," recalled Bill Lyon, who covered the Illini in those years for *The News-Gazette*. "He just floated through the air, tucked his legs up under him, and shot a jump shot that was unstoppable."

Away from the friendly confines of Huff Gym things weren't so easy for Jackson and Vaughn. Those difficulties were never more evident than on a trip they took down to Lexington in December, 1958.

"The night before the game Mannie and I went to a movie with a few of our white teammates," said Vaughn. "The lady behind the ticket counter turned to the two white players and said, 'You guys can come in but the two guys behind you can't.' Of course she was referring to Mannie and I."

Ironically Vaughn and Jackson were set to play against the Kentucky Wildcats in a building called Freedom Hall. It sure didn't live up to its name that evening.

continued on page 76

continued from page 75

"On one occasion during the game, I went to the free throw line," recalled Vaughn. "From the upper deck seats I heard, 'Hey, black boy, you're gonna miss.' After I made my first free throw, [the same heckler] used the 'N' word. One of the Kentucky players, Sid Cohen from New York, said to me: 'Don't let these ignoramuses get to you.'"

"I had always held the University of Kentucky in such high esteem and to have that experience there was specifically disappointing," said Jackson. "As we went out from halftime the band was playing all types of southern music and when I fouled out they were playing, 'Bye Bye Blackbird.'"

Vaughn received a more overt threat as he left the court that night after nearly missing a 25-foot jump shot at the buzzer that could have won the game for the Illini.

"As we were leaving the court, two white guys were standing nearby and one of them said, 'Hey, boy, it's a good thing you missed or we'd have cut off your ears and sent them back to your folks up north.' Believe me, I was glad to get back home. All that transpired 46 years ago, but it seems like 46 days," recalled Vaughn.

The unranked Illini nearly pulled off the major upset against the top-ranked Wildcats that night, losing 76-75, but Vaughn and Jackson were simply glad to be leaving "Freedom Hall".

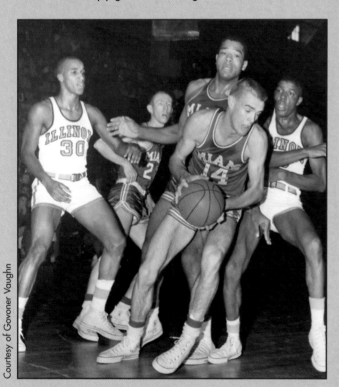

Courtesy of Govoner Vaughn

▲ Mannie Jackson (left) and Govoner Vaughn (right) play in a game against Miami of Ohio. The pair totaled a combined 1,923 points over the course of their three-year stint on the varsity team for a combined average of 28.9 points per game.

Through all the pressure, unique circumstances and difficult road trips the pair endured during their three years in the Illini's starting lineup, Vaughn and Jackson persevered.

"I never saw them ever turn around and confront someone who had said something to them," said Landt. "They were bigger than the low life around them, so to speak. Someone had to pave the way, and those two guys did for all of the guys who followed them."

Amidst everything else, Vaughn and Jackson had terrific careers at Illinois. Vaughn averaged 15.2 points a game and scored 1,001 points for his career, while Jackson averaged 13.8 points and finished with 922 points. Their point totals rank 35th and 43rd on the all-time scoring list.

In their second to last home game in Huff Gym, Jackson tore up the Iowa Hawkeyes in scoring a career-high 32 points on 15 of 28 shooting. Only two days later, on senior day, it was Vaughn's turn to end things on a high note. He scored 30 points, shooting an incredible 14 of 17 from the floor including a perfect nine for nine in the second half. Remarkably, Vaughn and Jackson both posted career highs in their last two home games in the Orange and Blue—and as always, they did it together.

Now 44 years later, Vaughn and Jackson are still side by side. Today, Vaughn also works for the Globetrotters as the director of alumni relations. Their offices sit about 20 steps apart.

When you listen to them talk about each other today you realize they are as close as they have ever been.

"I have known Gov literally my whole life. We roomed together for four years at Illinois, and I don't ever remember arguing with him about anything," said Jackson, reflecting on his best friend. "We hung around together a lot, we worked together for years and we shared dreams about where we wanted to go in the future."

There was no doubt who Govoner's biggest fan was.

"I used to sit on the bench and catch myself realizing that I pulled for Gov more than I pulled for the team," continued Jackson. "I hated to see him foul out and it hurt when he did. I would keep his scoring averages and would talk to him about ways he could get better."

"In rooming with Mannie for four years, I was just awed by how determined he was in his studies. He would get a project and not let it go until it was complete, because he was determined to excel," reflected Vaughn. "He is a true friend, and I am glad to have known Mannie my whole life."

They grew up together, played high school ball together, broke the color barrier at Illinois together and years later are still working together. They were teammates, best friends, and a lot like brothers. Mannie and Gov. Gov and Mannie. You can't say one name without mentioning the other. They wouldn't want it any other way.

continued from page 74

"At Purdue, Dischinger was one of the top three offensive guys I played against in college. His appearance on the court was anything but that of a skilled player. He had braces on his teeth, his jersey was always hanging out of his shorts, and his socks always sagged around his ankles. He looked rag-tag. Perhaps that was his ploy, to gain sympathy from his opponents and to have them feel sorry for his appearance. After the game ended, the PA [announcer] would say: 'Terry Dischinger led all scorers with 25 or 40 points.'"

Jackson was a 25-point sharpshooter in a 90-82 home win over Minnesota, and the UI's balance overcame Dischinger's 43-point eruption in an 81-75 thriller at Purdue.

But there was tough sledding ahead for Illinois. Hot-shooting Minnesota buried the Illini with a 17-5 run after halftime, prevailing 77-70 in Minneapolis even though, in the words of Bertine, "it was the first time in five Big Ten games that the Illini weren't mauled by the opposing center." Even so, Gopher center Ron Johnson scored 18 (he tallied 31 vs. Illinois earlier)

John Wessels' 19 points felled Notre Dame in the late-January Chicago trip, and Vaughn and Jackson combined for 37 to win at Michigan, 75-61. But the next five games turned up only one victory, that a double-overtime 93-89 verdict over Purdue. Dischinger scored 38 but none in the extra sessions. The unlikely Illini heroes were Landt and Frandsen, as each scored in the final 48 seconds. Two days later Ohio State put on a show at Huff when Havlicek and Lucas combined for 50 points in a 109-81 Buckeye blast. *The News-Gazette's* Bill Schrader called it "perfection personified."

Later in January, Indiana's Bellamy broke Phillip's Huff Gym record with 42 points as Indiana ruled, 92-78. Bertine stated that "Illinois' inability to defend against a good, big man was starkly underlined" in the game.

But Jackson and Vaughn were relentless to the end, and the Illini captured their last three games to finish 8-6 in the Big Ten—good for third place—and 16-7 overall. Team captain Jackson garnered 31 points in an 85-70 defeat of Iowa, while Vaughn drained 14 of 17 shots for a career-high 30 in his next to last game against Michigan. Vaughn and Jackson had 25 and 15 points respectively in the final win at Northwestern, and were among eight seniors leaving the program.

▲ *Govoner Vaughn receives the team MVP Award during his senior season. Left to right—Dave Downey, Harry Combes, Govoner Vaughn, [unknown], Mannie Jackson, and Jay Lovelace.*

When Vaughn received the team MVP award at the postseason banquet, he said: "We had aspirations of finishing higher in the Big Ten but that team out Columbus way disillusioned everybody."

Gov led the Big Ten in free-throw accuracy and was No. 4 in the nation in that category. His season mark of 86.5 percent is second in Illini annals only to Brian Cook's 87.3 in 2002.

Looking back now, Vaughn reflected: "It was a great experience at Illinois. Without hesitation, I'd do it all over again. The only reality check we had was in Kentucky. No problems anyplace else. For me, the University of Illinois was the place to be."

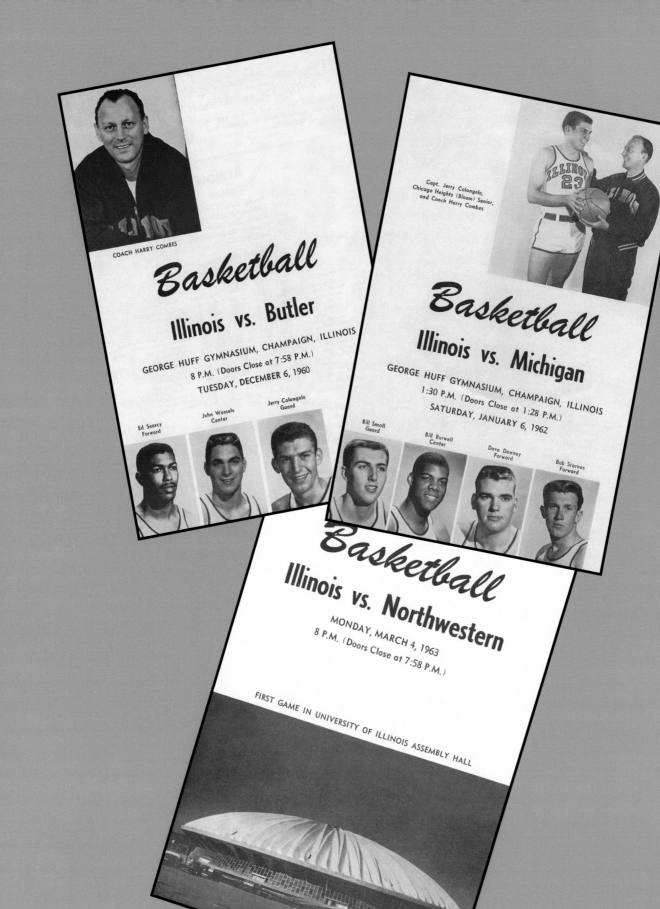

COACH HARRY COMBES

Basketball

Illinois vs. Butler

GEORGE HUFF GYMNASIUM, CHAMPAIGN, ILLINOIS
8 P.M. (Doors Close at 7:58 P.M.)
TUESDAY, DECEMBER 6, 1960

Ed Searcy
Forward

John Wessels
Center

Jerry Colangelo
Guard

Capt. Jerry Colangelo,
Chicago Heights (Bloom) Senior,
and Coach Harry Combes

Basketball

Illinois vs. Michigan

GEORGE HUFF GYMNASIUM, CHAMPAIGN, ILLINOIS
1:30 P.M. (Doors Close at 1:28 P.M.)
SATURDAY, JANUARY 6, 1962

Bill Small
Guard

Bill Burwell
Center

Dave Downey
Forward

Bob Starnes
Forward

Basketball

Illinois vs. Northwestern

MONDAY, MARCH 4, 1963
8 P.M. (Doors Close at 7:58 P.M.)

FIRST GAME IN UNIVERSITY OF ILLINOIS ASSEMBLY HALL

CHAPTER EIGHT

ASSEMBLING THE BIG TEN'S BEST

1960-61—1962-63

Harry Combes' quest to regain the Big Ten's top rung in the early 1960s appeared brighter as he attracted two exceptional prep scorers, Canton's Dave Downey and Aurora's Bill Small, along with big Bill Burwell of Brooklyn, New York. But it didn't develop as rapidly as he hoped. Chicagoans Pete Cunningham and Bernie Mills, both exceptional talents in that period, enrolled but never gained eligibility. And Jerry Sloan, who would become a two-time NBA all-star with the Chicago Bulls and eventual coach of the Utah Jazz, left the UI early.

"We'll always wonder what would have happened if Sloan had stayed," said Downey. "He was one year behind us. He never returned after going back to his McLeansboro home at Thanksgiving."

Sloan played on two small school national championship teams at Evansville. The Bulls retired his jersey in 1978.

But the Illini had another famous name in the fold. Jerry Colangelo, who had intended to play alongside Wilt Chamberlain at Kansas, was back in his home state and taking over the guard slot opposite Small.

The 1960-61 club lost four straight leading into Big Ten play and, after rallying briefly, lost seven of their last eight Big Ten games in posting 2-12 road record. Inconsistencies could be predicted early as Colangelo notched 19 points in an 84-52 rout of Butler, only to see the Bulldogs retaliate 70-68 as the Illini committed 21 turnovers in Indianapolis after Christmas.

"We started off scoring a lot of points," said Downey, now chief executive of The Downey Group, an investment firm in Champaign.

"When we flew out on the old DC-3 to Colorado, which was our first road trip for a young team (John Wessels was the lone senior), we learned what it was like playing at [a higher] altitude (a 90-81 loss). Then we traveled to Marquette and, playing well, we lost 96-87 ... still scoring a lot but giving up a lot."

A "sign of the times" occurred in Lexington where the Illini competed in the Kentucky tournament. The team felt obliged to leave a restaurant after they discovered the white players were being served, but not the two blacks, Burwell and Edgar Searcy.

"We found another place to eat in a downtown hotel," said Downey.

"I knew the great Kentucky coach, Adolph Rupp. He had actually come to Canton to recruit me. He visited the mayor, the superintendent of schools and others, and he walked in with this entourage and said, 'Boy, I've come to take you home.' I visited Lexington at a time when he was certainly the biggest name in college basketball.

"In the game, I don't remember any specific acts of racism. But early on, we were ahead and I had beaten Billy Ray Lickert several times with baseline drives. During a time out when it was quiet, Rupp walked out under the basket and said to the official, 'Mr. Shirley, that No. 40 is charging my boy Billy Ray.' I got two charging fouls in the next few minutes and had to sit down for the remainder of the half."

Kentucky won 83-78 with Downey scoring 23 and Wessels adding 18. The next night in Lexington, Illinois fell to California, the 1959 national champions, by a score of 72-54.

This was the era of Ohio State dominance. Thanks to Jerry Lucas and John Havlicek, the Buckeyes ruled the Big Ten with a 13-1 record and an NCAA title in 1960, a 14-0 mark in 1961 and a 13-1 record in 1962 The latter two teams lost to Cincinnati in the national championship game.

"When we went to St. John's Arena the first time (in 1961), it was a baptism of fire. We thought we were pretty good, but I can remember Larry Siegfried and

Mel Nowell at the guards and Havlicek and Lucas, and it was the first time I was ever up against an all-out defensive effort. Havlicek would force me out 35 feet from the basket, it seemed," said Downey.

"Lucas was just a machine. He was the most complete player we faced during that era. Against everybody else, I found something that I could do better. I even thought I was a better offensive player than Havlicek. But I couldn't find anything that I could do better than Lucas.

"The league was tough and we weren't up to it. Essentially the entire All-America team was made up of Big Ten players, not only Lucas and Havlicek but Walt Bellamy at Indiana, Don Nelson at Iowa and Terry Dischinger at Purdue," said Downey.

The 1960-61 team ended a disappointing season with a 9-15 record and a seventh place finish in the Big Ten at 5-9.

DOWNEY'S JUNIOR SEASON

A year later in 1961-62, a more mature Illini squad defeated eight of nine non-league opponents, triumphing at Oklahoma, 72-60, on December 9 to alleviate road concerns. Combes used just six players in that game with John Love sharing time with Bob Starnes alongside the set foursome of Colangelo (12 points), Burwell (16), Downey (19) and Small (21).

Against Iowa State at home, Downey tallied 24 points with 15 rebounds in an 82-73 triumph. The lone preconference loss came unexpectedly against unbeaten (6-0) Cornell, 72-60, despite Burwell's 25-point, 11-rebound effort. Bert Bertine commented that the Illini started their Christmas vacation two hours early.

In January, the Illini earned a third straight conquest of Notre Dame, 85-77. The win was marked by three busloads of Colangelo supporters from Chicago Heights turning out to honor the former Bloom captain.

"The game that stands out in that period was Creighton with Paul Silas, one of the few players who

The Big 3 under the basket for the Illini in 1960 were (left to right) Brooklyn's Bill Burwell, Canton's Dave Downey and Rockford's John Wessels. Burwell's arrival moved Wessels from center to forward.

averaged 20 points and 20 rebounds," said Downey. "During the warmup at Huff, Silas got hit in the face and his nose started to bleed, and Slim Stilwell couldn't stem the bleeding. We joked when Silas left with Stilwelll that he wouldn't be back. He wasn't."

Downey took over the game, posting his own 20-20 with 22 points and 21 rebounds in a 70-61 Illini victory.

"In the league in 1962, we felt that aside from Ohio State, we were as good as anybody," said Downey. "But this was a tough year because Combes got sick (bleeding ulcer). On our flight to Iowa,

▲ Bill Burwell (right) drives past a Butler defender as Bob Starnes (left) looks for the pass. Illinois defeated Butler 82-72 to open the 1961-62 season.

we had to land in Moline and they took him to the hospital, and Harry never returned (during the last eight games). Still, the Illini won at Iowa, 91-81, with Downey scoring 23, Colangelo 21 and Small 18.

The Illini stood 14-3 after whipping Northwestern 88-70 on February 12. Urbana scribe Bert Bertine noted that the team "won despite Burwell having the flu, Downey a head cold, Small a bad back and Starnes an arm injury."

The team recovered physically, but Combes' absence was deeply felt, and the Illini gave up 100 or more points in four of the next five games. It started with Purdue's Terry Dischinger running wild for 45 points in a 100-88 Boilermaker romp at Huff Gym. The Illini never found a way to stop him. Dischinger accounted for 239 points in six career games against Illinois—nearly a 40-point average.

"Dischinger was super quick for a 6-7 forward, had great touch and was relentless," said Downey. "He was always going to the basket. In a game the previous year, he made 17 free throws."

Wisconsin swept the Illini for the first time in 31 years, winning 103-101 to mark the third time that two

league members topped 100 in the same game. And Ohio State's reigning champs followed by putting six members in double figures (but not Bobby Knight) in a 102-79 triumph in Columbus. Two more losses continued the frustrating late-season slide that ended with a victory in the season's finale, 73-69, at Northwestern. The team finished 15-8, but only 7-7 in the conference.

That concluded Colangelo's career at the UI, but was only the beginning for him. Entering sports management with the Chicago Bulls, he became the youngest general manager in pro sports with the expansion Phoenix Suns. There he organized a group of investors to purchase the franchise in 1987 for $44.5 million, and he went on to spearhead drives to build America West Arena and Bank One Ballpark in downtown Phoenix. He brought major league baseball and the National Hockey League to Phoenix, his Diamondbacks winning the World Series in 2001. He was named NBA Executive of the Year four times. No UI graduate can match Colangelo's accomplishments in sports management. He was elected to the National Basketball Hall of Fame in 2004.

BACK ON TOP

Looking back on 10 years without a championship, the Illini were poised to break through against the powerhouse Buckeyes in 1962-63.

"We thought, particularly with the addition of Tal Brody, that we had the best team in the league," said Downey. "Ohio State lost a lot through graduation, and Indiana didn't have a big man."

Overlooked in the rankings for two years, the word was out early as No. 8-ranked Illinois began the season with a 66-49 defeat of Butler. Brody, a mobile recruit from New Jersey, led UI scorers with 15 and meshed perfectly with Combes' run-and-gun style.

"Tal was a prototypical Eastern Jewish guard who is a hero in Israel even today," said Downey. "He was someone who distributed the ball, a true point guard. Small was a shooting guard. They fit right in together. Tal was quicker than the rest of us, and he was looking to pass first. He was a sophomore playing with four seniors, and he created a good atmosphere for us. He had been committed to go with Frank McGuire at North Carolina before their scandal."

One early highlight of the season was Burwell's return to his home. The big Brooklyn center scored 26 points in a 98-66 defeat of Pennsylvania in New York's Holiday Festival. Illinois captured the tournament with Small carding 20 of his 25 points after intermission as West Virginia fell, 92-74.

The Illini were riding high on an eight-game streak but, back in Chicago after the New York trip, they were tiring as they entered their fourth game in six days. Notre Dame celebrated New Year's Eve with a 90-88 win over Illinois, their first loss of the year.

"That was bad scheduling," said Downey. "We were on a high from winning the country's biggest holiday tournament at Madison Square Garden. There were two issues. I had sprained my ankle before Christmas and played through it in New York. I was impaired throughout those three games. Then we were wearing down as we went straight to Chicago, and we lost by two."

They bounced back at Iowa, 85-76, and put a No. 3 ranking on the line at home against No. 5 Ohio State, breaking the Buckeye spell 90-78 before another standing-room-only crowd in the final season at Huff Gym.

▲ *Tal Brody (No. 12) was a "true point guard," according to teammate Dave Downey. The New Jersey native meshed well with Coach Combes' run-and-gun style of play.*

Downey, Burwell, Brody and Small scored 80 of those points.

"That was the best game we played during my three seasons," said Downey. "Ohio State was still good. Gary Bradds was the league's MVP. Tal was at his best in that game, spectacular at times."

But fans knew it would be a magical year when the Illini went to Northwestern January 14, fresh off a 106-point outburst that buried Purdue. After going nearly the first 10 minutes without a field goal and trailing throughout, Illinois caught up at 72-72 on a Downey basket, fell behind again and caught up again at 76-76. When NU missed its last chance, Brody was handed the

continued on page 85

GREATEST MOMENTS
(NO. 5) ILLINOIS 78, NORTHWESTERN 76
JANUARY 14, 1963 • MCGAW MEMORIAL HALL, EVANSTON, ILLINOIS

BOB STARNES' MIRACLE SHOT SINKS THE CATS

The Illini were happy just to be heading to overtime. After trailing the entire game, shooting miserably, and looking listless, overtime was all Harry Combes' troops could ask for. With the game tied at 76 apiece, Northwestern had the ball and stalled for the game's final 65 seconds. But Northwestern's Marty Riessen, later of professional tennis fame, threw an errant pass into the hands of Illinois guard Bill Small, who was able to get a time-out called with two seconds left.

All 7,200 people packed into McGaw Memorial Hall that evening were resigned that the game was going an extra five minutes.

"It's funny because I had a really good game that day," laughed Illinois captain and soon to be hero, Bob Starnes. "I had 24 points at the time and I thought to myself that if this game goes into an overtime or two I might be able to break the Illinois single-game scoring record."

The final Illinois huddle was an absolute mess.

"The crowd was going crazy during that timeout," remembered senior Dave Downey. "We were in the huddle and everyone was talking and asking for the ball. We had guys saying, 'throw me the ball at half court,' and guys saying they wanted to take the shot. By the time we broke the huddle, we accomplished nothing and didn't even know who was going to take the ball out."

The Illini had to go the entire length of the floor and the only thing that was predetermined was that Illini point guard Tal Brody was going to inbound the ball. What happened next is etched in Illinois basketball lore. Brody passed the ball in to Bob Starnes, who was being guarded by Northwestern junior forward Rick Lopossa.

"I was so tentative guarding Bob, because we all thought we were going to overtime," recalled Lopossa. "By the time he took those two dribbles, he was at the free throw line and I just waved my hands and backed away, because who is ever going to make a shot like that?"

▲ Bob Starnes' shot heard 'round the state—a combination of a baseball pass and a hook shot—sailed 60 feet through the air at McGaw Memorial Hall to land smack dab in middle of the bucket.

The Champaign-Urbana News-Gazette

Starnes got the ball, took two quick dribbles to the opposite foul line, and then launched into the air what Ed O'Neill of *The News-Gazette* called a "push-hook-throw" or as Starnes recalled, a combination of a baseball pass and a hook shot up. Even the man who threw it up never believed it would drop down.

"I just started to walk towards the bench because I didn't think it had a chance of going in," remembered Starnes.

Dave Downey saw the shot released and was doing his own kind of convincing.

"I was just yelling, 'It's good if it goes. It's good if it goes,'" remembered Downey. "And Jim immediately starts to swing his arms indicating that it would be good."

And then the impossible happened. Starnes' miracle chuck from 60 feet away dropped square in the middle of the basket, touching nothing but the bottom of the net.

"I was in a state of shock when the ball went through the hoop," Starnes said. "I don't think it hit me until we got back into the locker room."

After 40 minutes of playing, with the clock reading all zeroes, the Illini took the lead for the first time in the game and the only time that mattered.

Starnes wasn't the only one who was in a state of disbelief.

"I was just spell-bounded," said center Bill Burwell. "I remember sitting there just trying to drink in the fact that Bobby Starnes put the ball in from that distance."

"I remember being stunned and shocked and then thinking, 'Hey, we better do something.' So we went crazy," recalled Illinois guard Bill Small.

It was the shot of the century and something that probably won't ever be matched in Illinois basketball history. That fact wasn't lost on Illinois head coach Harry Combes, who sat with Starnes that night in a taxi to the airport.

"I remember Coach Combes telling me that I had made a fantastic shot," recalled Starnes. "He told me that my shot would be remembered forever and that I could tell my grandkids about it. He said they wouldn't believe me, but I could tell them."

Asked 41 years later if he had had a chance to tell his grandkids yet, Starnes laughs.

"I just told my nine-year-old grandson the other day," said Starnes. "I told him about the game, told him about the shot and you know what, Coach Combes was right. He didn't believe me."

And how could he? It was a miracle ending on a night where everyone in Illinois, as *The News-Gazette* headline so aptly put it, was thanking their lucky Starnes.

continued from page 83

ball on the far end with two seconds showing on the clock. He passed to Starnes who dribbled and launched what was reported as a 50-footer from behind the mid-court line—and it somehow found the net. The Illini would look back on this as their moment of good fortune in the title run.

"It seemed like the Starnes shot was a lot longer than 50 feet, maybe closer to 65 feet," claimed Downey. "It was certainly more than 10 feet behind the midcourt line."

Defense, the key to Cincinnati's consecutive national titles, keyed the Bearcats' 62-53 defeat of Illinois on January 26. The doubleheader drew the Chicago Stadium's largest crowd of 20,000-plus with top-ranked Cincinnati, California and Loyola on hand.

"Cincinnati was No. 1," said Downey. "They had George Wilson, Tom Thacker, Tony Yates and Ron Bonham. They were exceptional."

But this interlude did not dissuade the Combesmen from their high-scoring ways in the first of two extraordinary barn-burners with Indiana.

At home on February 4, Illinois rocketed to a 16-point lead with seven minutes left, and survived a feverish Hoosier rally by Tom Bolyard, Jimmy Rayl and the VanArsdale twins—Tom and Dick—in a 104-101 triumph. The 205 combined points in the game were the most ever at Huff. But 12 days later in Bloomington, the result was reversed, with Indiana winning 103-100 despite a record-breaking 53-point performance by Downey.

"Five days before, we had gone to Wisconsin and lost, and I had played terribly," said Downey. "It was the worst game of my career. I didn't reach double figures for the first time in 50-some games.

"We flew that old DC-3 to Indiana, and I felt too sick to work out the day before. I was miserable, and this was going to be the Big Ten TV Game of the Week. Early in the game, the VanArsdales were knocking me around, but the ball was falling my way and we were leading 50-41. I already had 29. It was like one of those days when all your putts go in.

"But they shot an incredible number of free throws (48) in the game and came back to beat us, 103-100."

Downey hit 22 of 34 shots on the way to 53 points—the most in a regulation Big Ten game to that point.

continued on page 87

GREATEST MOMENTS

INDIANA 103, (NO. 4) ILLINOIS 100

FEBRUARY 16, 1963 • INDIANA FIELD HOUSE, BLOOMINGTON, INDIANA

DAVE DOWNEY SCORES 53 POINTS

February 11, 1963, was an outright disaster for Dave Downey and the Illini, who lost on the road to Wisconsin, 84-77. For the first time in 56 games, Downey finished a game under double-digits in scoring on three of 11 shooting from the floor. His seven-point performance was enough to make him sick.

"When I got home from that game, I felt awful because I felt like I had let the team down," recalled Downey. "I was so emotionally down after that game and I spent those next few days worrying that the loss was going to keep us from winning the Big Ten title."

If that didn't make him sick enough, then the plane ride over to Bloomington, Indiana was going to be the icing on the cake.

"I wasn't a very good flyer in those days and I got extremely motion sick on that plane," remembered Downey. "The next night I was so ill I couldn't workout so I just sat on the bleachers and by the time the game rolled around I was still feeling terrible."

A crowd of 10,300 people packed the Indiana University Field House. Thousands more watched the game on the Big Ten Television Network. None realized that they were about to see quite a momentous game.

Downey's scoring barrage started early that day. First it was an "old-fashioned" three-point play off a Bob Starnes miss, then an easy lay-up off a Bill Burwell pass, and next his patented rising jumper from the foul line. It was evident to everyone that Dave was just getting started.

"Dave was hotter than a pistol that day," recalled teammate Bill Small.

After a deep two from today's three-point line, Downey drilled a baseline jumper and knocked in another put-back to give him a quick 11 points.

"It was Dave's kind of game, because we were going back and forth putting up a lot of shots and when that happened he could really light it up," remembered captain Bob Starnes.

The scoring onslaught continued at an incredible pace as Downey finished the first half with 27 points on 11-of-17 shooting, propelling Illinois to a nine-point halftime lead.

"I tried to guard Dave in that game and I guess 'tried' is the important word there," recalled Indiana senior forward Tom Bolyard, who was one of the men assigned to guard Downey that night.

The second half began and Downey didn't cool off. Only minutes in he converted a swooping reverse lay-up, a short baseline jumper, and a one-handed slingshot from just inside the foul line.

"I have never in my life seen so many various shots go in from different angles with so many people hanging over someone," reminisced sophomore guard Bill McKeown.

By the time Downey tipped in his final bucket in the closing seconds, he not only eclipsed the Illinois mark for single game points and field goals, but the Big Ten record for field goals and for single game scoring in a regulation game. Amazingly, his performance came in a losing effort as the Hoosiers came back to win the game, 103-100.

Even in a losing effort, Downey's performance left a lasting impression on everyone in the building that afternoon, especially the younger guys on his team.

"Watching Dave that night was a lesson on how to play basketball," said teammate Skip Thoren.

Downey scored 53 points on 22-of-34 shooting from the floor and nine-of-nine accuracy from the free throw line. Since that night in 1963, Illini basketball teams have played 1,205 basketball games, many with the added advantage of the three-point line, and only one player has come within even 10 points of breaking the record. (Andy Kaufmann's 46 points on December 3, 1990).

As Downey sits in his office in Champaign, now 41 years later, it's still something he looks back upon with a lot of pride.

"In that game I got closure," reflected Downey. "Most people, when they finish their career, wish they could play one more game so they could have done better or got it right. I got it right that one time and it allowed me to get on with my life."

He certainly did get it right that night, a remarkable 53 times.

continued from page 85

The '63 Illini bounced back with an 87-79 victory at Purdue before beating Wisconsin 89-77 in the last game ever played at Huff Gym. Illini teams posted a 339-79 record there since 1925-26.

"We really didn't want to leave Huff," said Downey. "Huff was a wonderful home court. We couldn't even practice at the Assembly Hall other than one shootaround."

THE HALL OPENS

An 84-81 stumble at Michigan didn't dim the general excitement for the opening of the special building—the Assembly Hall—on March 4, 1963 against Northwestern. It was both breathtaking with its revolutionary flying-saucer look and yet scary. Many fans wondered what was holding up the dome. There were even doubts expressed in the construction world.

Rich Falk, then a Northwestern star from Galva and now the Big Ten director of basketball officials, scored the first official basket. He commented later: "It's an amazing structure. We were in awe. We were frightened, too. We thought the darn roof might fall in."

Ahead of its time, the Assembly Hall emerged after years in which the Illinois General Assembly elected not to appropriate funds for a UI basketball arena, an idea that had been in the works since 1939 and for which plans had been drawn up in 1944. Two decades failed to produce state financing. UI president David Dodds Henry put forth the plan for a multipurpose building to handle sports and cultural events in the mid-'50s, with the idea of using student fees to service the bonds.

The design was created by New York architect Max Abramowitz, a UI graduate. He had the novel idea of laying two giant bowls edge to edge, with poured reinforced concrete and a folded plate design to use the corrugation of the concrete for added strength. The floor located in the middle provided flexibility, not limiting it to a stage on one end. Abandoning the rectangular seating arrangement of most arenas, Abramowitz placed permanent seats in a round bowl.

Dick Foley, a former Illini guard from Paris, was president of Felmley-Dickerson Co., the general contractors for the Hall. The winning bid came in at about $8 million, that cost reduced to $6.9 by eliminating outside work on parking lots and landscaping. Construction took 45 months. The building foundation was buried 30 feet beneath the ground to allow people to enter the hall in the middle of the seating area. It was said that 16,000 could vacate in little more than five minutes. Acoustics turned out far better than predicted.

In a revolutionary development, roof weight was cut by 25 percent by the discovery of a lightweight substitute for gravel in concrete, making the dome strong and yet light enough to avoid interior supports. Some 614 miles of one-fifth- inch steel wire was wrapped via 2,740 revolutions of a tractor at the base of the dome under tensions of 120,000 and 130,000 pounds per square inch. This tension squeezed the concrete and reduced its 400-foot diameter by two inches, lifting the dome two and a half inches off the supporting scaffolding. A circular ceiling platform connected by a catwalk was constructed for lights and devises that lower scenery and other equipment.

The general public was enthralled by the structure. Viewers were awestruck during an open house that preceded the first game. Likewise, students were open to the Hall, accepting the cost to them. Previously at Huff, many students received only three tickets for the basketball season. Now, with 16,000 seats, there was greater opportunity for tickets.

Unlike the building itself, the first basketball game at the Assembly Hall was not a work of art. With a crowd of 16,137 and a 110-piece band packing the space-age structure, tempo was shattered by 57 foul calls and various miscues. But Illinois outlasted NU, 79-73, as Downey scored 19 points to crack Kerr's career scoring record.

THE FINAL DAY

To share the 1963 Big Ten title and receive an NCAA berth, Illinois needed to defeat Iowa while Indiana knocked off OSU on a nail-biting Saturday. As they became more accustomed to the Assembly Hall, the Illini raced to a 46-33 halftime lead and hung on, 73-69, despite eight-for-30 shooting after the break. Small finished with 21 and Burwell 20 against the Hawkeyes.

Then Hoosiers Rayl and Bolyard, up to then winless against OSU and 90-65 losers one year before, carried

continued on page 90

GREATEST MOMENTS
(NO. 6) ILLINOIS 79, NORTHWESTERN 73

MARCH 4, 1963 • ASSEMBLY HALL, CHAMPAIGN, ILLINOIS

ASSEMBLY HALL OPENS FOR BUSINESS

The Illinois basketball team woke up on March 4, 1963, knowing it was going to be a special day. After over 38 years of playing basketball in the cozy confines of Huff Gymnasium, the Illini, with two games left to go in the 1962-1963 season, were moving into the spacious Assembly Hall to take on the Northwestern Wildcats.

Each member of that team was going to be a part of history, but only two guys had a hand in building it. The summer before their senior season, Illinois center Bill Burwell and guard, Jay Lovelace, worked construction on the Assembly Hall. It wasn't your run of the mill summer job.

"I remember pushing one of those buggies full of concrete on the roof of the Hall as it was being built," recalled Burwell. "We had to pour the concrete into the roof, which was a great way to get in shape and build muscles.

"It certainly wasn't a soft job, because we worked really hard," remembered Lovelace. "We were definitely laborers. We carried around a lot of wood and it was part of our job to move and pour the concrete up on the roof. I have always made the comment that if you would take out the concrete that Bill and I helped pour, the whole thing would come down."

There was a third member of the team working construction on the Hall that summer, but his stay on the job site didn't last long.

"I went up on the roof one time and I said to myself life is too short," laughed Dave Downey. "So I went right back and worked on a part of the Illini Union."

The Illini only had one practice in the Assembly Hall before they took the floor that evening. The question of who actually scored the first basket is still a heavily debated to this day.

▲ A sight to behold: The Assembly Hall opens to a capacity crowd of over 16,000. Everyone was wondering the same thing: Will the roof hold?

▲ *Illinois players partake in a shootaround at the Assembly Hall prior to tip off on March 4, 1963. It's a good bet that the Illini took plenty of shots to become familiar with their new shooting background. It was only their second look ever at the court.*

"The first time we practiced there it was so new that you could still smell the concrete," said Illinois reserve forward John Love. "Everyone raced out there to try and be the first one to score a basket and I remember thinking the janitors or construction guys had probably shot already."

The Illini recruiting class lass of 1961 consisted of Dave Downey, Bill Small, Bill Burwell, and Jay Lovelace. They were promised they would get two years in the Assembly Hall, and instead they would get just two games.

The move there was going to be a radical change. The tight quarters of Huff Gym would now give way to the bowl-like, fans-a-mile-away feel of the Assembly Hall.

A capacity crowd of 16,137—awed by the sight of the mammoth arena and fearful of reports that it might collapse—was in attendance on the eve of March 4, 1963. What they weren't awed by was the play on the floor. There were 57 fouls called and the change in depth perception wreaked havoc on both team's shooting. The Illini shot 36 percent for the game (25 percent in the first half), while Northwestern checked in at 30 percent for the game and a horrendous 23 percent in the second half.

The first basket in an actual game in the Assembly Hall was scored by Northwestern's Rich Falk, who later went on to become the head coach of the Wildcats and is now the Big Ten director of officials.

"I got the ball on one of the first possessions and I drove right to the baseline," said Falk. "I rose up, knocked down the baseline jumper, and I often joke that it was the last basket I would make because of the vastly different shooting background of the Hall. It was like nothing I had ever seen before."

The Illini outscored the Wildcats by 11 in the second half on their way to a 79-73 win, which kept their Big Ten Title hopes alive. The one bright spot of the night offensively was that Dave Downey broke Johnny Kerr's career scoring mark five minutes into the game when he sank two free throws.

But few remember Downey's feat, which was overshadowed by both team's awful play and poor shooting, and a looming fear that the roof might just collapse. Perhaps the only two in attendance who weren't a little bit concerned about the state-of-the-art structure the Illini now called home were Bill Burwell and Jay Lovelace—because only they knew the concrete was poured just right.

continued from page 87

Indiana to an 87-85 overtime victory that allowed Illinois to earn a share of the crown and the NCAA berth.

"Small and I watched the game in our apartment, and we had our bags packed to play in a national AAU tournament with a Chicago team," said Downey. "The game went to the wire and we knew we'd be the Big Ten representative if Indiana won. When it happened, we had a spontaneous campus celebration. There were 24 teams invited that year. The Big Ten representative was seeded into the round of 16."

That was the year Mississippi State won the SEC and had to sneak out of the state at midnight because the governor had decreed that they not play against teams with black members.

In the NCAA round of 16 in East Lansing, Chicago Loyola beat Mississippi State, and the UI's twin towers, Burwell and sophomore Skip Thoren, fought off Bowling Green's 6-11 Nate Thurmond to advance with a 70-67 victory. But Loyola, headed for the national title, ended the UI season with a 79-64 triumph.

"Loyola wasn't real big, but was quick and strong," said Downey. "That team was really the beginning of the modern basketball team."

Illinois finished the season with an 11-3 conference record and an overall mark of 20-6, which earned the team the eighth ranking in the final AP poll.

"I got good advice from Marty Blake, then the general manager of the St. Louis Hawks, who said, 'If you're going to play, we'll draft you first. But if you're my son, I'd say you ought to go on with the rest of your life. There are people who can't do anything else who would do anything to be in a uniform.' I never looked back.

"Later on, the Warriors offered me a $12,000, make-good contract for one year. I turned it down. Havlicek told me that he received $9,000 for his first year at Boston, made Rookie of the Year, and got a raise to $10,000 his second year. It was a different time."

▲ *Forward Dave Downey led the charge on a talented 1962-63 club that won the Big Ten and finished 20-6, ranked eighth in the country. Downey finished his senior year averaging a double-double for his career with 18.9 points and 11.0 rebounds per game.*

ILLINI ARENAS
ASSEMBLY HALL

1963-PRESENT

When the doors opened at 7 p.m. on March 3, 1963, the one-of-a-kind structure called the Assembly Hall became the new home for Illinois basketball. Now, more than 40 years later, it is widely known across the country as being one of the more intimidating arenas to play thanks to a "sea of orange" and the student cheering section, the Orange Krush.

The Illini opened the building with a 79-73 victory over Northwestern and since that night, the Hall has played host to 554 games—436 of them, or 79 percent, won by the Illini. There have been five undefeated home seasons and 150 sellouts in the rich history of the building.

"I always thought we had the best arena in the Big Ten and one of the best in the entire country," said Ken Norman.

The Hall has been the sight of unforgettable moments, great games and electric nights. For the players, the atmosphere within the Assembly Hall always got them ready to play a game.

"Just walking towards the Hall on game days got you ready to play," recalled Eddie Johnson. "When you walked down the tunnel towards the floor you could see the crowd staring right at you. When you walked out into that sea of orange it just got you ready to play. I loved the Assembly Hall and it is still one of my all-time favorite buildings."

Over the past few years, the sea of orange on game days has taken on a new meaning. Starting in February of 2001 with the inaugural 'Paint the Hall Orange' game, the building became an even more intimidating venue as now almost every single person in attendance is wearing orange.

If the I-Men spent years making Huff Gym an intimidating place to play for an opponent, then the Orange Krush student cheering section has taken that art form to a new level. Beginning in 1979, the Krush was placed on the Assembly Hall floor right under the basket and in front of the opposing team bench.

By the mid-1980s, the Krush began to grow in number and stature. They were quickly becoming known throughout the entire Big Ten as one of the best cheering sections in the conference.

"When I think of the Assembly Hall, I think of the Orange Krush, who were just awesome," said Kendall Gill, who played in front of the Krush from 1987-90.

During the 1990s the Krush continued to grow, and the section took off in 1996 when Coach Kruger became coach. Today the section is known as one of the best student sections in the country and opposing teams are fully aware their time in the Hall isn't going to be easy.

Over the last five seasons, the Illinois basketball team has dominated in the Hall, going 63-3 at home. In that span, perhaps no building in the country has produced as great a home-court advantage as the Assembly Hall.

The unique structure has a certain mythical feel to it on nights when the fog hovers as the sun sets. Some would say that mythical feel carries over to the inside of the building on game nights, when for four decades winning Illini clubs have shared in a unique experience with their fans—Illinois basketball at its best.

▲ *The Assembly Hall as seen from above. Thanks to the "sea of orange" and the Orange Krush, it's grown to be as intimidating a venue on the inside as it is an intriguing venue on the outside.*

Captain Bill Edwards,
Windsor Senior,
and Coach Harry Combes

Basketball

Illinois vs. Michigan State

1:30 P. M., SATURDAY, JANUARY 4, 1964

ASSEMBLY HALL, CHAMPAIGN, ILLINOIS

Tal Brody
Guard

Bogie Redmon
Forward

Skip Thoren
Center

Capt. Don Freeman,
Madison Senior,
and Coach Harry Combes

Basketball

Illinois vs. Kentucky

8 P.M., WEDNESDAY, DECEMBER 8, 1965
ASSEMBLY HALL, CHAMPAIGN, ILL.

Jim Dawson
Guard

Deon Flessner
Forward

Preston Pearson
Guard

CHAPTER NINE

OPENING THE OFFENSIVE FLOODGATES

1963-64—1965-66

The new look in 1963-64 produced two of the most prolific performers in UI history, center Skip Thoren and guard Tal Brody. They were juniors now at the peak of their scoring potential, and offensive records would tumble during their term on campus.

Combes, an all-league guard himself, always had backcourt sparklers. If the center position became a headache after BonSalle went ineligible, Combes' guards remained prolific.

Brody was a particular delight, following a long line of dashing marksmen dating to Bill Erickson and carrying through the likes of Don Sunderlage, Jim Bredar, Jim Wright, Paul Judson, Billy Ridley, Roger Taylor, Don Ohl, Manny Jackson, Jerry Colangelo and Bill Small. It was a running debate during that period as to which guard was best. Sunderlage had his supporters. So did Judson. But there were those who cast their vote for Brody, because he had the dash of Sunderlage with the shooting ability of Ohl.

With the UI's all-time highest single-season scorer, Don Freeman, joining Collinsville's big Bogie Redmon at the forwards, Illinois was ready to run up the points in 1963. They would average 84 points per game with Thoren checking in for the first of two double-double seasons, averaging 20.3 points and 13.8 rebounds for a 13-11 team.

It turned out to be two seasons in one. First, the Illini went 10-3 and seemed on the way to a successful campaign. They absorbed tough early losses to St. Louis, 81-78, and Oklahoma, 105-104, and hammered Butler twice before venturing to Los Angeles for two wins and a tough 83-79 loss to UCLA on December 28. Thoren and Brody were on the bench with fouls when John Wooden's Bruins, ranked No. 4, clinched it.

Illinois won the next five, starting with an 87-78 defeat of Notre Dame in Chicago. Said Combes after Thoren's 33-point effort: "Skip is one of the finest centers I have had in all my years of coaching. That includes Wally Osterkorn, George BonSalle, Johnny Kerr and others."

Moving into league play, Brody took charge with 29 and 28 points in wins over Michigan State and Iowa. Illinoisans weren't ready for what happened after the team reached 13-3, though. The defense collapsed in a 104-96 loss to Indiana and the VanArsdale twins, giving the Hoosiers 308 points in their last three dates with Illinois. Including that game, Illinois finished in a 3-8 tailspin and not even the persistent double-figure scoring of Thoren, Brody, Freeman and Redmon could turn it around.

Michigan's burly trio of Russell, Buntin and Oliver Darden shattered the UI defense in making 37 of 63 shots in a 93-82 outcome that solidified Michigan's No. 2 ranking. Guard Bill McKeown broke his wrist in that early February game, and captain Bill Edwards stepped in. But the struggling Illini were no match for Ohio State as Bradds threw in 49 points in a 110-92 runaway at St. John Arena.

It was Disastersville, and it didn't get any better on follow-up trips to Minnesota and Michigan State. Back home for Minnesota, the Illini broke a five-game slump with an 86-78 victory as Edwards, playing limit-ed minutes due to a severe cold, peppered the Gophers for 21 points. But Purdue threw up a zone two days later in West Lafayette, and Schellhase had 29 points for the Boilermakers in an 85-74 home win.

Cazzie [Russell] and Michigan were waiting in Ann Arbor where they overcame an Illini zone to prevail, 89-83, with Russell scoring 28. Thoren and Freeman converted 20 of 27 shots in throwing a brief scare into the Wolverines.

The Illini went 1-8 during this spell before winning their final two games to finish 13-11 on the season, but only 6-8 in conference play. The sixth-place finish was disappointing, but the team cast an eye toward the 1964-65 season, when their four mainstays would return.

PICKING UP THE PIECES

Reporting to the campus in the fall of 1964 was a Pinckneyville product, Ben Louis, who had been raised on southern Illinois basketball. The famous Duster Thomas had retired from coaching but social life in Pinckneyville still centered around the next game. In school, all basketball players had the same lunch and homeroom period, which allowed for morning practice. The last period of the day was reserved for physical education. This provided a one-hour jump on afternoon practices.

"Everybody bent over backwards to help the basketball program," said Louis, now an insuranceman in Champaign.

Thomas built a basketball empire amid the strong teams in that sector. Pinckneyville won the state championship in 1948 when it was still one class. Louis' team in 1964 lost in triple-overtime to the Cobden Appleknockers, who finished second to Fred Miller and Pekin.

Louis was on the UI freshman team in January of 1965 when Combes missed the UI's third Big Ten game with the flu. Braun filled in, but the Illini lost at Michigan, 89-83, as Russell and Buntin combined for 60 Wolverine points. For the Illini, Freeman had 27 points, Thoren added 24 and Brody had 21 of his own. These were high-scoring days.

Six-foot-three forward Don Freeman leaps above the pack for a rebound while teammates Tal Brody (No. 12) and Bill McKeown (No. 34) watch. Freeman led three Illini teams in the mid-'60s that could really put some points on the board in a hurry. By the time his college career was over in the spring of 1966, Freeman had amassed career averages of 20.1 points per game to go along with 10.3 rebounds.

continued on page 97

GREATEST GAMES
ILLINOIS 110, (NO. 2) UCLA 83
DECEMBER 4, 1964 • ASSEMBLY HALL, CHAMPAIGN, ILLINOIS

ILLINOIS CRUISES PAST DEFENDING-CHAMP UCLA

The Illinois basketball program couldn't have faced a more daunting task than to open the 1964-65 basketball season against defending 1963-64—and eventual 1964-65—champions UCLA. The John Wooden-led UCLA Bruins entered the Assembly Hall coming off a perfect 30-0 campaign. In that season they steamrolled through their opponents, including an 83-79 victory over Illinois in Los Angeles, on their way to the first national title in school history.

Gone from the previous Bruin team were three starters, but back were All-American Gail Goodrich and the famed "Wooden Press" that had driven teams crazy the year before. The Illini had been surprised and haunted by that press in Los Angeles, but swore they wouldn't let it happen again.

"We started to work as a coaching staff on how to attack that thing as soon as the previous season ended," said freshman coach Jim Wright. "We didn't stop preparing for that press until the day of the game."

When the players reported back to campus and started practice the coaching staff didn't waste any time.

"We worked the entire preseason on how to break that press," said sophomore Jim Dawson, who was getting ready to play his first ever college game. "Harry and his staff figured out a way to break through it and to make sure the guards couldn't trap us."

By the time the game rolled around, the Illini were a very confident bunch.

"We didn't see any way they could beat us that night," said Don Freeman. "We were so emotionally ready to play that game, and we just knew we could play with them."

"From the minute the ball went up that night I believed we were going to win that ball game," recalled senior guard Bill McKeown. "I don't think there was a guy on that team that doubted we could beat them."

From the opening tip, the Illini sliced through the press with relative ease. They were picking them apart, getting easy lay-ups and open jump shots, but more importantly, the Illini were red hot from the field.

"I just remember them hitting jump shot after jump shot," recalled Wooden, the legendary UCLA head coach. "I brought my team in and said, 'Don't worry, guys, they can't continue to play like this.' I kept telling them they couldn't continue, but they did. I remember calling a timeout late in the game to tell my team that I guess they would never believe me again."

The Illini's torrid shooting continued and by the time Jim Dawson drilled a shot over Kenny Washington right before the half-time buzzer, the Illini led 52-38 and were well on their way to cruising to the victory. By the time the game was over, Illinois came away with a 110-83 victory. Six Illinois players scored in double figures, led by Skip Thoren's 20 points. The team also set an Illinois and Assembly Hall record by shooting 58 percent from the field in the game.

"It was unbelievable to see us just dismantle them like that," said reserve junior guard Bob Brown.

"We overwhelmed them that day," said Illinois center Skip Thoren. "They were almost in shock."

UCLA went on to lose one more game that season before collecting their second straight national championship. Almost 25 years later, Coach Wooden recalled the game in his memoirs, *They Call Me Coach*:

"We were never close. And there wasn't much we could do about it. It was probably the worst lacing of my coaching career, a 27-point difference...It was no fluke. We just got slashed to bits."

continued from page 95

Combes was still in bed when the Illini whipped Minnesota, 75-72. Guard Jim Vopicka chipped in with 12 as all five starters crashed double figures and Illinois survived a late Gophers' rally. The late January interlude in Chicago found Freeman detonating his best game yet with flamboyant moves in a 28-point spree that felled Notre Dame 101-87. Thoren came right behind him with 25.

And Thoren was just warming up. He blazed for 37 as Illinois returned to the Big Ten against Purdue, romping 121-93. Dave Schellhase countered with 41, but Thoren had heavy backup: Freeman scored 22, Redmon had 21 and Brody added 19. It was the largest outpouring of Illini points up to that time.

On they rolled, ending the UI's dry spell at Ohio State with an 86-71 victory, stuttering briefly in a high-scoring 105-90 loss to Lou Hudson and Minnesota, but running up remarkable point totals in consecutive triumphs over Ohio State, 95-72, Michigan State, 113-94, and Iowa, 97-80. Twenty-point games were so routine that four Illini topped that number in East Lansing: Brody and Thoren with 26, Redmon with 23 and Freeman with 21. In setting a Jenison Fieldhouse scoring record at MSU, the Illini also established a school record for field goals, 50. Clearly, this was a Combes-type team.

Louis reminded: "Harry's philosophy was that a good offense is the best defense."

But the UI's title bid was foiled by Michigan as 16,128 Assembly Hall fans and millions on TV watched Russell score the Wolverines' last five points in an 80-79 barnburner. The Buntin-Russell duo tallied 53 for Michigan, and Russell's final free throw offset a hook by Thoren in the last two seconds. Michigan stood alone at 11-0 in the conference.

"Cazzie basically won that game for them," said Louis. "He was explosive. He wasn't one-dimensional. He was a power guard, and it hurt all the more that he was from Chicago."

Seniors Brody, Thoren and Redmon had one big burst left in them, rattling off another 121 points in the Assembly Hall against Michigan State. They finished 18-6 with the most points in one season (2,213), the most Big Ten points (1,277), the best shooting percent-

age (.481), the best individual shooter (Thoren with .560) and the most field goals in a Big Ten game (50). Their 10-4 mark in the Big Ten was good for third place.

Thoren, averaging his second double-double of 22.2 points and 14.5 rebounds, still holds the school single-season record for rebounds and the single-game mark with 24 rebounds against UCLA as a junior.

"Thoren was possessive of the post area," said Louis. "Skip was not a power center but he had sharp elbows. He had a lot of finesse and a patented short hook shot. He had a sense where the ball was going on rebounds, blocked out well and, in that period, had a lot of rebound opportunities. Thoren didn't spend a lot of

continued on page 100

▲ Forward Ben Louis—from Pinckneyville, Illinois—enjoyed playing for both the offensive-minded Coach Combes and the defensive-minded Coach Schmidt, pictured here with Louis.

GREATEST GAMES
ILLINOIS 91, (NO. 8) KENTUCKY 86
DECEMBER 19, 1964 • MEMORIAL COLISEUM, LEXINGTON, KENTUCKY

ILLINOIS BEATS RUPP AND KENTUCKY FOR FIRST TIME IN HARRY COMBES ERA

One would have to forgive Harry Combes if he got a little sick to his stomach when someone brought up the subject of Kentucky basketball. By the 1964 season, Combes' Illini teams had faced the Wildcats five times and had lost all five in heart-breaking fashion to Adolph Rupp and the boys in Lexington.

There was the crushing 76-47 defeat in the 1949 NCAA Tournament when the top-ranked Wildcats took off and never looked back. Two years later, Combes and the Illini met them again in the NCAA tournament in a game that went down to the wire before the Illini fell, 76-74.

"Harry would never get over those losses," said Dennis Swanson, who later would get to know Combes as a basketball manager in the late 1950s. "They cost him his shot at a national championship and he never forgot that."

In 1956, a Harv Schmidt-led Illini basketball team took an unblemished 4-0 record to Lexington and came away with a demoralizing 21-point loss. The next opportunity came late in 1958 when Mannie Jackson and Govoner Vaughn propelled Illinois to the final seconds against another top-ranked Rupp team only to see Vaughn's shot at the buzzer go astray.

The freshman group of Downey, Small and Burwell, along with junior Jerry Colangelo fought hard in 1960, but even they couldn't come out of Lexington with a win. Harry Combes just couldn't beat Adolph Rupp and it certainly bothered him.

"Harry had such a dislike for Kentucky," said Swanson, who witnessed the 1958 loss in person and today is the Executive Vice President and Chief Operating Officer of Viacom Television Stations Group. "He would rather beat Kentucky than eat."

On December 19, 1964, Combes received chance number six at Memorial Coliseum in the Kentucky Invitational Tournament against an eighth-ranked Kentucky team featuring star guard Louis Dampier and forward Pat Riley.

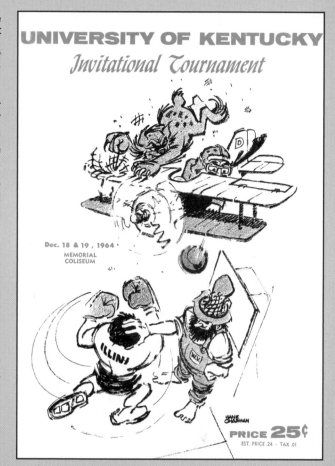

▲ *The cartoon image on the game program for Kentucky's matchup with Illinois in the 1964 Kentucky Invitational almost had it right. The Illini did indeed come out swinging, but unfortunately for the Wildcats, Illinois landed more than a few blows.*

"No one ever won at Kentucky, and especially in the Kentucky Invitational," remembered senior guard Tal Brody.

The Illini started the game out great, cutting up the 1-3-1 zone Kentucky played, to open up a 29-13 lead midway through the first half. Illinois' sharp shooting and hard work on the boards continued and after controlling the entire first half, the Illini took a nine-point lead into the locker room.

The second half was back and forth, but with two minutes remaining and Kentucky only down by three, Rupp decided they should foul Illini reserve Larry Hinton. In front a raucous crowd of 11,800 in the Coliseum, the junior guard calmly knocked down both free throws to give the Illini a five-point lead.

The free-throw barrage began. Next up was Tal Brody, who knocked two down with 58 seconds remaining. Then it was Bogie Redmon sinking two with 12 seconds on the clock. And, finally, Brody sank a pair with two seconds left to ice the game.

When the final buzzer sounded, Combes had finally beaten Rupp and Kentucky, and the Illini became the first Big Ten team to ever win the Kentucky Invitational with a 91-86 victory over the Wildcats.

"After that game was the happiest I have ever seen Harry," recalled Bill McKeown, who chipped in with a career-high 19 points that night. "He thought we had accomplished something pretty special and the smile on his face made that pretty clear."

"It was a great thrill and a great accomplishment for Coach Combes," remembered forward Don Freeman. "He finally defeated one of the legends in Rupp, and you could just tell it meant a lot to him."

Sticking with the tradition of the Kentucky Invitational, there was a final banquet to finish the tournament and this time the gifts didn't go as planned.

"Rupp bought watches for the first-place teams, and I am almost sure he did it assuming that [Kentucky] would get them," recalled Hinton, whose only two points of that game came on those late free throws. "They didn't get those watches that night."

Even his former players took notice that Combes finally beat Kentucky.

"I remember listening to that game on the radio," said former Illinois guard Ted Beach, who had been a part of that devastating loss to Kentucky in the 1951 Tournament. "I called Harry that Sunday morning when they got back and said that was one of the more enjoyable wins I have ever been around and he said to me, 'Ted, that is one of the more satisfying wins I have ever had, also.'"

Brody poured in 25 points, Skip Thoren scored 27 and grabbed 22 rebounds, and Harry Combes and his team got themselves a brand new watch. But to Combes, it wasn't just a watch. That watch became a symbol of getting over a major hurdle in his coaching career and of the day he finally left Lexington with a smile on his face.

Courtesy of Larry Hinton

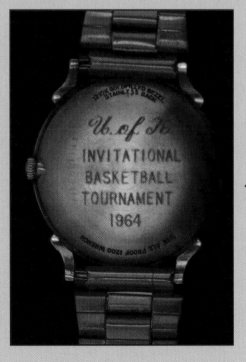

◄ *Adolph Rupp might have meant for his own Wildcats to wear these watches, but instead the Illini took home a new timepiece after upsetting Kentucky. This is Larry Hinton's watch. The inscription reads: "U. of K. INVITATIONAL BASKETBALL TOURNAMENT 1964."*

continued from page 97

time outside the post area. He didn't have the mobility of some of today's players but he took advantage of his abilities, and he had good players around him."

FREEMAN'S GREAT YEAR

With the three high-scoring seniors gone, Combes broke in sophomores Rich Jones and Ron Dunlap in the front line with Don Freeman in 1965-66. As a senior, Freeman would surpass Illini season and career scoring records.

"Freeman was deceptively quick, and he could play against bigger people," said Louis. "He was a good shooter and ballhandler. His size (6-3) didn't prevent him from scoring inside."

The Illini had a "bad trip" to New York after Christmas when they beat Georgetown but lost to Providence and Army.

"Those Army players were hard nosed under Bobby Knight," said Louis. "For us, the score of 78-69 was low. We didn't play very well. It was a different type of game."

The 1966 Illini were breezing at 3-0 in the Big Ten going to Purdue where, Louis said, "It seemed like Schellhase shot every time he got it."

Schellhase scored 38, while the UI's Jones went three for 18 and Freeman eight for 29. The .367 percentage did in the Illini, who lost 93-87.

After producing a withering 120-point blast against Notre Dame in Chicago, the Illini played their best game in upsetting No. 4 Michigan, 99-93, in Ann Arbor.

"We shot nearly 70 percent (.697) in the second half," said Louis. "This was the game where Cazzie Russell banged an attempted dunk off the rim late in the game. Freeman had 33 [points] and Jones 31. When they were on, they were hard to stop."

Jones and Freeman combined for 48 more points in a squeaky 78-77 defeat of Ohio State—sub Bob Johansen made two late free throws for the cushion—but consecutive home losses to Northwestern and Indiana by the almost identical scores of 80-77 and 81-77 ended Illini conference hopes.

"When you live like that, sometimes you die like that," said Louis. "We shot .364 against Northwestern, and then we fell off to .303 against Indiana. We had 20 more shot attempts

continued on page 103

◄ *Skip Thoren (right) was a monster on the boards and could score a little, too. He finished his career with a rebounding average of 11.2 boards per game to go along with 15.7 points.*

GREATEST GAMES
ILLINOIS 99, (NO. 4) MICHIGAN 93
FEBRUARY 1, 1966 • YOST FIELDHOUSE, ANN ARBOR, MICHIGAN

THE SHOOTOUT:
CAZZIE RUSSELL VS. DONNIE FREEMAN

In the spring of 1962, the Illinois basketball program lost a major battle. It wasn't a conference game in the friendly confines of Huff Gym and it wasn't a late-season road test, either. They lost in the quest for the top-rated high school recruit in the state of Illinois—and the country. Chicago Carver's Cazzie Russell was headed east to the University of Michigan instead of south to Champaign. Lead recruiter Howie Braun and head coach Harry Combes were absolutely devastated.

"I talked to Howie Braun years later about Cazzie Russell and Howie practically lived with him in his recruitment," said longtime Illinois play-by-play man Larry Stewart. "When Cazzie decided to

▲ Michigan always seemed to bring the best out in Don Freeman. In the Illini's 99-93 road victory over the Wolverines in 1966, Freeman matched Cazzie Russell bucket for bucket.

go to Michigan, I will never forget it. I thought Howie was going to kill himself."

Harry Combes was a coach who firmly believed Illinois boys should stay in Illinois and there is no doubt Cazzie going to Michigan bothered him.

"Harry felt kind of spurned by the fact that Cazzie didn't chose Illinois," recalled then senior Larry Hinton.

With Russell heading to Ann Arbor, the Michigan-Illinois rivalry immediately heated up. It turned out to be a one-sided rivalry. By 1966, Michigan had beaten Illinois all five times that Russell played, including a heartbreaking 80-79 defeat the year before in the Assembly Hall. To make matters worse the Illini were heading up to Yost Fieldhouse, a building where the fourth-ranked Wolverines had won 17 straight home games heading into the contest.

"That building was old, creaky and leaky," recalled Illinois center Ron Dunlap. "It was a real tough place to play."

Another member of the Illinois Class of 1962 knew this was his last shot at Michigan and Cazzie.

"Before the game I remember thinking to myself 'It is now or never,'" said Don Freeman. "I usually rose to the occasion on a challenge and what bigger challenge was there than Cazzie Russell and the Wolverines in Yost Fieldhouse."

When the game began it didn't take long for it to become the Don and Cazzie show. Russell nailed a bank shot and Freeman returned fire. Cazzie knocked down a 15-footer and Don answered the call with a jumper of his own. Before long it became pretty obvious that this was shaping into an all-time duel.

"It was an old-fashioned shootout," said Dunlap, who spent the night banging down low with Michigan center Oliver Darden. "[Russell and Freeman] just went at it head to head. Donnie at 6-3 and Cazzie at 6-5. There was no quit in either of them."

continued on page 102

continued from page 101

"Don had a real quick first step and he could get his shot off from anywhere on the floor," recalled Russell, who is now the head coach at the Savannah College of Art and Design. "He was a tough guy, a slasher, and a very intense player who always seemed to be in control of himself. He had a real good game that night."

At halftime, Michigan was clinging to a 45-42 lead, but not one of the 7,350 spectators could imagine what they were about to see. Someone forgot to tell Illinois super sophomore, Rich Jones, this was supposed to only be Donnie against Cazzie.

"I just remember Harry telling me at halftime not to be shy," recalled Jones, who finished the first half one of nine from the field. "He said if you have the shot in this half, take it."

Jones did just that. He came out firing and finished the second half hitting 12 of 13 shots to take a great deal of the pressure off Freeman.

As the dynamic duo of Jones and Freeman were firing away, Coach Combes had a new plan for Russell. It was time to turn to their defensive stopper, Preston Pearson.

"Harry told Preston at the half to not let Cazzie get the ball," said reserve guard Bob Brown. "I don't remember him touching the ball that much in the second half."

It was no surprise to those who knew the 6-1 Pearson well that he could step up and face a challenge as big as Cazzie.

"Preston was one intense competitor," recalled Bob Johnson, who grew up with Preston in Freeport and is currently the CEO of Black Entertainment Television. "He hated to lose, because losing to him was unacceptable and he always wanted to prove he could play against the best and guard the best whenever possible."

There wasn't an Illini player who had been guarded by Pearson in practice that doubted he could do it.

"Preston was a physical force," laughed Rich Jones, who once suffered a cracked rib from Pearson after Pearson tackled him in a fraternity football game. "He had such strong hands and when he put those hands on you, you didn't move where you wanted to go. Instead he moved you where he wanted you to go and there was no doubt that Preston was our stopper."

Pearson didn't completely shut Russell down in the second half, but he sure slowed him down. There was no slowing down the Illini, though, as they put together one of the greatest halves in Illinois basketball history. They shot a staggering 70 percent from the field drilling by 23 of 33 shots for 57 points. Freeman and Jones combined for 64 points in the game and the Freeman-Russell match-up lived to up its billing with both players netting 33 points on 14-27 shooting from the field and five points from the free-throw line. With a 99-93 victory, years of frustration against the Maize and Blue were over.

For Freeman, it was a night where he matched the great Cazzie Russell shot for shot. For Combes it was his 300th win in his Illinois career and for the Illini it was redemption against the Wolverines.

The next time Illinois returned to Ann Arbor they moved across the street to Crisler Arena or the "house that Cazzie built." For that one cold February night, though, the Fieldhouse became the "house the Illini tore down."

▲ *Preston Pearson—shown here on defense—was always on his opponent like a glove. He was the key to slowing down Michigan's Cazzie Russell in the second half of the Illini's thrilling 1966 victory over the Wolverines.*

continued from page 100

but we only made 27 field goals, and Indiana made 29 of 69."

Bertine's headline read: "Yikes!" Those home losses were unexpected.

After a 100-point outburst against Minnesota at home, the Illini fell to the same Gophers 94-92 in Minneapolis as they made a 21-point reversal despite Freeman's 35 points. Archie Clark scored 12 points in one four-minute stretch for Minnesota.

Such was the nature of the Big Ten's high-scoring era. Prior to 1955, no Illini teams reached 100 points. In the 12-season period beginning in February of 1955 and running through February 1966, Combes' teams had 32 scoring bursts of 100 or more. In the 38 seasons beginning in 1966-67, Illini teams hit triple figures 45 times, meaning that Combes' teams still enjoy 41.6 percent of the 100-point games.

The 1965-66 campaign wound up at 12-12 (third in conference at 8-6) but Freeman set marks that still stand today. He scored 668 points in 24 games for a 27.8 average that still remains the UI's all-time best. He averaged 20.1 for his three-year career, trailing only Weatherspoon (20.9) and Scholz (20.5) for career bests.

Still, Illinois had plenty of firepower returning in the fall of 1966. Little did they know what would happen next.

▲ *Forward Rich Jones clears out the lane as he grabs a rebound in an 80-64 win over Wisconsin in 1966. Jones lost his eligibility the following year due to the "Slush Fund" scandal.*

CHAPTER TEN

ADMISSION
TRANSITION
SUCCESS
1966-67—1969-70

Down through the decades, it has seemed as though a China Wall existed east of Danville, preventing the Illini from attracting Indiana prep stars. South Bend's Vic Wukovits—the exception—shared the center position with Dwight's Art Mathisen on the 1942 Whiz Kids squad. When the Illini landed sturdy southpaw Mike Price out of Arsenal Tech in Indianapolis and Bob Windmiller from North Manchester in the late-'60s, they became the only Hoosier basketball recruits to figure prominently into the Illini's plans in a quarter-century of Illini basketball between Indianapolis Attucks' Ed Searcy in 1960 and Noblesville's Scott Haffner in 1985. Searcy played parts of two seasons before losing eligibility, and Haffner transferred after serving as a sub one season. (This does not include Elkhart's Garvin Roberson, a pass-catching end who arrived on a football scholarship and served on Schmidt teams in 1972 and 1973.)

With no offers from Purdue or Indiana, Price credited William Moon, a music teacher at Arsenal, for hooking him up with the Illini athletic department. Price explained:

"Moon had attended Illinois, and he brought me to campus, and it moved from there. My older brother, Jesse, attended Millikin at that time and set some scoring records. But it was Moon who influenced me. I had a partial scholarship offer from Butler, and a full scholarship from Colorado. I wanted Illinois."

It was a nation in turmoil when Price and Bradley's Randy Crews arrived in Champaign-Urbana in the fall of 1966. Major civil rights legislation was being installed in the midst of the Black Power movement. Chicago was the scene of a July 1966 riot requiring a National Guard call-up. Campuses were hotbeds of anti-war protests. Martin Luther King was assassinated on April 4, 1968, and Bobby Kennedy's presidential quest ended with his death two months later. The Civil Rights Act of 1964 had long since revealed how few blacks were in attendance at white universities, setting in motion a surge that saw black student enrollments doubled in the next six years.

When Price became eligible as a sophomore in the fall of 1967, he was one of 223 black undergraduates who made up one percent of the UI enrollment. In response, the UI embarked on an affirmative action initiative called Project 500. A racially based admission plan, it was geared to correct the imbalance by offering special admissions to underprivileged minorities. Price, son of a Russellville, Kentucky, sharecropper, kept his concentration on basketball and studies. He was virtually oblivious to the national movement.

"In Indianapolis, we were aware of things happening around the country, but we were not totally in touch," Price said. "The term Naptown was deserved during that time, a city asleep.

"In Champaign-Urbana, the racial part never occurred to me that much because, in my freshman year, our pre-eminent players in football and basketball were black, at least until the 'slush fund' scandal. It was a rude awakening for me to lose close friends like Rich Jones and Ron Dunlap. I never fully understood what they did wrong. I know there are rules and you should follow them, but the rules in my estimation were always wrong. Those guys never harmed anyone. Looking back, it was the most devastating thing that happened.

"Then, later on, I was the only black player on the squad until we recruited Nick Weatherspoon, Nick Conner and Alvin O'Neal."

THE SLUSH FUND SEASON

The scandal became known in December of 1966, with Price nearing the end of his first semester. Records of three illegal funds were turned over to president David Dodds Henry by Mel Brewer, an associate athletic director and keeper of the records. Football coach Pete Elliott, poised to replace Mills as athletic director, was ultimately obliged to resign along with Combes and assistant Howard Braun.

This revelation shattered a quality UI basketball team as top-scorer Jones, center Dunlap and sophomore forward Steve Kuberski were declared ineligible. Guard Jim Dawson went on to capture Big Ten MVP honors (521 points for a 21.7 average) for a 12-12 team. Earlier, while still intact, Combes' last squad demonstrated great promise by serving Kentucky its 22nd home loss in 23 years, 98-97, in overtime on December 5.

"The Kentucky fans were pretty derogatory toward Jones and Dunlap," recalled then-junior Benny Louis. "But we beat a good team and our confidence was growing."

Five days later, a 90-88 loss at West Virginia had a "highway robbery" feel about it as the officials concluded it was possible for the Mountaineers' Dave Reasor, in one second, to leap up and catch a long pass, come down, fake and shoot a 20-footer. The basket counted over the outcries of Combes and the Illinois entourage.

"We all felt like we hadn't really lost the game," said Louis. "Going there was like walking into a deep, black hole. It was a loss but we still felt like we could go a long way with that team."

Later that month in Chicago, as the Illini prepared to face California, the three Illini were declared ineligible. At what Combes called "an absolute low point," the trio of Dawson (24 points), Deon Flessner (23) and Dave Scholz (22) keyed a courageous 97-87 win. But the Illini team had received a staggering blow that would linger beyond that season.

"I recall sitting around in the hotel in Chicago playing cards when Harry walked in and pulled out Rich, Ron and Steve," said Louis. "When they returned, they said they were ineligible. That put Scholz in the starting line-up and he went from there."

Guard Mike Price was the rare Illini recruit from the state of Indiana. Price starred on Harv Schmidt's first three Illini teams before enjoying a brief NBA career. ▶

The Illini traveled to Los Angeles and went 2-1 in the L.A. Classic, losing a 73-72 thriller to Southern Cal. Just as the earlier West Virginia game ended in dispute, the one-pointer with USC revolved around a no-call on what Combes believed was goal-tending on a late drive by Dawson. In that game, the officials warned long-time UI broadcaster Larry Stewart, stationed at courtside, about making derogatory officiating comments. Stewart waved them off, saying: "Be quiet, I'm on the air," a response that drew many laughs on the way home.

The Illini returned to Big Ten play in January and lost to Michigan State and Northwestern even as Dawson scored 21 and 29.

"Dawson was a great ballhandler and a good shooter," said Louis. "He had a lot of intensity. He played closer to 100 percent than anyone. He didn't pace himself like a lot of players.

"But as a team, we couldn't hold up. We played a lot of zone, which wasn't normal for Combes, in the last half of that season. Things were so bad that I moved from a guard to a forward position in the second half of the year."

Illinois defeated Michigan by the same score as the previous year, 99-93, but the meaning was different. Michigan, with Russell gone, was tumbling from first to last in one year. Illinois then lost twice in Chicago in late January, first to Notre Dame, 90-75, and then to No. 1-ranked UCLA, 120-82.

"They had [Kareem] Abdul-Jabbar, then known as Lew Alcinder, and he scored 45 points on 21 baskets in 27 shots," said Louis. "Combes was good at breaking John Wooden's press, but not in this game. I remember driving in with Alcinder at the free throw line, and he took one step back and blocked my shot."

Dawson finished with the fourth-highest single-season point total in UI history, and came in second to Minnesota's Tom Kondla in Big Ten scoring. He was voted Big Ten MVP over Iowa's Sam Williams. The Illini finished the season with a .500 overall winning percentage at 12-12, but a 6-8 mark in the Big Ten banished them to seventh place.

Despite playing for a 12-12 Illini squad in 1966-67, guard Jim Dawson (No. 24) captured the Big Ten MVP Award thanks in part to his 21.7 scoring average. It was one of the few bright spots for a team mired by scandal.

COACH SCHMIDT ARRIVES ON THE SCENE

As intense as his predecessor, Harv Schmidt left an assistant's position at New Mexico to become the third straight former Illini star to take the cage reins. Schmidt's regime started, as so many seasons before his arrival had, with a UI win over Butler. Scholz rolled in 37 points in the 75-57 win. The 6-8 Decatur product was a relentless scoring machine throughout his three seasons. But Scholz and the Illini were overmatched when they hosted Houston and the great Elvin Hayes and Don Chaney on December 9.

"Depleted as we were from the previous year, I was moved from guard to forward at 6-3," said Price, a sophomore starter then. "Houston's front line was 6-10, 6-9 and 6-9, and Hayes was outstanding (25 points, 20

continued on page 112

Center Dave Scholz was a rebounding and scoring force in the Big Ten, averaging 22.0 points and 9.6 rebounds per game during the 1967-68 season. The following year, sophomore Greg Jackson displaced Scholz to forward, thus creating one of the league's best rebounding and scoring frontlines.

GREATEST MOMENTS

ILLINOIS BASKETBALL: 1967-1970

HARV SCHMIDT REVITALIZES HIS ALMA MATER

The Slush Fund shattered the dreams of Illinois faithful everywhere. The basketball program endured an extremely difficult season in 1966-67, struggling to pick up the pieces and survive an emotional campaign in what was Harry Combes' final season on the sidelines. When Illinois and its athletic director, Gene Vance, went searching for the next coach, the University wanted someone that could reenergize the basketball program. Almost three weeks after the season ended they found the perfect guy in favorite Illinois son, Harv Schmidt.

▲ *Coach Schmidt (standing) reenergized the Fighting Illini and their fans by creating an unprecedented level of excitement at the Assembly Hall.*

Schmidt, a beloved Illini player from the mid-1950s, rode into Champaign under very challenging circumstances. But his love and passion for Illinois basketball soon wore off on the fan base.

"Harv was really loved in Champaign and Illinois really went through a down time there around the Slush Fund," recalled Schmidt's first recruit Rick Howat. "When he came in though, he was the savior and right off the bat he got things going."

Schmidt's first challenge was putting people back in the seats of the Assembly Hall.

"When I first got there, I didn't think the attendance figures were reflective of what it should have been for Illinois basketball," said Schmidt. "Believe me, I didn't win many battles with the Assembly Hall people, but I did convince them to put in platforms and the seats that now surround the court on the main floor."

While most coaches concentrate on their teams and recruiting, Harv worked tirelessly to make sure the students and the fans felt like part of Illinois basketball again.

"For years I went night after night to fraternities and sororities for their chapter meetings," remembered Schmidt. "I sat and talked with them for a while. I went to more of those things that you can ever imagine."

After struggling through an 11-13 season in his first year, the program saw something encouraging happen early in December of 1968. The fans flocked back, and while in attendance, they poured out their love for Schmidt with standing ovations.

"I went to a lot of games when I was in high school with my sister," remembered Otho Tucker. "All Harv had to do was walk on the court and the people went crazy."

"There wasn't a time that I was there that when he walked onto the court, Harv didn't get a standing ovation from the crowd," recalled Bob Brown, a former Illinois player and coach under Schmidt. "I was a young coach, but as a player I had been all over the country and I had never seen anybody received like that."

Many fans remember the standing ovations, but not how it all began. The ovations started in Schmidt's first season as head coach.

"Going out of the tunnel there were a few kids who sat right above it and they were always leaning over there yelling, scream- ing, and raising hell," recalled Schmidt from his home in Colorado. "It got to a point where I would chat with them and make a comment or two when I was going out at halftime or after the games. They starting giving me ovations, and God Almighty it took off from there."

"I remember it got somewhat intimidating to the opposition to see the response Harv got when he walked out," said Dick Campbell, who was Schmidt's right hand man during his tenure at Illinois. "I remember one time Johnny Orr from Michigan decided to wait until Harv came out and tried to walk out at the same time in order to offset it so it wouldn't affect his team. It really was incredible."

By the middle of that second season, Harv-mania set in. Whether he walked out at the beginning of a game or at half-time he was receiving standing ovations. "I Like Harv" buttons were passed out in the crowd and the Assembly Hall became a place to be again.

"The emphasis shouldn't have been on me, because it should have been on the kids," reflected Schmidt. "But in the course of the interaction I had with the kids, we got them com- ing to the games because by the third year we had that place filled up to the brim and people were doing anything for season tickets."

The team finished 12-0 at home in his second season and by the start of the 1969-70 campaign, no one wanted to miss a game in the Assembly Hall. When the season tickets went on sale before the season began the coaches couldn't believe what they saw.

"The students were sleeping outside the Assembly Hall for days trying to get season tickets," recalled Brown. "We would have to walk through the students on the way to work, because they were camped out there for three or four days at a time."

▲ Students line the inside of the Assembly Hall in 1969, camping out for their shot at Illini tickets. Coach Schmidt's tireless public relations efforts helped ensure that the Illini were a hot ticket.

"It was weeks before the season started and kids were camped out in tents just trying to get tickets," said Campbell. "We would be at work in the morning and they would all be looking through the windows at us as we were trying to get some work done."

The Illini finished the 1969-70 season 7-4 at home and saw the attendance average shoot up to 14,291 people a game, including five sell outs. Illinois basketball fever hit a high in the 1970-71 season when 177,408 people came through the turn- stiles during 11 home basketball games.

"You could count on there being 16,128 people [per game] in the Hall that year," recalled then senior captain Rick Howat. "There was a lot of excitement around the program and Harv had an electricity around his personality that brought that out."

Even though the team had an 11-12 record that season and only went 6-5 at home, every single game was sold out. In the history of Illinois basketball, including the 1989 season and the recent Big Ten Championship years, that has never happened again.

In three years, a program that had faced the depths of despair was back on the map. In the late 1960s, the Assembly Hall became the place to be again and it was all because a for- mer hero, Harv Schmidt, rode into town and brought life back to Illinois basketball.

continued from page 109

rebounds). Crews battled Hayes all the way. That game gave our team character."

The 54-46 score was Houston's lowest in 83 games, and the UI's lowest since 1951. The race-horse, high-scoring era of Combes was over.

"Schmidt was a defensive coach," recalled Louis, the team captain. "He wanted us to make a certain number of passes before we shot. With our talent, he demanded ball control. I played a defensive guard and an offensive forward. It really didn't matter because we were all trying to get the ball to Scholz."

At the Volunteer Classic, the Illini lost to Tom Boerwinkle and Tennessee, 66-42, and to an Army team featuring three Illinoisans including Chicago Weber product Mike Krzyzewski. The 2-5 Illini rallied in Chicago after Christmas with a pair of wins as Louis tallied 18 points in a 65-54 defeat of Georgia Tech, and Scholz went for 24 in a 68-50 defeat of Texas-El Paso. This came after Willie Worsley and Willie Cager, members of the 1966 national championship team, were sent home for curfew violations.

"The weather was terrible that week," said Louis. "We had a big ice storm, and we walked from the train station in Chicago straight down the middle of a snow-packed Michigan Avenue because there were no cars allowed. Instead of going to the stadium to practice, we went into a large conference room and did a walk-through with a rubber ball about the size of a volleyball."

An overtime loss to Indiana was the only setback in an eight-game stretch from late-December to early February. The Illini bounced right back from the loss to pull one out on January 13, 61-60, at Minnesota. Scholz's 25-foot buzzer-beater marked the UI's first lead in the game since 2-0. But after a 5-1 spurt in early January, the 1968 Illini fell out of the race. The February highlight was 62-61 defeat of Northwestern in which Scholz broke Dave Schellhase's Assembly Hall scoring record with 42 points. But the season record ended at 11-13 (6-8 in conference), only the second UI loser in 40 years.

"The core of that team was sophomores and, during that era, sophomores were relatively immature in the game," said Price. "We hadn't developed to a point where

we could hold up in a grueling league. Crews and I felt like we were pretty tough people, but we lacked the overall physical endurance to hold up."

Like Bur Harper during World War II, like Irv Bemoras, Jim Bredar and so many others, the graduating Louis made use of his basketball skills to ease military service. At the St. Louis induction center, Louis was interviewed by a second lieutenant from Notre Dame who reminded that the Irish had defeated the Illini in 1967. As a result of that conversation, Louis became a "physical activity specialist" and was put in charge of sports activity for 18 months at a base in Anchorage, Alaska.

SPRINGING FORWARD

For his second season at the helm, Schmidt had big Chicagoan Greg Jackson heading up his sophomores and was able to move Scholz out of the center position in 1968-69 for what was a stirring 19-5 run.

"I loved those guys," recalled the coach that year. "Jodie Harrison was a transfer from Alabama and he became a special leader. We finished second in the Big Ten, but that team unfortunately couldn't advance.

"We were big and strong by the standards of the day with Scholz, Jackson and Crews up front and Price and Harrison at the guards. We could rebound with most folks. These guys were extremely coachable. With Rick Howat, Denny Pace, Fred Miller and Bob Windmiller coming off the bench, we were nine deep. They never questioned anything. I would have liked to have had that attitude all the time I was there."

Price felt the key to the 19-5 season was "our five-finger defense." He explained: "Harv called it that because we fit like a glove. It was that defense that helped me get into the NBA."

The 1968-69 squad won their first 10 straight, electrifying a hungry fandom. They raced out of the gate with a 105-66 rout of Butler with Scholz (27 points) and Jackson (17) dominant. The lone single-digit victory in the 10-game spurt came in Omaha against Creighton. The Illini built a 13-point lead and held off the Blue Jays, 69-66, with free throws.

continued on page 114

GREATEST GAMES
ILLINOIS 97, (NO. 20) HOUSTON 84
DECEMBER 21, 1968 • DELMAR GYM, HOUSTON, TEXAS

ILLINOIS BREAKS HOUSTON'S HOME STREAK

December 21, 1968, wasn't a normal day in Houston, Texas. That morning at precisely 7:51 a.m., NASA launched the Apollo 8 mission as Frank Borman, James Lovell Jr. and William Anders attempted to be the first American space crew to travel to the vicinity of the moon. On that same morning at about the same time, the 6-0 Illinois basketball team was waking up at the Shamrock Hilton in Houston with their own mission at hand. That evening, they were set to face off against the 20th-ranked Houston Cougars, owners of a 60-game home winning streak that spanned over three and a half years.

The game was played at the Delmar Gym, which was a snake-pit-like facility seating 5,200. It was packed to the rafters that night.

"At the time, Houston didn't have a home gym, so they used to rotate to different high school gyms around the area," remembered starting Illinois forward Randy Crews. "We played that game in a very small high school gym."

"It was very hot and extremely humid in there," said guard Rick Howat. "Guys were slipping all over the court and I never, ever played another game on a floor like that."

About the only thing that went wrong for the Illini in the first half was the opening tip. Six-foot-eight Illinois center Greg Jackson couldn't believe what he saw as he got ready for the tip.

"I couldn't understand why the shortest guy on their team was jumping center until the referee threw the ball up," recalled Jackson. "After that ball left the ref's hand, all I saw was the bottom of his shoes."

After Cougar guard Ollie Taylor won the tip it was Illinois who became the aggressor in taking leads of 7-0 and 25-14 on the way to a 50-39 first-half lead.

"Houston sat in their 1-3-1 zone the entire game like we expected, but we had some good perimeter shooters on our team," remembered Illinois head coach Harv Schmidt. "Bob Windmiller, Rick Howat, and Dave Scholz could all shoot the basketball and they came out firing that night."

The Illini struggled to match the Cougars' physical play in the second half. The Cougars cut the lead to 66-61 before the Illini regained control on a Crews jumper and a Jackson lay-up.

Houston made one more late run and cut the lead again to only five points. But this time an Illini spurt capped by a Fred Miller steal and lay-up put the Illini up nine points with just over two minutes to go. Miller's steal turned out to be the final blow in a very physical and intense game as the Illini beat the Cougars 97-84.

"We knew we were going to have to play hard and keep the mistakes to a minimum," said Scholz, who along with Jackson scored 21 points that evening.

And the NASA space mission wasn't the only launch in Houston that day.

"They handed out miniature basketballs at halftime to all of the fans in the gym," laughed Miller. "At the end of the game we got most of them thrown right back at us."

"I guess they weren't used to losing at home," recalled Jackson.

For the first time in 60 games, the Houston Cougars fell on their home court. For the Illini, it was a huge win that launched them back into the national polls for the first time since the allegations hit two years earlier.

"I'll never forget Harv Schmidt standing in the antiquated dirty locker room that had very few amenities," said Illinois senior manager Jack Tuttle. "He wrote a big 7-0 on the portable blackboard and had a big smile on his face."

"I don't think I ever saw Harv as happy as he was after that game," remembered Howat.

News of the big Illini win spread everywhere, including 96,265 nautical miles into space. While reading the daily news of the day the next morning, Mike Collins at NASA informed the crew of the previous evening's events.

"We also notice that the University of Houston lost their first home basketball game in three and a half years last night as Illinois edged them out 97 to 84," Collins said.

The result of the game became the first college basketball score broadcast into space.

The Illini touched down at Willard Airport at 10:45 a.m. the next morning knowing they had accomplished something special. With a 13-point victory over the Cougars, their mission was complete.

continued from page 112

As the wins mounted, Schmidt became a campus hero, receiving standing ovations from adoring fans as he walked out before each home game.

"We always associated their feeling for Schmidt with how much they cared about what he brought back to the university," said Price. "We were a hard-working group from the moment he showed up. The people knew he was responsible for our tenacity."

The Illini stood No. 4 in the nation when they traveled to Purdue January 7. But Schmidt had no answer for Purdue, an arch-rival he never beat in seven seasons as coach. Without the aid of a three-point line, Purdue ace Rick Mount poured in 37 points on 16-for-24 shooting in a 98-84 backbreaker.

"Mount is to this day the purest shooter I ever saw," said Price, "and that Purdue team ran him through picks and screens until he was able to get off a

Courtesy of the Urbana Free Library

▲ *Center Greg Jackson was a dominant force under the basket before developing a chronic back problem that would later hamper his production. During the Illini's 19-5 season of 1968-69, Jackson averaged 16.4 points and 8.3 rebounds per game.*

shot. Jodie and I both tried guarding him, and Randy wasn't quick enough. That Purdue team reached the national championship game and lost to UCLA."

Nothing came easy for the 1969 Illini after the loss at Purdue. An overtime conquest of Northwestern was followed by three losses in five games, with all setbacks coming on the road. The team finished with a 19-5 overall record—with all five losses coming in Big Ten play—and an AP ranking of 20th. After two straight seventh place finishes in conference, Illinois leaped all the way to second place with nine Big Ten wins. Scholz continued his prolific scoring, checking in at 19.1 points per game for the season. He became one of three Illini to average over 20 for their career: Scholz at 20.5, Weatherspoon at 20.9 and Freeman at 20.1.

ONE STEP BACK

Without Scholz in 1970 and with Jackson developing a chronic back problem, the Illini lacked the scoring punch to hang with undefeated Iowa (14-0) and runner-up Purdue (11-3) in the Big Ten, but managed to tie Ohio State for third at 8-6. With the 1969 successes as background, and with Schmidt becoming the community's most popular leader, Illinois led the nation in attendance with 14,291 per game in 1970, and again in 1971 with 16,128.

Confidence remained high at the close of the 1970 campaign as the Illini finished among the top three in the conference for the 24th time in 36 years. But a downturn was in the offing.

"Jackson had periodic spasms," said Price. "He was kind of stiff and always walked as though his back hurt. He didn't receive the weight training and therapeutic work that we have today.

"Iowa's team precision that year was as good as I had experienced in college basketball. That team was super accurate, and they played better team defense than we did."

Price had 23 points and 12 rebounds at Northwestern in the team's only three-figure outburst of the 1969-70 season, a 101-80 victory. Illinois reached No. 17 in the national rankings, and climbed to 5-0 in the Big Ten with a 75-73 win at Michigan in which Jackson scored 26 points to offset Rudy Tomjanovich's 31.

The first league loss was hard to stomach. Ace free thrower Rick Howat missed a late toss, and Badger Al Henry's followed the miss with a goal that won it for Wisconsin, 66-65. It was the first Assembly Hall loss in two years. Consecutive road losses to Minnesota and Purdue stung. Rick Mount scored 28 in an 83-49 runaway that extended Purdue's home win streak to 30.

The brightest spot in a six-game losing streak was a strong bid to interrupt Iowa's perfect league season. John Johnson, Fred Brown and Glenn Vidnovic helped the Hawkeyes survive, 83-81, despite Howat's 32 points and Price's 15-point, 12-rebound effort. Price missed tying it with a 15-foot jumper with three seconds left.

"It was one of my better all-around games," said Price. "I later found out that Bob Cousy was there scouting. He told me that he put out the word that he was going to draft me in the second round.

"The New York Knicks got wind of that and drafted me with the 17th and last pick in the first round. I played for a little more than a year, then went to the Pacers in 1971 and on to the Philadelphia 76ers in 1972.

"Illinois was a great experience for me," said Price, who has been in the banking business in Indianapolis for 30 years. "From the standpoint of athletics, my sophomore year and the early part of my junior year were frustrating, a learning and transitional period. Then the last year and a half were fantastic. I enjoyed the whole school experience, socially and educationally.

Illinois finished the season on a losing note, dropping its final game to Michigan State, 81-76 to finish 8-6 in the Big Ten—good for third place—and 15-9 overall.

▲ Guard Rick Howat (No. 10) entered the starting lineup in 1969-70 and teamed with Mike Price to give the Illini a dangerous backcourt. Center Greg Jackson (No. 31) blossomed as a junior to peak in scoring (17.0) and rebounding (9.8) averages during the 1969-70 season.

ILLINOIS

December 2

'72

Price .25

Depauw U.

ILLINOIS

February 19

'73

Price .25

Minnesota

CHAPTER ELEVEN

NEW SHERIFFS IN TOWN

1970-71—1976-77

Harv Schmidt's honeymoon with the Illini fans was teetering when the "Ohio Nicks," Weatherspoon and Conner, and Peorian Alvin O'Neal joined the varsity as sophomores in the fall of 1970. The collapse at the end of the previous season had folks wondering about the team's stability and the coach's ability. The questions resurfaced after Illinois climbed to No. 18 in the national rankings with a typical 8-2 start against so-so competition, and then struggled in late January and went 1-9 from February on.

In an opening 113-102 defeat of Butler, the quintet of Rick Howat (28 points), Greg Jackson, Fred Miller, Weatherspoon and O'Neal attained double figures. A rebound in the last second saved Oklahoma, 74-72, but the Illini followed with three easy home wins. It looked all the more promising when Jackson dominated the paint with 29 points and 16 rebounds in a 96-79 defeat of Villanova in Honolulu.

At the outset of the 1971 Big Ten race, Illinois went 3-0 with a pair of clutch wins over Wisconsin and Michigan State. First, Howat bagged eight free throws in the final two minutes to repel the Badgers, 84-82, and then Howat and Weatherspoon built a 69-61 lead to survive the Spartans, 69-67. Both wins came prior to January final exams. When they returned, the Illini weren't the same. Purdue whipped the Illini twice, and Indiana won in Champaign, 88-86, as George McGinnis outscored Weatherspoon 32-24. A frustrated Schmidt drew two technicals that afternoon, including one in the final two and a half minutes.

The losing streak was at eight entering the season finale at Indiana, and Jackson went out on a winning note as he, Spoon and Krelle combined for 74 points in a 103-87 spanking of the Hoosiers. Jerry Oliver coached the Hoosiers on an interim basis that day following the resignation of Lou Watson, who would be succeeded by Bob Knight. The team finished 11-12 on the season, 5-9 in the conference.

THE 1971-72 SEASON

Weatherspoon was the big man on campus when Royal's Rick Schmidt arrived on the scene as a raw freshman in the fall of 1971.

"Spoon was very quiet, hardly said anything to anybody, but he was intense," said Rick. "He was thin but as hard as a rock, and he could jump."

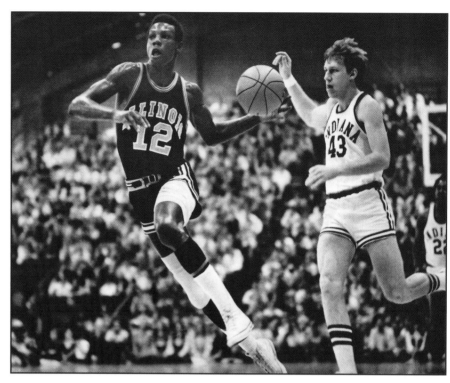

▲ Nick Weatherspoon—or "Spoon" to friends, fans and teammates—was the big man on campus in 1971. He increased his averages to 20.8 points and 10.9 rebounds per game during his junior year.

As was often the case, the Illini raised false hopes in early December with a 70-65 defeat of 20th-ranked Oklahoma at the Assembly Hall. Spoon had 16 points and received plenty of help from Ohio sidekick Nick Conner, footballer Garvin Roberson, promising young St. Louisan Billy Morris and captain Jim Krelle, who meshed eight baskets in nine tries. The win propelled the Illini to a 9-1 start and a No. 16 ranking.

This UI team was flashing balance and punch. Spoon racked 26 points and 14 rebounds against South Dakota, Krelle and Morris cashed 22 apiece at Tulane, Krelle enjoyed another big 25-point outpouring versus Loyola in New Orleans, and Weatherspoon and Morris combined for 50 in an 84-78 defeat of Georgia.

This was a team under a full head of steam. A 95-92 loss at Vanderbilt, with Spoon pouring in 34 points, seemed only a hiccup as the Illini traveled for a post-Christmas tourney in Jacksonville, Florida, where they rode the inside power of Weatherspoon and Morris to

wins over North Carolina State and Florida. Krelle hit the winning jumper in the 76-75 defeat of Florida to clinch the Gator Bowl title.

But all was not as it appeared. After opening the 1972 Big Ten race with an unimpressive 67-63 defeat of Northwestern, the Illini tumbled twice at home in Big Ten battles with Michigan (75-70) and Purdue (85-74). Suddenly, this wasn't the same team. Schmidt moved Jed Foster into the lineup at Michigan State, but his 18-point effort couldn't alter a disappointing 89-79 outcome. Losses to Michigan and Iowa followed and the Illini tailed off to 5-9 in the Big Ten.

Captain Krelle closed the season in a deep slump, his unhappiness culminating in a decision to leave the team after being benched for most of a 91-84 early March win over Iowa. A season-ending 97-84 loss at Wisconsin saw Spoon still pumping away, garnering 28 points to finish the season with 500 total points and a 20.8 average. Right behind was Morris with 15.2 points and 9.4 rebounds, excellent for a sophomore ... but he elected not to return, transferring to St. Louis.

"He was from St. Louis and went home to play in his home town. He was not happy at Illinois, and his classmates, Alvin O'Neal and Kris Berymon, also left early," recalled Rick Schmdt.

The squad finished 14-10 on the season.

SPOON'S SWAN SONG

With Morris gone, the hard-driving Schmidt moved in alongside Spoon and Conner in the 1972-73 front line while Duke transfer Jeff Dawson and Paris sophomore Otho Tucker started at the guards. Freshmen became eligible that year, but only one, six-foot-11 Bill Rucks, saw action, appearing in five games.

Spoon posted 37- and 29-point efforts in early romps over DePauw and Valparaiso, but another fast start was sidetracked in overtime during game three at Detroit, 79-77. Jeff Dawson, brother of Jim, had his first major outburst with 29 points in an 86-81 win over Furman two games later, but it would be an up-and-down 14-10 campaign overshadowed by the beginnings of a powerhouse revival at Indiana.

On a trip to Southern Cal for a December 22 match up, delays at O'Hare left the squad waiting in the airport.

"We got to Los Angeles about 1:30 a.m., and Weatherspoon and Conner were held out for the first 17 minutes of the game for disciplinary reasons," said Rick Schmidt. "We lost 75-72 in a game we should have won. Weatherspoon was terrific after he came in."

▲ *Illini center Nick Conner leaps into the air in an attempt to block the shot of a Wisconsin player, while teammate Nick Weatherspoon (left) waits for the rebound. Conner was regarded for being a tough defender and a solid rebounder.*

A highlight of late December was a date with UCLA and Bill Walton in New Orleans. The Illini battled the No. 1-ranked Bruins all the way before losing 71-64. Walton tallied 20 points, but the Illini hung in with Spoon scoring 18 and, in one of his top performances, Conner tacking on 17.

"We were down one point late in the game," recalled Schmidt. "I was dribbling down the court, and Larry Farmer head-butted me and cut the inside of my eye. Blood was gushing out. There was no call. They went down and scored a three-point play and won by seven. I went to the hospital and they had to put stitches on the inside of my eyelid."

It was UCLA's 53rd straight victory. The consolation for the UI was that Spoon and Conner made the Sugar Bowl all-star team. Conner was lauded for his defensive work against Walton.

Back in the Big Ten race, the Illini fell at Purdue in the opener and returned for their conference home opener against Wisconsin with only 8,607 tickets sold and fewer than that in attendance. Spoon and the Illini stalled out a 76-74 win against the Badgers, and then followed that with another two-point triumph as Jed Foster deposited a pair of free throws to turn back Dick Schultz's Iowa quintet, 80-78, before the semester break.

Spoon continued to move up the scoring chart with 30 in an 87-84 defeat of Notre Dame in late January, and the Illini fell into a win-lose syndrome in which they never won more than two straight down the stretch. Spoon waxed even hotter than before, corralling 34 points in a 76-75 win over Michigan in early February, and following with 32 in an 84-77 triumph at Northwestern.

"How do you stop a guy like that?" puzzled NU coach Brad Snyder said, calling Spoon and Minnesota's Jim Brewer "the two most dominating players in the Big Ten right now."

Indiana had an answer, turning loose Steve Downing for 41 points in an 87-66 verdict marked by Bob Knight's decision to bench Quinn Buckner "to get more patience on offense."

Weatherspoon scored 24 at IU, and added 28 in a win over Ohio State in which Otho Tucker and Garvin Roberson held the Big Ten's leading scorer, Al Hornyak, to 16 points.

"Garvin was a tremendous athlete but he didn't report from the football team until December," said Rick Schmidt. "He was a great defensive player."

In one of his most courageous efforts, Weatherspoon went for 23 points and 18 rebounds against Minnesota's powerhouse lineup of Jim Brewer, Clyde Turner, Ron Behagen, Corky Taylor and baseball great Dave Winfield. Bill Musselman's gang prevailed, though, 82-73 to serve the UI its first home loss of the year.

"Between Brewer and Winfield, Minnesota had two of the best athletes I ever saw," said Rick Schmidt. "They were big and strong and fast. I got in front of Winfield on a drive, and I crouched to take a charge, and he jumped over me. They both could have been tight ends in the NFL."

Spoon averaged 25 points a game as a senior, ranking second in UI annals to Don Freeman's 27.8 in 1966.

MISSING SPOON

A new world dawned in 1973-74 with the record-breaking Weatherspoon and the hard-rebounding Conner gone and, as it would happen, Otho Tucker being forced to redshirt due to a knee injury.

"Otho was my best friend and had been my roommate for two years," said Rick Schmidt. "He was a tremendous defensive player, and we didn't have much experience without him ... just Jeff Dawson and myself."

This was the beginning of consecutive 18-loss seasons, unprecedented in Illinois basketball. A 5-18 campaign that included just two Big Ten wins marked the end of Harv Schmidt's seven-year reign. Gene Bartow was hired from Memphis for an 8-18 campaign the following year that preceded his move to replace the great John Wooden at UCLA.

"We had no hint that Harv was in trouble that year," said Rick Schmidt. "We didn't know anything until around the first of March."

Nick Weatherspoon was absolutely dominant during his senior season with averages of 25.0 points and 12.3 rebounds per game. By season's end, Spoon had nudged past then Illini career scoring leader Dave Scholz with 1,481 points, an average of 20.9 per contest, which is still the best mark in Illini history.

Rick Schmidt became the go-to guy succeeding Weatherspoon. He opened the 1973-74 season with 27 points and 11 rebounds in a 101-80 loss at Arizona. He then joined Jeff Dawson, Dave Roberts, Tom Carmichael and Mike Wente in double figures while seven-foot Bill Rucks plugged the middle in a 99-78 home-opening win over Tulane.

But there was concern about Tucker when it was reported that he had "water on the knee" and would be sidelined indefinitely. Tucker's teammate at Paris, Brad Farnham, got his first start against Detroit on December 11, and sparked a 64-60 home triumph with 11 points and 10 rebounds. It was the first coaching loss after four wins for Dick Vitale, who went on to become more famous as a broadcaster than a coach.

Gibson City's long-shooting Dennis Graff popped into the lineup with 15 points in an 87-72 defeat of Northern Michigan, but the Illini reached conference play at 3-4 despite 30- and 26-point sprees by Rick Schmidt in New York losses to St. John's and Duquesne.

"I felt the need to score because I felt like I had as good or better a chance to score as anyone on the team," he said.

Fact is, this wasn't a strong Illini club. An opening 75-73 triumph over Ohio State ended a six-game skid at St. John Arena and made Illinois the only Big Ten road winner in the opening salvo. Schmidt scored 24 in the contest.

"Rick was superb again," said Illini coach Harv Schmidt. "He made all the big plays. He shows us a new shot every game."

But despite the best efforts of Schmidt, the Illini lost their next 11 in a row, including games against Bradley (in Chicago) and Jacksonville (at home).

"We lost to Purdue at home," said Rick. "John Garrett was six foot 11, and he went nine for 12 from the field. We couldn't guard anybody inside. That was our 10th straight loss to Purdue. We didn't have enough firepower."

On a personal note, forward Rick Schmidt put together impressive back-to-back seasons as a junior and senior, averaging 20.8 points and 6.2 rebounds per game over those two seasons. But the Illini as a whole failed to stand up to the rigorous tests of the Big Ten, winning just six conference games over two years.

The 91-69 margin was the worst ever in the Assembly Hall. It was Harv Schmidt's 10th consecutive loss to the Boilermakers, which would soon become 11 in early March. Dischinger, Schellhase and Mount were long gone, but Purdue still had a hex on the Illini.

Against Michigan State two days later, the smallest ever crowd of 4,685 attended the the Assembly Hall to see Illini break ahead 18-4 and lose, 90-82. Mike Robinson scored 24 and Terry Furlow added 21. Both were two-time Big Ten scoring champions in that era. After the game, MSU coach Gus Ganakas referred to the UI's all-white lineup while describing the Spartans as his "Greek ghetto team." The Spartans shot 72 percent in the second half.

Utterly defenseless, the Illini gave up more than 100 points on five occasions during the school's longest ever 11-game tailspin. The Illini became more shellshocked with each outing. Indiana won by its largest margin ever in Big Ten play, 107-67, despite Rick Schmidt's 27 points. The result caused Knight to say: "I don't enjoy seeing another team get beat that badly."

A 91-84 win over Iowa on February 23 was the only victory in the UI's last 15 games, coming as it did after an announcement that Harv Schmidt was handing in his resignation and would not return the following season.

"We had it going for a while but it got away because of failed recruiting," said the coach from his Denver home this year. "Some of the high school coaches weren't with us, and I don't know why. When I got the job, Vergil Fletcher (Collinsville) and Sherrill Hanks (Quincy) thought a top high school coach ought to get the job. That made it tough.

"We didn't have to get all the best prospects. If we had just gotten a few like Jim Brewer (Proviso East) and Doug Collins (Benton), we'd have been off and running. We couldn't get Jack Sikma from my own (St. Anne) area because he didn't think he was good enough. Ernie Kent was another [that we missed out on] from Rockford.

"Why we couldn't attract them, I'm not sure. I guess I feel like ... when I got the job, I thought I was prepared ... but I'm not sure I was prepared to handle some of the administrative responsibilities. I probably could have brought in a recruiter like Sam Miranda from Kansas for more money. There was too much recruiting responsibility on me, and I wasn't very good at it either, although I had pretty good success previously at New Mexico. Competition was strong. There is no place quite like it. Everybody recruits Illinois."

HERE AND GONE IN THE BLINK OF AN EYE

Gene Bartow had been highly successful at Memphis. The recruiting of assistant coaches Tony Yates and Leroy Hunt quickly bolstered the 1974-75 squad, as did new additions like Bloom All-Stater Audie Matthews, fellow freshmen Rich Adams, Tom Gerhardt

Courtesy of the Urbana Free Library

▲ *Guard Nate Williams—one of the UI's first ever junior college recruits—produced immediate results for new coach Gene Bartow in his lone season at the helm. The 1974-75 team doubled its Big Ten wins from the prior season, but still lost 18 games on the year.*

and Rick Leighty, and the UI's first ever junior college recruits, Nate Williams and Mike Washington. Tucker was also returning from his redshirt season.

"A big part of our recruitment was their desire to crack the Chicago market," said Nate Williams. "I had played at Crane Tech, and Mike played at Morgan Park.

"It was kind of a package deal. Mike pretty much wanted to go wherever I went. After I signed, he signed. We didn't know at the time that we were the first junior college recruits at Illinois. That didn't matter."

"Bartow was a good coach," Williams said, reflecting on his lone season with Bartow. "He wasn't really vocal, kind of laid back. Yates was more of a motivational driver. A lot of the coaching came from the assistants. Audie Matthews was an exceptional shooter but when he arrived on campus, he wasn't quite ready. His talent was raw, and needed to be developed."

Bartow's team left the gate with three early wins as Rick Schmidt notched a career-high 34 points and 12 rebounds at Iowa State.

"Bartow concentrated more on offense than Harv, and we continued to give up a lot of points," said Rick.

The Illini hit an early slick spot in the road when they lost to Arizona and Arizona State in the Fiesta Classic in Tucson. From that point, the losses piled up faster than the Illini could hold them off.

Bartow's 1975 Big Ten debut pitted Illinois against John Orr's Michigan Wolverines, who came to Champaign ranked No. 17 and boasted four regulars from the team that defeated Indiana in an Assembly Hall playoff a year earlier for the league's solitary NCAA bid.

"We played good enough to win," said Bartow after Michigan squeaked out an 86-84 double-overtime win. Schmidt, who led all scorers with 33 points, missed two free throw opportunities (his only misses after nine straight makes) after Illinois had forged ahead 82-78 with little more than a minute left in the first overtime. Oak Lawn's C.J. Kupec brought the last tie at 84-84, and Wayman Britt won it with a fall-away 10-footer.

"We had them beat twice," said Schmidt. "But we couldn't put them away. It was a complete letdown, to have the Big Ten champions down and let them get away."

Momentum slipped away after lopsided losses on the road to Iowa, 95-70, and Minnesota, 75-47. The dye was cast for a 4-14 Big Ten record in the first 18-game conference schedule since 1953.

"Bartow kept reminding us about not handling the pressure," said Williams, "and Rick was taking shots out of the offense. After the two losses by such big margins, we thought, 'Welcome to the Big Ten.'

"We couldn't keep Minnesota's Mark Olberding, Michael Thompson and Mark Landsberger off the boards. We've got to figure out something different."

Williams went on: "It was hard for Rick, an adjustment period under a new coach, and that senior year he never completely adjusted. But he was a strong one-on-one player."

The good moments were few and far between as the season rolled on. Against Northwestern on January 11, Tucker converted 15 free throws to tie the school record and as the Illini defeated Northwestern, 64-60. Tucker then scored 29 in what Bartow called "our best game of the year" in beating Wisconsin 72-56. But this was followed by two double-digit losses to Purdue and Tulane, a 66-62 win over Ohio State and then six more losses.

Indiana's unbeaten league champions toppled Illinois in Bloomington, 73-57. Later, in Champaign, the bruising Hoosiers ran up a 112-89 score to confirm their No. 1 ranking. Schmidt scored 31 in defeat.

At Purdue in mid-February, the Boilermakers racked 114 points, the most permitted by Illinois in a Big Ten game to that point.

Schmidt averaged over 20 points a game for the second year in a row—the last Illini to accomplish the feat—and now looks back on a career of "just misses." High school star of a terrific small school team at St. Joe-Ogden, he joined Rich Connell on a club that posted a holiday defeat of the state's top-ranked team, Joliet Central. But this was one year before the state split into two tournaments, and St. Joe-Ogden suffered a last-quarter loss to Danville on the Vikings' home court in the tournament.

"I just missed the Class A tournament, just missed the rule permitting the dunk, just missed freshman eligibility and just missed Lou Henson by one year," said

Courtesy of the Urbana Free Library

▲ Otho Tucker was a solid contributor for both Coach Bartow and Coach Henson. In a 64-60 defeat of Northwestern in 1975, Tucker hit 15 free throws to tie the school record, which has since been broken by Kiwane Garris, Frank Williams, and Deon Thomas.

Schmidt. "And I was the last player cut by the New Orleans Jazz. Then I went to San Diego in the ABA, was cut when two teams folded, and then the entire league folded.

"You'd never believe it, but George Halas gave me the best advice. He told me that I'd be a basketball reserve for four or five years, and then I'd be starting over in business, and I'd be way behind in terms of income. I had a chance to go to work for Dave Downey, so I dropped basketball and it worked out."

When Rick Schmidt left the UI, so did Bartow. Succeeding John Wooden at UCLA was too great an opportunity to turn down. The Illini were caught by surprise.

"Being young guys, it was like, 'What'll we do now?',"
recalled Williams. "Mike and I felt like we just got here,
and all of a sudden we don't have a coach.

"We didn't know what to expect. The Don DeVoe
rumor was out there."

HENSON GETS THE JOB

Both DeVoe, coach at Virginia Tech, and New
Mexico State's Lou Henson were in town for interviews
at the same time, and numerous media outlets were pre-
dicting that DeVoe had the job just hours before Illini
athletic director Cecil Coleman settled on Henson, who
had been Aggie athletic director while Coleman was athletic director at Wichita State.

"Here's the way that happened," said Henson. "I
knew Cecil from our director's meetings in the Missouri
Valley. He called and asked me to interview, and I was
interested because I knew a lot about the University of
Illinois."

But Henson was a hot item at the time. He had fielded three state champions at Las Cruces, and led New
Mexico State to the Final Four in 1970, one of six trips to
the NCAA tournament.

"The day before I was to come to Champaign, Wade
Walker of Oklahoma called, so I visited with him in Tulsa
on the way," said Henson, who preferred Illinois over
Oklahoma.

"Illinois hadn't won many games, but Audie
Matthews had just completed his freshman year, and
Otho Tucker was back for his redshirt year. Nate Williams
and Mike Washington had one year left, and Nate had a
tremendous season until he injured his knee against
Purdue late that first season.

"We had our work cut out. One of our goals when
I came in was to get into 400 high schools in the first
year, either myself or Tony Yates or Les Wothke. That's
what we concentrated on ... the state," Henson went on.

"Not only did we run into resistance in Chicago,
but in most areas in the state. The veteran high school
coaches throughout the state weren't particularly high
on Illinois. It was there, whether they'd say it or not."

As Henson's point guard, Nate Williams excelled.
And to this day, he has only good things to say about
the UI coach.

"He was a basketball teacher and a teacher of life,"
said Williams. "He had a knack for getting you where you
needed to be. I remember running wind sprints and he
pulled me to the side and said, 'You should win every
sprint every day.' I said, 'Every day?' He said, 'Yes, if you
do something every day that you don't want to do, it'll
make you a better person for life.'"

Henson's first game as Illini head coach was a winner. Rich Adams, who averaged just 5.1 points the previous season, opened the 1975-76 campaign with 25 points
including the tie-breaker with seven seconds remaining
in a 60-58 victory at Nebraska.

"We didn't use our high-post game when they pressured us, and we got inside for a lot of layups in that
first game. Adams and Washington did a good job
inside, and we used a zone defense to keep them out,"
said Henson.

Henson's gang started 5-0, and he was particularly
pleased with a 67-66 overtime win against New Mexico.
Matthews, known as "Audimatic" for his perimeter
shooting at Bloom High School, drained a 16-footer in
the last second to pull that one out of the fire.
Matthews scored 16 and Williams topped Illini scorers
with 20.

"It seemed like everything worked after Lou got on
us at halftime," said Williams. "He got his point across.
It was one of those good games against a tough team.
Our defense was solid."

But the next buzzer-beating shot went the other
way as Furman's Craig Lynch drained a 20-footer with
two seconds left for a 75-73 Illini loss on the road.
Illinois then dropped a second straight road game at
Southern Cal, 62-58.

The Illini reached the Big Ten at 7-2 on the heels of
a 106-64 rout of Rice, marking the only time in a four-
year stretch under Schmidt, Bartow and Henson that
the Illini topped 100. It was a balanced scoring burst
with Matthews, Adams, Washington, Williams, Tucker,
Ferdinand and Graff all hitting double figures.

The road hex at Iowa was extended—Illinois had not
won there since 1964—as the Illini dropped their 1976 Big
Ten openers at Iowa (84-60) and Minnesota (77-68).
Henson's first club found the home court more friendly,
though. The trio of Adams, Matthews and Williams sank
25 of 35 shots in a 74-69 defeat of Northwestern. After a

continued on page 128

GREATEST MOMENTS
ILLINOIS 60, NEBRASKA 58
NOVEMBER 28, 1975 • NEBRASKA COLISEUM, LINCOLN, NEBRASKA

RICH ADAMS' GAME WINNER GIVES HENSON HIS FIRST 'W'

There would be hundreds more to follow, but few would be as sweet as the first.

On November 28, 1975, first-year head coach Lou Henson took his Illini to Lincoln, Nebraska to open the season against the Cornhuskers and their all-everything guard, Jerry Fort. The Illini were heavy underdogs in the old and rickety Nebraska Coliseum, but Henson had a trick up his sleeve.

▲ *Lou Henson's first win as Illini head coach came in his debut, a road victory over Nebraska. It was the first of many for the longtime Illini coach.*

Coming from New Mexico State, he was known strictly as a tough man-to-man defensive coach. But on the first possession, the Illinois team came out in a zone.

"The whole time since Coach Henson arrived at Illinois we were working on a man-to-man defense," recalled assistant Tony Yates. "We practiced a little zone occasionally, but when Lou called for a zone at the beginning of that game it not only caught Nebraska by surprise, it also shocked the players on our team."

You could count the number of times Henson used a zone for a full game in his 21 years as Illini coach on one hand, but that night it worked to perfection. It was implemented to limit Fort's scoring and was a success as Fort scored just 12 points on five-of-13 shooting for the game. Nebraska, stunned by a look it never thought it would see, threw the ball out of bounds on its first possession to set the tone for the Illini defense.

A nip-and-tuck first half came to a close with the Illini clinging to a halftime lead of 26-23 on the strength of Otho Tucker's 12 points. Illinois started out quickly in the second half as Henson got a surprise he wasn't expecting. Sophomore Rich Adams was taking over the game.

"Rich got really hot in that second half and when he was on, teams had a real tough time stopping him," said Illinois guard Larry Lubin.

Adams racked up 19 second-half points to lead the Illini, but with just over a minute left to play, the game was deadlocked at 58 and Nebraska had the ball. The Cornhuskers set up their four corners offense, stalled for over a minute, and found forward Bob Siegel wide open from the left corner.

Siegel missed off the side of the rim and the ball went out of bounds to the Illini.

The possession before, Henson had inserted Lubin into the game to give the team more speed and better ball handling, and it turned out to be a great move. Lubin got the ball from Tucker off the in-bounds pass with about 12 seconds remaining and raced up the floor.

continued on page 128

continued from page 127

"When Coach Henson put me in he wanted me to try and penetrate," remembered Lubin, the first ever recruit of the Henson era. "I got the ball off the in-bounds and was fortunate enough to beat two defenders up the floor. Just as I almost got into the lane, I remember a big man coming towards me and I kicked it to Rich Adams."

Adams was wide open on the right baseline from six feet away and that night he wasn't going to miss.

"I got a real good pass from Larry and I have always liked to shoot the ball in a big spot," said Adams, who finished with a game-high 25 points that evening. "As I saw him racing up the court, I knew that if I had the shot I had to take it for the team and for Coach. It was a defining moment for me."

Adams' short jumper hit nothing but net, and the Illini were seconds away from getting Henson his first win. Jerry Fort raced down the court, double dribbled, and when the Illini in-bounded the ball into Tucker, win number one of the Henson era was in the books.

"I'll never forget getting that ball, covering up, and letting the clock run out," said Tucker, who finished with 19 points. "That locker room was great and it was almost like we won the Big Ten Championship. People were laughing, screaming, and slapping the lockers. I think we questioned whether we could beat a team of that caliber, but when we did, we kicked off the Lou Henson era on the right foot."

Illinois 60, Nebraska 58. For Coach Henson it was one down and 422 to more to go.

continued from page 126

home win over Wisconsin improved the team to 2-2 in conference, they hosted No. 1 Indiana. It wasn't close. IU forward Scott May scored 27 in an 83-55 blowout.

"Scott May had been elbowed in the eye in the previous game, and he could barely see," said Williams. "[But] that's why they were champions ... Scott May and Quinn Buckner and Bobby Wilkerson. They knew what it took. Defensively, they never let up the pressure. Wilkerson was the glue. He had arms you wouldn't believe."

A difficult January brightened toward the end when Williams, pairing off against fellow Chicagoan Rickey Green of Michigan, scored 26 points, and Rich Adams hit the winning rebound to nip the 17th-ranked Wolverines, 76-75.

"I grew up with Rickey Green, and we had been reading their boasts in the paper that week," said Williams. "At the end, I missed a free throw but we knocked it in. It was meant for us to win that game."

But just when Williams was hitting his stride, just as the Illini were ending Purdue's 13-game dominance on Henson's first try, Williams was injured. The press-breaking UI guard dislocated a bone below his knee and, as would happen with playmaker Steve Lanter in 1979, was lost for the season.

"We were a lot better club with Williams," said Henson. "We were 11-7 at the time. That was a blow."

"I was really down," recalled Williams. "I kept feeling I could come back, but it was one of those injuries where the chances were not good. I rehabbed for nearly a year. I was drafted by the Chicago Bulls but they wouldn't take a chance on me after they saw it wasn't strong enough in the physical exam."

Williams missed the last nine games, and the Illini dropped six of them against a heavy road lineup. Tucker tallied 18 in a 70-59 win at Wisconsin, and the Illini went from there to Indiana where they shot .564 and fought the national champions tooth and nail down the stretch.

Despite being lost for the season with a leg injury 18 games into the 1975-76 campaign, point guard Nate Williams, shown here driving for a lay-up against Ohio State, was awarded team MVP honors. Williams averaged 13.5 points per game on 53.4 percent shooting.

Matthews tied the game at 38-38 with 12 minutes to go, and the Illini were still within reach, 52-48, on Washington's jumper with 5:11 showing. But Indiana's Jim Crews cashed four free throws and the Hoosiers prevailed 58-48. This Bobby Knight creation went 32-0, winning Final Four games by 14 and 18 points, but felt the need to stall throughout the final eight and a half minutes against Illinois at home. Indiana's karate-chop defense was nearly matched by the Illini's tight zone. Henson pointed to four-for-11 free throw shooting and five consecutive misses at 52-48 as thwarting the upset. It was Indiana's 31st straight Big Ten victory. Illini hopes for a plus-.500 conference season died in a four-game slump at season's end. The road took its toll in losses at Michigan State, Michigan and Purdue to send Illinois to a 7-11 conference mark and a seventh-place finish. The team finished one game above the watermark with a 14-13 overall record.

▲ Center Mike Washington (with the ball) banged down low with Rich Adams on a balanced 1975-76 Illinois team. For a big guy, Adams was a good passer who averaged almost three assists per game during his senior year.

The Champaign-Urbana News-Gazette

"We realized right away that we had to step up our recruiting in the state," said Henson. "We worked hard to bridge some gaps because Illinois hadn't gotten the state's best in previous years."

Williams was named team MVP despite missing the last nine games. As an adult, he has spent large segments of his time in Chicago but now resides in Champaign. Washington became a state trooper in the Kankakee area.

HENSON'S SOPHOMORE SLUMP

Henson's second season was much like his first. Matthews and Adams again led Illini scoring for a 15-15 (7-11 in Big Ten) club in 1976-77. The addition of recruits Levi Cobb, Neil Bresnahan and Steve Lanter provided a lift as they beat St. Louis twice early and engaged in one cliff-hanger after another at home.

They nipped Nebraska again (67-63) with Cobb drilling 16 points, played poorly in blunting Cleveland State's upset bid (72-70), barely escaped Cal Poly (67-65) on freshman Rob Judson's 20-footer with four seconds remaining, and downed Arizona State (80-74) with Cobb

▲ Forward Rich Adams paced the Illini in scoring with a career-best mark of 15.9 points per game during his sophomore campaign. He also led the team's frontline in rebounding with 5.9 per game.

making all eight of his field goal tries and Judson converting four late free throws.

But Illini basketball wasn't back. And the fans knew it; a mere 6,938 attended on a Saturday afternoon in mid-December.

Traveling to the Rainbow Classic in Honolulu after Christmas, the Illini led late, 66-65, over Houston but fell 69-66 on the 25-point heroics of Otis Birdsong. That cast them in the loser's bracket. Henson's Illini dropped three of four heading into Big Ten play.

Then, in the 1977 opener at Ohio State, the team suddenly erupted for a series of offensive records. They converted 19 of their first 21 attempts, shooting 69.4 percent in an 89-72 triumph. That was an Illini percentage record, second best in Big Ten history and surpassed anything up to that time in St. John Arena. Matthews sank seven of 12 shots (and 14 free throws), Adams seven of eight, Cobb seven of 10, Ferdinand six of eight, Lanter four of eight and Bresnahan two of two.

Mike Woodson and the Indiana Hoosers cooled off the Illini, 80-60, in Bloomington, and another difficult Big Ten season was underway. Minnesota was undefeated when the Gophers came to town, and they rolled 83-69 as 6-10 Michael Thompson scored 25 while his eligibility was still under question in a legal hassle with the NCAA. Against Iowa, with 6-8 senior star Bruce "Sky" King sidelined, another of the Hawkeye recruits from across the border, Ronnie Lester of Chicago Dunbar, helped force 24 Illini turnovers as the Hawks rallied from a 13-point deficit to win in overtime, 84-81. The UI losing streak reached five in a 66-61 loss to No. 5 Michigan.

The slump ended as Matthews bagged 25 points in a 71-68 home win over Tex Winter's NU Wildcats. The only loss over the next four games was a tough 66-63 defeat at Purdue, which the Illini avenged two games later by knocking the Boilermakers out of the Top 20, 71-70, at home. Matthews, on a late-season scoring binge, hit the Boilers for 20 points and drilled the game-winning jumper with a second showing on the clock after Bresnahan knocked in a rebound to pull the Illini within one. Illinois followed that win with yet another thriller. Lawrenceville's Rick Leighty popped a 23-footer with two seconds left to defeat Northwestern in Evanston, 65-63.

That's the kind of season it was for Henson in his second go-round. Just when they appeared dead in a 62-

50 failure at Wisconsin on February 12, they rallied from 15 back against Indiana, going ahead 62-61 on Ken Ferdinand's tipin and winning 73-69 on late free throws by Lanter and Matthews.

But the Illini dropped their last five games, three of them in the final minutes. The 72-70 loss to No. 13 Minnesota was later forfeited by the Gophers for rules violations, just one of numerous Gopher records erased by infractions over the years.

As for the Illini, consistency was none too common, and the team finished the year in sixth place.

▲ Guard Audie "Audimatic" Matthews took over as the team's primary scorer during his junior season of 1976-77 with a 16.0 average on 51-percent field-goal shooting. But the team struggled in the Big Ten during Coach Henson's second season and finished the year in sixth place.

Fighting Illini

vs.
Southern California

Assembly Hall • Champaign, Ill. • Dec. 1, 1977
50¢

FIGHTING ILLINI BASKETBALL

IOWA
FEBRUARY 17

Assembly Hall • Champaign, IL • 50¢

FIGHTING ILLINI BASKETBALL

ILLINOIS VS. WISCONSIN

February 7, 1980 / 7:05 pm
Assembly Hall / Champaign, Ill.

CHAPTER TWELVE

HENSON HEADS ILLINI BACK TO TOURNEY
1977-78—1981-82

Eddie Johnson can still splash that jump shot. At 44, he can pop the net straight up in the air.

"If shooting was all there was to it, I'd still be in the NBA," smiled the Phoenix Suns TV colorman, looking back on 17 seasons and a 16.0 career scoring average at the highest level.

But it was at the University of Illinois that he enjoyed his most memorable basketball moment ... and his greatest disappointment. His corner jumper against Michigan State in 1979 upended the top-ranked Spartans, 57-55, and extended the UI's unbeaten record to 15-0. It capped a Mardi Gras day in Champaign where ticket scalpers made a fortune and celebrants went far into the night. It was called the UI's most memorable athletic event since the 1963 Rose Bowl.

"It's interesting how you can do things in your life that stick with people that you don't even know, something that they remember 20 or 25 years later," said Johnson. "I've had thousands of people come to me and say, 'I was there.' I know I'll always be in Illini folklore for that shot."

And then there was the final game in 1981 when he and his four-year running mate, Mark Smith, saw their college careers end in a 57-52 NCAA loss to Kansas State in Salt Lake City.

"That was my biggest disappointment," said Johnson. "We had a much better team. We had drawn a bye in the tournament, and we barely got by Wyoming in Los Angeles, 67-65," he recalled.

Johnson scored 19 and Smith made two free throws with three seconds left to break a 65-65 tie in what was only the UI's second NCAA win in 29 years.

"Then we came out and played one of our worst games," he said. "They got us into a slowdown game, and Derek Harper (0 for seven) and Craig Tucker (one for 10) couldn't hit. Kansas State had Rolando Blackman, who had a good pro career, but we had more talent. If we played them five times, we would have won

The Champaign-Urbana News-Gazette

▲ Once an Illini, scoring came easy to Eddie Johnson. It was getting him into an Illini uniform that was a real feat for Illinois, who struggled mightily in the late '60s and '70s trying to recruit in the Chicago area. The highly regarded Johnson's decision to attend Illinois was key to the program's success.

four. Our seed was great but we didn't take advantage of it. That was a terrible disappointment."

But for all the disappointments—and there were several during his college career—Eddie Johnson was a central figure in reviving a program that missed post season play for 16 consecutive years, advanced to NIT and NCAA events, and moved from there to become a perennial high seed in the 1980s.

The recruitment of Johnson from Westinghouse was not easy. Chicago, which became the mass producer of basketball talent in the 1960s and early 1970s, had not been kind to the Illini. The George Wilsons and Cazzie Russells made huge names elsewhere. Henson and his chief recruiter, Tony Yates, broke through with Levi Cobb from Morgan Park's champions in 1976. With Cobb and fellow freshman Neil Bresnahan gaining experience on a 15-15 team, and with Audie Matthews and Rich Adams figuring in, Johnson thought twice about where he had the best chance to play.

He was the state's top senior at Westinghouse, a McDonald's All-American. When Mark Aguirre left Austin to join then-senior Johnson, Westinghouse went 29-0 before losing to Wendell Phillips in the city final. Johnson was on everyone's "must recruit" list. He visited Southern Cal, listened to Lute Olson of Iowa and Johnny Orr of Michigan, and always considered DePaul.

"The recruitment of Eddie was a key for us," said Henson. "He was not only a terrific player but a bright young man. We saw him play a lot because the rules in that era weren't as tight on trips. And we had seen Mark Smith as a young player when we were recruiting Derek Holcomb at Richwoods. Johnson and Smith got things going for us."

"I had selfish reasons for choosing Illinois," Johnson recalled. "It was far enough away and yet close enough. Tony Yates won me over. I identified with Yates because I was in a single-parent household and he became a father figure."

Johnson returned from a basketball trip to Germany to announce his decision to attend Illinois. He was in for a shock.

"I had A-B grades my last two years in high school, and I was an All-American, but I wasn't ready school-wise or basketball-wise," he said. "I couldn't live up to expectations."

Neither could Mike Jones, a big guard from Joliet. He would ultimately transfer to Wichita State. Smith, meanwhile, was the best of the threesome early on.

"I was just a young colt," said Johnson. "I had never learned to maximize my time. I came close to not making it. Lou said I wasn't ready to play, and I had only a few decent games coming off the bench as a freshman. A lot of people in Chicago were disappointed, and rumors of me transferring weighed heavily on everyone. But Smith was a more complete player at that time. He could handle the ball and he understood the offense. He was my roommate and I was not jealous.

"We beat up some teams in the nonconference portion but when the conference started, we struggled, especially on the road. The Big Ten was then the best league in the country. There was no shot clock, and we lacked the ability to pressure defensively. Nor could we prevent teams from pressuring us. We didn't have much bulk inside. Those things were exposed. If the other team had a big guy, we were at his mercy."

Rich Adams exploded for 39 points in the second game of the 1977-78 season, a 113-107 defeat of Arizona. But problems became apparent in Portland after Christmas when a 5-1 Illini team couldn't handle the tall trees of Washington State and Washington. And who showed up in the first Big Ten game in 1978 but Joe Barry Carroll, a seven-footer who produced 20 points and 15 rebounds in a 95-85 Purdue triumph.

Illinois rebounded with a 65-64 upset at No. 11 Indiana, but the team dropped the next home game to No. 12 Michigan State and had losing streaks of three and four games down the stretch. The Illini defeated Iowa twice but dropped eight of their last 11 games to finish 7-11 in the conference—good for only seventh place—and 13-14 overall.

Neil Bresnahan was a steady contributor during Illinois' 19-11 season of 1978-79. He was named MVP of the Kentucky Invitational and was a brute on the boards, averaging 7.9 rebounds a game during the season.

TURNING THINGS AROUND

The sophomore season of Johnson and Smith remains the greatest enigma in UI basketball history. Smith's former prep teammate, Holcomb, was eligible after transferring from Indiana, and Mascoutah guard Steve Lanter returned after sitting out the previous season.

"It was a finesse team with a physical aspect," said Johnson. "I weighed 185 pounds as a freshman. I came back at 215. We worked together that summer and we were energized."

The 1978-79 Illini won at Missouri, 69-57, and took a 7-0 record and a No. 15 AP ranking to the Kentucky Invitational on December 22. Bresnahan, a backboard fanatic, pulled down 14 rebounds against both No. 8 Syracuse and No. 17 Texas A&M, the first-round conqueror of Kentucky. Despite scoring just 10 points in two games, Bresnahan was named the tournament's MVP as the Illini defeated both teams to win the tournament.

"Bresnahan is one of my favorite guys," said Johnson. "He never showed any attitude when he sat on the bench. I was excited to see him get the award. He deserved it."

continued on page 138

The Champaign-Urbana News-Gazette

GREATEST MOMENTS
(NO. 4) ILLINOIS 57, (NO. 1) MICHIGAN STATE 55
JANUARY 11, 1979 • ASSEMBLY HALL, CHAMPAIGN, ILLINOIS

EDDIE JOHNSON'S SHOT TOPPLES NO. 1 STATE

Illinois fans had waited over three decades for a game like this. Not since the great Indiana-Illinois battles of the early 1950s was there such anticipation for an Illinois home basketball game. The 15-0 Illini were welcoming the Michigan State Spartans into the Assembly Hall. The Spartans were the No. 1 team in the entire country and featured the most recognizable player in all of college basketball in Magic Johnson.

The week was full of intensity and anxiousness.

"Every day you thought more about the game and there was always something going on," recalled Illinois point guard Steve Lanter. "We were doing a ton of interviews, and just walking down the street everybody would stop you to wish you luck, give you a hug, and tell you that they loved you."

Everybody was coming to Champaign. *Sports Illustrated* was there, ESPN was broadcasting the game, Gov. Jim Thompson was there decked out in Illini gear featuring his patented orange hard hat, and by game time the hype had reached a feverish pitch.

Walking into the Hall that evening, fans felt a buzz. For the first time in the Henson era, the Assembly Hall was ready to rock and the players felt it immediately.

"When we came out of the tunnel that night the place exploded," said Lanter. "I can honestly say it was the only time in my life I couldn't feel my feet hit the ground."

"Right before the game began you needed a knife to cut through the tension in the building," said Illinois assistant coach Tony Yates. "It was like nothing I had ever seen before."

"I loved playing every game in the Hall, but that night was something special," recalled the game's hero, Eddie Johnson. "It was so loud in there and every time we scored, the fans acted like it was the last shot of the game. It was just unbelievable."

The Illini came out tense and it looked like the hype and atmosphere took them away from their game. Not surprisingly, they fell down early and when Michigan State's Ron Charles put in a lay-up off a feed from Magic Johnson, the Spartans enjoyed a 24-13 lead with nine minutes left to play in the half.

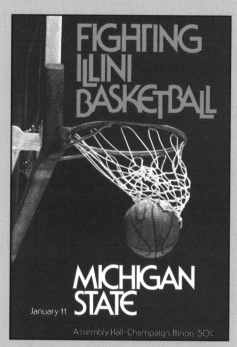

▲ *The game program from the Illini's historic victory over Magic Johnson's No. 1-ranked Spartans.*

Immediately after that basket, the Illini awoke from their doldrums. They went on a quick 11-0 run, and when the buzzer rang and the smoke cleared from the first half, the Illini finished on a 19-4 run to take a 32-28 lead into the locker room.

The unsung hero for the half was 6-8 Illinois sophomore Mark Smith, who scored 12 points and held Magic to just two.

"People forget about the match-up between Mark Smith and Magic Johnson and how great a job Mark did in containing Magic," remembered Illinois guard Perry Range. "Mark was the kind of guy who could do anything and was a great team player. He was able to neutralize Magic, which freed Eddie up to do the scoring."

The second half was nothing out of the ordinary.

"They were playing their zone, and we were playing our man to man and it was your typical physical second half of a Big Ten game," said Illinois guard Rob Judson. "It was back and forth, and you knew it was going right down to the wire.

It certainly would do just that. With the game tied at 55 and under a minute left to play, Illinois reserve forward Levi Cobb lost the ball off his foot and the ensuing struggle for the loose ball resulted in a jump ball. It looked like the Illini blew their chance, but Cobb was ready to win that jump.

"When the ball went up I was so keyed to go up and get it," recalled Cobb. "I got up so quickly that the Michigan State player hadn't even left the floor."

The Illini got the ball back and with 37 seconds remaining on the clock and the tension building they called a timeout.

"We were going to spread them out, penetrate, and hold for the last shot," recalled Judson. "When we got the penetration, we'd look for the best shot we could."

Judson in-bounded the ball to Johnson, who gave it back to Judson. Judson handed it to Lanter, who tossed it to Smith on the left side. It was Smith back to Lanter as the Illini spread into four corners. Lanter and Smith exchanged on a mini-weave one more time before Lanter ended up with the ball at the top of the key. He dribbled hard into the lane—beating his man—but pulled up and threw a short pass to Johnson who gave it right back.

"I remember I had the lane with about 15 seconds left, but I thought it was too early to take the shot," said Lanter. "I remember dribbling back up top thinking, 'Oh my God, I hope I don't have to take this shot.'"

As soon as Lanter got the ball back to the top of the key it was time to make his move. After two hard dribbles right he had a step on his man. At that exact moment, Michigan State forward Greg Kelser took one fatal step towards Lanter.

"When I saw Kelser make that stunt step, it was an easy decision to get the ball to Eddie," recalled Lanter. "I knew he was spotting up and ready for the ball."

Lanter dished it to Johnson, who took one hard dribble and rose up from 15 feet on the right baseline.

"Steve got the ball to me in rhythm and as a shooter that is all you can ask for," said Johnson. "From that point on I just had to make sure I had good mechanics."

"The ball had a great arch on it, you could see the backspin, and it looked so good," remembered forward Neil Bresnahan.

"I was directly in line with Eddie and when he let it go there was no doubt it was going in," recalled Illinois play-by-play man, Larry Stewart.

With four seconds left on the clock, the ball splashed through the net.

"There was a split second of silence and then the place exploded," said Judson.

Johnson, who was fading towards mid-court as the shot went in, raised both his hands in the air with jubilation as he did three hop steps towards mid-court before leaping into the air with a fist pump.

"Everything was in slow motion after I hit that shot. People were looking at me and they saw my reaction, but I had no idea what I was doing," said Johnson, reflecting years later on the shot that provoked bedlam in the Assembly Hall. "The euphoria of everything—your teammates, the crowd, and the fact that you just hit the game winning shot. You try to take it all in but it's too much."

There were still three seconds left on the clock and in an anti-climactic moment Magic Johnson threw up an air ball from beyond the mid-court line and the Illini came away with the 57-55 win.

As soon as the ball touched down and the buzzer sounded, the Orange Krush rushed the court to celebrate with the team. The noise was deafening, it was time to celebrate, and some say at that exact moment the Assembly Hall was shaking.

Larry Stewart described it best with his now famous words, "It's pandemonium in the Assembly Hall."

▲ The clock at the Assembly Hall reads four seconds as Eddie Johnson's game-winning shot swishes through the net.

▲ *Mark Smith (above) combined with Eddie Johnson to form a stunning one-two punch. Smith, a forward from Peoria's Richwoods High School, averaged in double figures in scoring in each of his four years at Illinois and shot 52.5 percent for his career in amassing 1,653 points.*

continued from page 135

The Illini were 12-0 and ranked fourth in the country when they reached the Big Ten opener, and they got off on the right foot with a 65-61 triumph at Indiana with Johnson tallying 18. After a dominant road win against Northwestern, Illinois' record reached 14-0 heading into an epic showdown with Magic Johnson and the No. 1-ranked Spartans at the Assembly Hall.

"When it came to the basketball skills and the ability to bring people to the game, Magic was arguably the greatest," said Eddie. "This was a team that would win the national championship. It seemed like everyone was there, including the governor. That one shot put Illinois on the map, and me too."

Lanter set up "the shot," breaking toward the basket with the score knotted at 65-65 to free up Eddie Johnson in the corner. Johnson nailed it and shouts of "We're No. 1! We're No.1!" echoed throughout the Assembly Hall.

"We had Ohio State coming up at home two days later, and the Buckeyes were huge," said Henson.

Unfortunately for the UI team, the No. 1 ranking didn't materialize. The Buckeyes snapped Illinois' 15-game streak in overtime, 69-66. Mark Smith tallied 28 points but Herb Williams, another of the big men who punished the Illini in that period, countered with 29. The key play was a dashing block by Carter Scott on Eddie Johnson's breakaway with Illinois leading by two in the final minute of regulation.

"We called time just to set up that out-of-bounds play," recalled Henson. "We set a screen and Eddie broke open, and Scott blocked it from behind. If Eddie had gotten that down, it would have virtually clinched the victory, although I saw a game last year when Stanford scored eight points in 20 seconds. Also in that Ohio State game, we missed two one-and-one free throw opportunities, and we lost in overtime."

So the Illini never reached No. 1, instead maintaining their No. 4 ranking heading into the following week. They were 16-1 after beating Wisconsin but Lanter injured his knee and was lost for the season. That was a distinct turning point. Suddenly, the Illini became vulnerable at the guards.

"Once again we couldn't counter pressure and teams started stalling on us. It was frustrating," Johnson said. "Teams knew they couldn't run with us and they attacked our negative."

After Purdue held at the end of both halves in a 69-57 Boilermaker win just a week after the Ohio State loss, Henson said: "The coaches need to address a shot clock in our meetings."

Lute Olson did the same thing in Iowa's 58-52 win at home in the following game, and an Illini team within a finger snap of being No. 1 on January 13 began their tumble out of the Top 20. By February 15, they were no longer ranked. A 15-0 team finished 19-11 (7-11 in conference play) as the offense failed to reach 60 points on seven occasions. The season ended with a thud—a five game losing streak that cost the UI a postseason birth. In the Big Ten, only three Illini cashed 20 points in a game for the seventh place team. On the season, Smith averaged 13.5 points per game and Johnson 12.1 after impressive starts.

NIT BOUND

"As juniors (in 1979-80), Mark Smith and I were the established leaders, and we came out strong again," said Johnson.

A 10-2 start included another victory over that season's national champion, in this case Louisville in Honolulu. Darrell Griffith scored 28 but UI balance, with Holcomb and James Griffin sharing center, prevailed for the 77-64 win on December 29, the Henson's 25th wedding anniversary.

"[Louisville] had a great club and we had them down badly," said Henson.

Eddie Johnson nailed 30 points in the Rainbow Classic finale against Hawaii, a 94-82 victory.

"Eddie just kept getting better and better," said Henson. "He improved all the time, each and every year."

But Illinois hadn't solved its road woes in the league, where they went 2-7 compared to 6-3 at home.

"We had some pretty good ball clubs during that period," said Henson, "but the league was so tough. It was hard to win on the road. So many of those teams were ranked. Go back and look. Bobby Knight was in his glory days at Indiana. Purdue was tough. Jud Heathcote came on at Michigan State and won the national title in 1979. Lute Olson had Iowa playing great. Ohio State was big and strong. Minnesota had Mychal Thompson and Kevin McHale. The whole league was tough."

"[Going on the road] was like going to the dentist," recalled Johnson. "The crowds were rough. It seemed like we had brain lock. We couldn't take what we did in preconference and apply it to the Big Ten."

But Johnson persevered. He made 13 of 17 shots in a 79-75 loss at Minnesota, and came back with 11 of 13 in an 80-60 defeat of Michigan at home.

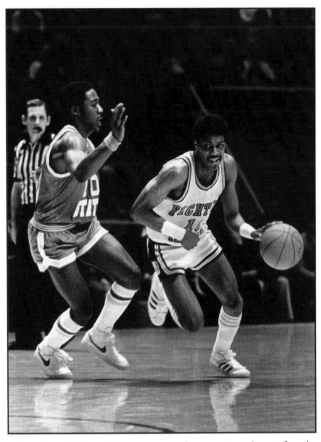

▲ Guard Reno Gray was another scoring threat for the 1979-80 Illini. The Chicago native poured in 25 points in an 89-68 rout of No. 20 Indiana at the Assembly Hall.

▲ *Eddie Johnson (No. 33) spreads his arms in celebration after scoring the winning bucket in overtime against Minnesota on February 21, 1980. The win secured the Illini a spot in the NIT Tournament.*

"Coach Henson allowed me to do pretty much anything I wanted, to shoot from outside or go inside," said Johnson. "I don't know if he has given many players that much leeway. I was on fire and those two games put me in the eyes of the scouts, though they still questioned whether I could play small forward in the NBA."

A stunning 89-68 home rout of No. 20 Indiana featured guards Reno Gray (25 points) and Perry Range (17) as they outperformed Hoosier freshman Isiah Thomas, who was one year removed from taking Indiana to the

national title. Johnson regretted the UI's inability to attract Thomas, figuring it was linked with the earlier recruiting failure with Mark Aguirre.

"Thomas and Aguirre were close friends in Chicago," said Johnson. "We had a lot of forwards on our team, and Mark was concerned because I didn't get to start as a freshman. He was an exceptional talent. If he had come to Illinois, there would have been a place for him. But he chose DePaul, and Isiah chose Indiana."

Illinois finished strong enough to grab an NIT berth, its first post-season opportunity since 1963. The clincher was a 60-58 overtime defeat of Minnesota on February 21. Range passed to Johnson for the game-deciding layup.

"We were happy to play in the NIT and have the home advantage in the first three games," said Johnson.

The Illini dispatched Loyola-Chicago (105-87), Illinois State (75-65) and Murray State (65-63), and again faced Randy Breuer, Kevin McHale and the tall Gophers in New York's Madison Square Garden.

"Their size frustrated us," said Johnson of the UI's 65-63 semifinal loss. "We played pretty well but Breuer (24 points) was out of his mind."

Illinois rebounded to beat Nevada-Las Vegas two days later, 84-74, to end the season on a good note. The team's sixth place, 8-10 finish in the Big Ten resulted in a 22-13 overall record. The 22 wins were the most since back-to-back 22-win seasons in 1951 and '52.

BACK TO THE BIG DANCE

When the Illini opened in 1980-81, they had a young point guard for the ages. He was a quick-handed defender and a lanky flying machine on the attack. Floridian Derek Harper had been leaning toward Michigan before coach John Orr decided to move to Iowa State. It was Tony Yates' repeated plane trips to Palm Beach that eventually paid off when Harper committed to Illinois.

In came a player who improved each year at Illinois, turned pro after his junior season, and improved his scoring for seven straight NBA seasons, peaking at 19.7 for Dallas in 1991. Harper retired from the NBA in 1999, finishing with 15,997 points, 6,571 assists and 1.958 steals.

"Tony did a good job," said Henson, "based on Harper's statements that he wanted to go to a Big Ten school. Back then, a lot of top players were leaving Florida to play elsewhere."

When arguments begin as to the all-time greatest UI guard, Harper's name must be considered. The Illini never had a more disruptive defender on the perimeter. His shot appeared to have the wrong rota-

tion as a freshman, but he became a deadly 54-percent shooter as a junior, once draining 19 field goals in a row. If Illinoisans wonder what might have happened in 1979 if Lanter hadn't been injured, if they wonder how the 1990 team might have fared with Nick Anderson, they must also wonder how the Elite Eight team in 1984 would have done against Kentucky if Harper had stuck around for his senior year.

Just as Harper arrived on the UI campus, so did junior college speedster Craig Tucker.

"I was excited," said Eddie Johnson. "We had added two point guards, and Reno Gray was still there. I watched Harper and I thought, 'There is a guy who really has it.' We were confident."

That season marked the beginning of the "Braggin' Rights" series with Missouri in St. Louis. In the debut

▲ Assistant coach Tony Yates' hard work paid off in full when Florida high school guard Derek Harper chose Illinois over Michigan. Harper became a leader and a forerunner to the Flying Illini of the late '80s.

game on December 10, Johnson bagged 16 points in the first half as Illinois built a big lead and coasted to an 84-62 win in the Checkerdome.

"Both sides felt it would be good to play in St. Louis," said Henson. "Later on, after we had had some success down there, Norm Stewart wanted to switch it to home-and-home, but it had become a tradition, people loved it and it couldn't be moved."

Three days later at Marquette, Tucker sank the winning free throw in a 69-68 thriller.

"This time, when we reached the Big Ten, we felt we belonged," said Johnson. "I have a particular memory of an afternoon TV game at Purdue when Smith and I dominated (87-65)."

Illinois had peaked at No. 12 in the rankings in the early season. On January 22, headed into a contest in Ann Arbor against No. 16 Michigan, the team was ranked No. 15 in the country. But the wrong Johnson,

The Champaign-Urbana News-Gazette

▲ *Perry Range closed his career on a high note in 1981-82 by starting each of the Illini's 29 games and posting career highs in points (12.9 per game), rebounds (4.4), and assists (2.4).*

Johnny Johnson, hit 12 of 14 shots in Michigan's 80-76 overtime win, and a balanced league began to take its toll on everyone. During that league race, five Big Ten teams showed up in the Top 20, and Indiana went on to capture the 1981 national championship.

"Down the stretch, we knew we had a shot at the Big Ten title," said Johnson. "We rallied to beat Michigan (67-64) and we had a chance to move into a tie with Indiana. But Isiah had a great game and Ray Tolbert hurt us with big baskets, and we lost (69-66) at home. There was an action picture from that game on the cover of *Sports Illustrated*."

The Illini finished the season ranked No. 19 after a 12-6, third-place conference finish (21-8 overall). It was the first time in 13 seasons that Illinois had finished the year as a ranked team. For their efforts, they drew a bye in the opening round of the NCAA tournament, their first time in the tourney since 1963, when only the league champion advanced. Facing Wyoming in Los Angeles, the UI squeaked by 67-65 as Johnson scored 19 and Smith made two free throws with three seconds showing on the clock. But nothing went right in a 57-52 loss to Kansas State. Harper and Tucker were stone-cold and the Illini picked a bad time for one of their poorest showings.

"We couldn't make a shot against Kansas State's 3-2 zone," said Henson. "We shot and shot and couldn't make anything."

Johnson passed his roommate, Smith, in career points down the stretch of their senior season, finishing with 1,692 points to Smith's 1,653. Johnson was drafted by Kansas City with the 29th pick and, along with Harper, became the UI's most prominent NBA players in the 1980s until Nick Anderson and Kendall Gill joined them in the 1990s. Over his NBA career, Johnson scored 19,202 points, averaging 16.0 for a 17-year career.

GOING SMALL IN '81-'82

With Johnson and Smith both gone in 1982, and slender forward candidates Jay Daniels and Anthony Welch learning at the collegiate level, Henson settled on a three-guard lineup in 1981-82. Sophomore Derek

Harper led the team in assists and steals, senior Craig Tucker paced scorers at 15.5 points, and the swift Perry Range posted a team-leading 52.1 shooting percentage from the field. The Illini got caught up in two overtimes during the first three games. In the first at the Horizon in Rosemont, Harper's steal and layup keyed an 87-83 defeat of Loyola that Henson called "undeserving." The Illini weren't so fortunate in the second overtime game at the St. Louis Checkerdome, falling to Missouri 78-68 as the Tigers made 41 trips to the free throw line. Norm Stewart's Tigers made 15 charities in the overtime alone.

The Illini went on to win five straight before falling apart, 71-51, at Toledo on December 29. They rebounded to kick off the 1982 Big Ten season with a 60-50 victory at Northwestern. This was a defensive gem as NU trailed 26-10 at the half. The Illini coasted even though the frontline starters, James Griffin and Bryan Leonard, fouled out with one basket between them.

But the win over the Cats was not a good projection for the conference race. Illinois scored just 50 points each in follow-up losses to Iowa and Ohio State, the latter another overtime defeat. Stalling was much a part of game strategies in this period, causing *The News-Gazette's* Tatelines to expound after a 55-51 win over Michigan State in mid-January:

"Please record this as a vote for the 30-second clock. Let's make the players perform. If they want to play keep away, take down the baskets and rename it tag. This feeling has been growing for years. ...The time is long overdue to set up some kind of shot clock. ... It would mark a return to sanity in an insane sport.

The UI's 10-8 conference run was highlighted by three wins over ranked teams—Minnesota twice and a home overtime victory against Iowa. A strong Gopher team was ranked No. 5 on the superb play of Trent Tucker, Randy Breuer, Tommy Davis and Darryl Mitchell. But James Griffin used his turn-around jumper for 19 points in a 64-57 upset. Later in Champaign, the Gophers were No. 8 and found themselves ambushed again as Craig Tucker went on a 32-point binge.

Road losses at Michigan State and Ohio State ended the team's NCAA hopes, but Illinois could still play the role of spoiler in the Big Ten race. The Illini trailed No. 11 Iowa by 16 points with 12 1/2 minutes to go on March 4 in Champaign. But, the tide turned in the game.

"We panicked," said Iowa coach Lute Olson after noting his athletes managed one field goal in 13 minutes of a 73-67 Illini comeback upset. Range scored eight key points in the late Illini rally, and the Illini used free throws to salt it away in overtime. The outcome gave Minnesota a one-game lead over Iowa in the Big Ten race.

Finishing Big Ten play in sixth place with a 10-8 mark, Illinois was invited back to the NIT. The Illini hosted two NIT games, blitzing Long Island 126-78 to set a major college record for postseason points, but then fell to Dayton, 61-58, for an 18-11 season mark.

▲ *Guard Craig Tucker dropped 32 points on the Gophers in the second of two season victories over the Big Ten powerhouse in February of 1982. On the season, Tucker led the Illini in scoring at 15.5 points per game.*

ILLINOIS

Assembly Hall • Champaign • December 2, 1982 • $1.00

Valparaiso

ILLINOIS

Assembly Hall • Champaign • December 7-8, 1984 • $1.00

Illini Classic

CHAPTER THIRTEEN

WELCOME BACK
TO THE BIG TIME
1982-83—1985-86

During his four seasons at Illinois in the early to mid-'80s, Quincy's Bruce Douglas held four important distinctions. For starters, Douglas and running mate Efrem Winters produced 95 victories. Douglas also dished out 765 assists, an incredible 263 more than UI runner-up Kiwane Garris. Third, he holds the school record for steals with 324, which is 106 more than runner-up Kendall Gill. And finally, Douglas was unsurpassed in breaking down game strategies in postgame interviews.

Douglas wasn't the best shooter or the fastest runner, but his head and his hands were in the forefront of every game he played. It all started in Quincy, a basketball hotbed on the far west side of the state where the Blue Devils once captured an uncommon level of greatness. Sell-out crowds turned Friday nights into the community's special kind of religion. A dozen members of the Douglas family have started on the varsity there, and Bruce was the best of the bunch. With him at the controls, Quincy went 123-5 in his four seasons, setting a Class AA record for consecutive victories (64) that still stands. On three occasions Quincy reached the state tournament undefeated under coach Jerry Leggett, finishing first, second and third.

For the 1982-83 season, Lou Henson tapped into this talent and, at the same time, landed a McDonald's All-American out of Chicago King, six-foot-nine Efrem Winters. This kicked off a four-year stretch in which Illinois won one Big Ten co-championship

and forged a path to the top of the NCAA mountain—but never quite reached the peak.

It all started November 26, 1982 in distant, frozen Anchorage where Douglas joined Derek Harper in the backcourt and the Illini were promptly pummeled by Vanderbilt, 58-47. Except for Winters' 17 points, there didn't appear to be much on the Illini plate.

"It was our first game and we were out of sync," recalled Douglas from his Woodridge home this year. "I didn't do much. It was normal acclimation to the next level."

The Illini bounced back with five straight wins, including a revenge game with Kansas State in which Harper—who was absolutely cold against K-State in the 1981 NCAA loss—scored 18 in spoiling the fans' fun in Manhattan, 59-55. The Illini dropped their second game of the season in Lexington to No. 2 Kentucky, a persistent headache for the Illini during the Douglas-Winters era and many other Illini eras. Douglas came out with a bloody nose.

"I got hit on a pick and fractured my nose," he said. "I had surgery to straighten it out."

After Kentucky, willowy sophomore Anthony Welch's late-game heroics pulled the Illini past the same Vanderbilt team that defeated them earlier. Welch scored 25, knocked in a rebound to bring about a tie in the first overtime, and hit clutch free throws in the second overtime to clinch the victory, 79-77. Two wins later, Wayman Tisdale was too much (34 points) for the Illini to handle as Oklahoma clobbered Illinois, 101-75, to complete the UI's pre-Big Ten portion of the season at 10-3.

Bruce Douglas penetrates against a Michigan defender. The high school star from Quincy, Illinois, quickly became the leader of an exceptional group of Illini teams in the mid-'80s. Douglas was a superb distributor of the basketball who doubled as a tremendous defender.

"Oklahoma just kept scoring in barrages," recalled Douglas. "We were thinking too much about going home for Christmas, and we got caught up in watching Wayman. He was great."

Minnesota handed out a 75-49 spanking at Williams Arena in the team's conference opener. Randy Breuer and his tall mates gave the young Illini a lesson on life on the road.

"That was a Big Ten wakeup call. I remember hearing Coach Henson shouting for a timeout because we were falling behind so fast and so early," said Douglas.

Nor was Illinois prepared a week later for No. 4 Indiana and its front line of Randy Wittman, Ted Kitchel and Uwe Blab. The Hoosiers beat the Illini 69-55 on the orange and blue's court. Knight gave his charges the green light to attempt their first ever three-point shots, and the Hoosiers responded by sinking four of four.

"It's a horse (bleep) rule, but if others are going to use it, we're going to use it," said Knight.

"The three-point shot was experimental in the Big Ten in 1983," explained Douglas. "We were a power team and we didn't shoot many. Our rule of thumb was that the ball had to go inside to Winters or Montgomery, and then back out. Coach Henson was a percentage player. The percentage rises about 15 percent once the ball goes inside."

No. 20 Ohio State was next, and senior Kevin Bontemps, who elected to play while classmate Quinn Richardson redshirted in 1983, came off the bench to help Harper (21 points) and Welch (16) repel the Buckeyes, 63-55, at home.

Back and forth the Illini bounced, losing 63-62 at Purdue as Dan Palombizio countered Harper's late basket.

"Palombizio made a turnaround shot from 15 feet," said Douglas. "I don't think he even saw the basket. That was a heartbreaker."

But the Illini hammered MSU, 78-71, with Harper outscoring Scott Skiles 25-18, and swept the Michigan trip as Harper (29 points) and Douglas (16) combined for 45 points in an 87-74 besting of the Wolverines.

"We were starting to jell in the backcourt, and we were stepping up the defensive pressure," said Douglas. "Derek was hitting his zone. We started looking for him to score more. And his on-the-ball defense allowed me to get steals off the ball."

Harper, a ball-deflecting whirlwind on defense, combined with Douglas for 150 steals that season. He was at that point performing as well as any guard in Illini history.

"Those two guys were excellent defensive guards," recalled Henson. "They had quick hands and they got a lot of steals."

Harper sparked a 62-61 home win over Iowa, but the celebrations were short-lived as Illinois fell on the road to Northwestern, 58-55, and Iowa, 68-66. The losses tarnished strong performances from Harper, who contributed 22 points against the Wildcats and 13 points and five steals against the Hawkeyes.

"We played Northwestern in the small DePaul Alumni Gym, and they shot lights out," recalled Douglas. "At Iowa, we built a good lead, and then they put a lid on the basket."

How different the three-point shooting was in those days. At NU, the Illini tried four three-point attempts and the Wildcats just three. At Iowa, Harper made the only Illini three-point attempt, and Iowa dared to attempt four, making two. Many coaches didn't believe in the shot.

Harper collected 52 points in home wins over Michigan and Michigan State in mid-February, but no one was ready for what happened next at the Assembly Hall. Illinois led Purdue by 20 points when coach Gene Keady, figuring "what did we have to lose," put in his reserves. That ignited an incredible rally as Illinois failed to record a field goal in the last 10:45. Former walk-on Jim Rowinski banked in the final Purdue basket in a stunning 54-52 upset.

"Those are the ones you try to forget," said Douglas. "We were young and we had a tendency to lose concentration. We never thought they could come back. We looked up and Rowinski banked it in, and that was characteristic of that year."

The Illini somehow recovered at Ohio State as Douglas scored 22. The Buckeyes' Larry Huggins was fouled intentionally late during the overtime period, forcing Ohio State to convert two free throws instead of attempting to tie the game with a three. Illinois won, 74-73.

"That was one of the thought processes to not let them tie it with a three," said Douglas. "We did well against Ohio State because they had smaller guards, and we backed them down."

But Indiana won at home without Kitchel, 67-55, and the regular season ended with a double-overtime home shootout with Minnesota. With the clock winding down, Harper drained a 27-foot trey to win it, 70-67, and send Illinois—who had tied for second in the Big Ten at 11-7—into the NCAA tournament in Boise, Idaho.

Any momentum gained from the thrilling regular-season ending win quickly dissolved against Utah. *The News-Gazette* noted that the Illini "played like awestruck seventh graders in their first school play, blowing lines and missing cues."

A 16-13 Utah club whipped Illinois, 52-49.

"We were shaky and just never relaxed," said Henson at the time. "We didn't get the ball to Efrem in the second half. You can't afford to go flat when you're in the NCAA tournament."

Following the conclusion of a 21-11 season, Harper, then a junior, decided to turn pro. His NBA scoring improved steadily to a peak of 19.7 for Dallas in 1991. He completed a 16-year NBA career in 1999, just three points shy of 16,000.

continued on page 152

Derek Harper ended his Illini career a year early to enter the NBA draft, where he was selected 11th by the Dallas Mavericks in 1983. During his junior season, Harper averaged 15.4 points per game, 3.5 rebounds, 3.7 assists, 2.3 steals, and shot 53.7 percent from the floor. As teammate Bruce Douglas said, Harper was in a zone.

GREATEST GAMES
ILLINOIS 70, MINNESOTA 67

MARCH 13, 1983 • ASSEMBLY HALL, CHAMPAIGN, ILLINOIS

HARPER'S BUZZER-BEATER SENDS ILLINOIS TO THE TOURNEY

Senior Day in 1983 against the Minnesota Gophers was for all the marbles. Win and you receive a bid to the NCAA Tournament. Lose and your season-long goal was dashed.

The 1982-83 season, an up-and-down year for the Illini in the Big Ten, began with an embarrassing 26-point loss to these same Gophers up in Minneapolis. It was a loss so devastating that it spurred an impromptu team meeting, and it was one that the team never forgot. Along with a trip to the tournament, the Illini were playing for pride—they wanted revenge.

Officially it was the last game in the Assembly Hall for seniors Bryan Leonard and Kevin Bontemps, but there was one more member of that team who pretty much knew he was walking out of the tunnel for the last time that afternoon.

"I did feel going in that it was my last game," recalled Illinois guard Derek Harper. "I thought I had a great year, and that my senior year couldn't have been any better. I felt physically and mentally ready for the NBA, because my confidence at that time was on a different level."

For Harper, it wouldn't be just another game. For the first time in his college career, his mother was in attendance.

"She was my confidant and a lot of her prayers got me through some tough situations in my life," said Harper. "For whatever reason, I just relax and play better knowing I have that kind of support in the stands. Having her there gave me a great deal of confidence, and I just felt going in that this was my game."

It certainly seemed that way early on as Harper and the Illini built a commanding 11-point lead in the first half and enjoyed a seven-point cushion at the half. Just when it seemed like the Illini had the game in control, things began to fall apart as 7-3 Gopher center Randy Breuer dominated the second half on his way to scoring 24 points and grabbing 12 rebounds in the game.

▲ Derek Harper celebrates with fans and teammates after his 27-foot shot swished into the net at the buzzer. The basket not only sent the Gophers packing, but it sent the Illini back to the NCAA Tournament.

With the game tied at 56 and the clock running down in regulation, Harper had a shot to win it, but missed from 24 feet.

"I remember thinking after I missed that shot that I was the goat," remembered Harper. "Walking back to the huddle, I just couldn't believe I had the chance to end the game and didn't do it. I told everyone who was around me that I wanted the ball in the overtime."

The teams remained deadlocked after the first overtime and when Illinois tied it up on an Efrem Winters alley-oop dunk with a minute left to play in the second extra stanza, Minnesota attempted to hold for a last shot. That plan failed when Jim Peterson launched a 15-footer that missed and by the time the Illini advanced the rebound to half-court and called a time-out there were four ticks left on the clock.

Going into the huddle, Harper let it be known that he wanted a second chance.

"I remember telling Coach Nagy, Coach Yates, and everybody else in shouting distance that I was taking the shot," said Harper. "I was saying it loud enough for Coach Henson to hear."

"Through both overtimes, Derek kept asking me to tell Coach Henson to give him the ball, because he was going to win the game for his mother," recalled assistant coach Tony Yates."I remember before Coach Henson drew up the play for the second overtime I said to him, 'Coach, get the ball to Derek because he is going to win the game for this team and his mom.'"

The play designed in the huddle had two options.

"We ran a lob play to Efrem Winters to tie the game minutes earlier so our first option was to set a back screen for him to see if we could get him the ball," recalled Henson. "If we couldn't get Efrem open we were going to give it to Derek and let him shoot."

"Coach Henson is drawing up a play with all these Xs and Os in the huddle and I am listening intently as he told us to do this and do that," reflected freshman Bruce Douglas, who was the in-bounds man on the play. "We come out of the huddle, Derek looks at me, and says with this serious look, 'Throw me the ball,' and that's exactly what I did."

Douglas threw the ball into Harper about 35 feet away from the basket and the rest is history.

"He got the ball, dribbled it a few times, did his shake and bake, and pulled up from the top of the key," remembered senior Kevin Bontemps.

With one second remaining, Harper launched a straightaway three-point shot from about 27 feet and hit nothing but the bottom of the net. It was time for the Illini to pack their bags for the NCAA Tournament.

It was a shot heard around the state and a moment that started a string of eight straight NCAA Tournament appearances. For Harper, it was a fairy tale ending to his days in the Assembly Hall.

"Personally that shot meant everything to me. Growing up as a kid I spent countless days on the basketball courts in the projects counting down the clock and dreaming of hitting a game-winning shot like that," said Harper more than 20 years later. "For my mother to be there to see it in front of a sold-out Assembly Hall was just amazing. It is one of the greatest moments of my basketball career, one that I will take with me for the rest of my life, and I get goose bumps even thinking about it."

It was a scene that seemed to come right out of a movie script. In his last game at the Assembly Hall, taking his last shot in the arena he starred in for three years, Harper was the hero one final time. He knew going into the game that he would walk out of the tunnel and into the locker room for the last time that afternoon, but he ended up being wrong. He wouldn't walk. Instead he would be carried into the locker room on the shoulders of his teammates.

continued from page 148

TOPS IN THE BIG TEN

The fall of 1983 dawned as one of the most promising and, as it turned out, memorable seasons in Illini basketball history. Derek Harper had departed early, and an injury forced Anthony Welch to take a medical redshirt. But Henson had redshirted Quinn Richardson, saving his senior season, and Richardson moved into a lineup that had long-shooting Doug Altenberger on the wing and rugged Chicagoans George Montgomery and Efrem Winters on the block. With the three-point shot back in moth balls (it returned as a national rule in 1986-87), the Illini started the season by whacking Utah, 99-65, in Rosemont.

"We got payback for our NCAA loss," said Douglas. "We were a year older and our preparation was better."

Montgomery's improvement was obvious when he scored 17 in a 78-47 rout of Southern Mississippi in early December. The Illini rumbled through the first six wins, all by 14 points or more, and stood 8-0 with No. 2 Kentucky coming up. But this wasn't your ordinary

Instead of paying the price of admission to watch Kentucky play at the Assembly Hall, these three fans got to don the stripes and referee the game. Due to poor weather, local Illini fans (left to right) Bob Hiltibran, Charlie Due, and Bill Mitze had to substitute for the NCAA refs, who were stranded on Interstate 57.

Curt Beamer/The Champaign-Urbana News-Gazette

game. It was Christmas Eve, 1983, and cars were stalled on snow-drifted streets in sub-50 degree wind chills. The Wildcats made it to Champaign, but the officials were stranded somewhere on Interstate 57. So a local trio of Charlie Due, Champaign Central High School's baseball coach, Monticello principal Bill Mitze and UI professor Bob Hiltibran climbed down from the stands and, with zebra shirts popping out of their Levis, officiated a game that was praised by both Henson and Kentucky's Joe B. Hall.

The Illini held big Sam Bowie and Mel Turpin in check, but the game boiled down to a last possession with Wildcats freshman James Blackmon converting a driving shot at the buzzer for a 54-52 Kentucky win. It was a tough loss, though not as tough as the next loss to Kentucky would be.

"It was the best officiated game all year," said Douglas. "They really let us play, and it was one of the best games of the year."

Illinois tuned up for the Big Ten season—and what a wild ride it would be—by building a double-figure lead and downing Missouri, 66-60, on the inside power of Winters (20 points) and Montgomery (15). Incredibly, the Illini played four overtime games and eight extra periods over their first eight league games, winning three overtime games and losing one. At Wisconsin on January 7, no Illini scored more than 12 points, the Badgers shot 52.9 percent, the Illini missed nine free throws as the Wisconsin crowd jeered ... and yet the Illini won, 63-62, in OT. Go figure.

"It was a defensive game and we made plays when we needed to," said Douglas. "We were still putting together a formula of how to win. We made big defensive plays late."

At Indiana four days later, the Illini weren't so fortunate. The Hoosiers reached 150-15 in their home Assembly Hall with a 73-68 overtime win. Altenberger tied it in regulation with a 20-footer but Steve Alford, converting 15 of 16 free throws, gave the Hoosiers a big charity edge that paid off in the extra session.

"I was at the point, and I didn't get to guard Alford much that time," said Douglas. "The next time around I guarded him. I remember late in that game Quinn was reaching out with his hand and touched him. They called a foul, and Alford shot them in."

The next game at Ohio State wasn't an overtime match but it was just as close. Illinois had to rally hard in the last six minutes to win, 55-53. But back to the overtimes, the January 27 date with Michigan lasted an additional half—four overtime periods or an incredible 20 extra record-breaking minutes. The five starters played at least 51 of the 60 minutes, and aches and pains were too numerous to count. Even the crowd of 15,000-plus was losing its collective voice. And why not? This game had five finishes.

First, a 46-46 score held for the last four minutes of regulation. After two back-and-forth extra periods, tension peaked as two delaying squads went scoreless for the first four minutes of the third overtime. Finally, in the fourth overtime, Richardson and Douglas made key steals and the Illini breezed to a 75-66 victory.

"I played every minute," said Douglas. "At the end of the first overtime, Michigan's Eric Turner made a basket to tie that was clearly after the buzzer. In the fourth overtime, we broke it open when we got back-to-back steals."

Next came Iowa in a contest the Illini led only once in regulation, 2-0, and yet rallied to win on clutch Douglas plays in the second overtime, 54-52.

"I got loose for a couple of creative shots on fast-break situations, and we were able to pull it out in overtime," Douglas said. "At that point, we began to think we wouldn't lose."

Out of that Iowa City firestorm, the Illini picked up steam with eight double-figure runaways interrupted only by narrow losses at Michigan (62-60) and Purdue (59-55). Winters was enjoying perhaps his best season. He speared 14 rebounds and combined with Douglas for 50 points in a March 1 defeat of Ohio State; then the pair combined for 44 points in a 70-53 home win over Indiana.

"We made some key assignment changes against Indiana," said Douglas. "I guarded Alford and did a pretty good job. We built up a good lead. And Efrem and I were playing like a 1-2 punch. We were in a good offensive mode."

Winters scored 25 points against Wisconsin as Illinois cruised past the Badgers, 81-57, to tie Purdue for the Big Ten title with a 15-3 mark. The UI's bid in the NCAA

▲ Coach Henson credited senior guard Quinn Richardson for successfully filling the gaping void left by Derek Harper's early departure. Richardson averaged 7.7 points per game on the season and shot 58.8 percent from the floor.

might have turned out differently if the big guy hadn't sprained his ankle.

No. 6-ranked Illinois roared into the playoffs, bypassing Villanova, 64-56, to reach the Sweet 16 for the third time in 32 years, and found themselves in Rupp Arena for the East Regional.

"We faced Len Bias and a good (No. 11-ranked) Maryland team that had won the Atlantic Coast Conference," recalled Henson.

The Illini expanded their late lead to 70-63, and staved off a Maryland rally to win, 72-70. But Winters injured his ankle when he landed on the foot of Bias in the second half. Questions arose at to whether he would be able to play against Kentucky in the battle for a Final Four slot.

"We put ice and water in a garbage bucket, and stuck Efrem's foot in it when the game was over," recalled trainer Rod Cardinal.

"Back at the hotel, we moved a student trainer out of my room and put Efrem in with me so I could continue the therapy. The team visited the horse farms

continued on page 156

GREATEST GAMES
(NO. 9) ILLINOIS 75, MICHIGAN 66
JANUARY 26, 1984 • ASSEMBLY HALL, CHAMPAIGN, ILLINOIS

FOUR-OVERTIME THRILLER ROCKS THE HALL

It was a three-hour marathon. A rugged, intense and physically exhausting battle between the Illini and the Wolverines that wouldn't be settled by the end of regulation—or even three additional overtimes. On this Saturday afternoon it would take a fourth overtime to decide a winner.

It was par for the course for the Illini, who were used to working hard and being physically exhausted. Overtimes and long practices were nothing compared to what strength and conditioning coach Bill Kroll put them through during the summer.

"There were nights in the off season when guys were late getting there so we would put cars out on the football field for lights and have them run sprints," recalled Kroll. "Those were the nights they were tired and it was a lot worse than anything they had to go through in season."

Calling this game intense is probably an understatement. The Michigan-Illinois rivalry dated back to the 1920s and by 1983 it had reached new heights. The rivalry on the football field boiled over with the contentious relationship between head coaches Mike White and Bo Schembechler; meanwhile, the basketball rivalry heated up after the recruiting classes of 1982. The Michigan and Illinois classes were billed as the top two in the country and the players on both teams were always out to prove they were the best.

"I had a couple of friends who also used to say that the next best thing to an Illinois win was a Michigan loss," said Scott Meents, a member of the Illinois Class of 1982.

This January matchup didn't look like it was going to be a barnburner early. The Illini sprinted out of the gate behind the play of Efrem Winters, who scored 15 first-half points on the way to a 27-16 halftime lead for the Orange and Blue.

The second half was a complete reversal of fortune as Michigan completely took Winters out of his game and hit their first nine of 10 shots to cut the gap to two points with eight minutes left to play. After Wolverine guard Eric Turner hit two jumpers to tie the game with a little more than four minutes left, both teams went scoreless and headed to the first overtime tied at 46.

Michigan took their first lead of the game on a Tim McCormick shot to start the first overtime, but the Illini fought back on consecutive shots by Altenberger and Winters. It looked like the game was over when Bruce Douglas hit both ends of a one-and-one with four seconds left, but Eric Turner drilled a controversial 20-foot shot at the buzzer to tie the game at 57 and send it into a second overtime.

"We weren't worried after Turner hit that shot because we were in good condition," recalled Illini captain Quinn Richardson. "All of the running we did in pre-season conditioning always helped us to maintain our stamina and endurance."

The second overtime was back and forth and when Michigan fumbled the ball away with only a few seconds left, the game headed into a third overtime tied at 62.

"That year we always figured out how to win games," recalled Altenberger. "I remember thinking if it takes eight overtimes, we are going to figure out some way to win this game."

Nobody scored in the first four minutes of the third overtime as both teams stalled and cautiously held the ball. After trading baskets in the last minute, Roy Tarpley deflected an Altenberger shot at the buzzer. Tarpley landed right on top of Altenberger, but to the dismay of the 15,952 in the Hall, no foul was called and the score remained tied at 64.

"That was the longest game I have ever been involved in," recalled coach Lou Henson. "Going into the fourth overtime, we knew that win or lose we had to end the game there."

Taking the advice of their coach, the Illini stormed out immediately in the fourth overtime. An 18-foot Quinn Richardson jumper from the left side ignited an 11-2 run.

"Michigan just wore down in that fourth overtime," said Douglas, who had two key steals in that offensive spurt. "They got sloppy with the ball and our conditioning was so good that we were able to suck it up for five more minutes."

After a grueling 75-66 win the players might have had a little energy left, but their coaches sure didn't.

"All I remember about that game is that when it was over I was so physically and emotionally worn out," said longtime

Fans could rest assured that Illini George Montgomery (left) and Efrem Winters (right) needed all the rest they could get following the Illini's four-overtime win against Michigan in 1984. If the game was not tiring enough, the team had to participate in a mandatory weight-lifting session afterward.

assistant coach Dick Nagy. "I was so tired I could hardly get home."

For the players on the team, their day's work wasn't nearly over.

"I will never forget what we did that day after the game," laughed Winters, who finished with a game-high 23 points. "We lifted weights. They weren't going to give us a break from that just because we went four overtimes."

In-season weight lifting was a staple of strength and conditioning coach Bill Kroll's program and an extra-long game wasn't going to change the schedule.

"Coach Henson came in to talk to us briefly and then we all got in our sweat suits," remembered Meents. "It was about five degrees outside, but we ran up the ramp and across Kirby to head into the Stadium. The fans were looking at us like we were crazy."

The weight circuit typically lasted 10-15 minutes and the team believed the program was essential to their success.

"We didn't think twice about going over there after four overtimes," said Altenberger. "If Coach Kroll said that is what

we needed to do to become champions, then that is what we were going to do."

There was one member of the Illini who wasn't going to make it to lift that night.

"I was exhausted after that game," recalled Henson. "I don't think I could have taken another overtime and I couldn't have even walked to the weight room from the Assembly Hall."

The Illini put in 60 minutes on the court and an extra 10 in the weight room. It was a very long day in a grueling year of hard work. Only a month and a half later, the hard work paid off when the Illini defeated Wisconsin at home to win a share of their first Big Ten Championship in 21 years.

They didn't celebrate it by staying in the locker room or walking back out onto the floor to talk to friends. While fans were clamoring to celebrate with them and reporters were dying to speak with them, the Illini were nowhere to be found. They had already run up the ramp, crossed Kirby Avenue, and were back in the weight room completing one more circuit.

continued from page 153

around Lexington on our off day, but Efrem stayed with me. But the ankle was badly discolored, and we really didn't have enough time. He lacked strength but he was determined to play against Kentucky."

Winters competed against Kentucky but was well below 100 percent. He managed just four rebounds to Sam Bowie's 14, and Kentucky prevailed yet another time as Dickie Beal scored the Wildcats' last five points in a 54-51 result. Controversy swirled around a half-court trap in the waning seconds. Illini coaches claimed that Beal traveled, but no call was made. Beal sank two free throws with 14 seconds left to clinch it.

"I thought it was a travel and a charge," said Douglas, "but they called a foul, and his free throws put an end to it. I won't say calls caused us to lose. But you never want to play for a Final Four berth on some-

▲ *Efrem Winters, hoisted up by his teammates, cuts the net after his 25 points secured an 81-57 win at home over Wisconsin to claim a tie for the Big Ten title. Illinois went 15-3 during the 1983-84 season and ended the year ranked sixth in the AP polls.*

one else's court, and we were the victims of that. They changed it after that year. No question it affects the referees when you're playing in front of 22,000, and all those fans are screaming for one team."

Henson looked back on that 26-5 Big Ten co-championship team, calling it "a team that should have reached the Final Four," and citing the performance of Richardson in replacing the departed Harper as one reason why.

"Certain types of players stand out as you look back over a career," said Henson. "Quinn had a lot of talent. Now, if you went over to the intramural building and watched him play, you might not pick him out. But he was a key to that team because we had other guys like Douglas who could penetrate, and Richardson and Altenberger were tremendous shooters. There was a drop off when Richardson graduated.

"I always remember what Adolph Rupp said at a clinic many years ago. He said, 'If you can't make the 18-foot shot, you're not going to get the others.' That's a basic shot in basketball. And now, with the three-point arc, the perimeter shot is the key to winning.

"There was a time when people said, 'Rebounding is the key to winning.' Well, when 33 percent was good shooting, that may have been true. There were a lot of rebounds in those days. But today shooting is the key, and ballhandling is next. It is a game of skill."

STAYING FOCUSED

Now entrenched among the national elite, Illinois entered the 1984-85 season ranked No. 2 in the nation with Winters, a first-team UPI all-league pick as a sophomore, entering his junior campaign on All-America teams projected by Street & Smith's, *Playboy* and *The Sporting News.* Douglas was rated *The Sporting News'* No. 2 point guard, after being named co-Big Ten Player of the Year by UPI the previous season.

This was a rugged team that would set the all-time Illini field goal percentage record (54.2) in a 26-9 season, and they were chosen to open against mighty fifth-ranked Oklahoma in the Tipoff Classic in Springfield, Massachussetts. Using high-percentage shots, the Illini put 10 players in the scoring column to overwhelm All-American Wayman Tisdale and the Sooners, 81-64. This kicked off an 11-1 run for a mature team that had Anthony Welch back from a redshirt year and could rotate Winters, Montgomery and Scott Meents at the two inside slots. Altenberger moved to guard alongside Douglas.

"I think we definately had good talent but it was a different makeup, and it changed the way we did things," said Douglas. "We may have had more talent but we had to make some adjustments. Anthony was more of a scorer, and Doug had a different role."

A cold-shooting affair with Alabama-Birmingham resulted in a 59-52 loss in Anchorage, but the Illini returned home to whip Oklahoma again, 73-70.

"You know it's a big game," wrote *The News-Gazette*, "when the 'sold out' sign goes up ... when the CBS-TV trucks are packed outside the Assembly Hall ... when 90-second commercials are scheduled every four minutes ... when a color photographer applies for a press pass from Delaware, Ohio ... and when reporters from the *Denver Post* and the *Fort Worth Star-Telegram* fly in."

Sub Tom Shafer became the sixth Illini to crack double digits, and the game turned in the UI's favor when the home forces swiped three balls while Oklahoma was trying to run down the 45-second clock before halftime. Tisdale scored 22 and the Sooners shot 50 percent, but the Illini won by holding turnovers down to five and making 13 of 15 free throws.

The preconference stretch ended on a highly controversial losing note when Loyola won at the Rosemont Horizon, 63-62, despite a foul by Alfredrick Hughes against Welch on a rebound at the end of the game. A review of game film, with the clock superimposed on the TV screen, showed Big Ten ref George Solomon calling the foul with two seconds remaining. But both the buzzer and whistle were almost indistinguishable in the din of 15,000 screaming spectators, and the two officials didn't have the option to seek help from a TV monitor in those days. So the refs turned to longtime Loyola official timer John Reilly, and he ruled that the game was over.

"It was one of those games where they just made a bad call," said Douglas. "I think they were determined

▲ Bruce Douglas (left) and Efrem Winters (right) made the cover of Basketball Times in 1984-85 as expectations ran high for the defending Big Ten champs.

to win. It was a game where we didn't play particularly well."

Two more devilish road losses followed as the 1985 Big Ten season opened. In the first, Minnesota rallied from a 56-45 deficit in the last 4:45 to win 60-58 on Tommy Davis' shot with two seconds left. In the second, Iowa broke a 58-58 tie to rule, 64-60, while coach George Raveling sat home with the flu.

Back home, the Illini finally won a close one, 64-58 in overtime, as Tony Wysinger applied the final touches against Michigan. This kicked off a six-game win streak that featured two coasting wins over ranked foes, No. 17 Michigan State, 75-63, and No. 13 Indiana, 52-41. The latter game, played in Champaign on January 27, attracted a whirlwind of criticism as Bob Knight, irate over the team's recent play, left junior starters Winston Morgan and Mike Giomi home, and started four freshmen while keeping most of his regulars, including

Olympian Steve Alford, on the bench. The rugged Illini outrebounded the young Hoosiers, 43-23, and maintained control after holding the Hoosiers to an Assembly Hall low 12 points in the first half.

"Knight was capable of doing anything so it didn't surprise us," said Douglas. "But it was kind of strange."

Writers had a field day with it. Bernie Lincicome's headline in the *Chicago Tribune* read "Knight benches his integrity."

▲ *Guard Doug Altenberger was a steady contributor for the Illini during his four healthy seasons of play. His accurate outside shot proved to be a deadly weapon when the Illini were in need of a big bucket.*

Gannett's Mike Lopresti wrote: "The shocker is in Indiana, where the keepers of the faith as spoken by Bobby Knight—usually in four-letter increments—have turned against their master. At least some of them. At least until he wins again. Knight wasn't playing with a full deck Sunday. Some may have suspected that for a long time, but on this occasion you could prove it by a body count."

Illinois was clearly playing without its full deck in the following game against Purdue. In what Henson called "the most inept performance by any team I've coached in 30 years," Purdue beat Illinois, 54-34. The UI's 15 second-half points set a record low for Mackey Arena.

"A lot of that inconsistency stemmed from veteran players trying to win by themselves and playing as individuals," analyzed Douglas.

The inconsistency showed up in the national rankings as well. Illinois bounced from their opening No. 2 ranking all the way to No. 15 in early January, only to climb back to No. 5 by late January and eventually fall as far as No. 17 after back-to-back losses in early February. Illinois, the favorite when the 1985 race started, did not repeat as Big Ten champion as a powerhouse Michigan team ended all doubt, 57-45, at Crisler Arena on February 9.

Scott Meents moved into the center position vacated by George Montgomery, who was lost for the season with a stress fracture. And the Illini were no match for Roy Tarpley and the large Wolverine rebounders.

"We had a lead late, but they came back strong. It was hard matching up with their size." said Douglas.

Michigan rolled on to a 16-2 conference record. Illinois garnered second place at 12-6 by winning six of their last seven games as junior college transfer Ken Norman began to make his presence felt. This UI team needed point production, with Winters falling off and Douglas seeing his average tumble to seven points per game in mid-February. Then, Montgomery was lost too, and Meents missed time due to a hand injury.

"We had become inconsistent in our offensive approach, and opponents were focusing more on Efrem," said Douglas. "We began to look to other people, and Efrem lost some confidence."

Norman scored 17 points in a 68-49 rout of Wisconsin, and Douglas came alive with 21 points in a 66-50 thumping of Indiana's "first team" in Bloomington.

"Our game plan always attacked Indiana's guards, and I had a good game over there," he said. "We usually played well against Indiana because of the matchups."

Then, as revenge for the earlier 54-34 loss at Purdue, the Illini doubled the score on the Boilermakers, 86-43, with Norman bagging 25 points off the bench. Fact is, by the end of the 1985 season, Norman was the UI's most dangerous offensive weapon. He combined quickness of foot with a fierce mindset, and would ultimately turn that combination into millions of NBA dollars.

"As he learned the system, Norman blossomed," said Douglas. "He was quick on the post, and very aggressive. And he was hungry. He jumped on his opportunity, and opposing teams didn't know what to expect."

Norman scored 23 and 15 in NCAA tournament victories over Northeastern, 76-57, and Georgia, 74-58. But the Illini's season ended when six-foot Mark Price, seven-foot John Salley and No. 6 Georgia Tech dumped the Illini in Providence, R.I., 61-53. Altenberger tried to rally the team from a 15-point deficit with 24 counters, but Illinois ultimately fell to conclude their season ranked 12th in the nation.

"Price made some phenomenal shots," recalled Douglas. "We stayed in the game but we never got on track."

ONE LAST SHOT FOR DOUGLAS

With Altenberger having early knee troubles and ultimately taking a medical redshirt in 1985-86, and with Douglas and Winters falling below 10-point production, forwards Norman and Welch emerged as the go-to scorers for Illinois. 1985-86 was a season much like the previous one, bubbling with potential thanks to a 12-2 start, but ultimately leaving fans a bit disappointed as the Illini were unable to keep pace with Michigan in the Big Ten scramble.

"We were seasoned, but I don't think we played well as a unit," said Douglas. "We had a lot of different types of players. The tough part was to stay within the team structure. We were not consistent."

Kicking off at home, the Illini gained revenge for the previous year's disputed loss to Loyola by burying the Ramblers, 95-64, as Winters (14 and 12) and Norman (16 and 10) hit double figures in points and rebounds. Oklahoma got even after the previous season's pair of losses to Illinois with a 59-57 victory over the Illini in Honolulu. Linwood Davis stripped Winters on a rebound and laid in the winning basket at the buzzer.

"It was a small, hot gym and we couldn't get any breaks," recalled Douglas. "That last play could easily have been called a foul."

Illinois won its seventh consecutive Illini Classic by a school-record margin of 51 points over Utah State, 115-64, as Scott Meents stepped forward to earn Classic MVP honors.

"Scott had a stretch of good basketball there," said Douglas.

Missouri was also not up to the task in St. Louis. Norman and Welch combined for 38 points in a 67-55 UI triumph.

"Those games in St. Louis were getting bigger every year," said Douglas, "and Missouri was becoming more competitive.

"We were seniors and we were trying to get the best out of our game, but the team struggled with things on the court at times ... like playing within the team framework, and putting more emphasis on wins than developing team numbers."

The Illini stood 10-2 after beating Minnesota 76-57 in the league opener. Then close-game losses turned against them. Roy Marble brought Iowa to ties at 55-55 and 57-57 before sinking the winning free throw in a 60-59 result at the Assembly Hall.

"We were struggling with consistency, and we let a lot of games get away from us," said Douglas. "There was not enough sacrifice that year, and our post defense went back and forth. Some days it was as good as any team I played on, but not all the time."

In any case, Illinois was no physical match for Michigan. The Wolverines had so much power in the front line with Roy Tarpley, Richard Rellford and Antoine Joubert that 6-9 Robert Henderson and 6-8 Butch Wade couldn't crack the starting lineup. Illinois challenged Michigan but fell short, 61-59, in Ann Arbor with Michigan native Glynn Blackwell scoring 13 points in place of the redshirted Altenberger and the ailing Tony Wysinger.

"Michigan threw a lot of big bodies against us, and Rice was an outstanding freshman who could really shoot," said Douglas.

Michigan State made it three straight losses when Scott Skiles bagged 22 points in a 58-51 Spartan win in East Lansing. The loss dropped the Illini out of the AP standings after debuting at No. 7 at the beginning of the season.

"We won the next three but we were on a roller-coaster," said Douglas. "As far as Efrem is concerned, it's hard for people to understand the different makeup of teams from year to year. He was asked to do different things. We didn't look to him to score as much because different scorers emerged. Efrem did go through some difficult times, but he never complained. I think he got better every year."

The Illini knocked off Michigan's champions when the Wolverines came to Champaign on February 8.

"We always got up mentally for Michigan, and we sustained our effort at home," said Douglas. "Efrem had 25 points. With Norman coming on, Coach Henson wasn't looking for Efrem to be a 20- or 25-point scorer but Winters played hard and was there when we went to him."

Controversy is always a part of one-point decisions, and the Illini got into another brouhaha in a 61-60 loss to Indiana at the Assembly Hall. Blackwell pulled Illinois within a point in the final minute. Then ref Eric Harmon called Indiana's Stew Robinson for an over-and-back violation at midcourt. But Verl Sell, the lead official, came running up to overturn Harmon's decision. Henson complained bitterly to no avail. The Illini got the ball back for a rushed shot at game's end, but Wysinger's 17-footer fell short. The Hoosiers took over first place in the standings (they finished second to Michigan) despite going scoreless in the last 4:50.

Television arranged for an Illini-Georgia Tech showdown on March 1, and the Ramblin' Wreck was ranked No. 4 when Illinois won at the Omni in Atlanta, 59-57. Illinois rallied from a 45-37 deficit on a rash of Wysinger and Norman baskets, and won it on Winters' 13-footer.

"Efrem played well again," said Douglas, "and we pretty much held Mark Price in check (14 points). That was a major win for us."

The win put the Illini back in the AP rankings at No. 19. But another southern team, Alabama, ended the Douglas-Winters era in another controversial finish—this one in round two of the NCAA Southeast Regional in Charlotte. With the score tied at 56-56 and the clock running out, Alabama guard Terry Coner drove into the lane and popped the game-winner after what Springfield scribe Jim Ruppert called "two-step harmony."

"Coner tried to get in and bumped into me," recalled Douglas. "He shuffled his feet so he could get a shot off, and he may have traveled. A lot of people thought so. It was a tough shot but he made it, off balance and all. That ended it for us."

The Illini finished tied for fourth in the Big Ten race with an 11-7 record and an overall record of 22-10.

"Looking back, it was a great time for me, a great opportunity," said Douglas. "I worked at it, and I tried to be a leader on and off the court. When I look back, I feel blessed."

Douglas became a youth minister while working on a degree in divinity at Moody Bible Institute, at the same time supervising meter readings in Chicago's southern region operations. Winters has been in the construction business for many years, and lives in Aurora.

Anthony Welch dunks the ball against Michigan State. Along with fellow forward Ken Norman, Welch picked up a lot of the scoring slack during the 1985-86 season. ▶

ILLINOIS

Assembly Hall • Champaign • December 12-13, 1986 • $1.00

Illini Classic

VS. MICHIGAN STATE / ASSEMBLY HALL, CHAMPAIGN / JANUARY 9, 1988

ILLINOIS

$1.50

FIGHTING ILLINI
35

ILLINOIS

INDIANA • ASSEMBLY HALL, CHAMPAIGN • JANUARY 28, 1989

FIGHTING ILLINI
13

$2.00

CHAPTER FOURTEEN

THE ILLINI TAKE FLIGHT
1986-87—1989-90

During the decades of Illini play, just two teams are recognizable by their nicknames: the Whiz Kids of the World War II era and the Flying Illini, so labeled by announcer Dick Vitale in admiration of their running, dunking style in the late 1980s.

The 1989 run to the Final Four had its beginning in 1986-87 when Henson brought in a superb freshman class of Nick Anderson, Kendall Gill, Stephen Bardo, Larry Smith and Phil Kunz.

Anderson was not eligible that year, and Bardo was the only freshman to crack the starting lineup after Christmas on a 23-8 team captained by Doug Altenberger, Ken Norman and Tony Wysinger. Norman, a mobile Chicagoan, averaged 20.7 points as a senior, second-highest among Illini scorers in the last 30 years.

"Norman was tremendous," recalled Henson. "He was a 6-7 postman who could run the court. He led the Big Ten in rebounding and was an accurate shooter. ...He became a valuable player for us."

Counting Duke among the early victims (69-62 in Hawaii), the 1986-87 Illini opened 7-0. In a 99-97 squeaker at Pitt, Wysinger set a school record for assists (16) and Altenberger took advantage of the new three-point arc by drilling five of seven treys.

"I think the coaches are going to vote against the three-point shot because you work hard for a game that you really deserve to win, then three or four of those and you get beat," Henson was quoted as saying.

Not exactly prophetic. Now, in reflection, Henson discusses the three-pointer:

"At first, I didn't like it because it put so much pressure on you defensively to guard the post, stop penetration and defend the perimeter. This and the shot clock revolutionized the game. And, in time, the three-point shot changed recruiting. You have to bring in guys who can shoot the three. You can beat anybody if you're making threes and they're not. ...The three-point shot is the reason you see more upsets today than years ago."

Easy home wins over Eastern Illinois, Baylor and Princeton brought the 1986-87 Illini to 7-0. The perfect season was snapped, 90-77, at North Carolina on December 20.

"We opened the Dean Dome in Chapel Hill, and that was the first time I was ever in awe of an arena," said

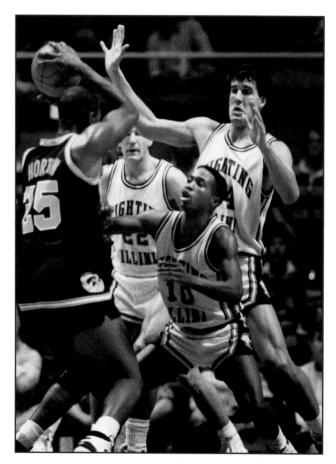

▲ Guard Tony Wysinger (No. 10) plays defense on his man as big center Jens Kujawa helps out. Wysinger averaged 11.3 points and 6.4 assists during his senior season of 1986-87.

Bardo, now a TV reporter in Chicago that also handles color commentary on the UI radio network.

"We led North Carolina early but they made a terrific run in the second half."

In St. Louis, Norman and Wysinger scored 24 and 18 points to dump Missouri, 92-74. This was the fourth win in Henson's 8-0 run against Mizzou coach Norm Stewart.

"What I remember most was that we had great leadership from Doug, Tony and Ken," said Bardo. "They took a young team and set the example through practice and communication, and forged a tight-knit unit.

"The Missouri game was the most physical we played up to that time—elbows flying, lips getting busted, the nastiest I'd been involved in."

No. 8 Illinois' 4-0 start in the Big Ten ended as Roy Marble, Brad Lohaus and B.J. Armstrong rallied unbeaten Iowa (15-0) from a 22-point, 61-39 deficit to win 91-88 in overtime in Champaign. The loss to No. 2 Iowa was one of the most devastating setbacks of Henson's career.

"As good as we played in the first half, we were the opposite in the second half," said Bardo. "It went south with 14 minutes to go. Their press just wore us down. And the shots they missed in the first half found the bottom of the barrel in the second half.

"We felt embarrassed in losing such a big lead. The next day all I felt was anger."

Eight days later at No. 5 Purdue, lightning struck again. Ahead 52-42 at halftime, and leading by three with a couple of ticks left, the Illini saw Doug Lee step in from out of bounds and tie it with a long three-pointer. The Boilermakers won in a wild overtime finish, 87-86. Altenberger missed a technical free throw with no time showing (Purdue celebrated too early) that would have forced the second overtime.

"Again, it was the same kind of feeling," said Bardo. "We had a lead and were playing well, and we didn't close out the game. That was our indoctrination into the Big Ten. They beat us up."

Illinois lost again at No. 4 Indiana, 69-66, but recovered from those setbacks to win the next four league games. Setbacks followed with additional losses to Iowa and Purdue (in OT again) that led to a rematch with now No. 3-ranked Indiana on March 1.

continued on page 166

GREATEST GAMES
(NO. 14) ILLINOIS 69, (NO. 3) INDIANA 67
MARCH 1, 1987 • ASSEMBLY HALL, CHAMPAIGN, ILLINOIS

ILLINI HAND HOOSIERS THEIR FINAL
LOSS OF SEASON

By 1987, the rivalry between Indiana and Illinois had risen to a new level. In the early and mid-1980s, the two staffs enjoyed a healthy and friendly relationship, but things began to change around 1986.

"It all started with the Lowell Hamilton recruitment," remembered Illinois assistant coach Jimmy Collins. "Lowell's high school coach was a big Bobby Knight disciple and he wanted

▲ *Lou Henson and Bobby Knight shake hands after a game. The coaches' relationship began to deteriorate in the mid-'80s once the Illini became a serious threat in the Big Ten— both on the court and in recruitment wars.*

Lowell to go to Indiana, but Lowell and I had developed a great relationship, and he decided to come to Illinois. It was a hot and heated recruitment, but when he chose Illinois the relationship between the two staffs went way south."

Illinois was beginning to beat Indiana on the court in games and off the court in recruiting battles.

"The series was starting to become a knockdown, drag-out battle with all the personalities from a coaching standpoint," said Illinois assistant coach Mark Coomes. "I think any time you started to beat Indiana, the relationship you had with them always changed. Bobby was good friends with Lou at one time, but when we started to beat them, it completely changed."

Heading into senior day for Tony Wysinger, Ken Norman and Doug Altenberger, the Illini were 10-5 in the league, but things could have been a lot better. The season had been a disaster against the Big Ten's big three of Iowa, Purdue and Indiana. In particular, this Illinois team had a bad habit of blowing big leads.

In mid-January, the Illini built a 22-point lead at home with 16 minutes to play against the undefeated second-ranked Iowa Hawkeyes before collapsing and losing in overtime. About a month later, Illinois held a 16-point second-half lead against sixth-ranked Purdue with 12 minutes left to play before letting that slip away and again losing in overtime. It had been a good season, but the brutal losses at home weighed on the mind of the Illini and especially their seniors heading into their final home game.

"We never forgot losing those big leads at home to Iowa and Purdue," said fifth-year senior Doug Altenberger. "Going into the Indiana game, I said to myself that I don't care what happens in this game, but there is no way I am going out of the Assembly Hall with a loss."

For Norman, playing Indiana was always something he looked forward to.

continued on page 166

continued from page 165

"I loved playing the Hoosiers, because you knew they were going to come after you and they always played man to man," said Norman. "I knew going into that game I could have a big offensive night, because they didn't have anyone who could stop me."

After getting 14 points from Norman and 11 from Altenberger, the Illini held a 40-36 lead at the half. The second half began with a Norman short jumper, an Altenberger three, and an emphatic Norman dunk over Keith Smart. Three minutes into the half the Illini had a 10-point cushion and were in that uncomfortable position of holding a big lead.

True to form, the Illini began to let that lead slip away.

"We had the lead early in the half and they just kept grinding away at it," recalled Wysinger. "We couldn't make any shots and I know I was missing shots that I should have made."

The lead was withering away, and with seven minutes remaining Indiana forward Rick Calloway tied the game at 57 on a spinning lay-up. Who could blame the record Assembly Hall crowd of 16,793 and the thousands of Illinois fans watching the game on ABC if they thought to themselves, "Here we go again"?

But the Illini wouldn't quit on this day. After a Norman 15-footer, Altenberger connected on back-to-back three point shots to give the Illini some breathing room.

With 39 seconds remaining and the Illini clinging to a two-point lead, the Hoosiers decided to hold the ball and try to get it to Alford for a three to win the game. Altenberger was guarding Alford and when he received a late screen up top, Norman jumped out to affect the shot. With Norman right there, all Alford could do was get off an off-balance, one-handed fling that hit off the front rim and fell into the hands of Stephen Bardo.

With two seconds left most thought the game was over, but that wouldn't be dramatic enough for that Illini group. Bardo missed the front end of a one-an-one and seconds later Alford got the ball at mid-court. He stepped up to launch a 45-foot heave, but Bardo recovered to block it, and the Illini pulled off a 69-67 victory.

It was a fitting end for Norman, Altenberger, and Wysinger, who scored 24, 22, and 10 points respectively that night to lead the team. They were such a huge part of the Illinois basketball program during the mid-'80s and it was a great way for the trio to go out.

Meanwhile, Indiana wouldn't lose another game that season on their way to the 1987 National Championship, but in the second half against Illinois that afternoon, it didn't matter how hard they fought to get back. This was one game where three seniors refused to lose.

continued from page 164

The 69-67 Illini victory was Indiana's last loss in a national championship season. With Ken Norman continuing his torrid stretch run with 24 points, Illinois led 69-67 with a half-minute left when coach Bob Knight elected to stall for a final three-point shot that would win it. But his ace guard, Steve Alford, had to shoot under pressure with five seconds left and his shot missed.

The Big Ten season concluded with road wins over Michigan and Michigan State, leaving the Illini's Big Ten record at 13-5, which was good for fourth place.

Unfortunately, that 1987 team will be remembered for its opening round, 68-67 loss to Austin Peay in the NCAA Southeast Regional at Birmingham, Alabama. Darryl Bedford, a 260-pound three-point shooter, looped five bombs as the Governors fought the Illini all the way, winning on two free throws by Tony Raye with two seconds showing. The Illini called time after passing to midcourt. Norman worked free for a makeable 18-footer at the buzzer, but it bounced off the rim while Norman lay sprawled on the court.

"It was my best offensive game but my worst in terms of turnovers (six)," said Bardo. "The feeling was strange all night, and Austin Peay was fired up after Vitale said he'd stand on his head if we didn't win. Ken had a good look at the end but it missed. I was hurting more for the seniors than for myself."

The Illini finished the season with a 23-8 mark and the nation's No. 11 ranking after peaking at No. 5 early in the season.

PREPARING FOR LIFTOFF

The 1987-88 team—a sophomore-laden squad which added Nick Anderson and Northern Illinois transfer Kenny Battle to its lineup—began with a 9-2 rush. After easily beating Baylor in the opener, the unranked Illini

Six-foot-seven forward Ken Norman was as dominant a player as there was in the Big Ten during his senior campaign in 1986-87. "Snake," as he was nicknamed, averaged 20.7 points per game on 57.8-percent shooting and hauled in 9.8 rebounds a game. Behind his steady play, the Illini finished the season with 23 wins and ranked 11th in the AP poll.

lost 78-76 to Villanova in Hawaii, but bounced back to upend No. 7 Kansas, 81-75, in the consolation round. They avenged the NCAA loss to Austin Peay, 100-62, on December 8 and topped 100 points in four consecutive games—including a 107-103 overtime victory over Auburn—as leapers Battle and Anderson meshed at the forwards and tall Jens Kujawa shared time at center with Lowell Hamilton.

J.R. Reid and North Carolina, ranked No. 4, ruled at the Assembly Hall, 85-74, but Henson maintained his dominance in St. Louis with a 75-63 thrashing of No. 17 Missouri.

The Illini entered Big Ten play still-unranked on January 4, and fell to No. 11 Purdue, 81-68, in the conference opener. Despite the loss, the team moved into the national rankings at No. 19 just three days later and celebrated with a 65-61 overtime win at Minnesota. However, a 1-5 spell in late January and early February put the club behind the eight-ball.

"We would show flashes of brilliance, and then we'd stink up the place, sometimes in the same game," said Bardo. "We could never maintain a consistent effort throughout. Battle came on at the end of the season and showed what we could expect the next season. It took all season for us to come together."

Just when the season appeared to be slipping away, the '88 Illini caught fire with an 8-1 Big Ten finish. With Gill slumping (five double-figure totals in the UI's last 17 games), Anderson and Battle emerged as the league's dominant forward duo down the stretch. They were effective and spectacular, combining for 51 points in a 118-86 rout of Ohio State, contributing 42 points in an 85-65 defeat of Wisconsin, producing another 44 points and 20 rebounds in dumping Indiana 75-65, and in full throttle as No. 11 Iowa came to town in early March.

Anderson was by now unstoppable, bagging 23 points and 11 boards to sink the Hawkeyes, 94-81. Three days later, in the final home game for Glynn Blackwell and Jens Kujawa, crowd-pleasing leapers Anderson and

Mark Jones

▲ Point guard Stephen Bardo was a solid contributor for some great Illini teams in the late '80s. There were always plenty of scorers around during Bardo's four seasons with the Illini, which left him the task of running the Flying Illini offense and tossing his share of alley-oop passes.

Battle ran wild for 50 points and 11 rebounds in an 85-74 rout of a 10th-ranked Michigan squad that was one year shy of the national championship.

"Guys were understanding their roles better and we were beginning to click," said Bardo.

Anderson, Battle, Gill, Bardo, Kujawa, Blackwell and company ended the Big Ten season on a four-game win streak, securing third place with a 12-6 record.

Postseason play looked highly promising as Lowell Hamilton bagged 21 points and Blackwell added 19 in a coasting 81-72 defeat of Texas-San Antonio in the opening round. What followed was a 66-63 loss to Villanova—the team's second of the season—that ranks high among the most disappointing setbacks in UI history.

◀ Kenny Battle led the Illini squads of 1988 and '89 with his awesome athleticism, tremendous defense, and breathtaking dunks.

The Illini—who had the potential to go far in the tournament—lost the game on missed free throws against a less talented team.

"(Villanova coach) Rollie Massimino told me later that he had pretty much given up, and just told his guys to foul in the hope we'd miss the free throws. And that's what happened. That was one of toughest losses I ever experienced," recalled Henson.

It boiled down to the Illini blowing a 14-point lead by missing five one-and-ones in the final minutes while Villanova cashed five treys down the stretch. Even so, Battle scored to put Illinois ahead with 14 seconds left, but Villanova responded, winning 66-63.

"That one hurt more than even the Iowa game a year earlier," said Bardo. "I could see us in the Sweet 16. We really dominated Villanova. They were down 14 and just started jacking it up, no pressure. Once a couple fell in, the basket got bigger. A reserve hit two of those five."

Illinois finished the season ranked 16th with a 23-10 record.

FLYING HIGH

By the time the 1988-89 season rolled around—even as the big German, Kujawa, elected not to return for his senior season—it was clear that the Illini had a flare for the dramatic.

Anderson was at times unstoppable in averaging 15.9 points during his first season. He would return to lead the squad once again, and along with Battle and Gill, this Illini team would make sure the crowd was with them in anticipation of every move. The center position belonged to long-armed Lowell Hamilton and backup Ervin Small. Marcus Liberty was eligible after sitting out his freshman year and ready to help the talented juniors.

What unfolded was the most magical season of UI basketball in modern times.

It started with a 17-game win streak over the course of two months that carried Illinois from No. 9 in the nation to No. 1. Victims among the 17 were 19th-ranked Florida (97-67), 10th-ranked Missouri, Louisiana State and Georgia Tech twice, 80-75 in Honolulu and 103-92 in double-overtime at the Assembly Hall.

In the annual encounter in St. Louis, Mizzou coach Norm Stewart was by now doing everything possible to end the Illini hex: traveling the same day, traveling the day before, altering practice times, staying in different hotels, changing restaurants. He would have taken a dog sled and cold sandwiches if it worked.

When Doug Smith, Byron Irvin and the Tigers broke out to an 18-point lead, Stewart's adjustments seemed to be working. But Battle (28 points) and Hamilton (21) brought the sixth-ranked Illini roaring back for an 87-84 victory that remains the UI's central jewel in the growing St. Louis bracelet. Battle was never better than that night.

"We took Missouri's best punch in the first half, and we made a furious close before halftime," said Bardo. "In the locker room, we felt we had them. I couldn't believe the type of athlete Doug Smith was. We couldn't stop him. But Kenny put on his cape and did what he did all season."

Far from weary, the Illini traveled to Louisiana State and hit the Tigers with their full salvo just three days later, steamrolling them 127-100. It was the most UI points in a game, the most field goals (53), and the most points in the Pete Maravich Assembly Center. The Illini shot 73 percent for 32 minutes before Henson cleared the bench, and even they were hot.

"We had 61 points at the half, and then we just exploded," said Henson. "In a short period of time, we had 100. Then the second team went in and shot better than the first team. It was an unbelievable game, and it was played the same day that John Mackovic was named athletic director."

"It was good of Lou to put in a few subs so they could get their three-pointers," quipped LSU coach Dale Brown, referring to P.J. Bowman and his two treys.

Gill scored 27, Hamilton added 24, Battle went for 17, Anderson chipped in 16, both Bardo and Liberty went for 12, and Larry Smith dealt out eight assists.

continued on page 173

A thing of beauty: Nick Anderson displays how the Illini got their new nickname. Dick Vitale, never short on catchphrases, coined the term "Flying Illini." ▶

GREATEST GAMES
(NO. 6) ILLINOIS 87, (NO. 10) MISSOURI 84
DECEMBER 19, 1988 • ST. LOUIS ARENA, ST. LOUIS, MISSOURI

ILLINOIS BATTLES BACK FOR BORDER WAR VICTORY

The sixth-ranked undefeated Fighting Illini faced their first major test of the season in the annual Border War game against the tenth-ranked Missouri Tigers, and 17 minutes into the ball game it seemed as if they were going to fail that test miserably.

Behind Chicago product Byron Irvin, who scored 16 points in the first 14 minutes of the game, Missouri raced out to a 39-21

▲ *Lowell Hamilton (left) and Kenny Battle (right) hoist the Braggin' Rights trophy after battling back to defeat Missouri 87-84 in the annual Border War.*

Mark Jones

lead with just over four minutes to play in the first half. The Illini were being embarrassed and it looked like they were going to be run out of the building.

"We had two ways to go when we fell down 18," said Illinois forward Kenny Battle. "We could get beat by 40 points or we could man up and show all of the Illinois fans that this team was going to be special—so don't ever give up on us."

Even down 18, the Illini refused to panic.

"We were never ever worried," remembered Kendall Gill. "I don't know if you ever saw Secretariat run in the Kentucky Derby, but he started out in last and all of the sudden he pushed some button and boom he won the Derby in record time. That's exactly what we did. When we fell down big we just said, 'All right, we have spotted them a big enough lead so now let's go get them.'"

The Illinois players might have been the only ones in the building who felt they still had a chance. The Tigers sure didn't.

"[The Missouri players] were running off at the mouth the entire first half saying, 'We have this game and it's over now,'" recalled Illinois forward Nick Anderson. "I just remember telling each and every one of them that this game is far from over."

First it was a Bardo three-pointer from the top of the key and minutes later Marcus Liberty hit a lay-up to cut the lead to 13. The Illinois defense became suffocating; while Missouri couldn't buy a bucket, the Illini continued to chop into the lead.

After Bardo hit one of two from the free throw line, Liberty put in a short jumper off a rebound, and to cap the run, Battle drilled a three pointer. Illinois finished the half on an 11-0 run to cut the lead to seven as they headed into the locker room.

"When we got to the locker room we knew we were going to win," said Illinois assistant coach Mark Coomes. "The run we made at the end of the half completely changed the momentum of the game and when the second half started we were ready to go."

The Illini were ready to go and more specifically they were ready to run and gun. The Illini came out flying, running up and down the floor on offense and pressing on defense. After two Lowell

continued from page 170

Hamilton jumpers and two Gill lay-ups, the Illini tied the game at 45 on a Battle put back off a rebound.

"Our conditioning played such a huge part in that comeback, because when we came out in the second half we ran Missouri's tongues out of their mouths," remembered Anderson, who only had seven points in the ballgame. "They didn't know what hit them and you could just see their legs coming out from under them. They just couldn't handle it and couldn't withstand what we were putting on them."

The Illini took their first lead of the half with 11:16 remaining on a Marcus Liberty three-pointer right in front of the Illinois bench.

For the Illini, the second half became the Kenny Battle show. He muscled, fought, and scrapped to score 19 points in the half and finish with 26 in the ballgame.

With two minutes left to play the Illini led by four, but a Lee Coward three-pointer and a Doug Smith dunk with one minute remaining gave the Tigers an 84-83 lead. After getting fouled with 26 seconds remaining, Battle calmly went to the line and sank both to give Illinois a one-point lead.

When Missouri turned it over on its final possession, the Illini completed one of the greatest comebacks in school history and one of the best games in the history of the Illinois-Missouri Border War.

"That win showed how explosive that team was," said Lou Henson.

They showed to the country that they were a team to be reckoned with, but more importantly, they proved to their fans that you could never give up on the 1988-89 Flying Illini.

"We expected to be that good because we had worked our tails off in the preseason," said Bardo. "We knew we had a special group, and the memory of Villanova haunted us."

Dunks were coming faster than the fans could count them. Hamilton slammed them down, Anderson tore out the nets, Battle southpawed his gorilla-style stuffs, and Gill electrified the crowd with left-handed breakaways.

In the Rainbow Classic after Christmas, with Illinois nursing a 74-73 lead on Georgia Tech, Anderson knocked in his own shot and blocked a Tech attempt to preserve the 80-75 win. Against Hawaii in the final, Anderson scored 26 points and Battle topped him with 29 to down the hosts, 96-87.

The Flying Illini posted three double-figure wins against Michigan State, Wisconsin, and No. 6 Michigan to open the Big Ten, then captured their school-record 17th straight victory on the 22nd of January in a double-overtime win against Georgia Tech. That propelled the Illini up one notch to No. 1 in the polls for the first time in 36 years and 952 games. It took 50 minutes of intense action to repulse Georgia Tech a second time. Dennis Scott was the long-shooting star for Tech, cashing 29 points. Battle countered with 25 points as five Illini hit double figures in an uphill struggle from a 16-point deficit at the start of the second half. Anderson broke the last tie (84-84) with a trey early in the second overtime, and Bardo came right behind with a short jumper in the 103-92 finish.

"What I remember is the Kenny Battle baseline dunk on the whole Tech team—the best I ever saw. His three-point play ignited us late in the second half," said Bardo.

"But we went from a highest high to a lowest low when we saw Kendall in tears in the locker room."

Gill had a stress fracture and would be sidelined for 12 games. Henson fretted about being ranked No. 1, and with good reason. With a target on their back and Gill on the sideline, the '89 Illini lost three of the next four to Minnesota, Purdue and Iowa in a series of tight games. So, the No. 1 ranking lasted only a week. By the time the 1-3 stretch was over, Illinois had fallen to No. 7 in the rankings. The three early Big Ten losses also meant that the Illini would have a difficult road to travel if they were going to capture the conference championship.

continued on page 175

GREATEST GAMES
(NO. 2) ILLINOIS 103, GEORGIA TECH 92
JANUARY 22, 1989 • ASSEMBLY HALL, CHAMPAIGN, ILLINOIS

ILLINOIS WINS 17TH STRAIGHT TO GO NO. 1

On January 19, 1989, Illini fans were glued to their television sets watching Duke play North Carolina in Durham. When the polls were released that week, the Blue Devils, who along with Illinois were the nation's only undefeated teams, sat just a few votes ahead of Illinois.

It wouldn't be for long. North Carolina demolished Duke that evening 91-71 and the stage was set for Illinois to garner the top spot in the polls.

"We certainly knew about it heading into the game," remembered forward Kenny Battle. "All we had to do on Sunday was win and then Monday we would be the No. 1 team in the country."

It was the talk of Champaign-Urbana all week long, but the opponent coming in for the matinee on Super Bowl Sunday was not going to be a pushover. Illinois had defeated the Georgia Tech Yellow Jackets earlier in the year, 80-75, in the Rainbow Classic in Honolulu, Hawaii. It was a hotly contested game that saw both teams' stars play extremely well. By the time they were getting ready to meet three weeks later in the Assembly Hall, the Illini were well aware of the challenge that lay ahead of them.

"We knew right away that Georgia Tech had a chance of beating us," said reserve forward Marcus Liberty. "At the same time we knew we had the talent to match-up with them since we had handled them earlier in the season."

The Tech line-up featured the likes of Dennis Scott, Tom Hammonds and Brian Oliver, who combined to score 57 of the team's 75 points against the Illini in Hawaii.

"We knew they were going to be really hungry to get us back," remembered Lowell Hamilton, who had hurt Tech with 22 points in the first match-up. "I had played in a lot of All-American high school games with Tom Hammonds and I knew he would be ready because he was a fighter."

The atmosphere in the Assembly Hall was electric. The fans entered the building knowing this could be the day that the Illini finally reached the top of the polls.

"The atmosphere was incredible," said walk-on Mark Steinberg. "It was Super Bowl Sunday, the whole nation was watching on television, and everyone was pumped up because of that."

Georgia Tech was ready and the Illini sputtered out of the gate. Before they even realized what hit them, Scott nailed five straight jumpers for 11 points to give the Ramblin' Wreck an early 16-8 lead. The Illini fought back and cut the lead to three with seven minutes remaining, but Tech finished the half on an 18-7 run to take a 14-point cushion into the locker room.

Ten seconds into the second half, Georgia Tech expanded their lead to 16 points on a Hammonds lay-up. Suddenly, things were looking extremely bleak for Illinois. After two Nick Anderson free throws, it was Bardo to Battle and then Anderson to Hamilton on back-to-back alley-oops that cut the lead to 10, forcing Georgia Tech to call a time-out and re-energizing the crowd.

"They came out on fire from the field in the first half, but in the second half we were flying around," remembered Illinois assistant coach Mark Coomes. "Everybody was all over the court to intercept balls, make threes, and throw down dunks."

The Illini kept scratching and clawing and eventually cut the lead to three on a Kenny Battle driving lay-up with six minutes remaining. The Flying Illini took their first lead just a few minutes later when Bardo knocked down a three from the left wing. The Illini held a two point edge with one minute remaining, but Tom Hammonds hit a short turnaround jumper in the lane to tie it up at 74 and the game headed to overtime.

On the scramble after that Hammonds shot went up, the Illini lost star guard Kendall Gill for the rest of the game—and a lot longer.

"I was trying to go for a rebound and my foot got caught with someone else's and twisted the wrong way," recalled Gill. "I knew my foot was broken and it ended up that I broke the fifth metatarsal. I tried to play on but the pain was too much."

Without Gill, the Illini fell down four with 2:27 remaining in the overtime. But four free throws by Bardo tied the game again at 82. Georgia Tech got the final shot of the period. Dennis Scott missed, his attempt falling right into the hands of Tech center Johnny McNeil. It looked as if he would have an easy game-clinch-

continued from page 173

ing lay-up but as he went up to take the shot, Battle swooped in to block it with both hands to preserve the tie. With the fans in the Assembly Hall exhausted, the Illini knew they had Georgia Tech right where they wanted them.

"Our conditioning played a huge factor in that game," remembered Nick Anderson, who finished the game with 18 points. "When we got ready to step on the floor for the second overtime we knew they didn't have much more left in the tank."

Not only was Georgia Tech running out of gas, but Oliver and Hammonds had fouled out. A minute into the second overtime, Anderson drilled a three from the left wing to give the Illini an 87-84 lead. Illinois never looked back. Bardo nailed a jumper in the lane, Hamilton hit one of two from the line, Larry Smith sunk two foul shots, and Battle put in an acrobatic lay-up.

The Illini pulled away, 94-84, sending the Assembly Hall into a state of euphoria. Before the fans could start their chant of "We're Number One" the Illini had to put the icing on the cake. Battle got the ball on the left wing off a pass from Smith and took it towards the rim.

"He went up for the dunk over 6-5 David Whitmore and it looked like he had gears going up," remembered manager Ryan Baker. "I don't know what he did or how he did it, but it seemed like the guy was going to block Kenny's shot until he hit that switch. [Battle] threw it down with his right hand over him, got fouled, and our bench and the Assembly Hall erupted."

"He dunked the ball so hard over that guy," said Gill, who called it his favorite Battle moment of all time. "It was unbelievable and it sealed the game."

"I wanted to put it down to end the game," remembered Battle. "That play put us over the top, and it was a great feeling because it was a three-point play and we knew after that we were going to be the number-one team in the country come Monday morning."

The Illini ran off 13 consecutive points to take a 97-84 lead with just over a minute remaining; it was celebration time in the Hall. The chants of, "We're number one," began, and just a minute later Larry Smith threw down a dunk off a fast break at the buzzer as the Illini walked away with a thrilling 103-92 victory in double overtime.

Coming away with their 17th victory in a row was a sweet feeling.

"It was tough to sit out those overtimes, but the guys took care of business," said Gill, who scored 19 points before the injury and would miss the next 12 games. "I had to get carried off the court by my teammates, but it was well worth it. We were No. 1!"

After a 72-52 loss—their fourth in Big Ten action—at the hands of an inspired Wisconsin club in Madison, the Illini came together for their most impressive finish since the early '50s. A 10-game win streak began with a shocking 102-75 rout of Purdue and carried through to the end of the Big Ten season with consecutive defeats of No. 3 Indiana (on the road), No. 15 Iowa (at home) and No. 8 Michigan (on the road).

The finish at Indiana was Hollywood-style. After Jay Edwards brought the Hoosiers even at 67-67 with a falling, pressured baseline looper that seemed to curve around the backboard, Anderson took Bardo's long pass and connected from beyond 35 feet to win it, 70-67.

"I took the ball out and we ran a play for Nick, and I threw it as hard as I could. He took a power bounce to evade the defense and used that 40-inch vertical jump to let it fly. It was a jump shot, not a throw. That's the biggest basket and win that I've been a part of, even bigger than Norman's jumper to win at Wisconsin two years earlier."

Gill returned for the Iowa game, a pin holding the fifth metatarsal bone of his left foot. He was one of six Illini in double figures as the UI splattered the Hawkeyes, 118-94, at the Hall thanks to spurts of 12-2 and 16-0 which erased an early 20-10 Iowa lead. Anderson had 29 and the Illini never looked better ... unless it was three days later at Michigan.

In Crisler Arena, facing the eventual national champions, Illinois assured a No. 1 seed by destroying the Wolverines, 89-73, before 13,609 disbelieving Michigan fans. Battle tallied 22 points, and Bardo's long arms held Glen Rice 11 points under his 25-point average.

"Except for the Indiana team in the mid-'70s, that's the best basketball team I've seen in my 16 years at Michigan," said U-M coach Bill Frieder. "If they'd had Gill all season, they could be undefeated."

"I felt as good as I could feel after Michigan," said Bardo. "We didn't show any weakness. We did everything Coach Henson wanted us to do. That was the perfect win going in [to the tournament]."

Despite their inspired play down the stretch, the Flying Illini failed to win a Big Ten crown thanks to those early Big Ten losses. Their 14-4 record landed them in second place behind Indiana.

Mark Jones

Entering the NCAA tournament ranked No. 3 in the nation, Illinois rolled past McNeese State and Ball State in Indianapolis, but was just one of four quality teams in the NCAA regional at Minneapolis. Louisville, Syracuse and Missouri—also in Illinois' bracket—were packed with future pros. The four competing teams sported no less than 13 future first-round NBA draft picks. This did not include Syracuse star Sherman Douglas, who was the first pick in the second round in 1989. Few regionals have been blessed with so much talent.

During tuneups the previous day, Battle slipped on a water spot and bruised his knee. He was up much of the night with trainer Rod Cardinal icing his leg, sleeping only from midnight to 5 a.m.

"Battle's knee was bruised from smacking the hard floor," said Cardinal. "The pit of my stomach went out when I heard it. We started icing him like crazy, and giving him Tylenol. The Minnesota trainers brought an exercise bike to the court so he could keep it warm. We basically nursed him through the game, using him for a segment in the first half and another segment in the second half."

Against 12th-ranked Louisville, Anderson carried a heavy load with 24 points and Marcus Liberty filled in nicely with 14 points and eight rebounds in a stirring 83-69 verdict. Battle scored just four points in 15 minutes but the Illini received a big lift from Larry Smith, who drew Henson's plaudits for "running the team."

That brought up No. 7 Syracuse, a convincing conqueror of Missouri. In addition to Battle's injury, Hamilton had a sore ankle. Just as Efrem Winters was limited five years earlier against Kentucky, Hamilton had landed on Felton Spencer's foot and was forced to leave the Louisville game with a swollen ankle.

"Battle and Hamilton were roommates," said Cardinal, "so I visited their room every few hours to give them treatments."

▲ *Center Lowell Hamilton stepped up his production for his senior season, the Illini's run to the Final Four. Hamilton averaged 13.6 points and 5.7 rebounds for a deep, talented team.*

Mark Jones

Ervin Small stepped in to share time at center against future pros Derrick Coleman and Billy Owens, and Battle (28 points) and Anderson (24) teamed up for an astounding 89-86 defeat of the Orangemen. The Illini never had a more impressive, more courageous pair of NCAA games than those two in Minneapolis.

"Growing up, I had watched a lot of Final Fours, and to have the opportunity to get there made it the biggest victory I was ever involved in," said Bardo.

In Seattle, with 39,187 on hand in the Kingdome, Illinois faced No. 10 Michigan a third time. This time around the Wolverines were coached by assistant Steve Fisher, who had replaced Frieder after Frieder was fired by athletic director Bo Schembechler for announcing

◄ *Kendall Gill lays the ball in with ease against Syracuse during the NCAA Tournament. When the 1988-89 Illini lost Gill to a stress fracture in his foot in late January, the team struggled through a three-week slump that saw them drop from No. 1 to No. 7 in the AP polls. Gill returned at the end of the Big Ten season to ease the team's transition into the tournament.*

continued on page 179

GREATEST MOMENTS
(NO. 8) ILLINOIS 70, (NO. 3) INDIANA 67

MARCH 5, 1989 • ASSEMBLY HALL, BLOOMINGTON, INDIANA

ANDERSON'S BUZZER-BEATER ARRESTS HOOSIER HEARTS

The Champaign-Urbana News-Gazette

▲ *An exhilarated Nick Anderson leaps into the air after his 35-foot jumper at the buzzer defeated Indiana on its home court.*

It was a classic back-and-forth battle between two of the best teams in the country. With a win, the Indiana Hoosiers would clinch the Big Ten title. But with 17 seconds left the Illini were clinging to a two-point lead. There was no doubt where the ball was going on Indiana's final possession.

Sophomore Hoosier guard Jay Edwards had already nailed two game-winning shots against Purdue and Michigan earlier in the season and was regarded as the best clutch player in the entire country.

With 10 seconds remaining Edwards, being guarded by Nick Anderson, got the ball from point guard Lyndon Jones. He drove hard left to the baseline and was forced back by Lowell Hamilton. With his foot inches from being out of bounds, he faded back and threw a high-arching shot over the outstretched hands of Hamilton into the tense air of Indiana's Assembly Hall.

"I swear that tear drop floater he threw up almost hit the ceiling of the Assembly Hall," remembered Illinois manager Ryan Baker. "It came down and didn't touch the rim at all."

Edwards had performed another miracle. Shooting from behind the backboard, he had tied the game at 67 with a virtually impossible shot which erupted the home crowd in celebration.

As the ball dropped through the hoop, Steve Bardo was aware enough to signal a time-out to official Ed Hightower, and a stunned Illinois group—barely able to hear their coach speak over the roar of the crowd—headed back to the huddle to draw up a final play.

"When he hit that shot, the crowd was going crazy," recalled Nick Anderson. "I just remember thinking that the game wasn't over until the buzzer went off."

There were two seconds left on the clock and Coach Henson's play called for Anderson to come off a screen and receive a pass from Bardo. Kenny Battle was going to set a screen for Bardo to give him some room, but Indiana Coach Bob Knight didn't have anybody guard the in-bounds. Battle dropped back and Indiana decided to double Larry Smith at half court. He became the perfect decoy. Henson gave one last bit of instructions to Anderson before they left the huddle.

"We told Nick that when he got the ball off the catch to make sure to take a bounce before he shot it," remembered Henson. "He was a much better shooter off the dribble than from a stationary position."

continued from page 177

Bardo got the ball, slapped it once and launched it all the way down the court.

"Bardo threw a strike," said Baker. "He put it right where Nick wanted to catch it."

Right before Bardo threw the pass, Anderson came off a double screen from Hamilton and Battle.

"When Kenny and Lowell set the screen on Jay Edwards, I came off of it wide open," recalled Anderson, who caught the pass, took a hard dribble with the left hand, and then rose up for a 35-foot jumper. "When I released it, you could see the rotation on the ball. It felt so good and the whole arena was dead quiet."

The ball seemed to hang in the air forever. As the clock struck all zeroes the ball simultaneously dropped through the rim hitting nothing but the net.

"When that ball went in I was like 'Oh my God,'" said Anderson. "It was a feeling like no other and the best feeling I have ever had on a basketball court."

The shot fell in right in front of the Illinois bench. The Assembly Hall went dead quiet as Anderson's teammates mobbed him almost immediately.

"When they piled on me it was the greatest feeling in the world," remembered Anderson.

As the Illini were celebrating, Coach Nagy took one quick look at the Indiana bench.

"I saw Coach Knight and you talk about going from jubilation to depression," recalled Nagy. "His face was 80 miles long and his chin basically hit the floor."

Edwards thought he had done it again, but this time he left a few seconds on the clock. One good miracle deserves another, and the Illini got theirs just in the Nick of time.

that he had accepted the Arizona State job. What followed was an epic struggle with 33 lead changes, not counting ties. Battle outscored Rice 29-28, but Michigan prevailed 83-81 as Sean Higgins knocked in Terry Mills' miss with only two seconds remaining.

"Battle was in great shape in Seattle, but Hamilton was never more than 80 percent," said Cardinal. "Against that Michigan front line, Hamilton needed to be able to jump, and he couldn't. He tweaked it again during the game and we had to re-tape it. That's when I got locked in the training room. I pounded until a security guard returned to let me out."

continued on page 182

▲ Forward Marcus Liberty didn't fully blossom until his playing time increased during the 1989-90 season, when he averaged 17.8 points per game. But his contributions were a key factor in the Flying Illini's depth.

GREATEST GAMES
(NO. 3) ILLINOIS 89, (NO. 7) SYRACUSE 86
MARCH 26, 1989 • HUBERT H. HUMPHREY METRODOME, MINNEAPOLIS, MINNESOTA

ILLINOIS HEADS TO THE FINAL FOUR

Mark Jones

▲ *Illinois celebrates its 89-86 victory over Syracuse at the Metrodome in Minneapolis.*

As they arrived in Minneapolis for the Midwest Regional, the Illini knew they had a very tough task ahead of them.

"We had Syracuse, Missouri and Louisville all going up to our regional," remembered assistant coach Mark Coomes. "You could have taken those four teams to Seattle and it would have been a great Final Four."

The trip north for the Illini looked disastrous from the get-go. With only a few minutes left in their first practice in the Metrodome, senior Kenny Battle slipped on a wet spot caused by a leak in the roof and severely sprained his knee. He was going to be extremely limited in the game against Louisville and just when it looked like things couldn't get worse, three minutes into the game Lowell Hamilton badly twisted his right ankle and would be out for the remainder of the game.

With Battle playing only 15 minutes and Hamilton just 13, the Illini gutted out a very impressive 83-69 victory over the Cardinals.

"I have never had a team in all of my years in coaching play with more emotion than we did that night," recalled head coach Lou Henson. "[Louisville] blocked 13 of our shots, but we never backed down and kept taking it at them. It was one of the greatest victories I have ever been associated with."

The win over Louisville set the stage for an epic battle against a very talented Syracuse team.

"They had Derrick Coleman, Sherman Douglas, Stevie Thompson and Billy Owens. They were loaded," remembered assistant coach Jimmy Collins. "There was a lot of trash talked before the game and some guys were billing it as New York against Chicago."

The hobbling Illini weren't going to be 100 percent for the game, but there was no doubt they were mentally prepared to play.

"I vividly remember the morning of the game when we went to our pre-game meal," said Collins. "Our guys were really quiet and it was almost like they were ghosts. There was almost nothing said and you could tell they were going to be about business."

Six minutes into the ball game, the game was tied at 13 but Syracuse quickly put together a 12-0 run to take a commanding 25-13 lead. On a Billy Owens jumper from the top of the key with 6:47 left to play in the half, the Orangemen took a 13-point lead, which was their largest in the game.

"They got up on us big in the first half, but we were never worried" said Nick Anderson. "We had made it a habit of coming back and we always believed that the game wasn't over until the buzzer went off."

The Illini ran together their own 8-0 run seconds later with Larry Smith capping it off with a lay-up on the right side, but Syracuse held them off to hold a 46-39 lead heading into the locker room.

The momentum swung immediately in the Illini's favor to start the second half. Anderson put in a short bank shot from the right side, Battle got a steal off the in-bounds, and Kendall Gill knocked down a three from the left corner to cut the lead to two. The next 10 minutes was a classic back-and-forth battle with the Illini tying the game for the first time at the 10:55 mark on a Gill three. After seven minutes of exchanging baskets and leads, the Illini built a three-point lead with three minutes remaining.

Off a long rebound, the Illini started one of their patented breaks. It was Anderson to Battle and Battle up for the lay-up. When Battle's shot came off the rim Gill flew through the air to slam it back down with one hand over Stevie Thompson to shake the dome and give the Illini an 83-78 lead.

The Illini seemed in control, but four missed free throws in the last minute gave Syracuse a chance. After a Sherman Douglas three from the top of the circle, the Illini were clinging to a one-point lead and the Orangemen fouled Marcus Liberty. The freshman went to the line, missed the front end of the one and one off the back rim, but Anderson tipped it back to Gill and this time Battle was fouled. Battle calmly went to the line and knocked down both free throws.

Syracuse rushed the ball down the floor and with nine seconds left Thompson pulled up from the top of the key, but left it short. Smith tipped the rebound into the hands of Gill. Before he could get fouled, Gill launched the ball up the floor to Battle who took it up towards the rim as the buzzer sounded. For the first time since 1952, the Fighting Illini were headed to the Final Four. The bench swarmed the court and the celebration was on.

"It was real intense," recalled Battle, who was rolling around on the Dome floor with Bardo. "This was what we had set out to do from day one in the preseason and all that suffering, all that yelling, and all that pain finally paid off."

"When the buzzer sounded it was such an incredible moment," recalled Gill, who—still bleeding from a Coleman elbow earlier in the game—was on the floor in an embrace with

▲ *Coach Henson celebrates with Kenny Battle (left) and Nick Anderson (right) after advancing to the Final Four.*

Anderson and Smith. "Jumping all over each other on the floor is something I will never forget and it was the best moment I have ever had in basketball."

The party didn't stop in Minneapolis and when the Illini finally arrived back in Champaign the celebration continued.

"The airport was just packed with people and the streets were mobbed," remembered Coomes.

"It was crazy to see the effect it had on the campus and it really hit home then," said Hamilton. "It was almost like being a rock star."

Battle, still suffering from a bum knee, finished with 28 points while Nick Anderson put together an incredible 24-point, 16-rebound performance.

"Derrick Coleman was 6-11 and played in the NBA for many years," remembered assistant coach Dick Nagy. "Nick dominated Derrick Coleman that afternoon and his performance, especially on the boards, was unbelievable."

It was a season filled with adversity that capped a trip 37 years in the making. It was almost fitting that the Illini dealt with the injuries they were forced to endure up in Minneapolis, because nothing was going to stop this team from achieving their "Battle 4 Seattle."

continued from page 179

Bardo said the team was "heartbroken at first, to be so close to a national championship and not get it." But the response of a packed house of Illini fans in Champaign reminded of what a special season it had been.

"The Assembly Hall was dimly lit," recalled Cardinal, "and when the team came out of the tunnel, the spotlight brought into view the 'yellow brick road' theme. It was a special moment when Lou and Mary came out arm in arm."

The magical season ended early, but the memories remain fond for many fans of the 31-5 Flying Illini, who finished the season ranked third in the nation.

MAINTAINING THE MAGIC PROVES TOO DIFFICULT

With Hamilton completing his eligibility, Anderson turning pro and Larry Smith ineligible in 1989-90, the trio of Bardo, Gill and Liberty went to work with a new group including freshman Andy Kaufmann and junior college centers Andy Kpedi and Rodney Jones. Again, the Illini started fast with 11 straight wins and a No. 4 AP ranking.

"Florida was ranked in the Top 25, and the win there (74-69) was a boost for us," said Bardo. "Also, the win (78-61) over Temple at home was big when we shut down Mark Macon."

Liberty scored 20 points and Gill added 17, but both Henson and Temple coach John Chaney lauded Bardo for his nine points, nine rebounds, six assists and strong defense.

"Bardo is first class," said Chaney.

The annual Border War on December 20 pitted No. 5 Illinois against No. 4 Missouri, and the Illini exploded in a 101-93 win.

"To top 100 points in the Border War was special, and Kendall and I finished 4-0 against Missouri," said Bardo.

But Bardo and Gill were being investigated by the NCAA based on their purchase of personal cars from a Decatur dealership. The NCAA had been tipped off that something about the paperwork might be improper.

"Two hours before the Big Ten opener at home against Wisconsin, we didn't know whether we would play," said Bardo. "They dropped the charge. I never found out why. I didn't ask. I was just happy to be playing.

"My car was a $4,000 used Corolla, and my parents had the financial means to pay in cash. My dad, Harold, was a professor at Southern Illinois University at the time, and later became interim athletic director there. My parents were upset because the NCAA went into their financial records without their knowledge. As for Gill's part of it, I never talked to him or his parents about it."

This was a small part of a broader NCAA investigation related to the recruitment of Chicagoan Deon Thomas, who had chosen Illinois over Iowa and was sitting out as a freshman that season.

With Gill and Bardo on board for the Wisconsin game, Illinois won 73-59 as a fired-up Gill went seven for seven from the field—his way of responding to the NCAA.

"The rest of the Big Ten season was up and down, back and forth," said Bardo. "We could never win three in a row. Probably the most satisfying, the most emotional was Senior Day against Iowa. We clobbered them, 118-85, and it was a realization for Kendall and me that our Illini careers were pretty much over. Before the game, our four years flashed before our eyes. That was our best game of the season by far."

Bardo and Gill closed the Big Ten season with a 69-63 victory at Indiana, making them 6-2 against the Hoosiers. Gill hit late free throws to clinch the victory and win the Big Ten scoring title. He was the UI's first individual champion since Andy Phillip in 1943.

But for the third year in four, Bardo and Gill left the NCAA tournament prematurely, losing to Dayton 88-86 in Austin, Texas, in the opening game.

"I just remember that game as one where nothing went right," said Bardo. "I was called for an intentional foul (against Norm Grevey) before halftime and it inflamed their coach and the fans. Grevey was on a breakaway, and he went up on the left side and tried to switch in mid-air to go right. I was going to foul him hard but he was in an awkward position and he hit the floor. That wasn't a good way to end it."

continued on page 185

▲ Memorabilia from the Illini's 1989 trip to the Final Four—the "Battle for Seattle".

GREATEST GAMES
(NO. 18) ILLINOIS 118, IOWA 85
MARCH 4, 1990 • ASSEMBLY HALL, CHAMPAIGN, ILLINOIS

ILLINOIS SMOKES IOWA IN WAKE OF DEON THOMAS INVESTIGATION

The wounds were wide open on March 4, 1990, and everybody associated with the Illinois basketball program couldn't wait until Iowa arrived at the Assembly Hall. The always-heated Iowa-Illinois rivalry turned vicious the previous June when the NCAA, acting on a complaint by the Iowa coaching staff, began an investigation into Illinois' recruitment of Deon Thomas. The investigation scarred the season, forced Thomas to redshirt, and placed a black mark on the Illinois basketball program and assistant coach Jimmy Collins.

Illinois lost a 69-67 heartbreaker to Iowa in late January at Iowa City, and by the time Senior Day rolled around the Illini were ready for revenge.

"The hype and intensity around that game was like none other," recalled junior forward Marcus Liberty. "There was a lot of frustration built up between the two teams and every time we played them we wanted to beat them real bad."

The Illinois crowd was out for blood. They were angry, frustrated and upset with the events of the season and it didn't help that their team had a rough go with the fans up in Iowa City.

"I noticed over the years watching the Illinois fans that if someone said anything bad about the team or any of our players they were going to find out and let the other team have it," said Liberty. "They knew how Iowa treated us when we went there and they were going to let them have it."

You could feel the tense atmosphere around campus as the game approached. It got so intense that Coach Henson and his seniors asked for the fans to be rowdy, but also to stay orderly. Iowa coach Tom Davis got a police escort to and from the court, Iowa stayed over in Peoria the night before the game, and they were one guy short on arriving in Champaign.

"[Tom Davis] didn't let Bruce Pearl come to that game," remembered Collins. "Lou tried to keep me from going to Iowa, but I told him there was no way in hell I wasn't going."

At 3:07 p.m. when the ball was thrown up for the opening tip, Iowa might as well have left to go home. They were intimidated,

scared, and the Illinois players didn't waste any time taking it to them. Ervin Small came out fired up and scored the first four Illinois points on two short jumpers in the lane.

"Ervin Small and I were really close and it was like we had a big brother-little brother relationship," said Collins. "He played that night with a real vengeance."

The Illini led 8-6 with 16 minutes to play in the first half before they put on one of the most fierce and impressive runs in the history of the program. Gill scored six points, Kaufmann and Liberty picked up nine more, Bardo added three, Rodney Jones chipped in with two, and by the time the smoke cleared the Illini went on a 29-6 run and enjoyed a 37-12 lead.

During the run, the Hawkeyes looked lost. They missed six consecutive free throws and shot an abysmal 29 percent from the field. By the time the first half ended, the Illini had built a commanding 48-23 lead.

As the Illinois fans chanted, "Run up the score," it only got worse for the Hawkeyes in the second half. The Illini remained red hot and staked their first 30-point lead on a Bowman three from the left wing. With two minutes left, Bardo knocked down the teams' 13th three-point shot of the game to give Illinois a 41-point lead.

Luckily for the Hawkeyes the final buzzer was about to sound. Illinois finished with six players in double figures, with Gill's 25-point, seven-steal, and six-assist senior-day performance leading the way to a 118-85 victory. The Hawkeyes missed 16 free throws and turned the ball over 26 times on their way to the worst drubbing in the long history of the series.

"It was a game of emotions, and for me I was so angry going in that a lot of the details of that game slipped past me," said Collins reflecting on that game almost 15 years later. "I harbored a lot of anger and it almost caused me to go to counseling. It was a game that pacified me somewhat, because we beat them pretty bad."

By the end of the game, Iowa was right back where they wanted to be all along—on a bus back to Iowa City.

continued from page 182

Even with the crowd of 11,000 vocally against them, the Illini pushed Dayton to the end with Gill scoring 28, Liberty contributing 18 and Andy Kaufmann adding 15. But Bardo had six turnovers and went zero for six on three-pointers. The loss typified a 21-8 season (11-7 in conference) that showed promise—the Illini were ranked as high as No. 4 in the nation before finishing the season ranked No. 18—but is remembered for an NCAA investigation and the innuendo surrounding it.

Gill, who finished the season with a 20.0 scoring average, and Liberty, who finished with a 17.8 scoring mark, both entered the NBA. Gill is entering his 15th season in 2004 after spending the previous 14 years with Charlotte (first round draft choice), Seattle, New Jersey, Miami, Minnesota and Chicago. Gill carries a 13.5 career scoring average into the 2004-05 season. Liberty was drafted in the second round by Denver and spent four years in the NBA with the Nuggets and the Pistons, posting a career scoring average of 7.3.

Mark Jones

▲ *Kendall Gill throws it down with his left hand. Gill flourished as a senior on a 21-8 Illini club, setting career high averages in scoring (20.0), rebounds (4.9), and steals (2.2).*

$3.00

UNIVERSITY
OF **ILLINOIS**

DEC. 1, 1990

versus

EASTERN ILLINOIS

ASSEMBLY HALL

CHAMPAIGN

ILLINOIS

Illinois-Chicago • December 4, 1993 • Assembly Hall

BASKETBALL

$2.00

ILLINOIS

BASKETBALL

VS. PENN STATE
January 21, 1993
Assembly Hall
Champaign, Ill.

$2.00

CHAPTER FIFTEEN

TURBULANCE LEADS TO NCAA GROUNDING

1990-91—1993-94

Like Nick Anderson the year before, lanky Chicagoan Marcus Liberty turned pro after his junior season, and the Illini fell from the national spotlight in 1990-91. Alton's Larry Smith, who sat out the previous season, was the only member of the Gill-Anderson-Bardo class still on the court. Smith and Springfield's Rennie Clemons were the guards for a front line of Deon Thomas, junior college transfer Andy Kpedi and Jacksonville's Andy Kaufmann.

Henson's revamped unit was stung by two early losses. The first came at the hands of Nebraska, 100-73, in San Juan. Then, with Smith sidelined by an ankle sprain, UI-Chicago embarrassed the Illini, 71-60, on a 27-point outburst by 5-7 guard Tony Freeman.

"That's our biggest win in four years," said UIC coach Bob Hallberg.

Smith returned for 23 points, seven rebounds and six assists, and Kaufmann bagged a personal-high 40 points in a 106-87 rout of Eastern Illinois. And Kaufmann, a spinning, muscling forward, topped that with 46 more points against Wisconsin-Milwaukee, giving him 86 points in three days ... but he still took a back seat to Milwaukee's Von McDade who accumulated nine treys and 11 free throws in an

Assembly Hall record 50-point show. In that game, Thomas scored the most overlooked 34 points in UI history. By the way, Illinois won, 120-116, in overtime.

"That was a back-and-forth battle between the two guys, Kaufmann and McDade, to see who could top who, not something Coach Henson was happy about," said Tom Michael, then a UI freshman from Carlyle's Class A state champions. Already signed prior to the state tournament, Michael justified Henson's decision by scoring 45 points against Prairie Central in the IHSA semifinals and 28 vs. Rock Island Alleman in the title game.

Michael still holds the UI school record for three-point accuracy in a season, hitting 49.3 percent as a sophomore in 1992 when he led the Big Ten in all games (49.3) and league games (55.7). He has remained with the Division of Intercollegiate Athletics, now serving as an assistant director in charge of academics.

The most vivid memory from December of 1990, however, was yet to come. In the Illini's eighth consecutive triumph over Missouri, an 84-81 thriller, Kaufmann

Tom Michael (left), Scott Pierce (center), and the rest of the Illini had their hands full when Shaquille O'Neal (right) and No. 10 LSU came to town in 1990. But the big man fouled out and Illinois held on to win, 102-96.

Lou Henson said that Illini guard Rennie Clemons was "the best I've ever coached at penetrating the defense." Despite that claim, the legendary tale of Clemons dunking on LSU's Shaquille O'Neal is untrue.

banged out 33 points. Thomas scored 18 of his 23 points in the second half as Illinois roared from a 41-34 deficit.

"Whatever I said in the last seven years, just put that down, and change the names," grimaced Mizzou coach Norm Stewart in St. Louis. "Is it fun? Oh, it beats a poke in the eye with a sharp stick."

Next came a home date against No. 10 Louisiana State and Shaquille O'Neal, who both proved no match for Rennie Clemons and his 17 second-half points. Like Babe Ruth's fabled "called shot" against the Chicago Cubs, the six-foot Clemons didn't actually do what has been handed down in storybook fashion. He didn't dunk over Shaq. But he did score a soaring three-point play directly in O'Neal's face with 50 seconds to go, fouling out the LSU star and ensuring the 102-96 Illini win.

"Rennie is the best I've ever coached at penetrating the defense and getting the ball in there," said Henson.

"Our defense was keyed around Shaq with someone behind and someone in front," said Michael, "and that put a strain elsewhere defensively. He wasn't nearly the specimen that he is now, but he was still huge.

"I had met him the previous fall when he was on an official visit. When I shook his hand, I thought he was the largest person I ever met. It was an experience to play against him."

But Illinois' defense wasn't ready for the Big Ten opener at No. 5 Indiana, as Calbert Cheaney scored 30 in a 109-74 runaway.

"Cheaney started out by getting six or seven layups, and I think that got him feeling like he could make anything," said Smith, who scored 21 himself.

Three days later, the Illini were smiling again as Kaufmann nailed two late three-pointers and Michael another as the UI rallied from a 59-52 deficit in the last 2:35 to edge Purdue, 63-61 on a Thomas rebound during the final seconds.

"Deon was able to find his way around the basket and to come up with the basketball at the right time," said Michael.

The thrills continued as Illinois nipped Minnesota, 67-66, thanks to Clemons' acrobatic three-point play at the game's conclusion. But Steve Smith popped in 35 points to help Michigan State crack through the UI's home-court advantage, 71-68, and the Illini got another taste of a future pro star when Jim Jackson led 15-0 Ohio State—ranked fourth in the nation—to an 89-55 romp.

"This was the first of two Buckeye championships," said Michael. "They had five guys who could pressure all over the floor."

The Illini were 2-3 in the league when they ignited a six-game win streak at Michigan, winning 72-67 via a 28-point outpouring by the versatile Smith. The veteran playmaker was enjoying his best season, and would be rewarded with the team MVP award. But the Illini, who finished third in the conference with an 11-7 record, were not eligible for postseason play as a result of the NCAA's unspecified "institutional control" violations stemming from the Deon Thomas investigation. The team swept Purdue and Iowa, as well as Michigan and Northwestern, and stood 11-5 before dropping the last two games to Wisconsin and No. 3 Indiana.

Smith had 144 assists, 168 rebounds and a 13.6 scoring average, while Kaufmann averaged 21.3 points per

Mark Jones

▲ Larry Smith was the only holdover in 1990-91 from the recruiting class that netted the Illini Kendall Gill, Stephen Bardo, Nick Anderson and Smith. After sitting out the previous season, Smith contributed 13.6 points, 5.8 rebounds and 5.0 assists per game.

game. Thomas, who shot .577 percent from the field in his redshirt freshman season, average 15.1 points and 6.8 rebounds per game.

A LOSING SEASON

Suffering the pangs of NCAA sanctions, just three years removed from the Final Four, Henson reflected on his personnel losses as he looked on hard times in the fall of 1991. Smith, the last of the Flying Illini, was gone. Kaufmann, who averaged 21.3 points as a sophomore, was ineligible. Jamie Brandon, the state's Mr. Basketball from Chicago King, left the UI's summer bridge program and transferred to Louisiana State. And 6-10 Juwan Howard of Chicago Vocational joined the Fab Five at Michigan. His decision came while Illinois awaited NCAA word on the prolonged investigation.

Henson's chief recruiter, Jimmy Collins, would be withheld from recruiting on the road for more than two

▲ With Andy Kaufmann ineligible, forward Tom Michael stepped into the starting lineup and provided a boost of offense for the Illini during the 1991-92 campaign. On the season, Michael nailed 75 three-point shots on 49.3 percent shooting.

years, and Henson was limited to two scholarships, handing them out to forwards Robert Bennett and Marc Davidson.

"Probably as much as anything, there was frustration," said Michael. "Being in the middle of it, we didn't feel the punishment was fitting. Being Deon's roommate as a freshman, I didn't think what was happening was going to equate to what we ended up getting ... no tournament and the loss of scholarships. That probably held us back until the late '90s, when we finally won the Big Ten title in 1998."

In 1991-92, Illinois sustained only the second losing season under Henson, going 13 for 15. T.J. Wheeler was back after losing eligibility in the second semester of his freshman year, and Michael moved into the front line. The campaign's opening game—a 65-60 loss to future Big Ten member Penn State—set the tone for what developed into a long bumpy ride.

"Temple of Doom" read one headline after a 92-56 loss at Temple that was one of the most decisive in Henson's long career. Mik Kilgore (27 points), Aaron McKie (21) and Eddie Jones (20) left no doubt in serving the Illini their worst loss since 1974.

"First of all, playing in that gym, it was like playing in Huff, and the end balcony seemed so close that you thought you'd hit it with baseline shots. It was bad all around," said Michael.

Missouri not only snapped the UI's eight-game St. Louis streak but did so 61-44. And the Illini needed an overtime to eke out a 94-87 win over UIC, thanks to Thomas' 39 points.

"Deon was so silky smooth on the post," said Michael. "He had a high release that was difficult to block. He was a great teammate. He was even keel, and never negative, even in the circumstances surrounding his first year when he elected to redshirt on his own."

Power forward Deon Thomas (No. 25) rises in the lane for a shot attempt as fellow Illini Robert Bennett readies for a rebound. Throughout his Illini career, Thomas responded well to adversity—whether it was allegations of recruiting violations or Illinois' losing season in 1991-92. As teammate Tom Michael said, Thomas never had a negative attitude.

Mark Jones

Severely overmatched, the Illini played 10 ranked teams in their last 21 games. They defeated just one of the 10, No. 13 Michigan State. During one tough stretch, the Illini lost three games by a total of six points. First, in a 54-53 loss at Minnesota, Henson questioned a foul call on a rebound that sent Dana Jackson to the line for the winning free throw with no time remaining. Wrote Paul Swider of the *Daily Illini:* "For the third time in as many road games, the Illini lost following a disputed call by the officials."

"When you're trying to fight through a season with all the things we couldn't control, it's hard to take when you lose games in that manner," noted Michael.

Then came No. 10 Ohio State in the Assembly Hall. Michael drilled six three-pointers and Thomas scored 26 as Illinois rallied from a deep hole (49-31), only to lose 74-72.

"We struggled, no question, but I think we played hard and competed, as difficult as things were," said Michael.

Next came Northwestern in Evanston. Thomas lost his dribble as he tried to break a 43-43 tie, and Wildcat Cedric Neloms raced down the court with the turnover and banked a once-in-a-lifetime 30-foot trey to end NU's 29-game Big Ten losing streak.

"All six Illini league losses were winnable in the last 20 seconds," reported *The News-Gazette.*

"Once again, we found a way to lose in a crazy way," said Michael. "I was just devastated. We didn't want that streak to end against us.

"It wasn't easy on Coach Henson. You look back at all those off-court things, and our place of real comfort was the court, and that was tough because we were losing so many close games."

The bad luck reversed as Illinois won overtime duels with Purdue and Iowa. In West Lafayette, Thomas converted 14 free throws in a 32-point outburst that felled the Boilermakers 77-71. At the Assembly Hall on February. 23, Hawkeye forward Chris Street, who was killed in a snowy automobile accident the next year, had 12 points and 14 rebounds but the Illini somehow held on in overtime, 77-72. T.J. Wheeler (22 points), Clemons (16), Michael (14) and Thomas (13) joined in a balanced offensive attack.

Illinois' NIT hopes were dashed as No. 2 Indiana, No. 5 Ohio State and Michigan's young Fab Five, ranked No. 14, proved too much for the Illini in early March. The team ended conference play with a 7-11 record in eighth place. Thomas' scoring average improved to 19.3, but that was one of only a few highlights for the weary Illini.

REBOUNDING IN '92

The next season started on a distressful note for Henson, who left the team for four days prior to an Alaska trip due to the death of his son, Lou Henson Jr., in a single-car accident between Urbana and Danville.

"It was a tough situation for anyone to have to deal with," said Michael. "Basketball was and still is everything to Coach Henson, and maybe that helped him get through an extremely difficult time."

Henson announced a starting lineup that included long-shot artist Richard Keene of Collinsville, a McDonald's All-American who chose the UI over Duke. Michael, the seventh-leading three-point shooter in the nation the previous year, opened at the small forward as Kaufmann steadied the grades that cost him the previous season.

Opening in Anchorage, Kaufmann came firing off the bench (18 points) to help Thomas (25) and the Illini edge Dayton in overtime, 86-78. Kaufmann popped 27 more points in a 93-77 rout of Vanderbilt, and the Illini entered a title-game shootout with New Mexico State, where Henson coached before and after his Illini days. The Aggies took advantage of Clemons' absence (thigh bruise) as speedy Sam Crawford erupted with 32 points and 10 assists in a 95-94 win.

"Andy was a one-man offense," said Michael. "You knew when he got rolling, there wasn't much anyone could do to stop him. He was deceivingly quick and his

After sitting out the 1991-92 campaign, forward Andy Kaufmann returned in 1992-93 as the Illini rebounded from a disappointing season. Kaufmann averaged 17.3 points per game in his senior season and nearly went out with a bang in his final home game, coming within two points of defeating Michigan's Fab Five in overtime. ▶

physical strength helped him get to the hole, and he was very good at the free throw line."

Kaufmann's Jacksonville High coach, Mel Roustio, once offered the opinion that no prep in Illinois history made as many fourth-quarter free throws as Kaufmann. The statistics would support that belief. Kaufmann averaged 29.8 points over 106 contests in a four-year prep career, and claimed a national record of 918 free throws while shooting 86 percent from the line. Kaufmann was often unstoppable in one-on-one situations. Henson sometimes complained that when the ball got in his hands, everybody stopped to see what he was going to do. Most of the time it was a headlong drive toward the basket.

Back from Alaska, the Illini edged UI-Chicago 70-68, as Kaufmann followed Henson's orders to foul with the score 70-67. Kenny Williams made one of two free throws with three seconds left as the Illini avoided a possible three-point shot to tie.

Illini fortune wasn't so good in St. Louis as the Missouri Tigers prevailed in a 66-65 squeaker to give Illinois their second loss. Follow-up losses to Texas and Marquette sent the UI into Big Ten play on a three-game losing streak. They promptly turned it around by winning eight of their next 10 games. During that span, Henson earned win No. 600 in an 82-66 lashing of Penn State.

"The loss to Missouri was hard to deal with because of everything that surrounds that game," said Michael. "Then, going to Texas on the day after Christmas, we didn't play well at all."

When fans look back on Assembly Hall games in 1993, none will be relived more often than the February 4 date with Iowa. To begin with, Chris Street had died, reviving Henson's memories of his own son's misfortune. Then too, bitterness lingered from the NCAA sanctions that were initiated when Iowa assistant coach Bruce Pearl taped telephone conversations in 1988 with then-Simeon star Deon Thomas.

Andy Bagnato wrote in the *Chicago Tribune:* "Many at Illinois blame Pearl for setting up Illinois' NCAA probation by taping calls with Thomas. Thomas supposedly acknowledged that he had received financial inducements from the Illini. Thomas later said he did-

n't know he was being taped, and that he was merely agreeing with Pearl in hopes that he'd leave him alone."

There was no mention of this when the NCAA infractions committee passed out two years of probation, generalizing on the reasons in citing "lack of institutional control."

The undercurrent was strong leading into this game. UI fans were steamed up, and the contest was nip and tuck. Keene's trey brought Illinois even at 75-75 but Iowa had seemingly won in the final seconds when a rebound caromed off the shoulder of Thomas into the Iowa basket, putting the Hawkeyes up 77-75. The clock was reset at one-point-five seconds, and Wheeler fired a long pass to Kaufmann who speared the ball on the right sideline, turned left and drained a 30-foot three-pointer to win it.

"Had all those things not happened with Iowa in the previous few years, it wouldn't have been so sweet," said Michael. "But it being Iowa, and the way we were able to get that done, it was an incredible experience to be a part of. I remember running out and being on the bottom of the pile with Rich Keene."

February was not otherwise good to the 1993 Illini, although a double-overtime 78-70 defeat of Purdue assured the Illini of an NCAA slot. It was the sixth straight defeat of Keady's men, the last three in overtime. Kaufmann, who missed the previous trip to Penn State in a dispute with Henson over class attendance and playing time, hit two free throws to tie the Boilermakers at the end of the first overtime and scored 20 overall in his first game back.

With Kaufmann, Clemons and Brooks Taylor playing their final home game, the Illini came within a finger snap of upsetting Michigan's Fab Five. Twenty-one offensive rebounds saved the Wolverines in overtime, 98-97, as Jalen Rose scored 23, Chris Webber added 22, and Juwan Howard and Jimmy King both chipped in 18.

"With Howard and Webber inside, they were so strong," Michael reflected. "That's the thing that stands out. And they were very confident. They weren't afraid to talk to you, especially Rose. That sort of thing happens all the time, but they did more of it.

"With all the hype that surrounded that group, it was fun to compete against them. You always like that

continued on page 197

GREATEST MOMENTS
ILLINOIS 79, (NO. 9) IOWA 78
FEBRUARY 4, 1993 • ASSEMBLY HALL, CHAMPAIGN, ILLINOIS

ANDY KAUFMANN BURIES HAWKEYES AT BUZZER

There's absolutely no way it was supposed to end like this. Fate couldn't be this cruel, especially on their home floor against Iowa. After fighting back the entire game to tie it up on a Richard Keene three-point shot, the Illini saw Acie Earl's 15-foot jumper from the baseline fall short.

What happened next was a miracle for the ninth-ranked Hawkeyes and absolutely devastated the Fighting Illini.

"I remember the shot bounced hard off the side of the rim," said Illinois center Deon Thomas, who was battling for rebounding position with seldom used Hawkeye forward Jim Bartels. "I reached for the ball. It hit my arm, flew back up there and kissed off the backboard and went into the basket [to give Iowa the lead]. I mean what are the chances of something like that happening? I remember thinking did it have to happen in the Iowa game?"

"You could do that a thousand more times and it isn't going to get close to going in," said guard T.J. Wheeler. "When that shot goes in you are done. The game is virtually over, and I was just like, 'You have to be kidding me.'"

With an entire Assembly Hall crowd in shock and the Iowa bench in jubilation, only one guy was aware enough to make sure he got a quick timeout.

"When that ball went in, Rennie Clemons immediately ran to the referee to signal timeout," remembered soon to be hero Andy Kaufmann. "I was in such disbelief that I couldn't have thought about doing that, but Rennie did a great job of saving the game."

With the referees deciding how much time to put back on the clock, the Illinois huddle was the definition of disbelief and disarray.

"Everything was swirling and nobody was really saying too much," recalled Kaufmann, who was pacing back and forth. "I don't think things were really coherent and the coaches were con-fused because they were trying to figure out how much time would be put on the clock."

During the huddle, Kaufmann made eye contact with T.J. Wheeler and immediately they knew what they were going to run.

"For some reason the two practices before that game we worked on that exact play," recalled Wheeler, speaking of a play in which he, a former high school quarterback at Christopher High, was going to be in the in-bounds passer. "It was the first time we ever worked on it in practice and why we did on those two days I will never know."

With the play set, Wheeler walked to the baseline still stunned over the turn of events.

"Before the referee handed me the ball, I was still thinking 'How in the world did this happen?'," remembered Wheeler. "When you are throwing that kind of pass you don't want to throw it out of bounds and you don't want to throw it like a base-ball so there is spin on it."

Being guarded by 6-8 James Winters, Wheeler ran towards the Iowa bench, getting a pick from Clemons. Almost simultaneously on the other end of the court, Kaufmann cut hard toward the Illinois bench using a double screen set by Robert Bennett and Thomas. The next 1.5 seconds have gone down in Illinois basketball folklore.

"T.J. fired a strike to Andy coming off a double screen," recalled reserve guard Gene Cross. "He caught the ball, took one hard dribble, and boom—the shot went up."

About a half a second later the ball dropped through the hoop, hitting nothing but the net.

"It looked good all the way and it felt good all the way," remembered Kaufmann, who was fading back to mid court as the shot went in. "Instantaneously there was this feeling of elation and it was such a big rush."

continued on page 196

continued from page 195

When the shot dropped in the Assembly Hall erupted. It was bedlam on the court as teammates, coaches, and the Orange Krush swarmed to celebrate the miracle shot.

"I made the mistake of falling on my back and I got pinned on the bottom of the pile," recalled Kaufmann. "I remember thinking if this gets any bigger I am never going to get out here. I couldn't move a finger, but it was just great."

"At that exact moment you could hear the eruption all the way in the bowels of the building," remembered Illinois athletic director Ron Guenther, who caught the second half of the game on television in order to watch the officials. "It was amazing and I raced to get to the locker room."

"I don't know who was happier at that moment, Andy Kaufmann or Coach Collins," laughed Wheeler. "Coach Collins came running over to me and we hugged right in front of the Iowa bench. I didn't know if I was going to be able to leave because he wouldn't let go."

In 1.5 seconds, the Illini turned a demoralizing loss into an exhilarating win. The victory was made even more special because it happened against Iowa.

"There's no question that it meant more to us to beat Iowa than any other school," said Illinois forward Tom Michael. "To win the way we did that day was extra sweet."

"The wounds were still open and we were still going through Hell from the investigation," remembered Illinois assistant coach Mark Coomes. "That shot was vindication at its best."

Perhaps Deon Thomas summed the feelings up best when he remembered the moment years later. "When the shot went in I just remember the first thing going through my mind is, 'We got them'. We beat them and we put them out of their misery."

▲ *Andy Kaufmann launches his game-winning shot that defeated No. 9 Iowa 79-78.*

Mark Jones

continued from page 194

challenge. They were the elite group and it was a great challenge that everyone looked forward to."

Michigan enjoyed a 12-2 record against Illinois around the Fab Five period. Due to infractions (large payments by a booster), many of those U-M wins have since been removed from the record.

Illinois finished Big Ten play with an 11-7 record and a share of third place. They were directed to Salt Lake City for the 1993 NCAA West Regional. Illinois handled Long Beach State, 75-72, but couldn't stop Vanderbilt, which avenged its Anchorage loss to Illinois, 85-68. Kaufmann closed as the UI's No. 4 scorer up to that time, but was struggling at the end and didn't score a point against Vandy until the final three minutes.

"Vanderbilt knew our plays as well as we did," said Michael, "and that made it difficult to run set stuff."

The loss didn't overshadow a slight comeback for the Illinois program after seasons of controversy and strife. The 1992-93 club finished the year at 19-13, with Thomas (18.3 points per game, 8.0 rebounds per game) and Kaufmann (17.3 points) leading the way.

GARRIS ARRIVES, THOMAS THRIVES

The 1993-94 season opened with Chicago King giant Rashard Griffith enrolling at Wisconsin, his huge teammate Thomas Hamilton unable to meet his Illini commitment due to test shortcomings, and UI veteran Rennie Clemons losing eligibility. But Henson had a 6-9 junior college transfer in Shelly Clark, who would average 11.8 points and 8.3 rebounds on the season. And joining Keene in the UI backcourt was one of the premier four-year guards in UI history, Kiwane Garris of Chicago Westinghouse.

Opening the season ranked No. 16 in AP's Top 25 rankings, the Illini compiled 200 points in their first two blowout wins over LaSalle and UI-Chicago. But, the team sustained two tough December losses to Marquette, 74-65, and in St. Louis to Missouri, 108-107, in triple overtime. Garris scored 31 points against Mizzou but, despite being an excellent free throw shooter over his career (86 percent over 116 games), missed 10 charities including two with the score knotted 97-97 and no time remaining in the sec-

Mark Jones

▲ *Wheeler provided consistent play and an impressive touch from the free throw line during his three seasons in the Illini's starting lineup.*

ond overtime. Looking back, the Illini blew a nine-point lead in the final 1:23 of regulation, a five-point lead with 47 seconds showing in the first overtime, and the golden opportunity in the second overtime with Norm Stewart risking a technical as he charged onto the court and motioned wildly behind Garris on the first miss.

"Forget those two free throws," said Michael. "We had many opportunities to close it out, and we couldn't do it. After being around that St. Louis game so much, maybe it was fitting. Over the years, we've gotten a lot of breaks. That was the longest 10 days (from the Missouri loss to the team's next game on January 2) before we played again."

In Big Ten play, Henson's 19th team fell out of the Top 25 in an opening 79-74 loss at Michigan State. They rebounded by manhandling Northwestern, 81-53, and then rode Garris' hot hand past Ohio State and Iowa. Garris tallied 64 points in those two games, sinking 27 of 32 free throws as those clubs couldn't keep him off the line.

"Kiwane was a scorer. He always found a way to get to the hole," said Michael. "It was different because the previous point guards didn't have that kind of scoring mentality. He had a knack. He was totally different from Rennie. Rennie didn't look to score, and took a lot of pride in getting the ball to the open man. Kiwane's mentality was to be a scoring threat."

No. 15 Michigan, while losing Webber to the NBA, still had Howard and Rose. Those two combined for 48 points to maintain their mastery over Illinois, 74-73, despite T.J. Wheeler's 23-point outburst. It was the Illini's first game of the season against a nationally-ranked opponent.

"I think Michigan had lost something but they still had that air that they were part of the Fab Five," said Michael. "That was an important time in college basketball because of what Michigan was able to do with that class. Mention the Fab Five, and everybody knows what you're talking about even though they never won a Big Ten title or a national title. They brought a lot to college basketball. We wanted to beat them and we came close but we couldn't get over the hump. You look back now and it's all mental."

If Illinois had lucked out in playing their first ranked opponent in game 14 of the season, their luck was about to change. Next up was a road game against No. 16 Wisconsin, who boasted Rashard Griffith at center. The Badgers hammered the UI, 66-56, with former Illinois preps Michael Finley and Tracy Webster joining Griffith in the assault.

"As a high school player growing up in the state, there was one place you think about playing (Illinois)," said Michael. "When that doesn't happen, there is added fire for those players to do better when the time comes."

Illinois rolled out of January with their third straight game against a ranked team. This outcome went in their favor—an 88-81 defeat of No. 11 Indiana. Five Illini players cracked double figures in scoring:

Keene, 19; Thomas, 18; Wheeler, 13; Garris, 12; and Robert Bennett, 11.

"That was the first time in my four years that we beat Indiana in Champaign," said Michael.

But February was another roller-coaster ride, and the Illini dropped all their road games at Northwestern, Iowa, Michigan, Indiana and Purdue. Their biggest March victory was a 90-75 verdict over 20th-ranked Minnesota in which outgoing seniors Thomas, Michael and Wheeler scored the first 14 points in their home finale. Freshman Jerry Hester provided a look into the future with 20 points.

"I came out and hit my first three three-pointers and it was a nice way to leave the Assembly Hall, to play well and take that energy into post season play," said Michael.

But the Big Dog was waiting in West Lafayette. All-American Glenn Robinson punished the Illini with 49 points in an 87-77 Purdue win to wrap up the Big Ten season.

"He got part of those on me," smiled Michael.

Said Henson at the time: "I feel fortunate that we only played against him twice in two years."

Paired against Georgetown in the NCAA Midwest Regional at Oklahoma City, Illinois saw its 73-67 lead disappear in the last 5 1/2 minutes of an 84-77 Hoya triumph.

"That is a reminder of the importance to play well during the season so you don't get an 8-9 draw," said Michael. "The winner of our game had to go on against Arkansas, who won it all that year."

Thomas scored 19 points in the loss. While he never made the first All-Big Ten team in an era featuring contemporaries like Glenn Robinson, Chris Webber, Jimmy Jackson and Calbert Cheaney, Thomas remains the UI's career scoring leader with 2,129 points. He shot .663 percent as a senior and had a four-year accuracy mark of .601.

Illinois finished the season at fourth place in the conference (10-8), with an overall mark of 17-11.

Kiwane Garris (left) and Deon Thomas (right) share a laugh at mid-court. The duo became a deadly one-two scoring punch for the 1993-94 Illini, with Thomas contributing 19.6 points per game and Garris adding 15.9 points in his freshman season.

94 ILLINOIS 95

BASKETBALL

$2.00

vs. Purdue
March 4, 1995 • Assembly Hall

KIMBERLY-CLARK IGA NIGHT!

BIG TEN CENTENNIAL

ILLINOIS
40

vs. Michigan

March 2 or 3, 1996

Assembly Hall

ILLINOIS

1995-96 Basketball Program

Americ... Software & Ha... Day!

ILLINOIS

BASKETBALL

$2.00

vs. Northwestern

February 5, 1997

Assembly Hall

News-Gazette/WDWS Night!

CHAPTER SIXTEEN

SAYING GOODBYE
TO AN OLD COACH,
WELCOMING
A NEW ERA
1994-95—1999-2000

If Chicagoland has been the most-traveled recruiting ground for Illini basketball coaches, Peoria is close behind. Lou Henson had good luck with Richwoods' Mark Smith and Doug Altenberger and Central's Tony Wysinger, and made a strong pitch for sleek Manual forward Jerry Hester as the Deon Thomas era wound to a close in the early 1990s. Hester was an easy catch.

"Growing up, I always watched the 1989 team on television, and Wysinger and Altenberger were influences," said Hester. "I was aware of Bradley University, and I knew the Missouri Valley produced a lot of good players, but not like the Big Ten. Guys want to get away from home a little bit."

Beginning with Hester, a fifth-year varsityman in 1998, and running through 2003, Manual stars played dominant roles for the Illini on three Big Ten co-championsnhip teams. Hester moved in as a sophomore starter in 1994-95 on a unit with Shelly Clark at center, Garris and Keene at the guards and Robert Bennett at the other forward. Learning the ropes were promising freshmen Matt Heldman of Libertyville, the Chicago Simeon duo of Bryant Notree and Kevin Turner, and St. Martin's Jerry Gee.

But things didn't develop quite as Henson hoped. Notree's start was hampered by a clearinghouse delay, and Clark was suspended for two exhibitions and the first three games for off-court problems.

An opening trip to Puerto Rico found Illinois winning the tournament with Garris, who scored 27 in an 85-75 title-game defeat of Virginia Tech, receiving MVP honors. Breaking into double figures in that game was Brian Johnson (10), who walked on from Maine West the previous year.

Mark Jones

▲ *Center Shelly Clark had big shoes—namely Deon Thomas'—to fill in 1994-95. Clark averaged 11.8 points and 8.3 rebounds per contest.*

"The memorable thing about Puerto Rico was the slippery floor," recalled Hester. "We felt like we were playing on ice skates. They kept wiping off the floor every five minutes. That was the worst until I got to Poland where the wood was warped from rain coming through the ceiling. The floor had big bumps in it."

Hester played professionally five years in Poland after starting with the Rockford Lightning in the Continental Basketball Association. After joining Gee in Poland during the 1999 season, Hester became league MVP in 2000. He moved to London in the Euro League, but decided to return to Poland in January 2001, making the Polish all-star team in 2002 and 2003.

"But I was away from my family too much," said Hester, now working in sales for a telecommunications company in downtown Chicago.

"The Polish people are great, but it's backwards there, in some ways like the 1940s, and I didn't want to bring my family over."

Back at the outset of the 1994-95 season, Illinois met Duke, ranked No. 6, in the first-ever college game at Chicago's new United Center. The Blue Devils built a big lead, but Garris and Keene knotted the game at 54-54 with seven minutes to play, and Garris gave the Illini their last lead, 65-64, with a trey at 1:23. But Duke's nine-for-16 three-point shooting won out, 70-65, as Steve Wojciechowski hit three and Trajan Langdon and Kenny Blakeney nailed two late ones.

"That game started the annual United Center series," said Hester. "There was a lot of excitement in playing on the same floor as Michael Jordan. That was Shelly Clark's first game after being suspended, and we were adjusting. Duke really hit some wild threes to beat us."

Illinois went from there to a five-game win streak and carried a No. 23 ranking into the Border War in St. Louis, where brokers were selling sets of four tickets near the court for $110 apiece. With memories of the previous year's triple overtime thriller, it figured to be a classic. It wasn't. Not for an Illini team shooting 26 percent in the second half and being outscored 41-21 after the break. Missouri ruled 76-58.

"That's a great way to open the Kiel Center," said Norm Stewart.

"That was a group effort in which nobody shot well and nobody played good defense," recalled Hester. "We struggled all the way, and Missouri took advantage. That was a wakeup call. Practices became a lot more intense after that."

No. 8 Connecticut made it made it back-to-back losses for the Illini, as they fell 71-56 on the road. But the team rebounded as Hester racked up 29 points in an 86-76 defeat of Memphis. That kicked off a four game win streak to open 1995 league play, the last two victories over Purdue and Indiana. Keene was the hero of the 62-58 stunner in West Lafayette; his three-pointer with a minute left reversed a 56-55 deficit. Henson, on his 63rd birthday, became the fourth coach in history to win 200 Big Ten games. Back home against Indiana, Hester and Garris sparked a late 14-0 run and the Illini bombed 11 treys for a 78-67 win.

But the Big Ten season wouldn't be that easy. Illinois dropped their next three games, and the spiral continued as the Illini dropped eight of their last 14 contests. Two riotous February wins over Iowa kept the NCAA ball rolling. First, with Shelly Clark ailing (flu) in Iowa City, Robert Bennett made all nine of his shots, and Illinois shot 72 percent in the second half to win, 79-74. Back home 10 days later, Hester sank a critical trey, and Bennett stole the ball from Jess Settles and made a free throw to force Iowa into overtime. And Illinois won again, 104-97, with Clark bagging 25 points and 15 rebounds, and Garris scoring 27.

The biggest 1995 win thereafter was another overtime nail-biter, 94-88, over Minnesota, which avenged a road loss to the Gophers earlier in the year. Sam Jacobson brought the Gophers back from a 67-57 deficit and the Gophers' new all-time scoring leader, Voshon Lenard, made one of two free throws to force overtime at 73-73. Garris broke the last tie with a free throw to make it 82-81, and Illinois ran wild with 21 points in the extra session.

The Illini had their foot in the NCAA door, and they survived a 2-3 finish to make the field. But it was a short-lived experience. Tubby Smith's Tulsa club was the opponent in Albany, N.Y., and the Illini again failed to hold a late lead in NCAA play. Records show the Illini were "out" of only one NCAA game in 12 under Henson, that being a 17-point loss to Vanderbilt in 1993. Otherwise, imminently winnable NCAA games were lost via free throws and late turnarounds by margins of five, three, three, eight, two, one, three, two, two, seven and six points.

Such was the case in the Tulsa game in 1995. Illinois led by 11 with just over 13 minutes to go, but Tulsa shot 60 percent in the last 20 minutes with Shea Seals and Pooh Williamson drilling big treys, and the Illini tailed off to 32 percent after the break. The season shooting percentage of 44.7 was the UI's lowest in 20 years.

"We were up (62-61) in the final minute when I blocked Williamson's shot," recalled Hester. "The ball went straight up in the lane, and I remember it like slow motion. Robert Bennett tried to tap it out, and it went right back to Williamson, who shot a three to put them ahead."

That made it 64-62 with 43 seconds remaining, and the Hurricanes added free throws to close out a 68-62 win.

END OF A LONG ROAD FOR HENSON

There was speculation in the media, particularly as Henson's recruiting difficulties mounted, but the players didn't realize Henson was entering his final UI season in 1995-96.

"We didn't suspect anything," said Hester. "I don't remember hearing a lot of talk about him retiring. Of course, I didn't read newspapers a lot because, good or bad, I was taught not to in high school."

No. 12 Duke was on a 16-for-17 run against Big Ten teams that December and carried a 95-game streak against non-ACC foes at Cameron Indoor Stadium when the Illini surprised almost everyone and turned the tables. Kiwane Garris, returning from a groin strain, came off the bench for 19 points while Bryant Notree, Richard Keene and Jerry Gee chalked up double figures. Illinois raced ahead 38-22 before halftime, fell behind 52-47 late but rallied with key goals from Hester, Garris and Notree to win 75-65.

"Playing against Duke is great, and their fans are legendary," said Hester. "It was one of the most exciting experiences other than the NCAA tournament. When we hit the floor, we really got charged up. Gee had two big dunks and wound up with a double-double (13 points, 12 rebounds). Notree was a sophomore and that was his 'coming out' party (14 points). We came together as a team. I remember being on the free throw line with the fans jumping back and forth, and I saw the basket move. I thought they really did have home-court advantage."

Illinois was 7-0 going to St. Louis for the annual matchup with Missouri, ranked No. 15 to Illinois' No. 14. The Illini outlasted Kelly Thames and the Tigers, 96-85, in overtime. While the Tigers missed three free throws in the last minute of regulation, Garris was zoned in as he made 15 of 16 charities, and Hester sank

two threes in overtime. For the second time in two seasons, the Illini scored 21 points in a five-minute overtime session. Six Illini cracked double figures including sub Kevin Turner (12 points).

"Everybody was thinking revenge going to St. Louis," said Hester. "I played back in the lane defensively because my man, Julian Winfield, didn't shoot that much. Overtime makes some players tense, but we had a good feeling."

Back in Chicago three days later, the Illini breezed past Cal, 83-69.

"Chris Gandy started and guarded Shareef Adbur-Rahim, and did a good job," said Hester.

In a showdown of unbeatens in Honolulu the following game, No. 13 Syracuse topped No. 12 Illinois, 75-64. Coach Jim Boeheim's zone prevailed as only Gee (21 points, 12 rebounds) was able to solve it. Garris, Keene and Hester went five for 28 from the floor.

"They had big guards and that zone really stifled us," said Hester. "I see Syracuse on television, and it's still the same zone, and a lot of people have trouble preparing for it."

Reaching the Big Ten with an 11-1 record and a No. 13 national rank, the 1996 Illini promptly lost five straight to drop out of the Top 25 for good. It began at Minnesota where coach Clem Haskins, aware that Garris, Keene and Hester missed 20 of their first 22 shots against Syracuse, moved his Gophers into a zone that befuddled the Illini shooters. Those three went 0 for 12 in the first half. The Gophers added 20 offensive rebounds in posting a 69-64 verdict that sent the Illini swirling downward.

Garris injured his shoulder and cold-shooting losses followed against Michigan State and Michigan as Henson shook up the lineup without improvement. The Illini nearly broke out at No. 16 Iowa as Notree's trey put the visitors ahead 73-71 with four minutes left, but Andre Woolridge countered and the Hawkeyes pulled it out, 82-79. Finally, with Garris returning for a tug of war at No.

Sharpshooter Richard Keene was a four-year starter for the Illini and averaged 38.4 percent shooting from beyond the arc during his Illinois career.

Mark Jones

17 Purdue, Henson spread the court in the closing posses-sions and let Garris score the last five points in a 71-67 vic-tory.

"Purdue had won two straight titles, but we had won there the year before as well," said Hester. "I liked play-ing at Purdue. When Big Dog (Glenn Robinson) scored 49 points against us in 1994, that was the loudest gym I ever heard. We really quieted them down. We had Garris back and that was our first Big Ten win."

It was Henson's ninth win in the last 12 with rival Gene Keady, although Keady reversed it (74-71) later in their final confrontation in Champaign.

February arrived with Wisconsin in town, and the result was called "devastating" by *The News-Gazette.* Garris went one for 11, including a miss on the final shot after Hennssy Auriantal, a 6-1 freshman from Montreal, put the Badgers ahead, 57-56. Hester scored 22 but UI outside shooting was off once again.

The Illini faced nine Top 25 teams during an 18-13 season. They beat their last ranked foe, No. 18 Iowa, 91-86 on February 24. After the game Henson announced he would retire at sea-son's end.

"I could see us having a real difficult time recruiting this spring," said the coach, "and we might get shut out in the fall. It's tough attracting young men when they don't know who their coach

will be a year or two down the road. You've got to have players, and we only have one freshman."

That freshman was Ryan Blackwell, and he depart-ed with Henson, returning to his Syracuse roots as a sophomore.

"We were in shock when Coach Henson made his announcement," said Hester. "He shook everybody's hand in the locker room. He started tearing up a little bit. We hadn't seen him that emotional. We sat there and nobody said anything.

"It was a frustrating time for me, because I hurt my ankle earlier at Ohio State, and I was trying to

Chicago Simeon product Bryant Notree was a key contributor on the 1995-96 Illini squad whose season highlights included road victories at Duke and Purdue and another Border War win. On the season, Notree averaged 10.5 points and 6.1 rebounds per game.

Mark Jones

play although I wasn't fully healthy. I wanted to help send Coach Henson out on a happy note. But it was rough in the stretch."

Henson was a 67-66 loser in his final conference game against visiting Minnesota. For the Gophers, it meant the end to a 16-game losing spell at the Assembly Hall. The retiring coach received a Henson Day proclamation from Gov. Jim Edgar, a worldwide tour from the Alumni Association, a golf cart and various other gifts, but his Illini blew a 14-point lead and saw a last-second hook by Garris roll off the rim in the heartbreaking loss to Minnesota.

With its weakest-rebounding, poorest-shooting team in two decades, Illinois still made the NIT field despite a 7-11 league record and ninth-place finish. The NIT granted the Illini a home game, but they couldn't take advantage of it, falling to Alabama despite a strong, 21-

point, seven assist effort by Garris, who was named All-Big Ten even though injuries forced him to miss three full games and late portions in two others. Keene closed his career with nine assists, but Alabama's Roy Rogers blocked eight shots in a 72-69 Alabama triumph.

As Ron Guenther began his search for a replacement, Henson looked back on 21 years in which he ran the UI program with class and dignity. He met resistance from the first day when he inherited a club on probation and limited by two scholarship sanctions. Just when he reached the heights of the Final Four in 1989, unsubstantiated charges of recruiting irregularities by Iowa assistant coach Bruce Pearl led to "institutional control" sanctions that chilled recruiting. Finally, speculation regarding his age—63—influenced him to step aside ... only to return for another seven years at New Mexico State.

COACH K—KRUGER—IS HIRED

Even the Illini players got caught up in wild "Coach K rumors" after Henson stepped aside.

"Coach K has bought land over near Mahomet," the joke circulated. "He's going to build a big home there."

"We heard all of it," said Hester, "and it turned out to be true. Coach K was Coach Kruger. I knew about him. I thought that was a step in the right direction. He had proved he could win when he took Florida to the Final Four."

Lon Kruger became the 14th men's basketball coach at Illinois. He opened his debut 1996-97 season at UI-Chicago on November 22. Garris scored 26 points and Hester added 17 in a 68-63 victory.

"That was Jimmy Collins' first game coaching against Illinois," said Hester, "and it was a weird feeling. We knew the whole UIC coaching staff. It was

Mark Jones

▲ Coach Lon Kruger turned around the Illini's fortunes in his first two seasons, taking them to the NCAA Tournament in both years and winning the Big Ten in his second.

Guard Jerry Hester was a regular in the Illini starting lineup beginning with his sophomore season in 1994-95. For his career he averaged 11.4 points per game, but peaked at 14.7 points and 5.3 rebounds per game for the 1997-98 Big Ten co-champs. ▶

family, and we wanted to win badly. Down the stretch, Kiwane and I had a big run of points and we put it away."

Off to Hawaii for a tournament, Hester enjoyed one of his best games—20 points, eight rebounds and five assists—in a 73-67 defeat of Texas Christian, only to injure his back in the second game, a 70-60 loss to Louisville.

"I came down on a rebound," said Hester, "and I tried to run but I couldn't. I knew something was wrong. I thought it was just back spasms or a muscle pull, and that I'd be okay after I sat out the Virginia Tech game," which Illinois easily won, 92-68.

Amazingly, when Illinois stopped to play California on the way back, Hester came off the bench for 20 points in one of his best performances. The Illini fought Cal into double overtime before losing 89-88 despite Garris making 17 of 17 free throws.

"I was in pain the whole way," Hester said. "But I played well so I thought I could get through it. But the next day I could hardly walk. We took an MRI and determined that it was a herniated disc. I had to have surgery."

The Illini reached the 1997 Big Ten race 10-1 by whipping No. 24 UCLA, 79-63, in Chicago and splattering Missouri in St. Louis, 85-69. In the UCLA game, Matt Heldman (19 points), Chris Gandy (18) and Bryant Notree (14) took full advantage of their new opportunities in Hester's absence.

"Gandy was coming into his own," recalled Hester. "He became the next scorer after Kiwane, and Coach Kruger did a good job getting him to take the challenge. Gandy took advantage of his redshirt season."

Sneaking into the AP's Top 25 at No. 24, Kruger's 1997 Illini split their first four Big Ten games before hosting No. 7 Minnesota. Garris and Turner popped 24 apiece in a 96-90 barn burner. Then they squeaked out a 66-63 decision at Michigan State, lost at Wisconsin and Iowa, and defeated No. 17 Indiana on the road, 78-74, in the team's lone duel of the season. This marked the beginning of Kruger's 6-2 run against Bob Knight.

"Kruger's preparation was great, and in the game he made excellent adjustments," said Hester. "Knight is one of the all-time best and you know what you're going to get, but things change during the game, and Kruger was real good at matching up, taking advantage of positions, and changing defenses. Under Kruger, we had plays where we'd trap, and sometimes change defenses in the last 10 seconds of the 35-second clock."

Illinois later avenged its loss to Iowa, knocking the Hawkeyes out of the Top 25, and nearly upset No. 2 Minnesota in Minneapolis. The Gophers survived, 67-66, on two free throws by 275-pound John Thomas, who went to the line after a phantom call against Gandy on the baseline.

Still, the 1997 Illini bounced back with three impressive wins, outscoring a ranked and star-studded Michigan team 41-9 at the end of a 70-51 decision that clinched an NCAA berth for the Illini. Garris was soon named the sixth Illini to receive first-team All-Big Ten honors on two

Mark Jones

▲ *Matt Heldman started at guard on Coach Kruger's first two teams and provided the Illini with an accurate touch from the three-point line and the charity stripe.*

Kiwane Garris capped a successful Illinois career with a strong showing his senior season—19.2 points and 5.4 assists per game. Garris is currently second on the Illini career scorers list with 1,948 points, an average of 16.8 per game. ▶

occasions. On the season, Garris averaged 19.2 points and 5.4 assists per game, and made 73 three-pointers.

Off to Charlotte for the opening round of tournament play, the 19th-ranked Illini appeared to be catching fire as Garris tallied 27 and Gandy 20 in a 90-77 rout of Southern California. Then the Illini hit another NCAA detour. Tennessee-Chattanooga shot 51.1 percent, and the Illini trailed off to eight for 23 in a second-half shooting slump that resulted in a 75-63 loss.

Afterwards, all the talk was about respect, as Chattanooga coach Mack McCarthy and his players claimed they heard the Illini chanting "Final Four" and singing before the game. An irate Kruger telephoned McCarthy later, and reported the incident as a fabrication "that was blown out of proportion."

In his first year, Kruger had done an impressive job of righting the ship, finishing tied for fourth in Big Ten play with an 11-7 record (22-10 overall).

RETURN TO GLORY

Hester returned for his redshirt year in 1997-98, and joined an all-senior lineup featuring Gee, Johnson, Heldman, and Turner with freshman Sergio McClain as sixth man. Kevin Turner was a "new man," heading for an All-Big Ten season and a 17.1 scoring average.

"Turner had some big games as a junior," said Hester. "As a senior, he shot lights out in practice every day. We had a lot of confidence in him."

Turner scored 17 points in an opening 69-59 defeat of Bradley, signaling his readiness to become a major force.

"I had extra incentive playing Bradley, and not just because I'm from Peoria," said Hester. "The Bradley coach, Jim Molinari, was my coach on the World University team in Italy that summer. I played well, but I was the only one who didn't play in the championship game. And he gave everyone else an evaluation for the pro scouts, but not me. I took exception to that. For me, when we played Bradley, it was more about him than the game."

The third game, however, nearly derailed the Illini as UIC coach Jimmy Collins came close to pulling off an upset for the second straight year. Only the strong

▲ Power forward Jerry Gee gradually improved each of his four seasons at Illinois, eventually becoming a key piece of the Illini's 1997-98 team. As a senior, Gee averaged 8.5 points per game on 52.3 percent shooting.

inside play of Gee (26 points) and the marksmanship of Hester (21) snuffed the Flames, 71-70.

"That was Gee's best game. I remember Kevin throwing a lob intended for me, and Gee jumped over me and dunked it," recalled Hester.

A trip to Bayamon, Puerto Rico, uncovered more early-season shortcomings as the Illini dropped two of three games there by blowing a 10-point lead against No. 19 Louisville, 58-57, and falling to a powerhouse St. John's club (83-66) that was packed with stars Zendon Hamilton, Felipe Lopez and Ron Artest.

"Artest was just a freshman but extremely strong, and he could handle the ball," said Hester. "And Hamilton was 6-11 and too big for Gee."

Later that December, Illini fans had a field day at the Assembly Hall as both Tom Penders and his assistant, Ed Oran, were ejected during Illinois' riotous 105-80 defeat of Texas. This win came on the heels of a 71-61 defeat of No. 17 Clemson.

However, two losses in St. Louis, 57-51 to the Billikens and 75-69 to Missouri, offered no indication the banner Big Ten season that was about to unfold. And Illinois' final tuneup resulted in a 74-69 loss at UCLA even though Turner exploded with 32 points.

"That's when Turner really felt within himself that he could do it on an every-game basis," said Hester.

"My aunt, Ella Maupins, had died in a car accident in St. Louis, and I really didn't feel like playing at UCLA. She was one of my favorites and she loved to joke around with me. No excuse, but I wasn't into that game. UCLA got way ahead of us, and Turner just took over. That made Kevin a leader on our team."

Turner was still hot when the Illini hosted Indiana in the 1998 Big Ten opener, and he rattled in 35 points as Illinois built a 63-41 lead and hung on, 74-72. It was a tough game for Kruger, whose father, Don Kruger, had just passed away in Silver Lake, Kan. A follow-up 76-64 win at Iowa, with the 11th-ranked Hawkeyes installed as prohibitive favorites, showed the Illini were serious about a title march. Just when Iowa caught up at 44-44 and the Hawkeye crowd was its loudest, the Illini pulled away with a powerful run. Hester scored 20, Heldman added 19, Turner netted 17 and freshman McClain chipped in 14.

"I don't believe we were thinking about the Big Ten race at that time," said Hester. "Two years before we had started 11-1, and we were just going game by game. We knew the bottom could fall out.

"In our win at Iowa, Ricky Davis literally jumped over Matt Heldman to dunk the ball. We joked on the way home, 'Hey, Matt, what did the bottom of his shoes look like?' And I remember those older ladies sitting on the sideline and heckling me, and I shut them up with three-pointers right in front of them."

Consecutive losses to No. 9 Purdue and Michigan State in mid-January stalled the march. Against the Spartans, guard Mateen Cleaves put a dagger in the UI's heart with 27 points.

"I've never seen Mateen that hot," said his teammate Mo Peterson. "I thought he was Michael Jordan, just hitting shot after shot. After awhile, I didn't even bother to go in and rebound."

"Cleaves hadn't been known as an outside shooter until that point," said Hester. "Kruger tried four different defenders on him but nothing worked."

The Illini turned that disappointment into a seven-game win streak. Kruger meshed his athletes skillfully, mixed defenses and kept opponents guessing. That's how they edged No. 16 Michigan, 64-53, even though they were outrebounded for the 10th time in 11 games, shot a mediocre 41 percent from the field, and missed 13 of 24 free throws. Seven UI opponents to that point were averaging less than 60 points per game.

"You don't realize it when you're going through it," said Hester, "but collectively, as five seniors, we were all on the same page defensively. I knew if I got beat, we'd rotate. We didn't even have to talk. I've never played on a team with that much cohesiveness."

An overtime 53-47 win at Wisconsin boosted the streak to six. Turner stole the show again by converting a difficult spin shot to bring about a tie at the end of regulation.

"That was the biggest shot of all," said Hester. "He just manufactured a basket out of nothing. Then we pulled out the victory. And I had my career high in rebounds (13)."

That set the stage for a showdown with No. 13 Michigan State, and the Illini hit them with a full salvo, 84-63, with sub Arias Davis (12 points) becoming the fifth member in double figures. This time, the Illini mixed 63 percent second-half shooting with superior defense that held Cleaves to 12 points and six turnovers.

"Watching the Illini at home against Michigan State this past season (a 75-51 win February 10, 2004), it reminded me of our game," said Hester. "We were upset because we had blown such a big lead earlier, and the way Cleaves danced off the court. We wanted them to know we were for real. And that was the loudest I heard the Assembly Hall."

Still, Illinois couldn't handle Purdue, ranked No. 8 in mid-February and featuring Chad Austin, Brad

continued on page 214

GREATEST GAMES
ILLINOIS 84, (NO. 13) MICHIGAN STATE 63
FEBRUARY 12, 1998 • ASSEMBLY HALL, CHAMPAIGN, ILLINOIS

ILLINOIS DESTROYS STATE ON WAY TO SHARE OF BIG TEN CHAMPIONSHIP

When the 1997-98 Illini began their preseason schedule with exhibition losses to the Australian National Team and the NBC Thunder, no Illini fan could have ever imagined they would get to this point. After an up-and-down nonconference season that saw the senior-laden squad go 8-5 out of the gates, the Illini got hot to start the Big Ten season. By February, they were staring down a monumental showdown in the Assembly Hall with the first-place Michigan State Spartans.

Earlier in the season, the Illini had the Spartans on the ropes at the Breslin Center as they stormed out to a 21-5 lead. But they were unable to finish the job as Mateen Cleaves scored 24 of his 27 points in the second half to lead the Spartans to a 68-64 victory.

It was a game and a performance the Illini didn't soon forget.

"We had a lot to prove that night," remembered Illinois center Jarrod Gee. "We blew the lead up in East Lansing and we thought we should have won that game. We wanted revenge and we wanted to get them back."

For the first time in a few years, the Assembly Hall and the Illinois crowd had a game they could get really excited about.

"That was the first game in a while that brought everybody to the Hall where everyone knew it mattered," said starting forward Brian Johnson. "It was our first game on a national stage—ESPN was there—and it meant we were competing for a Big Ten title."

Mark Jones

▲ Fans swarm the court after the Illini easily defeated Michigan State at the Assembly Hall.

The Illini featured a team with five seniors in the starting line-up and each of those guys knew this would be their chance at a Big Ten Championship.

"Our guys were jacked," said head coach Lon Kruger. "I think the buzz around town and campus especially indicated it was going to be a special night."

The Illini, spurred on by the emotion of the home crowd, bolted out of the gate to take a 16-7 lead on the strength of two Kevin Turner threes from the right wing. Leading 25-13 with just over seven minutes to play, the Illini struggled to close the half and the Spartans went on a 14-7 run to narrow the gap to 32-27 heading into the locker room.

"The first half of that game was like the first round of a boxing match," said Jerry Hester. "We threw the first good jab, they threw one back, and it was just like both teams were feeling each other out."

Behind six early second-half points from Hester, the Illini increased their lead to nine by the 16-minute mark. Then came the fireworks. First it was a Matt Heldman three off a screen from Sergio McClain, then a Hester uncontested lay-up, and next a Victor Chukwudebe turn around shot from the left block.

The Illini were rolling and their fans were deafening.

"We really fed off their energy the entire game," recalled Turner, who finished the game with 20 points. "The Krush was unbelievable and the entire crowd was propelling us."

Up 13 points with about 12 minutes left to play, Matt Heldman threw a no-look pass to Arias Davis who knocked down a wide-open three on the right wing. On the ensuing Illinois possession, Davis returned the favor. This time he drove the lane and kicked it out to Heldman who drilled his three to give the Illini an 18-point lead.

The consecutive buckets sent the Assembly Hall faithful into pandemonium.

"That was the knockout punch," remembered Hester. "When Arias and Matt hit those two threes the sixth man was going crazy and they had us so pumped up. We took it from there and never looked back."

With Heldman and Davis delivering the dagger, all that was left was to finish the Spartans off. The lead got as high as 24 late in the game and the Illini shot 63 percent from the field on their way to scoring 52 points in the second half. When the final buzzer rang, the Orange Krush darted onto the floor to celebrate an 84-63 victory that put the Illini in a first-place tie in the Big Ten race.

Illinois finished the game with four starters in double figures and received great bench contributions from Davis, Chukwudebe and McClain. Cleaves, who lit up the Illini in East Lansing, was held to just 11 points and committed six turnovers under heavy defensive pressure. With the blowout win, the Illini showed that they were no fluke.

"At that point, we really arrived on the scene and it gave us a lot of confidence," said Johnson. "It showed us that we could beat anybody in our league."

"A lot of people had written us off, but we always believed in ourselves," said Turner. "Our fans, and everyone around Champaign, believed in us too and that game kind of put the stamp on things."

It was the game that defined the upstart Illinois team that went on to share the Big Ten Championship. Now six years removed, the players still marvel at the passion of the Assembly Hall crowd that evening.

"It was a legendary atmosphere and something I will never forget," said Hester. "I watched Illinois as I grew up and went to a lot of basketball games over the years where I heard the Assembly Hall loud, but that night was something special. It was the night that brought on what we see going today, because it was the night we got back to the top of the Big Ten."

It was an evening that won't ever be forgotten and when Illinois fans talk about the greatest atmospheres and loudest nights in the history of the Assembly Hall, one thing is certain—February 12, 1998 will always be on that list.

continued from page 211

Miller and Brian Cardinal, son of UI trainer Rod Cardinal. The lanky Cardinal, hailing from nearby Tolono, went 9-0 against Illinois during his years at Purdue.

Having already whipped the Illini in Champaign, the Boilermakers bumped them again 75-72 in West Lafayette as Hester and Turner missed late treys. They also overwhelmed the Illini in the semifinals of the first Big Ten tournament in Chicago, 68-47.

"Miller was the key," said Hester. "He always played well against us. He was taller than Gee and he was so efficient."

Despite their success against Illinois, Purdue dropped four games in the conference, allowing Illinois and Michigan State to tie for the Big Ten title at 13-3.

No. 22 Illinois set up the championship with an 82-72 win at Indiana where an irate and potentially explosive crowd booed the officials after Knight was ejected for his infamous run-in with ref Ted Valentine. Knight was later reprimanded for calling it "the greatest travesty in 33 years of basketball as a college coach. That goes beyond anything that's even ridiculous."

The final dispute revolved around Knight's reason for walking onto the court when Luke Recker had been knocked down. Knight said he was attending to Recker, and Valentine felt otherwise. Two technical fouls ensued. It is noteworthy that Valentine did not work Big Ten games the next year.

"That was bizarre, the way it was handled," said Hester. "I didn't know what to think. I never saw a crowd so angry. Sergio was hanging on the rim after Luke Recker missed a drive-in, and when goal-tending wasn't called, Knight went ballistic."

"Even after we beat Indiana, we didn't talk much about the championship," said Hester. "We needed Purdue to beat Michigan State to get a share, and Michigan State already had its championship banner flying at the Breslin Center. We watched on television at Kruger's house. It went into overtime and Purdue won (99-96). We were starting to celebrate when Cleaves threw a long shot, and it caromed off the front of the rim. It was that close."

There they were, Big Ten co-champions with five senior starters: Brian Johnson, a former walk-on; Kevin

Turner, a recruiting afterthought who tagged along with All-Stater Bryant Notree from Simeon; Jerry Hester, a medically redshirted fifth-year senior; Matt Heldman, a diminutive jump shooter remade into a point guard; and Jarrod Gee, undersized center.

Seeded into the NCAA tournament at Sacramento, the Illini beat South Alabama but fell to No. 20 Maryland, 67-61, despite a 14-point, 13-rebound effort by Gee.

"That was a heartbreaker," said Hester. "Their guards made some great shots. I remember a particular three-pointer late in the game, with Heldman all over (Terrell) Stokes, and he shot it in from the corner. Then they made some big free throws at the end."

Illinois finished the '98 season with a Big Ten banner hanging in the Hall and a 23-10 record. Hester is sure that senior experience made the difference for the Illini.

"Age and experience made all the difference in 1998. We didn't think we'd win simply because we were seniors, but when we look back, we realize what an effect it had. We had been through it so many times. Brian and I were fifth-year guys," said Hester, who favors redshirting as a valuable option for high schoolers entering college.

"I take pride in being an Illini, in being there in the late '90s when the Orange Krush returned as one of the great student sections in the country, and in seeing Illinois win those Big Ten championships," said Hester. "Our team in 1998 wasn't looked upon as being a top team nationally, but we brought back the winning pride."

Kevin Turner became the go-to guy on offense in 1997-98 with the departure of Kiwane Garris. He averaged 17.1 points per game for the Big Ten champs and knocked down 78 three-pointers on the season.

MOMENTUM SWING

The advantages of employing five senior starters on 1998's Big Ten co-champions evolved into a distinct disadvantage when Kruger met with a young squad the following fall. Cory Bradford, a long-range bomber from Memphis, became eligible after sitting out his freshman season, and accepted a heavy scoring role. But the Illini's guard play was so shaky in 1998-99 that sturdy sophomore Sergio McClain often found himself teaming up with Bradford in the backcourt. Meanwhile, Victor Chukwudebe, Fess Hawkins, Robert Archibald, and Rich Beyers were tested in the block. Junior college

Craig Jones/Getty Images

▲ *Sophomore Sergio McClain became a defensive force during the 1998-99 season as the Illini battled their way through a difficult season. McClain ended the campaign averaging 8.6 points and 2.3 steals per game.*

transfer Cleotis Brown took Hester's wing position. Kruger mulled the possibility of redshirting Damir Krupalija through the first seven games, then decided to use him.

The club split an opening pair at New York's Madison Square Garden, losing 75-73 in an overtime thriller to Wake Forest and thumping Georgetown, 65-50, as Bradford scoring 19 points, Archibald added 14 and Beyers chipped in 10. Back home, the quick hands of five-foot-four Shawnta Rogers rallied George Washington from a 57-53 deficit to a 64-58 triumph that shocked the Illini faithful.

This was a warning sign. Illinois went on a six-game win streak against weak competition—Tennessee-Martin, Texas-Pan American, Bradley, Eastern Illinois—but then lost to No. 13 Kansas, 65-55, and No. 15 Missouri, 67-62. The team rallied to beat No. 14 Clemson, 67-50, in Greenville, S.C. to finish off their non-conference schedule at 8-4.

The stage was set for the team's first last-place finish in Big Ten play since the mid-'70s. A wintry road debut at No. 8 Indiana, with only 7,249 able to attend due to a fierce storm, ended Kruger's three-game streak against Knight in a 62-53 loss.

The overmatched Illini dropped their first seven Big Ten games, many by double figures. It would be a 3-13 conference season, but there was more here than met the eye. First, the Illini faced 15 Top 25 teams between their matchups with Kansas on December 19 and Indiana on February 24. Second, the Illini broke their winning drought with a 61-59 win at Michigan as Chukwudebe popped a baseline 12-footer with four seconds remaining. Three games later, the toppled No. 11 Wisconsin, 53-51, on the sharpshooting heroics of Bradford.

That they were improving was even more evident from the final home losses to Iowa, 78-72, and Indiana, 70-64. But no one was ready for what would happen in the second annual Big Ten Tournament in Chicago. Inspired by rookies Lucas Johnson and Krupalija, and led by the scoring of Bradford and the defense of McClain, the 1999 Illini took advantage of Minnesota's six-for-24 first-half shooting and outlasted the No. 23 Gophers, 67-64.

continued on page 218

GREATEST GAMES
MARCH 4-7, 1999

ILLINI SURPRISE ALL WITH RUN AT BIG TEN TOURNAMENT CHAMPIONSHIP

The 1998-99 Illinois basketball season was a rebuilding year for a program that lost a plethora of seniors. Featuring five freshmen in their rotation, the Illini struggled all season due to inexperience and a lack of confidence. They carried a 3-13 conference record into the Big Ten tournament. Even for an eternal optimist it seemed like it would be "one and done" for the Illini in the tournament. To make things worse, the team's final practice before leaving for Chicago's United Center might have been their worst of the year.

"After we got done with that practice, I took one of the suits out of my bag because I figured we were only going to play one game up there," said assistant coach Rob Judson. "I was prepared to go out and start recruiting [activities] the next day."

"I didn't think there was any way we could make a run in that tournament," remembered forward Lucas Johnson. "I even had plans for that Thursday night back in Champaign."

Their first opponent was the 23rd-ranked Minnesota Gophers, who had beaten them handily up in Minneapolis in early February. The Illini and Cory Braford started the game red hot and by halftime built a 38-23 lead. It seemed like they would coast to an easy victory, but two minutes into the second half the Gophers went on a 15-0 run to pull within one point. The young Illini seemed doomed.

"When Minnesota made that huge run a lot of people thought we would crumble," said Damir Krupalija. "We found some courage, made some huge shots, and found a way to win the game."

Behind Bradford's 22 points, the Illini became the first ever 11th seed to win a game in the Big Ten tournament with a 67-64 victory over the Gophers.

"After the first game you could just see the attitudes change," said Johnson, who had to quickly cancel his Thursday night plans. "Everyone seemed to have increased confidence and all of the sudden things started to click."

Next up was 17th-ranked Indiana, who had defeated the Illini twice during the season. In a game that was never in doubt, the confident Illini steamrolled the Hoosiers 82-66 behind 17 points from Lucas Johnson and 16 from Bradford.

"It was good for the team to play Thursday, Friday and Saturday without any break," said Judson. "We got hot and were able to stay hot."

Their semifinal opponent was the 11th-ranked Ohio State Buckeyes, who featured the great backcourt of Scoonie Penn and Michael Redd. In a classic back and forth battle, the Illini led by three with two seconds to go and Redd, who scored 32 in the ball game, was heading to the line for two. He made the first, intentionally missed the second, and in a scramble for the ball Redd recovered the rebound and launched a potential game tying shot. The desperation shot missed off the back of the rim and the Illini came away with another win.

"For me, the Ohio State game was the most special," remembered Krupalija. "It was a close game and one that we would have blown in the regular season. Ohio State went on to play in the Final Four that year so it was a big win."

By this point, the Illini were one win away from earning a surprise bid into the NCAA Tournament. The city of Chicago jumped on the Illinois bandwagon.

The fourth and final opponent was the second-ranked Michigan State Spartans, who had annihilated the Illini in East Lansing and won a close game in the Assembly Hall during the season. It was the fourth game in four days and the Illini would need a miracle to win it.

"We were a very tired team at that point," remembered head coach Lon Kruger. "Our biggest concern going into the game was that we couldn't get behind because then fatigue and emotion would catch up to us."

The Illini kept it close early and were only down 21-19 with seven minutes to go in the first half, but that would be all she wrote. The Spartans closed the half with a 17-6 run to take a 13-point lead into halftime. Illinois' astonishing run had ended at the hands of the Big Ten champion Spartans, who coasted to a 67-50 victory.

The run was over and their season was done, but the Fighting Illini provided their fans with a magical four days that would forever have its place in Illinois basketball history. Their three wins sent a message to the Big Ten and more importantly sent a message to the guys on the team.

"That postseason run gave the team a lot of confidence heading into the off season," remembered Kruger. "More than anything it motivated them to work hard over that summer to improve on their games."

The Big Ten Tournament in 1999 proved Illinois basketball was back—and wouldn't be going anywhere for a while.

continued from page 216

Nice upset. But it was only the beginning. Hawkins chipped in 16 points in a rollicking 82-66 defeat of No. 17 Indiana. No. 11 Ohio State couldn't keep pace in the semifinal as the balanced attack of Bradford (17 points), Chukwudebe (13), Johnson (12) and Brown (11) overcame a 32-point spree by Michael Redd, who missed the final off-balance shot in a 79-77 shocker.

The clock struck midnight for Cinderella, however, in the finale as Michigan State, ranked No. 2 in the nation, prevailed 67-50. But the last-place Illini stood proud after tangling with 19 ranked teams over the course of the season and turning the league tournament on its ear in the early days of March.

"I saw a little fatigue (in the Illini)," said MSU coach Tom Izzo, "but I also saw a lot of players that I'm not looking forward to playing next season."

After finishing the season on a high note despite a 14-18 overall record, next season couldn't come quick enough for this young Illini team.

FINDING THEIR GROOVE

With gifted guard Frank Williams gaining eligibility and talented lankies Brian Cook and Marcus Griffin joining the lineup, the Illini drew an opening AP ranking of 17 as they blistered Western Illinois, 76-53, and Bradley, 72-62, to open Kruger's final season in 1999-2000.

A late Illinois rally couldn't catch the Illini up to No. 17 Duke in Chicago (72-69), nor were the Illini up to the showdown with No. 24 Maryland at the MCI Center in Washington, D.C., losing 69-67 on a shot by Juan Dixon. The squad reached 6-2 and drew more

▲ *Frank Williams (left), Coach Kruger, and Cory Bradford (right) discuss strategy on the sidelines during a 1999-2000 game. Williams and Bradford provided the much-improved Illini with a one-two scoring punch from the backcourt during Kruger's final season as coach. Bradford broke his own Illini record by nailing 96 three-pointers during the season.*

Mark Jones

national attention on December 18 in Chicago when they erupted for 53 second-half points and demolished No. 8 Kansas, 84-70. Williams and Bradford outplayed backcourt rivals Jeff Boschee and Kenny Gregory in that showdown.

But the news wasn't good from St. Louis, where No. 15 Illinois fell to unranked Missouri, 78-72, for the third straight time. Tiger guards Clarence Gilbert and Keyon Dooling combined for 49 points in the win. And after Frank Williams nailed a three-pointer to nip Ohio State 80-77 in the Big Ten opener, a three-game losing streak—coupled with a series of injuries)—sent Kruger back to the drawing board in mid-January as his Illini fell from the AP's Top 25.

"Rod (Cardinal) just kind of throws his hand up with the number of appointments he has for rehab. I don't know that we've ever been around a situation with more injuries," said Kruger.

But the Illini forged ahead, losing only to power-house Michigan State over their next 10 games, and finished fourth in the conference with an 11-5 record. Perhaps the key game in the late-season surge was a 51-50 victory at Penn State, which was followed a couple weeks later by an impressive 87-63 home win against No. 16 Indiana.

In a 63-30 romp at Northwestern, the Illini held the Wildcats scoreless for more than 15 minutes in building a 23-0 lead. More good fortune followed the No. 21 Illini into the Big Ten Tournament in Chicago. Bradford extended his three-point streak to 60 games with a game-winner on a feed from McClain in another triumph over Indiana, 72-69. Brian Cook, Big Ten co-freshman of the year, scored 18 in the win, and Illinois improved to 11-2 in games that Cook started. Krupalija extended his uncanny string of hard-rebounding performances against Indiana. The Illini then downed Penn State, 94-84, before bowing once again to Michigan State in the tourney finale, 76-61.

Illinois' quest for an NCAA Sweet 16 appearance was over in a flash, unfortunately. After bumping Pennsylvania in the opening round, 68-58, the Illini fell to Florida, 93-76, as only Bradford (27 points) seemed to be on his game. It marked the 11th straight year that the Illini failed to advance beyond the NCAA's second round, and ended the team's season at 22-10.

Then, in May of 2000, came the shocker. Tom Izzo declined the head coaching job of the Atlanta Hawks and recommended Kruger, who made a stunning decisions to leave Illinois for the NBA dollars after just four seasons.

Athletic director Ron Guenther remained upbeat, saying, "I would always rather replace coaches because of their success. This was a personal, career and financial decision by Lon and his family."

Within days, the even shorter era of Bill Self would be underway as Guenther, the one-man search committee, made a swift, roundly applauded decision.

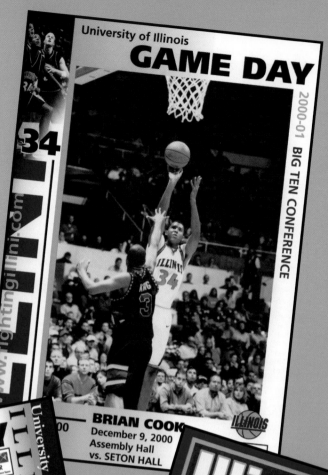

University of Illinois

GAME DAY

2000-01 BIG TEN CONFERENCE

34

www.fightingillini.com

BRIAN COOK
December 9, 2000
Assembly Hall
vs. SETON HALL

ILLINOIS

GAME DAY

February 26, 2002
Assembly Hall
vs. Indiana

ILLINOIS POWER
Part of the Dynegy Performance Team

University of Illinois

ILLINI BASKETBALL

www.fightingillini.com

2001-2002

HONORING THE CLASS OF 2002

The Official Game Program of the University of Illinois

30

33

Archibald Bradford Krupalija Johnson Williams

Illinois Basketball

Game Day

The Official Game Program of the
University of Illinois
$2.00

Senior Sean Harrington

Illinois vs. Michigan State
February 18, 2003
Assembly Hall

24

ILLINOIS

verizon wireless

2003 program courtesy of Larry Boyd

CHAPTER SEVENTEEN

SELF-IMPROVED
ILLINI
2000-01—2002-03

Bill Self, a coach on the rise after his 32-5 season at Tulsa in 1999-2000, hit the court running with Lon Kruger's UI athletes as the school calendar turned to fall of 2000. Self was hired basically without an interview. Athletic director Ron Guenther settled on him after a scheduled meeting with Oklahoma's Kelvin Sampson in Norman was called off due to media recognition. Guenther simply flew home and offered the job to Self.

Self's three-year term overflowed with excitement. He was "Aw, shucks," but smooth, at ease with a college president or exchanging street lingo with a junior college recruit. His gregarious nature wowed fans at luncheons. On the practice court, he displayed amazing recall of every player's moves throughout up-and-down action.

Careening from one stirring assignment to another, Self's three UI teams played 22 ranked opponents (splitting even, 11-11), won 78 games, defeated Missouri all three years in the St. Louis Border War, showed a 10-1 record at Chicago's United Center, shared in two Big Ten championships, won the Big Ten tournament in 2003, and were 6-3 in NCAA tournament action.

"It was an exciting time, a lot of big-time games," said Sean Harrington, a sophomore guard in 2000-01 who upon graduation followed Self to Kansas as an administrative assistant. "It always seemed like we were going up against a high-ranked opponent. The fan base was great. The highlights were winning Big Ten titles."

The Self era got off to a great start as the eighth-ranked Illini blew by Maine, 86-57, and headed off to Maui. The spotlight burned bright in November 2000 as the Illini entered competition in the Maui Invitational. There, Illinois defeated UNLV, 74-69, and No. 6

Mark Jones

▲ Marcus Griffin was the second leading scorer for the Illini in 2000-01 under first-year coach Bill Self. Griffin teamed up with fellow Peoria Manual players Sergio McClain and Frank Williams to account for roughly 40 percent of the team's scoring and rebounds and 50 percent of the team's assists.

Maryland, 90-80, before bowing in a thriller to No. 1 Arizona, 79-76. The five starters—Peorians Sergio McClain, Marcus Griffin and Frank Williams plus Cory Bradford and sophomore Brian Cook—attained double figures against Maryland. And Williams, on a late tear, wowed the Hawaii crowd with 27 points in a rally that fell short against Arizona.

Remarkably, Illinois played its second No. 1 team a week later when Duke hosted the ACC/Big Ten Challenge game at Greensboro, N.C. Again, Illinois' late rally fell just short, 78-77. Williams, who tallied 19 points in the game, went to the line with three and a half seconds remaining to shoot three free throws with Illinois trailing 78-74. He made the first two and was directed by Self to miss the third. But his hard throw caromed off the backboard and directly into the basket for the final 78-77 score.

"It was unusual to play different No. 1 teams in back-to-back weeks," said Harrington. "It made us stronger as a team. We lost two close games, but we felt we were making strides. We knew we could play with any team in the country, but we also knew we would have to eventually win some of these games."

Back home on December 9, the No. 9 Illini did just that in a 87-79 win over No. 7 Seton Hall. Williams and Griffin combined for 45 points as Illinois staged the biggest comeback in school history, spotting Seton Hall a 42-21 lead shortly before halftime and charging back to win, 87-79 in overtime. Bradford had no treys in regulation but popped two in overtime.

In Chicago on December 16, the Illini outmuscled a now seventh-ranked Arizona, 81-73, with coach Lute Olson complaining about the rough play as all five UI starters hit double figures and Harrington came off the bench to make three straight treys. Bradford broke the NCAA record for three-pointers in consecutive games during the contest, and would extend the streak to 88 before being stopped by Wisconsin nearly two months later (February 13).

"When you look at our team, we were big and physical that year," said Harrington. "We had depth, and that was the style we played. I don't really think Olson was looking ahead, but it ended up working to his advantage in the Elite Eight where so many fouls were called."

continued on page 224

GREATEST GAMES
(NO. 9) ILLINOIS 87, (NO. 7) SETON HALL 79
DECEMBER 9, 2000 • ASSEMBLY HALL, CHAMPAIGN, ILLINOIS

ILLINOIS WINS WILD ONE WITH COMEBACK;
BRADFORD TIES NCAA RECORD

The ninth-ranked Fighting Illini and their legion of fans couldn't wait for December 9, 2000.

"CBS was coming into town and we were real excited about it," recalled Sean Harrington.

The seventh-ranked Seton Hall Pirates, behind head coach Tommy Amaker, entered the game with a 5-0 record boasting one of the best freshman classes in the country in Eddie Griffin and Andre Barrett. The Assembly Hall was packed and by game time the atmosphere was electric. But, 20 minutes into the game the only electricity left in the building came from the Pirate bench.

The first half was a disaster for Illinois. The Illini came out flat and Seton Hall came out smoking hot. The Pirates built a 24-12 lead eight minutes into the ballgame and then looked to run Illinois right out of their own building. By the time the halftime buzzer sounded, a shocked Illini team headed to the locker room down 42-25.

"We underestimated them … and we were just really nonchalant" recalled Cory Bradford, who struggled in the first half trying to get his NCAA record-tying three-point shot.

Coach Self was furious with the indifferent play of his team, especially that of guard Frank Williams, who took only four shots in the first half.

"Coach was really disappointed in Frank's energy level and [aggressiveness]. He came into the locker room and lambasted Frank," said assistant coach Norm Roberts. "He really got on him and said, 'This is on you, because we go as you go.'"

The Illini were getting embarrassed on national television and Coach Self wasn't about to let up on Williams.

"He started to raise his voice and said to Frank, 'You are giving us absolutely nothing!' Then he turned to the team and said, 'We can do it without him,'" remembered Roberts. "Coach's final words as we left the locker room were 'Let's go out there and win this game in spite of Frank.' You could tell Frank was mad, and I really didn't know how Frank was going to respond."

The verbal lashing from Coach Self wasn't your normal pep talk.

"It was the hardest I have ever gotten on any single player by triple," said Coach Self.

The Illini and Williams responded immediately. The second half opened with a Brian Cook dunk and a Williams lay-up to cut the lead to 13. Williams trimmed the lead to 10 with just under 14 minutes remaining, and then just a few possessions later he drilled a three to cut the Pirate lead down to five.

"We were down 17 at the half and 21 in the first half, but the crowd never gave up," remembered Johnson. "All of the sudden we started hitting our shots and getting stops."

Just 11 minutes into the second half, the Illini fought all the way back to tie the game at 55 on a Marcus Griffin free throw. The rest of the game was a back-and-forth battle. To no one's surprise the Illini turned to Williams and he delivered, first putting in a tough lay-up and then knocking down a short jumper to give the Illini a two-point lead with 43 seconds remaining.

But the Illini were unable to stop Seton Hall on their final possession as Greg Morton knocked down two free throws to tie the game at 68. When Griffin's jump shot at the buzzer clanged off the rim the game was headed to overtime.

Coach Self decided to call the first set play of the overtime for Bradford, who had yet to knock down a three and had sat on the bench during the last five minutes of regulation.

Bradford came off a double screen, got the ball, rose up, and rattled the shot down, sending the Assembly Hall into a frenzy. With that three, he tied the all-time record for consecutive games with a three pointer and gave Illinois a lead they would never relinquish. An emotional Williams added four more points in the overtime session, giving him 17 since halftime and 21 for the game. When the buzzer sounded, the Illini completed the largest comeback in the history of the program by defeating the Pirates 87-79.

"After the game, instead of being mad, Frank walks by me, pats me on the butt, and says, 'Is that good enough for you?,'" remembered Self.

This was a new Illini team—and a special group, one that would never quit.

continued from page 222

Careening from the frying pan to the fire, Illinois won its second overtime game, 86-81, over Missouri as Cook exploded with 23 first-half points, and Williams came through in the clutch.

"That was a rough stretch for us," said Harrington. "The Missouri game went into overtime and was very emotional. We didn't get back to the hotel until late, and we were still excited. Then we had to catch an early-morning flight to Texas. It was hard to bounce back."

A weary Illini team, promoted to No. 5 in the rankings for their recent success, lost at Texas, 72-64. But the team was ready for a successful Big Ten run. The league in 2000-01 had slipped in prestige from two years previous, and Illinois opened by steamrolling Minnesota (Griffin scored 27) and Ohio State. Iowa rose up to knock the Illini off in Iowa City, 78-62.

"The Iowa game was a wakeup call. We needed a loss like that to grab our attention," said Harrington.

The Peoria trio excelled as the Illini recovered for four straight wins before dropping an overtime battle, 98-95, at Penn State.

"That Penn State team might have been overlooked but it was good with Titus Ivory and the Crispin brothers," said Harrington.

Three clearcut wins followed. First came an 84-59 laugher over Northwestern, then a 77-66 home-court thumping of No. 4 Michigan State in which Bradford, struggling all season on a gimpy knee, sank six treys.

"That was the second-biggest home game after Seton Hall," said Harrington. "There was so much orange in the Hall that I had to stop and look around. Cory was the key in the win. Michigan State started both halves with runs, and we fought right back. That was the game that put us in position for the Big Ten title."

Finally, after nine straight losses to Purdue, the Illini served up the most decisive setback in Mackey Arena history, an 82-61 victory, with nine Illini scoring six points or more. The win moved Illinois up three slots in the national rankings to No. 4.

No. 19 Wisconsin was a different story at the Assembly Hall. And it was Griffin's turn to pull one out of the fire. The UI center soared high for an in-bounds pass with less than a second left to flip in the winner, 68-67.

John Biever/SI/Icon SMI

▲ *Cory Bradford broke the NCAA record for most consecutive games with a three-point basket during the 2000-01 season despite playing on an injured knee. His six threes against Michigan State in a 77-66 home win was just one short of his career-best mark for a single game.*

The Illini continued their winning ways at Indiana, 67-61, and went on to share the Big Ten title with Michigan State at 13-3. Indiana and its pepperpot guard, Tom Coverdale, got revenge in the Big Ten tournament, 58-56, as Kirk Haston rejected Williams' driving bid to tie the game. But that only made the Illini better prepared for a run to the NCAA's Elite Eight.

In Dayton, Ohio, as a No. 1 seed, the Illini breezed. The three Peorians joined Cook and Bradford in dominant performances as the Illini dispatched Northwestern State, 96-54, and Charlotte, 79-61, to set

continued on page 227

GREATEST GAMES
(NO. 7) ILLINOIS 77, (NO. 4) MICHIGAN STATE 66

FEBRUARY 6, 2001 • ASSEMBLY HALL, CHAMPAIGN, ILLINOIS

ILLINI PAINT THE HALL ORANGE
WITH WIN OVER STATE

It was the most anticipated home game since the 1989 season. The fourth-ranked Michigan State Spartans were coming to town and this was the year the Illini were going to dethrone them. If the Illini wanted to win a Big Ten Championship in 2001, they had to go through the three-time defending Big Ten Champs Michigan State.

"Everybody marked that game down," said forward Damir Krupalija. "They beat us for three years in a row and we couldn't wait to get them back."

In fact, the only player suiting up for the Illini that evening who had ever tasted victory against the Spartans was Sergio McClain. He was a freshman reserve when Illinois beat them in February of 1998.

"They had Final Four talent every year and they had physically abused us in the past," said center Robert Archibald. "We wanted to come out and make a statement. We wanted to show them they weren't the only team in the league who could play that style and be successful with it."

A local radio station declared it the first ever "Paint the Hall Orange" game and Illinois fans woke up that morning with a jump in their step.

"The hype for the game was ridiculous," said Lucas Johnson. "It was ESPN, [Dick] Vitale and a Tuesday night game. That week I kept hearing how much the tickets were being scalped for and I just couldn't believe it."

The Orange Krush lined up at noon for a 6 p.m. start and when the building opened it was evident this wasn't just a normal regular-season Big Ten game.

"I was coming out of the tunnel and the entire place was orange," remembered Krupalija.

The Illini came out with emotions running high and were so excited that they started very tight. Michigan State jumped out to a 7-0 lead and held an edge until two Frank Williams free throws tied the game at 23. Sparked by threes from Lucas Johnson and Cory Bradford, Illinois finished the half on an 11-6 run to take a 34-29 lead into the locker room.

In the first 10 minutes of the second half both teams traded punches, but neither team could deliver the knockout blow. It was

turning into a physical battle and with 9:35 remaining the Illini were clinging to a one-point lead. Illinois continued to fight and finally delivered their knockout punch in the form of sharp-shooting Cory Bradford.

"Dick Vitale came up to me before the game and asked me how my knee was feeling and I remember that it felt really good," recalled Bradford, who had had trouble with his knee stiffening up all season long. "For some reason I woke up that day and had no problems with it. It wasn't stiff, it wasn't tight, and it just felt great."

At 51-50, Bradford came off a Krupalija screen and drilled a three from the top of the key. Two minutes later, Bradford got a feed from Archibald and swished a three right in front of the Illinois bench to give the Illini their biggest lead of the ball game at 59-53.

"I felt so loose during the game. ...It seemed like I was throwing the ball in the ocean," remembered Bradford, who finished the game with 22 points on six three-point shots.

A little more than a minute later, Sergio McClain gathered a rebound, pushed it up court, and skipped a pass cross court to an open Bradford again standing right in front of the Illini bench. He lifted up, flicked his wrist, and there was no doubt about it. The Illini led by nine and Michigan State immediately called a time-out.

On Illinois' next possession, Brian Cook took one step in the lane and dished the ball out to Bradford. With no hesitation and Marcus Taylor right in his face, Bradford launched a three that hit nothing but the bottom of the net. The Assembly Hall erupted, the Illini increased their lead to double digits for the first time, and the Spartans were dead, eventually falling 77-66.

"It was an exhilarating game and it was great to share the win with the students who rushed the court," recalled Johnson.

"That game was so indicative of the way that team fought," said Coach Self. "It was one of the more memorable basketball games I have ever coached in and I will always have the picture of the scene of that game in my office because it was just awesome."

With a hard-fought 77-66 victory over the Spartans, the Illini announced they were heading to the top of the Big Ten.

GREATEST MOMENTS
(NO. 4) ILLINOIS 68, (NO. 19) WISCONSIN 67

FEBRUARY 13, 2001 • ASSEMBLY HALL, CHAMPAIGN, ILLINOIS

MARCUS GRIFFIN'S SHOT
SENDS BADGERS HOME SULKING

It was an uphill battle the entire game. The 19th-ranked Wisconsin Badgers had come into the Assembly Hall and dominated the fourth-ranked Illini in all facets of the game. By the end of the first half, the Badgers shot an incredible 61 percent from the field and knocked down six of their nine three-point attempts on their way to building a 35-23 advantage heading into the locker room on February 13, 2001.

"We were in a really tough spot there," remembered forward Lucas Johnson. "We had such high expectations for the finish of that season and they came in and took it to us on our home court."

The Illini began the second half trying to scratch and claw their way back, but when Roy Boone hit a three-pointer seven minutes into the half to put the Badgers back up by 12, it seemed like the lead was insurmountable. Then, almost immediately after Boone's three, Frank Williams came alive. He scored 18 of his 22 points in the second half and when he drilled a three-pointer with four minutes remaining, the Illini pulled within one at 59-58.

After a see-saw battle in the last three minutes, Marcus Griffin grabbed an offensive rebound off a Williams missed shot and put in the lay-up to give the Illini a 66-65 lead. It seemed like they were going to pull it out, but Sean Harrington fouled Kirk Penney with 10 seconds left and Penney made both free throws to put the Badgers back up by one. The game looked over when Williams missed a shot on the final possession, but the ball tipped off a Badgers' hand and went out of bounds with 2.5 seconds left on the clock.

Illinois' 16-game home winning streak, its Big Ten Championship dreams, and its chance at a No. 1 seed in the NCAA Tournament all hung in the balance.

"We called out of bounds play number four," remembered head coach Bill Self, who made one slight adjustment to the play. "Usually Frank always took it out, but we decided to let Sean be the passer on that one. We thought if Frank set the screen, there wasn't anyway they weren't going to help on him because they would be nervous about him getting the ball."

The in-bounds passer, Sean Harrington, had two choices with where to go with the pass.

"That play was in our play book all year and we used it a lot," recalled Harrington. "If Marcus was open off the screen, I was going to lob it to him and if not Frank was going to post up on the block."

Sitting in the huddle, Griffin was confident he could knock the shot down.

"I had a good game that night and already had 16 points," said Griffin.

Six-foot-eight senior Maurice Linton guarded Harrington on the in-bounds pass while Griffin was being checked by 6-11 freshman Dave Mader. When Harrington got the ball in his hands, Williams came down to set the back screen, and Mader took one step towards Frank.

"As soon as I [saw that Griffin was open] I just put the ball up high enough so he could go get it," said Harrington.

When Harrington threw the ball over Linton it only hung in the air for a split second, but it surely seemed longer than that.

"It seemed like the ball was in the air forever," remembered Griffin. "I just went up, caught it, and guided it back the other way.

"It was one of the biggest shots I made in my career. Just hearing the crowd's reaction after it went in was amazing and it helped us keep our Big Ten Championship hopes alive."

Back the other way was right into the hoop. When the shot splashed through the basket with only 0.8 seconds remaining, the Assembly Hall erupted. Wisconsin threw a long in-bounds pass the length of the court that was intercepted by Williams and the celebration was on.

Somehow, someway the Illini got out of that game with a victory.

"We stole that game after they had executed everything they wanted to and basically had the game won," recalled Robert Archibald.

Great teams find a way to win close games and the Illini sure did that night. With one big shot from big Marcus Griffin the Illini moved one step closer to a Big Ten title and the No. 1 seed in the NCAA Tournament.

continued from page 224

up a showdown with No. 12 Kansas in San Antonio. It was no contest. Nick Collison, Drew Gooden and Kirk Hinrich were dwarfed. Frank Williams, who won the *Chicago Tribune* Silver Basketbnall Award as the UI's first Big Ten MVP since Jim Dawson in 1967, broke free for 30 points. And Lucas Johnson came off the bench to contribute 15 points in an 80-64 runaway.

"Frank carried us throughout," said Harrington.

That set the stage for a rubber match between the nation's fourth- and fifth-ranked teams—Illinois versus Arizona. Lute Olson laid groundwork by complaining about the rough play of Johnson, Archibald and the muscular Illini. His strategy worked as officials called an incredible 59 fouls, sending six Illini to the bench with five personals in an 87-81 losing result for Illinois.

Mark Jones

▲ *Senior center Robert Archibald moved into the starting lineup for the 2001-02 season, the Illini's second Big Ten championship in a row. Archibald shot 65.9 percent from the floor and averaged 5.5 rebounds and 10.6 points per game in helping the Illini advance to the Sweet Sixteen.*

Arizona guards Gilbert Arenas and Jason Gardner combined for 39 points as Arizona advanced to the Final Four, and the Illini went home.

"We were playing in foul trouble, and it hampered us the entire second half," said Harrington. "It was tough because we were right there. If we could have made a few stops, we would have gone to the Final Four."

Illinois finished out its most impressive season in years with an Elite 8 appearance, a share of the Big Ten title, a 27-8 overall record, and a peak at No. 3 in the AP rankings in late February. With the exception of a one-week stretch at No. 11, Self's debut club went wire-to-wire in the AP's Top 10. Williams finished the year with a 14.9 scoring average, 4.4 assists-per-game, and 2.0 steals per game.

ILLINI IN SHARING MOOD AGAIN

McClain and Griffin had graduated, but Bradford returned for his final year and Robert Archibald and Damir Krupalija were ready to step up on a defensively stout Illini squad in 2001-02 that began the season ranked No. 3 in the AP poll.

Highly touted Gonzaga was no threat in the opener at home. The scoring balance of Cook (18 points), Bradford (17), Archibald (16) and Williams (13) proved too much for the Zags, who fell 76-58. The Illini went unthreatened for four games until a November 24 showdown with Bruce Weber's Southern Illinois Salukis in Las Vegas. In the finals of the tournament, SIU led 66-63 with 7:40 to go but didn't get another field goal until the final 12 seconds. Harrington shot the Illini ahead 71-68 with a triple, and the Illini drained nine straight free throws. Even so, 23-point scorer Kent Williams had a last-ditch shot to tie, but missed as the 75-72 score stood.

"All summer long, we talked about our chance to beat Illinois," said Kent Williams. "It's hard but it still feels good to say we played the No. 2 team in the nation down to the wire."

The No. 2 ranking didn't last long as the Illini fell at No. 5 Maryland, 76-63, three days later in the

continued on page 230

GREATEST MOMENTS
NOVEMBER 11, 1998—FEBRUARY 10, 2001

BRADFORD DEMOLISHES THE NCAA
THREE-POINT RECORD

It was the 22nd game of his Illinois basketball career and Cory Bradford wasn't thinking about anything except trying to get a road win for his team. The Illini were playing at the Barn in Minnesota and three minutes into the game, he rose up from behind the three-point line on the left side and knocked down a relatively easy shot. He didn't think anything of it, but after the game he learned that his only three-pointer that day had a little extra significance.

"After the game our sports information director, Barb Butler, said that I had just tied Matt Heldman's record for 22 consecutive games with a three," remembered Bradford. "That was the first time I knew I had a streak going, but it never hit me as to how important it was going to become until the end of my sophomore year in the Big Ten Tournament."

Thirty-seven games separated that Minnesota game and Illinois' first game in the 2000 Big Ten Tournament. Bradford hit at least one three-point shot in every single one of them.

On March 10, 2000 in a first-round match-up with the Hoosiers, the Illini were caught in a dogfight. In a back and forth game that was close throughout, no one seemed to notice that Bradford had gone 0-5 from downtown and was in serious jeopardy of losing the streak.

With 7.3 seconds left and the game tied it was Illini ball and Coach Kruger drew up a play for point guard Frank Williams.

"They double-teamed Frank so Serg (Sergio McClain) couldn't get him the ball," recalled Bradford, who had struggled all afternoon from the field. "Serg drove the baseline and Coach Kruger taught us that every time a guy drives baseline, he has to have a bail out guy in the weak side corner. It was just a reflex for me to slide down to the corner."

A wide-open Bradford got the ball in the corner, rose up into the air, and hit nothing but the bottom of the net to send Illinois into the semifinal of the tournament. When he knocked it down he didn't even realize it was his only one of the game.

"It wasn't going through my mind at all and it didn't hit me until Barb told me in the locker room that I hadn't hit one before that," said Bradford. "That game showed me that I had some-

thing good going and that is when she told me that Wally Lancaster held the NCAA record of 73 [consecutive games of hitting a three-point basket]."

Bradford entered his junior season with the streak at 64 games. The record was in sight, the local media picked up on it and the pressure started to grow.

"I felt the pressure to start that season," recalled Bradford. "It got to a point where the media wasn't asking anything about the team and it was always about the streak. It was coming really close and I was thinking that I was ready to get it over with."

He hit two threes against Maine, three against Maryland, one against Arizona, and one against Texas Southern.

"It seems the closer and closer it got the harder it was for me to knock down that three," remembered Bradford.

By this time Lancaster had become a household name in Champaign and everyone was waiting for the first three of each game. There were three against Duke, two against Kansas State and two against Wisconsin-Milwaukee to move one game short of tying the record.

On December 9, 2000, against the seventh-ranked Seton Hall Pirates in front of a national television audience on CBS, Bradford was shooting to put himself in the record books.

The script didn't go as planned. The team fell down early and Bradford wasn't shooting well.

"There is no doubt in that game he was pressing," remembered assistant coach Norm Roberts. "He was pressing so hard and there were even a couple of situations where they were bad shots out of the flow of the offense."

Bradford went 0-6 from behind the arc in the first half and none of his shots looked good.

"I had some good looks but I just looked timid shooting them," said Bradford. "I short-armed a couple of threes and I looked like I had never shot a three-pointer in my life."

As the game went on the pressure continued to grow.

"I started to put up shots thinking that I had to get this out of the way, because I came too close not to get it," remembered

Bradford. "Eventually Coach Self sat me down and told me to calm down and think about it."

Having missed his only two three-point shots in the second half, Bradford sat the last five minutes of regulation. It wasn't easy sitting on the bench and knowing he might have missed his chance.

"As it was nearing the end of regulation, I just thought that I can't be selfish," said Bradford. "All I was thinking about was myself and it was more important to win the game. I just told myself that if it doesn't happen, then, oh well."

But Bradford would get one last chance. Marcus Griffin missed a shot at the end of regulation and the first set play of the overtime was called for Bradford.

"Coach Self said, 'This is it,' and they ran a play for me. It was play number one and it called for me to come of a double screen," remembered Bradford. "Coach said, 'As soon as you catch it let it go.'"

Coming open off the screen, Bradford rose up and launched a three that rolled around the rim a few times before dropping in.

"It still didn't seem like it wanted to fall for me," laughed Bradford. "But when it went down it was a huge load lifted off of me."

The Assembly Hall crowd erupted as number 73 was in the books.

A week later, Bradford attempted to break the record against Arizona in the United Center. It wouldn't take him long this time.

"I ran a pick and roll with Marcus Griffin and we knew they were going to go under the screens. Coach Self taught our big guys to roll into them if they did that," said Bradford, reflecting back on the shot that put him in the record books in sole possession of the longest streak in NCAA history. "As soon as Griff did that, I stepped up and looked at the first line I saw, which was the NBA line, and just pulled it."

The shot dropped and the United Center crowd went crazy. A continuous buzz lasted for three minutes as the crowd rose to give Bradford a standing ovation. After the game the team presented him a ball as they carried him off the court.

"It was amazing that the crowd waited around after the game to give me another standing ovation," said Bradford from his home in Hungary, where he played professional basketball last season. "When I got the game ball and my teammates picked me up, it was probably one of the biggest moments of my life."

The streak ended later that season as Bradford failed to hit a three-point shot in February against Wisconsin. He etched his name into the record books with 88 consecutive games with a three-point shot. His teammates are still amazed at his accomplishment.

"As a three-point shooter, you are going to run into droughts where you are not shooting the ball well or games

where you don't get that many shots," said Illinois guard Sean Harrington. "For one individual to hit a three-pointer in 88 straight is incredible."

Over the course of his streak Bradford collected 25 games with one three-point basket, 23 with two, 17 with three, 12 with four, five with both five and six three-pointers made, and one with seven three-point buckets.

Bradford finished his career with 1,735 points, 275 assists, and 363 rebounds. Those are all great numbers, but for Cory Bradford only one number will always follow him as the years go on. That number is 88.

▲ *Cory Bradford acknowledges the crowd after breaking the NCAA record for consecutive games with at least one three-point basket. The moment came in December of 2000 in a game against Arizona at the United Center in Chicago.*

continued from page 227

ACC/Big Ten Challenge. The squad then dropped another two games later to No. 7 Arizona, 87-82, in Phoenix. But Frank Williams was on his game with 22 points in St. Louis as the Illini shot 50 percent to throttle Missouri, 72-61. The Illini stood 11-2, their only losses to elite powers, as they began their run for the Big Ten championship.

"Missouri put us back on track after two tough losses on the road," said Harrington.

For half the conference race, it didn't appear that a repeat could happen. Wisconsin won 72-66 in kicking off its long run of Big Ten home wins under Bo Ryan. The Illini fell at Purdue, 84-70, but Cook and Archibald shared 39 points and 15 rebounds in igniting a three-game win streak that began against Michigan.

Suddenly, in late January, the No. 9 Illini hit a wall. Unable to stop Indiana's long-range bombs, the Illini succumbed, 88-57, in Bloomington as Tom Coverdale,

Dane Fife and Kyle Hornsby led the Hoosiers on a league-record 17-trey explosion.

"I'm still trying to forget that one," said Harrington.

Nor did the Illini recover at No. 25 Ohio State or against Michigan State at home.

Surely the 67-61 loss to the Spartans—one of only three Assembly Hall losses in the last five seasons—would end title hopes ... but it didn't. After plummeting to No. 21 in the AP poll, the Illini finally recovered and took charge at Michigan with a 68-60 victory, and went on a stirring eight-rebound game win streak—that included a non-conference win over Seton Hall—to share the Big Ten title at 11-5 with Wisconsin, Indiana and Ohio State.

"The loss to Michigan State at home was an eye-opener. We realized we could be considered an under-achieving team," said Harrington.

continued on page 233

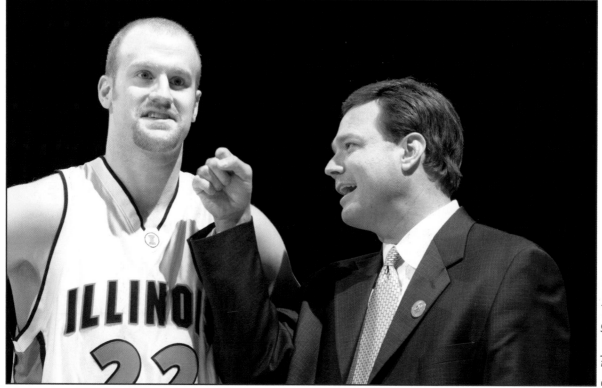

▲ *Coach Self gives forward Lucas Johnson a playful punch. Once Johnson was inserted into a game, however, any sign of playfulness was left on the bench. Johnson served as a hustling, intense igniter for Illinois, often putting the fight back into Fighting Illini.*

Tom Pidgeon/Getty Images

GREATEST MOMENTS
(NO. 15) ILLINOIS 67, MINNESOTA 66
MARCH 3, 2002 • WILLIAMS ARENA, MINNEAPOLIS, MINNESOTA

WILLIAMS BUZZER BEATER WINS BIG TEN

The dream run was seemingly over. After fighting their way back to the top of the Big Ten standings with seven consecutive conference wins, the 2001-02 Illini watched their hopes for a second straight Big Ten Championship fade away when Minnesota guard Kerwin Fleming knocked down a three-pointer with 3:12 remaining to give the Gophers a nine-point lead in the final conference game of the season.

Most, including many Illinois fans, thought the game was over. But this Illinois team had gone through too much to just quit. They faced adversity with injuries, they suffered through a midseason funk, they stuck together when nobody believed in them, and they stuck by their star player, Frank Williams, while many questioned his passion and desire.

Down nine with three minutes to go, Illinois was in deep trouble.

"We had no chance to win that game at that point," remembered head coach Bill Self. "But what I loved about those teams at Illinois is that no matter what happened during the game, it was always going to come down to the last two minutes."

After a three-point basket by Cory Bradford and two free throws by Robert Archibald, the Illini cut the lead to four with just over two minutes left to play. After recovering a blocked shot from Brian Cook, Archibald was fouled again, but this time he missed his two free throws and again essentially ended Illinois' chances at a comeback.

With 31 seconds remaining the Gophers had the ball and a four-point lead. But, the Illini refused to be put away. Frank

continued on page 232

Mark Jones

▲ *The shot: Frank Williams' short jumper sealed the deal as the Illini defeated the Gophers to clinch a share of the Big Ten championship.*

continued from page 231

Williams tied up Fleming, ripped the ball from his arms as he was falling back, and it trickled into the hands of a wide-open Bradford at the top of the key. He rose up and nailed a three-point shot to bring the Illini to within one.

Illinois trapped the Gophers' Kevin Burleson on the ensuing in-bounds pass. When Burleson tried to pass it cross-court to a teammate, he threw it out of bounds. With 6.9 seconds left on the clock, the Illini had one more shot to bring the trophy back to Champaign.

There were no surprises in the Illinois huddle.

"I remember Frank saying, 'Give me the ball,' and you could see it in his eyes that there wasn't another person on that team that was going to take that shot," recalled Lucas Johnson. "Everybody in the building knew it, everyone watching on television knew it, and Frank knew it. He was going to take the shot."

Self had gone through his ups and downs with Williams throughout the season in trying to get his star player to perform with consistent energy. But he still knew whom to call the play for.

"There is no telling how many e-mails I got that year saying I should bench him and be a tough coach," recalled Self. "But to the very end Frank was my guy. I knew Frank gave us a chance to win any game and without Frank, we didn't have a chance to win most games."

"What Coach wanted was for a big [guy] to come and set a pick for Frank on the wing so he could penetrate," remembered

assistant coach Norm Roberts. "He told Frank, 'When you turn the corner, if you can get all the way, just go,' and our big guys were going to get to the other side of the floor so if Frank missed it they would be there for the rebound."

Frank caught the ball on the wing guarded by 6-7 Big Ten Defensive Player of the Year Travarus Bennett. He got a brush screen, dribbled hard right and turned the corner. As the lane opened he rose up, glided through the air, and put up a soft bank shot from the right corner. As the shot went up, everything seemed to move in slow motion.

"It wasn't an easy shot," remembered forward Damir Krupalija. "It was one of those where he put it up and you said, 'Oh my God,' but he was able to get it over the defender's outstretched arms."

"For Frank to be able to elevate over Bennett was amazing. He didn't shoot when everybody expected him to shoot," remembered Johnson. "He hung in the air, let Bennett fly by him, and then shot it off the glass with ease."

"I sealed my man off, because I knew the shot was coming," remembered Archibald. "I had a feeling it wouldn't matter, because when the game is on the line Frank isn't going to miss those. He just loves that spotlight when he gets the chance to shine."

After all the criticism and all the doubts, Frank Williams put the entire team and the weight of the Illini nation on his back and delivered a Big Ten Championship with a short little kiss shot off the glass. It's a moment frozen in Illinois' rich basketball history in typical Frank Williams fashion.

"People don't know this, but it really bothered him when people got on him that year," said Self. "It was just fitting that Frank made that play to give us another title."

The shot set off a wild celebration in Minneapolis. The Illini were champions again, but this year something made it all the more special. This one didn't come easy and it took almost every second of the season to climb out of the hole they dug for themselves in January and early February.

"That win meant so much to the team, and personally it reassured me that I made the right decision in coming back from my injury," said Johnson, who missed part of the season due to ACL surgery. "That moment and feeling was the reason I came back. ... Just holding that trophy in the locker room knowing I couldn't have asked for better teammates to share it with was one of the greatest feelings I have ever had."

With a great comeback capped by an amazing shot, for the first time since 1951-1952, an Illinois basketball team could claim one thing: they were back-to-back Big Ten Champs.

▲ *The reaction: The usually even-keel Frank Williams leaps into the air and pumps his fist after clinching the 2001-02 Big Ten Championship in dramatic fashion.*

AP/WWP

continued from page 230

Purdue led a February 19 contest by 18 points in the first half before Cook rallied the home forces in a 17-0 run that set up a 69-67 victory. Surviving that nail-biter, the Illini found themselves right back in another one at Michigan State where Frank Williams turned in a sparkling 22-point, 8-rebound game to fend off the Spartan rally, 63-61.

"He has been criticized for his effort, chided for his laid-back nature and circled in red as the one player most responsible for Illinois' disappointing season. But Tuesday night Frank Williams played with a rage," wrote *Decatur Herald & Review* columnist Mark Tupper.

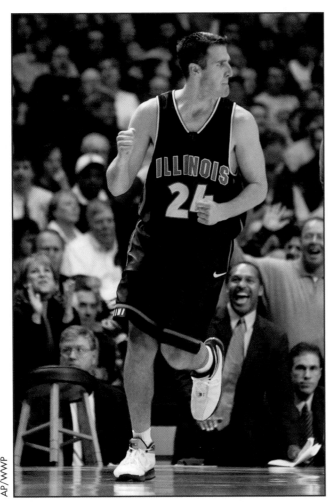

AP/WWP

▲ *Sean Harrington celebrates after another clutch three pointer. Harrington hit 191 three-point shots over the course of his Illini career on 42.8 percent shooting, good for third on Illinois' career list.*

"The treatment of Frank by the media was very unfair," said Harrington. "We were playing bad as a team, and the focus was on Frank. He played a very emotional game at Michigan State, and that was another turning point. He proved a lot that night. He got a lot of abuse for things that nobody was doing well.

"As a player, you try not to let outside forces come in, but people were bringing it up, and that drew us closer together."

On the Illini rolled, devouring Penn State, Northwestern and No. 25 Indiana down the stretch, setting up a tough final assignment at Minnesota. The Gophers, with Rick Rickert and Dusty Rychart starring, had this one in their grasp before Illinois came out of nowhere to score the last 10 points and win, 67-66. Minnesota had the ball and a 66-62 lead in the final half-minute. But turnovers proved the Gophers' undoing. Bradford popped a trey to cut the lead to one, and Williams took advantage of Minnesota's switch to a man-to-man defense by making a dramatic drive for his only basket of the second half with two ticks left on the clock. When the Gophers threw the last pass away, it was their third turnover in the final 17 seconds.

Williams' soaring drive-in, captured in a remarkable wide-screen photograph, showed an entire fandom open-mouthed and gasping. There have been many unbelievable Illini finishes over 100 years, but none that caught the opposing crowd more astonished and off-guard.

"That was a reflection of the whole season," said Harrington. "Just when it looked like we were down and out, we pulled it off."

Illinois beat the disappointed Gophers again in the Big Ten tournament, this time without a hitch (92-76) as the three-point shooters, Bradford (25 points) and Harrington (16), were on the beam. But the magic ran out in the second tourney game against Ohio State, 94-88, and the No. 13 Illini left Indianapolis and headed for Chicago and the NCAA Tournament.

Comfortable in the Windy City surroundings, Illinois had no trouble in dispatching Steve Fisher's San Diego State team, 93-64, and held Creighton's Kyle Korver to 14 points as Frank Williams and Brian Cook led a 72-60 triumph. But Kansas was waiting at the

Kohl Center in Madison, and the Illini fell into a 38-percent cold spell as the No. 2-ranked Jayhawks ended the UI run, 73-69.

"We looked back on two Big Ten championships but the ending was bittersweet," said Harrington. "We wanted to go farther."

Still, the Illini ended a respectable season and a wild Big Ten ride with a share of the conference title and a 26-9 overall record. Williams improved his scoring average to 16.2; likewise, his rebounding average improved to 4.7 while his steals (2.0) and assists (4.4) remained consistent with his career norms. Williams (late first round) and Archibald (early second round) were both selected in that year's NBA draft.

(RE)BUILDING STEAM

Senior Brian Cook was the only full-time starting lineup returnee entering Self's final season, but Illinois remained among the nation's elite thanks in no small part to a trio of freshman—Dee Brown, Deron Williams, and James Augustine—and a pair of sophomores—Roger Powell and Luther Head. In a 7-0 start, six of the wins came by double figures, including a 92-65 rout of No. 12 North Carolina that started the big ball rolling and the coaching dominoes ultimately falling. Coach Matt Doherty, hampered by the injury loss of Sean May, could never get the Tar Heels turned around, was ultimately fired and replaced by Roy Williams, leaving the Kansas job open for Self.

December's highlight was an 85-70 thrashing of No. 11 Missouri. Red-hot freshman Dee Brown produced 21 points and seven assists while Cook cashed 17 points and nine rebounds for the No. 12 Illini. But the first Illini flaw became apparent in Memphis on December 28 when big Chris Massey, dominating the paint, rallied Memphis for a 77-74 decision.

"We felt like we had a good non-conference season," said Harrington. "We were definitely young with five seniors gone and freshmen stepping in."

Illinois reached the Big Ten opener vs. Minnesota with a 10-1 record and a No. 10 ranking. This rebuilt club promptly dispatched the Gophers, 76-70, with Cook and

Harrington scoring 25 and 22, and defeated Wisconsin, 69-63, with Cook collecting a career-high 31 points.

But No. 8 Illinois couldn't handle road assignments at Iowa and No. 18 Indiana, dropping both games. They rebounded with three clearcut wins, and then dissipated a 14-point lead in dropping a 68-65 scorcher at Michigan State.

"We had control of the Michigan State game out of the blocks," said Harrington. "We took the crowd out of it in the first half but Alan Anderson hit a three at the halftime buzzer. It shouldn't have counted and it changed the tide of the game."

That mistake by the officials gave impetus to a rule change whereby halftime shots may be analyzed by the refs on the TV moniter.

The Big Ten race boiled down to a showdown at No. 24 Wisconsin, winner take all. The Badgers hadn't lost a Big Ten home game in two years under Bo Ryan, and they maintained the tradition on March 5, 2003. The UI's big guns, Cook and Brown, scored 25 and 20, and Illinois rallied from a 10-point deficit in the final minutes to tie it. But Badger balance and precision prevailed in the end. Devin Harris drew a foul with four-tenths of a second remaining, and converted the second of two free throws to cinch it for the Badgers, 60-59.

"It was intense," said Harrington. "The crowd was into it every play—very loud. There were high stakes involved. With Wisconsin, you can't pinpoint one thing. The fans are great, and the Badgers play with a lot of confidence at home."

Illinois ended up second in the conference with an 11-5 mark, and entered the Big Ten Tournament ranked No. 13 in the nation.

continued on page 237

Frank Williams entered the NBA Draft following the 2001-02 season after posting career-best marks in scoring (16.2), assists (4.4), and rebounds (4.7). In each of his three seasons with the Illini, the team won at least one NCAA Tournament game. ▶

GREATEST MOMENTS
(NO. 13) ILLINOIS 67, MICHIGAN 60
JANUARY 29, 2003 • ASSEMBLY HALL, CHAMPAIGN, ILLINOIS

COOK'S SECOND HALF FOR THE AGES

If Illinois had any hopes of challenging for the 2003 Big Ten title, they needed to beat the Michigan Wolverines in the Assembly Hall in late January. The Wolverines entered the contest on a 13-game winning streak and boasted a 6-0 conference record.

After the first 20 minutes of play, the lackluster Illini were happy to be down only five points at the break. As Coach Self lit into his team in the locker room, he concentrated that outburst on the team's senior leader, Brian Cook, who finished the first stanza with only four points on three shots.

"Coach really challenged Brian at halftime," remembered assistant coach Norm Roberts. "He told him he had to bring it, he had to be a force, and that he had to be our guy."

The lecture wasn't necessarily needed, because Cook knew he wasn't playing up to his ability.

"I knew we needed to play better as a team and I wasn't playing like myself," recalled Cook. "I was having a horrible game in the first half."

The locker room speech didn't spur the Illini on to immediate success, however. Michigan opened the second half scoring five straight points to increase its lead to 11. After a time-out by Illinois, it was time for Cook to get going. He knocked down a short turn around jumper from the left side and then followed it up on the next possession with a three-pointer to cut the Wolverine lead to six.

Yet while Cook was beginning to heat up, the rest of the Illini remained ice cold. After four straight Illinois turnovers with 12 minutes left to play, the Illini fell behind by 10 points as their defense continued to be shredded by the Wolverines.

"They were a better team than us that day," recalled Self. "I remember a few minutes into that game, I turned to one of the assistants and said, 'We can't guard them.' When they got up double figures late, I thought we were in trouble."

The Illini were in trouble, but then a confident Cook started to catch fire. After hitting six straight free throws to cut into the lead, Cook followed with a baby jumper in the lane and then a three-pointer right in front of the Illini bench to cut the lead to one.

"[Cook] came out in that half with a mindset of just get the ball to me," said Roberts.

With just under four minutes to play, Cook muscled in a lay-up after spinning away from a double team to give the Illini a one-point lead. He was destroying the Wolverines.

"He dominated the game in the second half in every way you could," recalled guard Sean Harrington. "He was going inside, he was going outside, and they played some zone so he would step up and make some threes. It got to the point where we were running him off screens just to get him shots."

By that time the players on the team heeded Coach Self's message in one of the huddles. Every time they got the ball they were told to "feed the beast".

"Whenever we needed a basket he told us to give [Cook] the ball and every time we did in that half he scored," said Dee Brown. "He just kept scoring and scoring and he set the tone for the whole second half."

"The basket started looking so big," remembered Cook. "I became more and more aggressive as the half went by and it seemed like every shot I put up was going down."

After two-free throws by Cook put the Illini up 60-56, he capped his magical half just seconds later when on consecutive possessions he put in two lay-ups to give the Illini an insurmountable five-point lead.

The Wolverines scored 27 points in the second half to Cook's 26. For the game he finished with 30 points on nine of 13 shooting from the field.

"We jumped on his back and he carried us," said Self. "In one half, he became a bona-fide All-American and the Big Ten player of the year. It was an unbelievable performance."

After the game, Cook was so tired he couldn't make it to the interview room due to dehydration.

"It was real emotional for me, because I knew we needed to win the game to be in position to win the Big Ten," remembered Cook. "I was just so excited—maybe a bit too excited."

Cook didn't need to come to the interview room, because anyone who watched the game fully understood what he did that night. In 20 minutes of play, he single-handedly dismantled the Wolverines and willed his team to a much-needed victory.

continued from page 234

TOURNEY CHAMPS

The disappointment didn't last long as the Illini roared into Chicago and captured the Big Ten tourney. Northwestern upended Minnesota but was no match for Illinois, 94-65, to set up a semifinal showdown with Indiana. Sophomore Luther Head helped rock the Hoosiers, losing a portion of a front tooth but popping 16 points to back Cook's 25-point effort. The Illini built a double-digit lead with 2:53 showing and then hung on to win, 73-72.

"Luther went on a run before half and we had a lot of momentum," said Harrington. "Then they came out and hit a bunch of shots. Coverdale sank some difficult threes late in the game."

Reaching the Big Ten finals for the third time in five years, the Illini blasted defending champion Ohio State, 72-59. Harrington made four of five treys, Augustine had a double-double (12 points, 10 rebounds), Roger Powell tallied 16 points, and Cook added 15. Cook, the Big Ten MVP, was also named the tournament MVP; meanwhile, Powell, who led the Big Ten in percentage shooting (.641 in league games only), was named to the all-tourney team. In additional honors, Brown was second-team All-Big Ten, a member of the league's all-freshman team and was tops in all-games assists with 159, though one behind Deron Williams (76) in league games.

But there was tough sledding directly ahead in the NCAA tournament.

"I don't think it hurt in the sense of our playing on the previous Sunday," Harrington opined about opening NCAA Tournament play just four days after Big Ten Tournament play ended. "It was nice to win the Big Ten Tournament after the loss at Wisconsin. We at least got a championship out of the deal. But we were disappointed when we didn't get a two or three seed (in the NCAA tournament). We wound up (as a four seed) in a stacked bracket."

Notre Dame was resting, having been eliminated early from the Big East Tournament, while the Illini played hard through Sunday. First, Illinois advanced with an unimpressive 65-60 victory over a Western Kentucky squad that shot 31 percent in the first half. The Hilltoppers' Patrick Sparks, who had attained double figures in 15 of the previous 17 games, went two for 13 from the field as the UI's secret weapon—defense—provided the margin of victory. Opponents shot just 37 percent against the 2003 Illini, second best in the nation, and the UI's best percentage-against mark since 1956.

"I think it was a very sound defense," said Harrington. "We didn't have many breakdowns, and team speed was a huge factor. We were good in previous years also. The 37 percent figure wasn't a huge jump.

"Cook was definitely a good defensive player and covered for others' mistakes. His entire game improved greatly over the years at Illinois. Each year he got stronger."

But No. 22 Notre Dame's Irish had their long gunners tuned up. After barely escaping Wisconsin-Milwaukee, they rocked Illinois with 13 treys in 24 launchings as Dan Miller cashed a career-high 23 points. Defensively, the Irish played behind Cook, daring him to shoot, and he was off the mark on a six-for-23 day. The result was a 68-60 Irish triumph that ended the Self era.

The finish was out of character for Cook, who must receive consideration when Illinois fans choose their best scorer-rebounder of all time. Averaging exactly 20 points a game as a senior, he closed his Illinois career as the No. 3 scorer in UI history with 1,748 points to go along with 815 rebounds. And, more important, the Lincoln product started on four teams that won 22, 27, 26 and 25 games, shared two Big Ten titles and won a Big Ten Tournament championship.

Said his running mate, Harrington: "We had four very exciting, fun-filled seasons. That's why I came to Illinois, to play in those games and to win Big Ten championships. It was a great experience. I hold a lot of memories."

The 2002-03 squad finished with a 25-7 mark and the 11th spot in the AP rankings. They also finished under speculation of Self's departure. Self anguished over his decision to leave, fluctuating back and forth. But he was drawn by the tradition at Kansas, where he had once worked, and by family-geographic ties.

Bruce Weber took charge without missing a beat, lending credence to the suspicion that continuity, so widely valued, may be overrated. In five seasons under three coaches, Illinois has produced an average of 25.2 wins, and is 63-3 at the Assembly Hall, a remarkable 15-3 at Chicago's United Center, 4-1 vs. Missouri in St. Louis, and 9-5 in the NCAA tournament. During that five-year span, the Illini have run up some remarkable records against some of their stiffest Big Ten rivals: 10-0 vs. Minnesota, 9-1 vs. Michigan (winning the last nine in a row), 8-2 vs. Indiana, 7-2 vs. Iowa, and 5-4 against a Purdue squad that completed the 2000 season with a nine-game win streak against the Illini.

But here is the most amazing—and possibly most overlooked—statistic of all. Where once the Illini were renowned for lackluster finishes down the stretch of Big Ten play, where a 15-0 start in 1978-79 faded to a 4-11 finish, an 11-0 getaway in 1989-90 tailed off to 10-8 finish, and a 9-0 beginning in 1995-96 drifted to 9-13 completion, note how the last five UI teams have finished: Taking the last 15 games prior to the NCAA tournament, the Illini entered the playoffs with a 12-3 record in 2000, and followed that with 11-4, 12-3, 12-3 and 13-2 ... demonstrating why the Illini boast the best Big Ten record and the strongest finishes over that span.

That good fortune has not fully carried over into the NCAA postseason, however, where the Illini have never been able to sustain quality shooting in their most challenging contests. The common denominator in the last five NCAA losses was sub-par field goal accuracy. In order, Illinois shot 38.8 percent against Florida in 2000, 39.7 versus Arizona with the Peoria trio of Frank Williams, Marcus Griffin and Sergio McClain going 4 for 26, a shaky 38.1 percent vs. Kansas in 2002 with Williams and Cook going 12 for 35, a weak 34.9 vs. Notre Dame with Cook shooting 6 for 23, and finally 40.6 against Duke last March with Head and Deron Williams seven for 24 and the bench going one for nine. Arguments will rage as to whether strong defenses or the tension of pressurized playoff games numbed the Illini elbows. But reviews of the Duke game show that the shots weren't much different from the UI's previous game against Cincinnati, when the Illini blistered the nets at a 63.6 clip.

With national powers like U-Conn, Kentucky, Duke and Kansas losing key members, expectations are soaring in Illini Nation for the 2004-05 season. Not only

does the starting lineup return intact, but all the key reserves are back, plus two additions from the Chicago area: Simeon's Calvin Brock and West Aurora's Shaun Pruitt. So the buildup is mounting daily. Can Dee, Deron and the gang meet out-of-sight expectations? Can they keep their road magic going against Missouri in St. Louis, Oregon in Chicago, Gonzaga in Indianapolis, Arkansas in Little Rock, and whoever finds their bracket in Las Vegas?

And, most important, can the Illini break through when the going gets tough in the NCAA Tournament?

The talent is there. Roger Powell and Luther Head are primed for big senior campaigns. So hang on. We're about to embark on another wild ride.

Brian Cook's four-year rise to Illini legend was complete after an amazing senior season in which the forward averaged 20.0 points and 7.6 rebounds per game in leading a surprising Illinois squad to a second-place finish in the Big Ten. ▶

CHAPTER EIGHTEEN

ILLINI HEAD COACHES

RALPH JONES
1912–13—1919–20

Nearly hidden in the dustbin of Illini basketball history is one of the most extraordinary coaches of his time—Ralph Jones. During the early days of the 20th century, Jones simultaneously coached a high school, a college and a YMCA team, won two Big Ten championships at both Purdue and Illinois, and was later the head coach of the Chicago Bears.

Less than 10 years after Dr. James Naismith introduced the world to the game of basketball in 1891, Jones laid the foundation for the sport at his alma mater, Shortridge High School in Indianapolis. He was listed as player-coach as a junior in 1899, and he was a key factor in the formation of a four-team league in 1901 when Shortridge, Butler College, Manual High School and a local YMCA joined allegiances.

Moving to Crawfordsville, Indiana in 1904, Jones coached the high school, Wabash College and the YMCA, often pitting them against each other. Wabash claimed four state college titles during the period in which Jones was head coach and, in 1906, included Yale and Big Ten champion Minnesota among its victims. Wabash lost just two games in 1907, both to a high school that boasted Ward "Piggy" Lambert—later an assistant to Jones—as a squad member. Lambert later went on to fame as a coach at Purdue.

The 1908 Wabash team claimed the national title with a 24-0 record. Moving to Purdue in the fall of 1909, Jones led the Boilermakers to a shared Big Ten title in 1911 and a perfect 12-0 season in 1912 before accepting a position as head basketball coach, assistant baseball coach and freshman football coach at Illinois.

The third of Jones' eight Illini teams went 16-0 in 1914-15 and claimed the school's only national title, mythical as it was. That team featured captain Sven Duner and the Woods brothers, Ralf and Ray. The brothers returned for consecutive 13-3 seasons, sharing the conference title with Minnesota in 1916-17.

Jones remained for three more seasons of wartime turmoil before moving to a prep school in Lake Forest, where he coached for nearly a decade. Then, his relationship with George Halas—a three-sport UI star during Jones' term and the founder of the Chicago Bears—led to being selected as the Bears head coach in 1930. His Bears teams went 24-10-12 in the early-1930s and won the franchise's first NFL title in 1932. Halas nearly lost his franchise to bankruptcy during the depression and reportedly paid Jones with I.O.U. notes. Jones elected to return to a more dependable paycheck at Lake Forest, where he continued to turn out exceptional basketball teams—two of which were undefeated—until 1949.

Halas called Jones "a coaching genius" greatly responsible for developing the "Monsters of the Midway." Jones is also credited with the revival of the T-formation and the use of a man in motion. On the basketball court as Illini coach, some credited Jones with originating the fast break. No one can question the man's coaching intellect, nor his accomplishments in producing seven winning basketball seasons at Illinois and an overall record of 85-34.

▲ Coach Ralph Jones won two Big Ten titles during his eight seasons with the Illini. His 1914-15 club was deemed national champions.

▲ Coach J. Craig Ruby left behind his coaching duties at the University of Missouri to take the head coaching job at Illinois in 1922.

J. CRAIG RUBY
1922-23—1935-36

It is something that seems inconceivable today, but when athletics director George Huff went in search of a new basketball coach in 1922 to replace the departed Frank Winters, he looked to the University of Missouri to find his man. There he found J. Craig Ruby, a two-time All-Missouri Valley Conference forward for the Tigers who had led his teams to consecutive 17-1 seasons under head coach Walter "Doc" Meanwell. In 1921, Meanwell left to coach his alma mater, Wisconsin, and the Missouri players petitioned to have Ruby take over.

After compiling a record of 32-2 in two seasons at Missouri, Ruby was offered the head coaching position at Illinois. When Ruby accepted the position—and the almost 3,000 dollar raise that came along with it—he became the eighth head coach in the history of Illinois basketball.

▲ *Coach Ruby—wearing dark, long pants on the right-hand side of the photo—oversees a practice in 1933.*

At Illinois, Ruby's team didn't waste any time in putting together winning seasons. After a 9-6 campaign in 1922-23, the Illini tied with Wisconsin and Chicago for the league title in 1923-24.

As a person, Ruby was well respected by his players.

"He was a fine gentleman who had a good sense of humor," remembered Alfred Kamm, who played for Ruby in the early 1930s. "I know we all got along him with him real well."

"His manners were perfect," recalled reserve Sidney Port. "He would never offend anybody or ridicule a guy in public. He was a very nice gentleman."

As a basketball coach, Ruby was an innovator and was known as one of the great tacticians of his time. He campaigned with Phog Allen for higher baskets to offset the advantage of tall centers. He also advocated the elimination of the dribble to offset stalling and wanted

the hoop's diameter enlarged to 20 inches rather than 18. Ruby was also an instrumental factor in organizing the Basketball Coaches of America Organization, which he later became president of in 1930.

Ruby began his Illinois coaching career advocating the short pass system that his mentor, Meanwell, had employed at Missouri. In this system, only set chest shots from short distances to the basket were permitted. Later in his tenure at Illinois, Ruby allowed his teams to play with more abandon and the fast break replaced the slow break.

On the sidelines, Ruby was known for his habit of nervously chewing a handkerchief during the games.

"He chewed on the handkerchiefs all his life," remembered his daughter, Joyce Fowler. "He was always chewing on the corner of them and I remember one Christmas my grandmother gave him a dozen nice linen handkerchiefs. She said, 'If you are going to be chewing, at least you will be chewing on something nice.'"

Ruby coached 14 years at Illinois and won 61 percent of his games. In 13 of those seasons, the Illini finished in the upper half of the Big Ten and in 1934-35 Ruby collected his second and last Big Ten Championship at Illinois.

Right before the second semester began in 1936, Ruby announced it was going to be his last season at Illinois.

"I believe it's unwise for my family and myself to depend on basketball entirely for our livelihood in the later years of my life," wrote Ruby in his statement. "I do not choose to face the prospect of coaching basketball at 50 or 60 years of age."

February 24, 1936—the final home game of the season for the Illini—was named "Ruby Day." Illinois was losing a great coach and college basketball was losing one of its greatest pioneers. That morning in *The New-Gazette*, people from all over the college basketball world shared their thoughts on Ruby.

"The world at large has benefited by the life and work of Craig Ruby through the manly men he has developed," said James Naismith, the inventor of basketball. "Basketball in particular has benefited through the splendid techniques that he has devised and through his scientific attitude toward the best interests of the game."

After leaving coaching, Ruby dove right into the business world. From 1937 to 1946, he worked as personnel manager for Hallmark Cards and then he operated the Friendship Gift and China House from 1946 to 1961. After a brief retirement, Ruby began selling commercial real estate and eventually retired in 1976. He passed away on September 9, 1980, at the age of 84.

He won 148 games in his time at Illinois and helped to usher in Huff Gym, but his greatest legacy from his 14-year tenure at Illinois was the young men he molded into great players—Doug Mills, Harry Combes, Howie Braun and Wally Roettger. Those four guys led the Illinois basketball program and athletic department all the way until 1966.

DOUG MILLS
1936-37—1946-47

Illinois fans were sure familiar with the name Doug "Gaga" Mills by the time he became the head coach of the Illinois basketball team in 1936. Growing up in Elgin, Illinois. Mills first exploded onto the scene as an all-state forward for the Elgin Maroons, winning two consecutive state championships in 1924 and 1925. All set to go to Iowa, Mills was convinced by Illinois head coach J. Craig Ruby, to stay in-state and come to Illinois.

There are few athletes in the history of the University that enjoyed the success that Mills did in his time in Champaign. On the football field for coach Bob Zuppke, he was the starting halfback but also played safety and place kicked on teams that went 20-2-2 in his three years, which included the Helms national championship team of 1927.

As a guard for Coach Ruby, Mills didn't enjoy the same team success but individually starred for the Illini, earning second team All-Big Ten honors in 1929 and first team honors in his senior year, 1930.

At the age of 22, Mills was offered the head coaching job at the University of Kentucky but turned it down to become the head coach of Joliet Township High School. The Wildcats were forced to hire their second choice, a high school basketball coach that had just led Freeport to a third-place finish in the state tournament. They gave the job to Adolph Rupp.

After a five-year football and basketball coaching stint at Joliet Township High School, Mills returned to his alma mater in 1935 as an assistant basketball coach to Ruby. Only a year later, Ruby resigned and the stage was set for Mills to be named head coach. At first he turned down the position, because he hadn't received assurance that he would also be allowed to continue on Zuppke's football staff. When he finally got that assurance on April 3, 1936, at the age of 28, Doug Mills became the ninth coach in the history of the Illinois basketball program.

"As a basketball coach he was second to none," said Gordon Gillespie, who played for Mills in the mid 1940s. "He is the only one that I knew at the time that used the Illinois weave, which was an offense that weaved around the center position with four men rotating. He taught that offense better than anyone I know of then or now."

During his 11-year tenure as head coach, Mills won almost 70 percent of his games and had a 55-35 record against twelve different coaches who went on to be inducted into the Hall of Fame.

"I wanted to go to Illinois, because I wanted to play for Doug," remembered Illinois guard Walt Kirk. "Doug Mills was a huge figure at the time who was right up there with the likes of Adolph Rupp."

Mills won a Big Ten title in his first year at the helm while coaching players like Lou Boudreau and Harry Combes. He then went on to win two more Big Ten titles with the Whiz Kids in 1941-42 and 1942-43.

Like many coaches in his day, Mills wasn't a yeller or a screamer; in fact, it was very rare to see any emotion of out him.

"I remember sitting there in Huff Gym watching games with my Dad and there was very little emotion," recalled Doug's son, Peter Mills. "You could tell when something went right he appreciated it and when something went wrong he might tense up a bit, but I don't ever recall him vocally responding to anything."

In 1941, at the age of 33, Mills succeeded Wendell Wilson as the athletics director and held that post until he resigned in 1966. With a lot more than basketball on his plate, he left a lot of the practice responsibilities to his trusted assistant, Wally Roettger.

"Together they made a very strong tandem," said Bob "Chick" Doster.

"Wally was the guy who ran most of the practices and was the defensive coach," said reserve Ken Parker. "He would always show us exactly what our opponents were going to do."

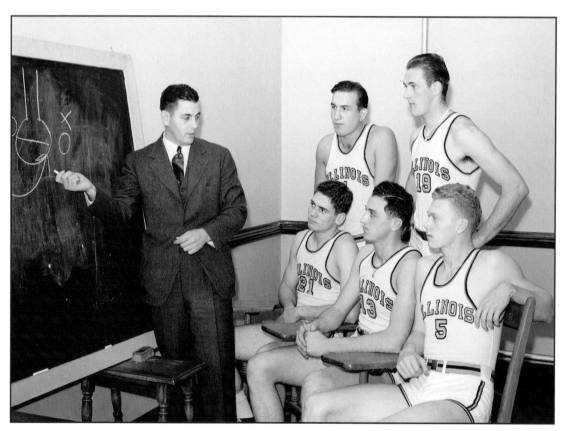

▲ Coach Mills (left) goes over Xs and Os with his players. Mills became the ninth Illini head coach in 1936 at the age of 28.

In his tenure as head coach, Mills began what would become a 30-year tradition of Illinois coaches wearing a particular color of socks.

"He would always wear the same red socks when we were one a win streak and was very superstitious in that way," recalled Gillespie.

Mills is best known for his days with the Whiz Kids, but perhaps his best coaching jobs were done while those star players were away at service. He compiled a 38-23 record in the three years while the Whiz Kids were gone, including a 19-point win over George Mikan and DePaul in December of 1945.

Off the court he was a man of integrity.

"As a person I have never met a finer man," said Gillespie. "He was a gentleman and a marvelous person who had a big heart."

Mills was ready to relinquish his head coaching duties after the 1945-46 season, but showed that integrity by staying on for one more season. He knew the Whiz Kids were going to be returning from the war, and he felt they wouldn't be the same. Mills thought that was too much pressure to put on a first year coach.

Mills left his post after a 14-6 season in 1946-47 and handed the job over to a former guard on his first Big Ten Championship team, Harry Combes. His 25-year tenure as athletics director was marked by success in all sports and included the great year of 1951-52 in which Illinois won eight championships out of a possible 12.

He was a major part of University of Illinois athletics for over 30 years as a head coach in basketball, assistant coach in football and athletics director.

"Illinois was his life," recalled Peter Mills. "He truly loved the university and its athletic department."

Mills passed away on August 12, 1983 at the age of 75, but will forever be known as one of the greatest coaches and athletics directors the University has ever seen.

HARRY COMBES
1947–48—1966–67

Before he made the unprecedented leap from high school coach to the head man at the University of Illinois, Harry Combes was already a legend in Champaign. Born in nearby Monticello, he became a star guard in the mid 1930s for the Sages, earning him a scholarship to the University of Illinois. As a player at Illinois from 1935-37, Combes became a big part of two Big Ten championship teams under coaches J. Craig Ruby and Doug Mills.

Combes' head-coaching career began in 1939, just two years after he graduated college, when he accepted the head job at Champaign High School. In nine years

▲ Harry Combes was a star for the Illini as a player before becoming their head coach in 1947. As a starting forward, Combes was a member of two Big Ten champion teams in 1934-35 and 1936-37.

at the helm in Champaign, Combes won about 85 percent of his games, leading his team to three state championship games in a row and winning the title in 1946.

When Doug Mills left the head coaching position to concentrate on being the athletics director in 1947, he remembered the guard who had helped him win his first Big Ten Championship 10 years earlier. On July 10, 1947, Combes made the short trek across town to become the 10th coach in the history of Illinois basketball.

His first five seasons at the helm produced three Big Ten Championships and three third-place finishes in the NCAA Tournament. As the head coach, Harry Combes was off and running, and so were his teams—literally.

"Harry believed in the concept that the best defense was a good offense," recalled Benny Louis, who

▲ Coach Combes won 316 games and four Big Ten titles during his 20 seasons as Illini head coach.

played for Harry late in his tenure at Illinois. "You weren't inhibited about putting the ball up and in fact, if you didn't you were probably sitting on the bench."

Illinois forward Bogie Redmon remembered a rare time when Harry got very upset with the team.

"There was this one game where we weren't shooting that much in the first half," recalled Redmon. "We got into the locker room, Harry threw his clipboard down, and said, 'I want 60 shots in this half.' I remember Dave Downey, Bill Small and Bob Starnes said 'no problem' to that."

As a rule, Harry wanted his players to put up 100 shots a game, and for the time period he coached, his teams racked up an incredible amount of points.

"He loved to have us fast break, and his whole philosophy was to get the ball down court and get up a good shot," said Illinois guard Bill McKeown, who played for Combes in the early to mid-'60s. "It was fun to play for him, and he loved the run and gun."

"Harry Combes taught the fast break like no one I have ever seen since," remembered Illinois guard Bill Ridley. "We would work on it all the time in practice and he taught us that the best fast break was when the ball never touched the floor. He was such a great tactician when it came to that."

He coached in an age where Adolph Rupp of Kentucky, Branch McCracken of Indiana, Everett Case of North Carolina State, John Wooden of UCLA and Fordy Anderson of Michigan State were the cream of the crop. But Harry Combes was right there with them. They all had a healthy rivalry and at least one member of that elite group always respected Combes.

"I liked Harry as a person from the time I first him," said Wooden. "We only played against each other a few times, but it was evident that he was a very fine basketball coach."

As a coach and an innovator, Harry Combes was one of the best.

"I thought he was an offensive genius," recalled Dave Downey. "You hear everyone talking about a motion offense today, and I guess that is what we had, because everyone on those teams had an equal opportunity to score."

In Champaign there were few people, if any, more well known than Combes.

"He owned the town and was a revered individual," recalled Illinois center Johnny Kerr, who played for Combes in the early 1950s. "I can't think of any time that anybody said something negative about him."

Combes was high strung. He had a very intense personality, and many times on the bench he became very emotional.

"Outside the game he was a very mild-mannered guy, but it was different on game days," said Illinois guard Larry Hinton. "He was very into the games and every now and then he would explode. When he did he would get all red-faced and yell at the referees, but you knew it was coming from his passion for the team."

A forward for Combes in the late 1950s, Govoner Vaughn recalled Combes' intensity and that it was very rare to ever see him joke around.

"There are a couple of times where he cracked a joke and actually laughed," remembered Vaughn. "The entire team's jaws dropped because he actually smiled."

Yet despite a winning smile, Combes was a stand-up guy and certainly a straight shooter.

"Harry was probably one of the most honest people I have ever met in my entire life," said Jim Wright, who was one of the few people to have played for and worked under Combes in his time at Illinois. "People don't know this, but he worked at Illinois without a contract. His contract was a handshake with the athletics director Doug Mills."

Combes didn't have a room-lighting charisma and wasn't what you would call a people person. In fact, he rarely went out on the road on recruiting trips; he left most of that up to his trusted assistant of 20 years, Howie Braun.

"I don't think he enjoyed going out into people's homes," recalled Ted Beach, who played under Combes for seven straight seasons at Champaign High and Illinois. "He was more of a nuts-and-bolts, hands-on basketball-type guy, and he didn't really enjoy the speech giving and recruiting aspect of his job."

His relationship with his players was a distant one, and few had personal moments away from the court with Combes.

"He would come into practice, blow his whistle, and then after practice was over he was gone," said Irv

Bemoras. "You couldn't really get close to him, but when we needed it he gave us a lot of time and was a good coach."

On game days, Combes was seen in his traditional Illinois blazer, gray slacks, and his patented red socks, the center of his superstitious streak.

"When he got the job at Illinois, Doug Mills gave him a pair of red socks as a present," recalled Harry's daughter, Jane Austermiller-Combes. "He never ever went to a game without a pair of red socks on—that was his trademark."

In all, Combes coached 20 years at Illinois and compiled 316 wins and a .678 winning percentage. He went on to win four Big Ten titles and was a part of numerous great games and moments in Illinois basketball history. His tenure at Illinois abruptly ended in 1966 when the Big Ten and NCAA slapped allegations of rules violations against the Illinois basketball program. The end for Combes came on the recruiting front, which ironically was something he almost never had his hands in.

For the first time since he was a boy growing up in Monticello, basketball was taken away from him.

"I think the slush fund was the turning point in his demise," said daughter, Jane, reflecting back on those circumstances almost 40 years later. "It literally broke his heart, and I think it made him sick to the point he never got well."

Combes passed away on November 13, 1977 at the age of 62.

He didn't go out leaving the people of Champaign and the University of Illinois empty handed, however. He left behind him a legacy of success and unforgettable games, and enough spectacular memories to last a lifetime.

HARV SCHMIDT
1967–68—1973–74

March 29, 1967 was a day that Harv Schmidt will never forget. That afternoon, he was named the 11th coach in the history of Illinois basketball. For

Schmidt, who played forward for Illinois from 1953-57, it was a dream come true.

"When Harv first got the job I met with him to talk about staying on as the freshman coach," recalled Jim Wright, who had been a senior when Schmidt was a freshman at Illinois. "He sits down and the first thing he says to me is, 'I would rather be the head coach at Illinois than the president of the United States.' It was his dream and ambition to be in that position and he was so pleased to be there."

If Harry Combes once believed that the best defense was a good offense, Harv Schmidt was the exact opposite.

▲ Coach Schmidt and his towel—where one went, the other was likely to follow.

"Our practices were very difficult and we were always concentrating on defense," remembered reserve Paul Nitz. "Even with that leftover team in his first year we were able to stay in a lot of games because we were such a great defensive team. I blame Harv to this day, because I can't go to a high school basketball game and enjoy watching it. I always notice sloppy defense."

His teams were physically tough and they took pride in their defense. In his first game in the Assembly Hall, Schmidt's Illini held the Houston Cougars and their superstar, Elvin Hayes, to just 54 points in a losing effort. Schmidt was extremely meticulous in his preparation and alongside top assistant Dick Campbell they laid things out in the finest details for their teams.

"With Dick and Harv preparing us for the games you could almost go stand and wait for people to make their cuts," said Otho Tucker, who played for Harv at the end of his tenure. "You would know their defenses, their shifts, and exactly what the opponent was going to do."

After an 11-13 season in his initial campaign, Schmidt led the Illini back into prominence and the national spotlight with a 19-5 season in 1968-69. In only two years he had brought Illinois back from the depths of despair and it seemed like things were rolling.

Schmidt is one of the more intense coaches who has ever roamed the Illini sidelines. On game days he was fired up, nervous, uptight and tense all wrapped up into one.

"He would pace as much as anyone I have ever seen in the locker room before the game," remembered Illinois guard Jeff Dawson. "You could tell he was getting charged up and that was when the adrenaline was flowing. It was easy to see that he had quite a bit of Fighting Illini in his blood and we would run out of those locker rooms ready to go."

"At halftimes he always paced back and forth, back and forth," recalled forward Fred Miller. "He had his head down, he was mumbling something, and we always sat quietly waiting to see what he was going to say. The longer he paced the more we were in trouble."

Through a lot of that pacing there was a cigarette right there with him.

"It seemed like Harv could take two puffs and have that cigarette down to the little bitty butt that you could hold between your fingers," said Tucker. "He would suck on that thing so hard and the lower it got the faster he would pace. Finally he would throw it down and stomp on it."

The pacing and the cigarettes weren't the only things that helped him to keep that fire, passion and intensity in check.

"He popped those stomach pills and Digels like crazy," recalled Wright. "He ate them like they were popcorn."

"Sometimes he would walk around with a bottle of Maalox," recalled Nitz. "He would mumble something to himself, chug the Maalox, and then mumble something again."

No one did a better Harv Schmidt impersonation than Illinois forward Randy Crews. His impressions in the locker room were frequent and are legendary, but one time it didn't go as planned. Illinois guard Rich Howat was there to see it.

"Randy was doing his Harv impression and he wasn't facing the door that Harv came in at," said Howat. "We didn't know how he would react, but Harv broke out laughing and the whole team followed. We had a really good game that night because it relaxed everybody."

On the sidelines, Harv always carried a towel in his hands and he stalked up and down the sidelines flailing his arms, pumping his fists and yelling instructions to his guys.

"He was very animated," remembered forward Dave Scholz. "He made sure he got his point across and sometimes when things weren't going well he would sit there with his arms folded hoping it would come around. If it didn't he would let us know about it."

After a 15-9 season and a third place Big Ten finish in 1969-70, the Illini struggled mightily in 1970-71, losing eight of their last nine games to finish under .500 for the first time since his initial season.

For a guy as emotionally involved as Harv, the losses were extremely difficult.

"He took the losses very hard as any competitor would," recalled Andrews. "After a lot of the games he was just drained. He gave 100 percent in every game and after the game he was like a dishrag when there was nothing left to squeeze out of it."

"He was totally absorbed in the game," said Scholz. "There were times in the locker room after the game that I would see him throwing up because of how intense he had been."

Even with his intense and tough exterior, Schmidt was a coach who his players really enjoyed being around.

"As a coach and a person they don't come any better," said Randy Crews.

"He was always consistent, and as a player that is all you can ask from your coach," said Garvin Roberson, a guard for Schmidt in the early '70s.

"Harv was a father figure to us all," recalled Nick Weatherspoon. "He was one of the main reasons I even came to the University of Illinois. When I met him you could tell he had a burning desire to win like I did, and I was drawn to that."

The Illini enjoyed back-to-back 14-10 seasons in 1971-72 and 1972-73 behind Weatherspoon, but internally, things were starting to go downhill. The culture of America was changing, and Schmidt's style wasn't rubbing off very well with the "new" ballplayers. In those two seasons, he lost three highly regarded recruits in Kris Berymon, Alvin O'Neal, and Billy Morris to transfers. His recruiting was never the same.

Losing Tucker to injury before the 1973-74 season began, the Illini lost 14 of their last 15 games to finish in last place in the Big Ten. It was a very difficult ending for a man who spent many years revered in Champaign. At the end of the season, Harv's seven-year tenure as Illini coach ended when he handed in his resignation to new athletics director Cecil Coleman.

Over 30 years later, Illinois fans look back on those great early years with very fond memories. They remember an Illini hero riding back onto campus in 1967 and giving them hope again. They recall the sold-out Assembly Halls and the atmosphere Schmidt created.

What they may not realize is how much Schmidt loved his alma mater. Three times during his tenure he was offered an NBA job and every single time he turned it down. He could never envision leaving the University of Illinois.

It was a dream come true in March of 1967, and although it didn't turn out the way he would have liked, one thing remains certain—Harv Schmidt was, and always will be, a Fighting Illini.

GENE
BARTOW
1974–75

By the time Gene Bartow arrived in Champaign to take over for Harv Schmidt, he was already known across the country as a master builder and one of the best coaches in college basketball. He coached Valparaiso to a 93-69 record from 1964-70 before moving on to Memphis State and performing miracles there. He took the Tigers from 6-20 to an 18-8 record in his first season on the sidelines, and three years later took the team all the way to the national championship game before losing to Bill Walton and UCLA.

After the 1973-74 basketball season, Coach Bartow received a call from Illinois athletics director Cecil Coleman.

"When I first heard from Cecil my impulse was that things were good at Memphis State and I should stay there," recalled Bartow. "But as I began to think more about it, the lure of the Big Ten, a beautiful arena, and the great University of Illinois prestige was too much to pass up. One thing led to another after that and soon after I was on my way to Champaign."

His coaching philosophy was a definite contrast to the defensive style and intense nature of Harv Schmidt.

"Gene was a southern dude and very much an offensive coach," recalled senior forward Rick Schmidt, who had his best year under Bartow. "He wanted us to throw the ball up and play. It was a big change in philosophy, but I liked him a lot."

"We used to call him Clean Gene," said freshman Rich Adams, who was part of Coach Bartow's first recruiting class. "He was a very nice guy who was full of energy and definitely a straight shooter."

"Gene was a very dynamic guy whose greatest strength was his practice situations," said Illinois for-ward Otho Tucker, who played for three head coaches in his five years at Illinois. "He did an amazing job of breaking down his practices into a teaching mode. The thing I learned most from him was how to make every moment in practice effective."

Illinois assistant coach Lee Hunt spent four years with Bartow at Memphis State before following him to Champaign.

"Gene was intense, but he wasn't the type of guy to scream the entire two hours of a game or practice," recalled Hunt. "He never tried to embarrass a player, and I think the guys who played for him over the years always respected that."

One of Bartow's first orders of business as the head coach of Illinois was to shore up recruiting and reconnect with the Chicago area. His decision to hire assistant coach Tony Yates proved to be very important in the eventual resurgence of the program.

Yates looks back fondly on working for Bartow.

"He was a great person, a class individual, and it was a very special year for me," said Yates. "He was an excellent motivator as a coach and was a very likeable person, but he was also very fiery at times under that nice, neat, old smile of his."

Bartow's first and only year in Champaign got off to a good start as he ironically beat his former school, Valparaiso, by 11 to get his first win on the Assembly Hall side-lines. Before long though,

▲ *Gene Bartow flashes a signal from courtside. Bartow's stay at Illinois was cut short due to an enticing offer from UCLA.*

the team began to struggle and ended up with a 8-18 record for the year, winning just four Big Ten games.

"I think the guys lost so much the previous years that they always thought something bad was going to happen," remembered Bartow. "In the first Big Ten game of the season we had the defending Big Ten champs in Michigan on the ropes but just couldn't pull it out and lost in double overtime."

In February of 1975, with a month to go in the season, Bartow received a call from UCLA athletics director J.D. Morgan saying that John Wooden was going to step down and he asked him if he would be interested in the job. At first Bartow didn't think he would take it.

"I told him in that first conversation that I wouldn't go to UCLA, because I just got to Illinois and I couldn't do that," said Bartow, reflecting back on the circumstances 30 years later.

Morgan told Bartow to think about it for a couple of weeks and then Bartow took that fateful trip up Interstate 57.

"I was traveling to Chicago to meet with Lou Boudreau, who was a great Illinois alum who was helping me recruit up in that area," recalled Bartow. "On the way back to Champaign that evening, I slipped in a ditch on an icy road and while I sat there waiting I thought the warm weather would sure be nice."

Soon after that, Bartow accepted the UCLA job and was off to Westwood.

"I don't regret leaving Illinois," said Bartow from his home in Memphis. "But I do think if UCLA hadn't called, I would have stayed 20 years in Champaign and won a championship or two. I really think you can get those types of players there."

Bartow's stay following John Wooden was short lived. He spent two years at UCLA, even making it to a Final Four, before leaving the west coast to be the athletics director and head coach of the University of Alabama-Birmingham. He spent 23 years at UAB where he is known today as the father of the program. In that span his teams made nine NCAA Tournament appearances, including an Elite Eight trip in 1982. Currently, Bartow is a scout for the Memphis Grizzlies.

He was here one day and gone the next, but Bartow's decision to hire Yates was instrumental to bringing the program back to prominence. His depar-

ture set the stage for a relatively unknown coach—Lou Henson—to come on board and bring the Illini back to prominence.

LOU
HENSON
1975-76—1995-96

For 21 years the name Lou Henson was synonymous with Illinois basketball. He coached in 647 games, and nobody in the history of the program has won as many as Lou. His coaching tenure spanned three decades and produced countless unforgettable moments and winning seasons along the way. In the past 100 years, few people, if any, had the impact on Illinois basketball that Lou Henson did.

When athletics director Cecil Coleman hired Henson in the spring of 1975, a lot of people were shocked. Prior to coming to Champaign, Henson had successful head coaching stints at Hardin-Simmons and New Mexico State, but a lot of people around the community were proclaiming "Lou who?"

It didn't take Coach Henson long to change those feelings.

"When Lou came in, there was no beating around the bush and all of that public relations stuff was gone," remembered Otho Tucker, who played on Coach Henson's first Illinois team. "He said, 'Fellas, here is the way we are going to do it, here is what we need to get done, and here is our plan.' With Coach you always knew exactly where you stood."

In his first three seasons at the helm, Henson and his assistants struggled to get Illinois basketball back on its feet. While his teams might not have been winning on the court, Henson and his assistants—Tony Yates, Les Wothke and Mark Coomes—were battling off the court in recruiting and doing everything in their power to prepare their teams for what lay ahead. Whether you played for Henson in those early years, in the late 1980s, or at the end of his tenure there is one thing that was universally true: you were always going to be well prepared.

"He was a wonderful practice coach in terms of preparing you for the games," remembered Lowell Hamilton. "He obviously studied a lot of tapes and he would statistically assign us to do certain things in a game that enhanced our chances of winning. Coach Henson was second to none in terms of preparation."

As the recruiting off the court improved so did Henson's Illinois teams. With highly recruited athletes like Eddie Johnson and Mark Smith in the fold, the 1978-79 team started 15-0 and rose near the top of the national rankings.

The following year the team finished 22-13 and placed third in the NIT. In Johnson and Smith's senior year, Henson and staff added another superstar guard in Derek Harper and for the first time since 1963, the

Coach Lou Henson and his trademark orange blazer became a staple at the Assembly Hall during the 1970s, '80s, and '90s. Henson's 21-year tenure is the longest in Illini coaching history.

Illini returned to the NCAA Tournament and ended the season ranked 19th in the country.

His work ethic was phenomenal and nobody loved being around basketball more than Lou Henson.

"He was a student of the game," said Illinois guard Gene Cross, who today is an assistant coach at DePaul. "Whenever I talked to any of the assistants and asked where Coach Henson was, they always said he was upstairs watching film or was down in the locker room breaking something down."

For Henson, his time at Illinois was a 365 day-a-year, 24-hour-a-day job, and he never stopped thinking about ways to improve his team and the program.

"I don't think anybody ever worked harder than Coach Henson," said assistant coach Dick Nagy, who spent 17 years at Illinois with Henson. "He had as much dedication for the game as you could possibly have. I used to think I was real dedicated until I spent time around him, because he set a new standard. Basketball was his life."

"We would be driving down to a golf outing in June and he would be diagramming plays all the way down there and all the way back ... trying to plan the offense for next season," remembered assistant coach Bob Hull.

Coach Henson is the definition of a basketball lifer. He is someone who is around the game at all times and enjoys every single minute of it.

"He lived and breathed basketball," recalled T.J. Wheeler. "I always thought if something was going to happen to Coach it was going to be in his office or on the basketball floor, and that is probably how he wants to go out."

After getting back to the NCAA Tournament in 1981, Henson's teams almost never looked back. Struggling to replace the scoring and leadership of Johnson and Smith, the 1981-82 group went 18-11 and lost in the second round of the NIT. The next season Harper stepped to the forefront and led the 21-11 Illini back into the NCAA tournament. That year started a run of eight-consecutive NCAA Tournament appearances.

In 1983-84, Henson produced one his best teams ever. The Illini went 26-5, losing those five games by a combined total of 16 points on the way to their first Big

Ten Championship since 1962-63. That team's style was typical of a Lou Henson ball club, because they were tough minded and played suffocating defense.

"Defensively, he was one of the best coaches in the country," said Bruce Douglas, who was the best defender in the Big Ten during his time at Illinois. "He was able to take us as individuals and develop us, but more importantly, he was able to instill the principles and strategies surrounding team defense."

The next two seasons after the title in 1984 brought high expectations and two more NCAA Tournament trips capped with hard-fought losses. The NCAA Tournament became the norm under Henson, but he had yet to get over that hump and get to the Final Four.

On the sidelines, Henson was famous for his animation.

"It was so funny the way he did that little strut when he paced in front of the bench," laughed forward Nick Anderson. "He always used to point that finger and when he pointed that finger you knew he was mad about something."

On or off the court, you never heard Henson use foul language.

"The one thing he never, ever did was swear," remembered Quinn Richardson. "He never used a cuss word regardless of how upset or how frustrating a situation was during a game, in practice, or behind closed doors."

Behind his soft-spoken voice and Oklahoma drawl, Lou Henson was a feisty and competitive guy.

He never backed down from anybody or anything.

"I was right there when Bobby Knight and Lou had their confrontation," recalled Illinois' all-time leading scorer Deon Thomas. "I couldn't believe what I saw because Coach Henson is yelling to Bobby that he is not afraid of him and that he is just a big bully. I was like, 'Wow, look at Coach.'"

Lou finally got over the NCAA Tournament hump in 1989. He led the Flying Illini to a 31-5 record and a trip to the Final Four in Seattle where they lost a heartbreaker to Michigan in the semifinals.

After the departure of Anderson to the NBA, Henson's team in 1989-90 finished 21-8 and 18th in the country but was also faced with the NCAA investiga-tion into the recruitment of Deon Thomas, which resulted in probation for the program. The first three seasons of the 1990s produced 53 wins and 38 losses as Henson and his staff struggled to recover from the allegations. Through it all, Henson handled himself with class and dignity.

"You can judge a person by how they react to situations both good and bad," said assistant coach Hull. "Coach Henson handles himself with class after the greatest win and the toughest loss."

For Henson, it wasn't just about teaching his kids about the game of basketball.

"I don't think people realize how much he cares about his players," reflected Richardson. "There were a lot of practices where we would take 15 minutes out to talk about life and how to earn a living after basketball."

"If it wasn't for Coach Henson I wouldn't be the man I am today," reflected Ken Norman. "Most coaches just roll the ball out and hope you go to class, but that wasn't the case with him. He made sure you went to class. He made sure you were respectful on and off the court. And, he tried to mold you into a quality human being. I have the utmost respect for him because of that."

On February 24, 1996, Henson announced that the current season would be his final season at Illinois. The reaction from fans and the University of Illinois was an emotional farewell to a man who had spilled sweat and tears to bring Illinois basketball into national prominence.

It has been almost a decade since Lou Henson coached his last game at Illinois, but fans still reminisce about the man who roamed the sidelines in his orange blazer. For 21 seasons he battled and coached his heart out for the Orange and Blue. For 21 seasons he shined a positive light on Illinois basketball and Champaign-Urbana with his high moral values and class.

For over two decades, Lou Henson was Illinois basketball.

LON
KRUGER
1996–97—1999–2000

When it came time to hire a head coach to replace the legendary Lou Henson in the spring of 1996, Illinois athletics director Ron Guenther knew exactly whom he wanted. In fact he had his eye on this coach for a long time.

"I had a friend, Jim Dawson, who is a former Illinois basketball player, turn me on to someone who was fairly close to the Kansas State program. So I actually began to look at Coach Kruger when he was there," remembered Guenther. "If you look back at the photos of when Florida and Lon were in the Final Four, I was sitting four rows behind the Gator bench. I didn't know if I could get him, but he was definitely the coach I wanted."

Guenther got his man, and on March 21, 1996, Kruger was named the 14th basketball coach in the history of Illinois. It didn't take him long to prove himself to the guys on the team.

"The first impression I had of Lon is that there was a real ease in talking to him," recalled then junior forward Brian Johnson. "We got the best of both worlds, because we had a coach we had a real good working relationship with and someone who knew the game of basketball."

As far as a tactician, Kruger is second to none.

"He is a guy that knows his Xs and Os better than any coach I have ever been around," said Lucas Johnson, who was a part of Kruger's second recruiting class. "He knows the game like the back of his hand and from the point guard position to the center spot, he knows every little nuance and can teach with the best of them."

"Coach Kruger was a basketball nerd," laughed guard Cory Bradford. "He is so smart and he sees things so quickly. If we were ever in need he would call a time-out and run a play that would put us over the top in any situation we were in."

In his first season at the helm, Kruger was able to guide the Illini to a 22-10 record and into the Round of 32 in the NCAA Tournament. Going into his second season, the 1997-98 campaign, the Illini weren't expect-ed to do much and actually were picked to finish in the bottom half of the Big Ten.

In one of the greatest team efforts and coaching jobs in the history of the program, Kruger guided his senior-laden team to a 23-10 record and a share of the Big Ten Title. The title was the Illini's first since 1984, ending a 14-year championship drought.

As a person, there aren't a lot of guys out there as classy and genuine as Kruger.

"He is a stand up guy and someone I looked up to," said Lucas Johnson. "He has high morals, high standards, is a real good guy, a great family man, and someone you would want to model yourself after."

While he knew the 1998-99 season was going to be a struggle on the court, Kruger and his assistants, Rob Judson, Rob McCullum and Mike Shepherd, were taking care of business off the court. By the time the season began, guys like Sergio McClain and Cory Bradford were already on the court and Frank Williams and Marcus Griffin were waiting in the wings.

The 1998-99 season was a tough one for Coach Kruger as he tried to replace the five graduating seniors with young players. The team finished 14-18 overall, but made a magical run to the finals of the Big Ten Tournament, beating three ranked teams in three straight days before falling to the Michigan State Spartans.

In his public persona, Kruger portrayed himself as a cool, calm and collected guy who rarely got upset and was always very low-key and controlled. What most people didn't get a chance to see was how passionate and intense he could be.

"He is one of the biggest competitors you are ever going to meet," recalled forward Victor Chukwudebe. "He just didn't let the whole world see his emotions and intensity all the time."

"I don't think people realize how fiery he can be," said Rob Judson, who was an assistant for the entire Kruger tenure. "If he felt practices needed to be more competitive or if the guys weren't performing well he could be extremely fiery."

The Illinois team realized that at halftime of a Michigan State game in Kruger's last season at Illinois.

"They were killing us and we were down a lot," remembered Bradford. "He went down the line and flat out went off on us. Usually he was calm, even behind closed doors, but there were certain situations that really ticked him off. Once you saw that bottom lip start to curl you knew you did something wrong."

He also had a knack for getting his teams to play extremely hard.

"He was a master motivator and sometimes I don't even know how he did it," laughed Chris Gandy. "He always made you think that the guy you were playing against in practice was going to take your spot. It didn't matter if you scored 40 points in the previous game, you always felt you had to fight."

His final season at Illinois produced a 22-10 record and a final AP ranking of 21. For the third straight year his team fell in the NCAA Round of 32, but Illinois fans were already looking forward to the following season and the great team he had coming back.

Out of nowhere, on May 24, 2000, Lon Kruger accepted the head coaching position of the Atlanta Hawks. He coached two and a half seasons with the Hawks before being let go and later took an assistant coaching position with the New York Knicks. He returned to the college ranks as the head coach of the UNLV basketball program in the spring of 2004.

He was only at Illinois for four years, but he certainly left a lasting impression.

"I look back on his tenure and the one knock locally was that he couldn't recruit," said Guenther. "Then you look and see he brought in Sergio McClain, Frank Williams, Brian Cook, Marcus Griffin, and other guys who have done a great job for the program winning championships."

He certainly wasn't the flashiest coach in the history of the program and he only spent four years on the sidelines, but Lon Kruger's lasting legacy is that he built upon the solid foundation on which Illinois basketball stands today.

▲ *Coach Kruger talks to Cory Bradford on the sidelines during the 2000 Big Ten Tournament. Kruger was a masterful tactician who was able to think on his feet. His high basketball IQ sometimes drew playful teasing from his players. Bradford, in particular, called him "a basketball nerd."*

BILL
SELF
2000-01—2002-03

When Lon Kruger unexpectedly left for the NBA in May of 2000, Illinois athletics director Ron Guenther was forced to begin his second coaching search in four years. In Ireland on a pre-planned golfing trip, Guenther spent a great deal of time on the phone between rounds of golf and really liked what he heard about this young guy down in Tulsa.

"The more I found out about Bill Self the more I liked him," said Guenther. "He had a more outgoing personality, he was younger, and there was no doubt he was going to be a real popular guy. He met all of the criteria in terms of being a god coach who had a strong work ethic. In the end everything led me to Bill."

The opening at Illinois caught Self off guard.

"I think Coach Kruger surprised a lot of people when he left for Atlanta, because it kind of came out of left field," recalled Self. "I was on vacation with my family in Disney World, and I got a call from [ESPN analyst] Andy Katz explaining the situation. I wasn't contacted directly or right away, but after studying the situation I decided if they [did come after me] Illinois was probably a place I would like to coach."

On June 9, 2000, Bill Self became the 15th coach in the history of the University of Illinois basketball program. He was coming off three great years with Tulsa and the guys on the team took to him right away.

"At the time he came in, I think Coach Self was just what the doctored ordered," recalled Robert Archibald. "We were very, very hungry for success and with Coach coming off an Elite Eight appearance the year before he certainly had a blueprint that worked to get us there."

"He is a real down-to-earth guy and is just real good with people," said Rob Judson, the lone holdover from Lon Kruger's staff who spent one year under Self before becoming the head coach at Northern Illinois. "When he came in he won that group over quickly and his offensive philosophy fit them perfectly. Those guys were definitely worried when Lon Kruger left, but he made a real big impression with them immediately."

"Coach Self definitely thinks in terms of the player," recalled Cory Bradford. "He is always thinking if I was a player what I would do or if I was a player how would I think or feel? The way he approached things helped us to feel real comfortable around him right away."

If they didn't know it already a few days into his tenure, the Illinois basketball players soon realized how intense Coach Self was going to be.

"The first real team meeting he ever called was around three days after he took the job," remembered Damir Krupalija. "He was walking into his office from the Ubben parking lot and we were playing a pickup game. While he was walking we had two behind-the-back passes that hit the wall. He comes downs, calls a team meeting, and when we get in the room he goes off [on us] and we barely knew the guy. He went right down the line, you are stealing the school's money. You are overweight. You go get treatment because you look hurt. And, I mean he said something about everyone. We were sitting in that room shocked, but from that point on everybody knew what to expect and what we had to do."

In his first season as Illinois head coach, Self led the Illini to a 27-8 record and a share of the Big Ten Championship. The team entered the NCAA Tournament as the No. 1 seed, but fell in the Elite Eight to Arizona, 87-81.

On the court, Self was able to balance being a player's coach with being a disciplinarian.

"As a person he is a guy's guy and the type of guy you would like to hang out with off the court," said Lucas Johnson. "He would get on you, but it was always constructive criticism and it wasn't so much that he was mad at you but more that he wanted you to get better.

Expectations were sky high going into Self's second season at Illinois, and when the team lost three games in a row in late January, Self faced his first real adversity in Champaign. Many people don't realize how hard he worked, especially when things weren't going according to plan.

"I would come into the office at four in the morning and see the light on over at Ubben," remembered Guenther. "I would go over there with my coffee and find him wrapped up with 16 Cokes re-watching the tapes."

After starting 4-5 in the Big Ten, Self's group won their last six Big Ten games, including the conference finale at Minnesota that the team took in dramatic fashion to finish 26-9 and again clinch a share of the Big Ten Championship. The team advanced to the Sweet 16 in the NCAA Tournament before falling 73-69 to Kansas.

With six players leaving, Self's third team at Illinois was challenged to blend his recruits with holdovers like Brian Cook and Sean Harrington. The Illini started the season by winning 12 of their first 13 games and then fell one point short at Wisconsin of winning a third straight Big Ten Title. 11 days later the Illini captured the school's first Big Ten Tournament title.

The Illini earned a fourth seed in the NCAA Tournament, but lost a disappointing second-round game to Notre Dame to end their season. With another good recruiting class coming in, it seemed the sky was the limit for Self, but much to the chagrin of Illinois fans everywhere, he departed in April of 2003 to replace Roy Williams at Kansas.

"It was tough to leave that group of guys," reflected Self from his office on Naismith Drive. "They are great kids who formed a terrific group. I certainly appreciated all of their efforts, how hard they worked, and the type of people they are. I loved all of the problems we had, loved dealing with the guys being irresponsible, and loved dealing with them not playing hard enough. I loved it all with that group."

In his three seasons, Self won 78 games, two Big Ten Championships, and finished with a winning percentage of 76 percent. He became the first Big Ten coach since 1912 to win titles in his first two seasons. Incredibly, his teams went 39-1 in the Assembly Hall. If the team's success wasn't enough to position the Illini among the nation's elite, Self's engaging personality brought the program an incredible amount of additional national exposure.

▲ Frank Williams (left) and Coach Bill Self react to the Spartans crowd following the Illini's 63-61 win over Michigan State in East Lansing on February 12, 2002.

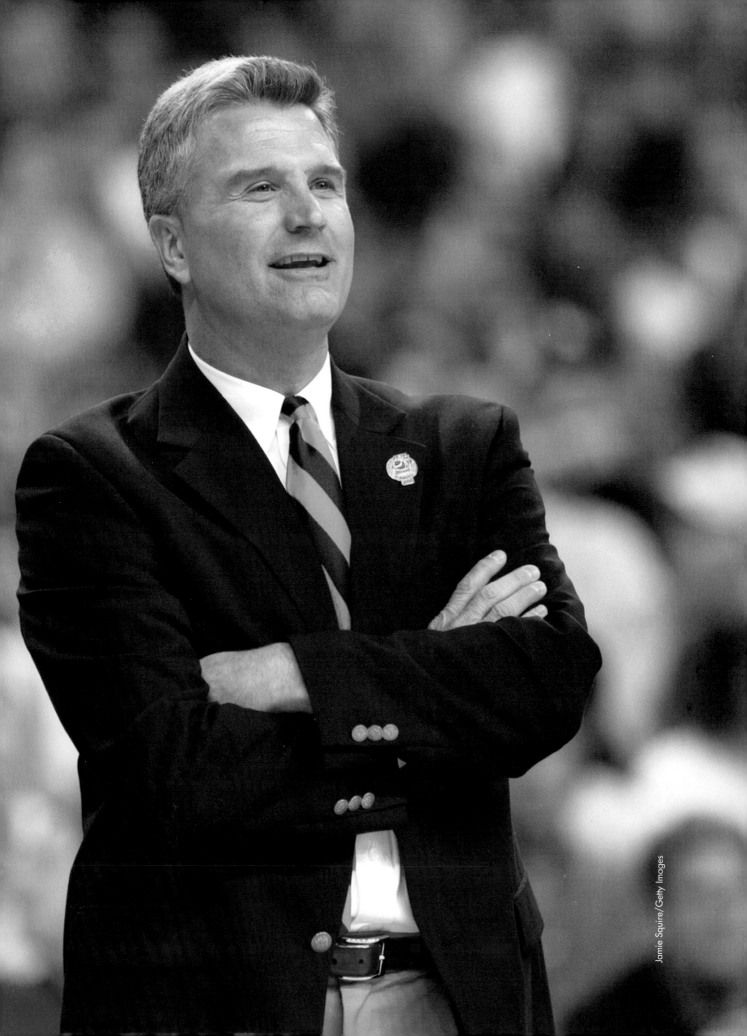

Lon Kruger brought Illinois back to the top of the Big Ten and then Bill Self came in and took it to an entirely new level. His departure passed the torch on to Bruce Weber, who so far hasn't stopped running with it.

BRUCE WEBER
2003–04—PRESENT

Bruce Weber is the perfect example of the right man at the right time. Under less-sturdy leadership, it's difficult to imagine the 2003-04 Illini winning a Big Ten Championship.

Weber learned a thing or two about leadership during an 18-year apprenticeship as an assistant coach under Gene Keady at Purdue. With the help of Weber, Keady's Boilermakers won six Big Ten championships and made 17 postseason appearances. While other assistants in college coaching were schmoozing and networking to get a leg up with another program, Weber remained close to home as Keady's strong right arm. He coached on the court, scouted the opposition, traversed the recruiting trail and kept tabs on his player's academics. In the six years following Weber's departure from Purdue to become head coach at Southern Illinois University, Purdue has captured no Big Ten championships and has finished with a losing record in conference play on four occasions.

Moving across the border in 1998, Weber strengthened recruiting ties with Illinois high schools while compiling a 103-54 record during five seasons at Southern Illinois. He laid the groundwork for his next move by capturing two Missouri Valley championships and reaching the NCAA Sweet Sixteen in 2002 as the Salukis downed Texas Tech and Georgia before falling to Connecticut. Earlier that season, the Salukis battled the Fighting Illini to the wire in Las Vegas before falling 75-72.

UI athletics director Ron Guenther sought certain qualities in a candidate to replace Bill Self—loyalty, honesty, energy and expertise. In Bruce Weber, who was named Missouri Valley Coach of the Year following the 2002-03 season, Guenther had found his man. And Weber, who after hearing Guenther's criteria remarked to himself, "Why not me?", seemed up to the task.

But the rewards didn't tumble in overnight for Guenther and Weber. The introductions were barely over when trouble reared its ugly head in an excess of on- and off-the-court concerns.

Recounted *Chicago Sun-Times* writer Herb Gould: "Between legal issues that resulted in suspensions for Luther Head, Aaron Spears and Richard McBride, Deron Williams' fractured jaw, Nick Smith's moody behavior, Dee Brown's shooting problems, James Augustine's nagging injuries, a small dryer fire at his home and a minor house break-in, Weber has had a lot on his plate."

Sounds like a disaster. But as the saying goes, what doesn't kill you only makes you stronger. Weber blended the emotions and lessons-learned from the hardships into an epoxy that solidified a courageous team, sending them on a 12-game winning streak down the stretch. At the finish line was the Illini's first outright Big Ten championship since 1952. He topped off a marvelous season with a 92-68 rout of Cincinnati in the NCAA Tournament, which marked the first time an Illinois team has ever beaten a higher seed in the tournament.

Not a bad start for a "gym rat" who began his coaching career as a volunteer assistant coach at Madison High School in Milwaukee. By any standard, Weber has paid his dues. And for the Illini, Weber is now paying big dividends.

◄ *For Bruce Weber, the position of Illinois head coach was a long time coming. The 2003-04 Big Ten Championship and the team's subsequent success in the NCAA Tournament made it well worth the wait.*

CHAPTER NINETEEN

THE FIGHTING ILLINI
ALL-CENTURY TEAM

RAY
WOODS
GUARD: 1914–15—1916–17

Raymond J. Woods came to the University of Illinois from Evanston with his brother Ralf in the fall of 1913. Under second-year coach Ralph Jones, Woods spent his first year in an Illini uniform on the bench learning from guys like Sven Duner of Wheaton, Dudley Crane of Montclair, New Jersey, Frank Bane and Helmuth Kircher of Chicago, and Edward Williford of Nokomis.

Woods cracked the starting line-up during his sophomore season of 1914-15 on a team that breezed through their non-conference schedule with wins over Arkansas A.C., Illinois Wesleyan, Millikin and the Peoria Tigers. The Woods brothers helped the Illini storm through the conference season, culminating with a 19-18 victory over Chicago in which the brothers stole the show. The 1915 Illini went 16-0 and were named national champions; for his part, Ray Woods earned Helms All-America honors.

Before his junior year began, Woods was named captain of the 1916 Illini. Amazingly, Ray Woods played every minute of every game in that 13-3 season on his way to his second straight All-America award.

Not always a major scoring threat, Woods was known for just about everything else. He was an exceptional rebounder, a floor leader with great passing skills and a guy who worked hard on the defensive end of the court.

By the time their senior year rolled around the Woods brothers were the talk of the conference. Ray scored six points in a win over Purdue at West Lafayette, eight points in a lopsided victory over Northwestern in the Gym Annex (Kinney Gymnasium), four in a huge late season win against Minnesota and netted a game-winning basket against Wisconsin in his last home game in an Illini uniform. The 1916-17 team finished 13-3 and in a tie for the Big Ten title with Minnesota.

Ray Woods finished his Illinois career as a three-time Helms All-America selection, three-time All-Big Ten member and the first great guard in the history of Illinois basketball.

▲ *Ray Woods starred on a pair of Big Ten champion teams along with his brother, Ralf.*

CHUCK CARNEY

GUARD: 1919–20—1921–22

From the beginning of his life, Charles Carney learned how to be resilient.

"He was from an Irish family that had a lot of kids," explained his grandson Walter Robb. "He lived on the wrong side of town and he had to establish his toughness. He told me a lot of stories about going places and getting into scrapes or fights."

When Carney left Evanston High School to enroll at the University of Illinois, no one could have ever imagined the feats he would accomplish or the records he would set. Over the next four years, he excelled on both the gridiron and the hardwood, becoming one of the greatest athletes to ever don the Orange and Blue.

But back in August of 1919, Carney's great career at Illinois almost ended before it began.

"He was close to never making it down to Champaign, because right before he was supposed to leave for school his father passed away," recalled Carney's only child Roslyn Leydet. "He was being approached to play professional ball, but before my grandfather passed away he made him promise that he would get an education."

Carney's basketball career at Illinois began in 1920 when as a sophomore he burst onto the scene with his unique ability to score. Before the season even started, Coach Ralph Jones replaced team captain Kenneth "Tug" Wilson with Carney in the starting line-up. In his first ever game against Northwestern, he scored 14 of the team's 24 points on the way to a victory over the Wildcats.

At 6-1 and 195 pounds, with slicked-back long hair, Carney was big for his day. He played center on the team, could score from all over the court with his nice touch, and was chosen as the designated free throw shooter. (In the early part of the 20th century, teams chose one person to shoot all of their free throws during the game.)

Carney scored 202 points (71 from the free throw line) in his first full season on the court and accounted for 52 percent of the Illini's scoring production on his way to first-team All-Big Ten honors. His 188 points that season in 12 conference games stood as a Big Ten record for 22 years.

But Carney's abilities on the football field cost him playing time on the basketball court. In the last game of the 1920 football season against Ohio State, Carney tore ligaments in his knee during the second quarter and missed the first nine games of the basketball season. Under new head coach Frank Winters, Carney returned February 5 in West Lafayette, but he wasn't the same player. He scored only 38 points in limited action the rest of the year. Still, it was no surprise that Carney toughed it out after the injury.

"He was a very tough man and he never really did any complaining or whining," recalled Robb. "That was true right up to the very end of his life."

Carney was named captain of the 1921-22 Illini and shifted over to the forward spot before the season began

▲ *Illini forward Chuck Carney starred on Coach Ralph Jones' last team in 1919-20 and Coach Frank Winters' second team in 1921-22. Carney led the Big Ten in scoring both seasons and was named an All-American.*

as Slim Stillwell and Wally Roettger manned the middle. Carney began the year tearing up Illinois Wesleyan for 15 points, and his torrid scoring pace continued throughout the season. On February 20, 1922, Carney became the first Illini basketball player to hit for 10 baskets in one game scoring 23 points in a 41-22 rout of the Ohio State Buckeyes in the Gym Annex. He finished the year scoring 172 points and again earned first-team All-Big Ten honors.

▲ *Chuck Carney's letterman's sweater and the Varsity "I" Association Award of the Year presented to him in 1979.*

Carney finished his Illinois career with 497 points and held the career scoring record until Andy Phillip eclipsed it in 1943.

Carney's diversity as an athlete earned him a unique distinction. He was a two-time basketball All-American (1920, 1922) as well as a football All-American in 1920. That made him the first Big Ten player ever to be an All-American in both sports. After his outstanding senior campaign, he was named the National Basketball Player of the Year. He later was inducted into both the Basketball and College Football Hall of Fame, becoming one of only two people to be a member of both.

After leaving Illinois, Carney went on to be an assistant football coach at Northwestern, Wisconsin and Harvard before entering the investment banking business as a New York Stock Exchange representative for the firm of Dominick and Dominick.

He credited the University of Illinois for affording a young kid from the wrong side of town a chance to move up in life.

"He always said the University was a bridge in his life," remembered Robb. "His time there rocket-propelled him from his beginnings in that rough neighborhood into coaching and eventually into the investment business."

In his later years, he resided in Boston and retired from Dean, Witter, and Reynolds in 1978. Carney passed away in 1984 at the age of 84, but he will always be remembered for being one of the greatest two-sport athletes the University has ever seen.

For Carney, his time at Illinois is something he never got tired of talking about.

"I remember he took a trip back to Illinois just to see their new gym and we always had people visiting us from the University," recalled Leydet. "He was always very happy when his friends from Illinois came to Boston and I remember they used to sit down for a while and reminisce. My father loved the University of Illinois very, very much."

GENE VANCE

GUARD: 1941-42—1942-43; 1946-47

Doug Mills and his assistant, Wally Roettger, hit the jackpot with the class of 1940, eventually bringing to Illinois all five of *The News-Gazette's* first-team all-state squad. They landed Andy Phillip from Granite City, Ken Menke from Dundee, Dike Eddleman from Centralia, Ed Parker from Cicero and Gene Vance from Clinton.

Ellis Eugene Vance grew up in nearby Clinton, Illinois and was the only Whiz Kid who came from the Central Illinois area. With his proximity to the school he didn't have much of a choice when it came down his recruitment.

"My folks pretty much decided on it for me," said Vance. "I remember my mother saying, 'You can go anywhere as long as it is on the corner of Wright and Green.' Most kids were staying in state and I wanted to come to Illinois."

Spending his freshman year getting acquainted with Andy Phillip, Ken Menke and Jack Smiley, who along with Art Mathisen would form the now famous Whiz Kids, Vance and his fellow classmates were ready to make an immediate impact in the 1941-42 season.

Vance scored six points in his first ever collegiate game against Marquette and scored 10 in a huge win against the defending national-champion Wisconsin Badgers in his first Big Ten game. He added a season-high 12 against Michigan one week later and for the season averaged four points a game.

There wasn't much on the basketball court that Vance couldn't do.

"He had great balance in his total game," said guard Walt Kirk. "He rebounded, he passed well, he could move, and he had great speed for a bigger guy. He was just a solid, all-around player and his whole game was good."

Vance began his junior season, the 1942-43 campaign, on a roll. He scored 10 points against Nebraska in the second game of the year and hit a 55-foot shot at the end of the first half against Missouri that sent the Huff Gymnasium crowd into a frenzy. He poured in 12 points against Northwestern, 11 against Ohio State, and 12 against Minnesota en route to averaging seven points a game and earning a first-team All-Big Ten selection.

While he picked up his scoring in his junior season, Vance was better known for his prowess on the defensive end of the floor.

"He wasn't a very flashy player, but he was consistently good, especially on defense," remembered teammate Ray Grierson. "He was always on his man and aware of where he was. If you ever had Gene Vance guarding you in practice you knew it because he was on you like glue."

Standing 6-3 and weighing 210 pounds with wavy dark hair, Vance was very big for a guard and had an incredible stature both on and off the court.

"He had the body of a Greek idol and my wife at the time was in love with him," remembered reserve guard Ken Brown.

"He would be up in Lake Geneva over the summer life guarding and then he would report for basketball in the fall," recalled Kirk. "We wore white uniforms then and he would have that holdover sun tan, which made him quite [popular] with the girls. He was a glamorous guy and a very imposing man."

For all of his accolades, athletic ability and achievements, Vance was a man of few words.

"Gene was really quiet, but he had this confidence about him," remembered Grierson.

"The thing that impressed me about Gene was that he didn't act as if he was better than anybody else, which would have been easy for him to do because he was a big shot in a lot of ways," recalled guard Cliff Fulton.

After the 1943 season, Vance served three years as first Lieutenant in the Infantry in the Army, which

▲ *Gene Vance was a big guard for his day—standing an impressive six foot three and sculpted "like a Greek idol." Like the other Whiz Kids, Vance opted to serve his country during World War II, hence interrupting his college education.*

included 16 months in Europe. He returned to Champaign in 1946 to team up with Phillip, Menke and Smiley for their final season at Illinois.

In his first game back in an Illinois uniform, Vance netted five points against Cornell. He continued to play well throughout the season, scoring seven against Marquette, nine against Pittsburgh, and nine against Missouri in the first four games of the season. In late February he put together the two best offensive performances of his college career when he scored 16 points to lead the Illini to a one-point victory over Ohio State and then netted 15 points, including the game-winning basket, against Northwestern at Chicago Stadium.

For the season, he averaged just under seven points a game and earned second-team All-Big Ten honors in guiding the Illini to a 14-6 record and a second-place conference finish.

After completing his Illinois career, Vance was drafted by the Chicago Stags, where he played from 1948-49. He moved over to Tri-Cities in 1950-51 and finished his professional career with Milwaukee in 1952.

After serving for a year in the Korean War, Vance was named the head basketball coach at LaSalle-Peru and spent four years there before returning to Champaign in June of 1956 to work with the Alumni Association. He became the director of the Alumni Association in 1959 and held that post until he was called on to become the athletics director in 1967 to help the University recover from Big Ten and NCAA sanctions. After a five-year stint as director, Vance joined the University of Illinois Foundation as a fundraiser and retired after 18 years in that post on July 31, 1990.

Vance, the last living member of the Whiz Kids, currently resides in Champaign and still looks back fondly on the great teams he was a part of in the early 1940s.

"It was such a great thing to be a part of," reflected Vance. "When I look back now at the two Big Ten championships and the Whiz Kids name, which has always stuck with us, it is something I am very proud of."

ANDY PHILLIP

GUARD: 1941–42—1942–43; 1946–47

Andy Phillip didn't waste a lot of time making Huff Gym his second home, nor did it take long for the Illinois fans to fall in love with him. He first stepped foot in the gym in the 1940 high school state basketball tournament, where his Granite City Warriors defeated Herrin 24-22 in overtime to win the state title. Phillip scored 15 of his team's 24 points in the championship game, 53 points in the tournament and gave Illinois fans a taste of what was to come. With that exceptional performance, the Andy Phillip legend was born.

Phillip came to the University of Illinois in the fall of 1940 along with Ken Menke, Gene Vance and Jack Smiley. Those four recruits, along with Art Mathisen, went on to win two Big Ten championships, set numerous school records and become the group that would forever be known as the Whiz Kids.

Within the Whiz Kids group, Phillip was the star—the go-to guy on offense.

"Andy was the finest basketball player I ever saw in all of my years of watching basketball," said Gordon Gillespie, a former Illini who watched Phillip play up in Chicago Stadium during his high school days. "He was the type of player that made all the hard things look easy."

On the basketball floor there wasn't anything that Phillip couldn't do well.

"He was an all-around player, and as a forward, he always impressed me with the way he was able to handle the ball," recalled Johnny Orr, who played with Phillip at Illinois and later went on to coach at Michigan and Iowa State. "He could dribble the ball as well as anybody."

At a time when scoring was at a premium, Phillip could put the ball in the net. In his three-year Illinois career, he scored 729 points—demolishing Chuck Carney's Illinois scoring records in the process—and broke the Big Ten record for total points and total baskets in one season. On March 1, 1943, Phillip broke both the Big Ten and Illinois record for points in one

game when he netted 40 against Chicago in the Whiz Kids last game before they were broken up due to World War II.

That record stood for 20 years and it still is the fourth-best single-game scoring total in Illinois basketball history.

In addition to his scoring prowess, Phillip was an early playmaker.

"He was such a great passer," remembered Illinois guard Jack Burmaster. "It seemed like he could see out of the rear of his eyes."

To the younger guys on the team and the people in the community, Phillip was a legend.

"When I was a junior and senior in high school, Andy Phillip was my idol," recalled Dick Foley, who grew up in nearby Paris, Illinois. and lettered for the Illini in the late 1940s.

▲ *Andy Phillip broke all kinds of scoring records during his time with the Illini. But scoring wasn't all the legendary guard could do. Teammates also noted his amazing court vision as well as his brilliant leadership.*

"Andy was a leader by example and a guy who never put anyone down," recalled Illinois center Robert Rowe. "He was always constructive in what he said and how he said it when he was trying to help you out."

Off the court, the 6-3, floppy-haired Phillip wasn't a very talkative guy. He was so quiet and reserved, in fact, that his former coach Doug Mills once joked that in Phillip's case the old saying should be changed to, "Do as I do and not as I say."

"He was a very quiet individual unless you really got to know him," recalled Phillip's high school and UI teammate Ken Parker. "He wasn't stand-offish, but you had to really be around him a lot before he would open up."

After the 1943 season, Phillip became a lieutenant in the Marines and was stationed in Iwo Jima in the South Pacific. After returning from the War, he rejoined his teammates Menke, Smiley and Vance for the 1946-47 season, but struggled to return to form and to recover from a sickness he came down with while serving.

After leaving Illinois in 1947, Phillip was drafted by the Chicago Stags and went on to have an illustrious 11-year career in the NBA, leading the league in assists in two of those seasons. He amassed 6,384 points, was a five-time NBA-All Star and a member of the 1957 world champion Boston Celtics. For all of those accomplishments, he was inducted into the Naismith Memorial Basketball Hall of Fame in 1961.

Even after retiring from the NBA, Phillip always remained true to his roots.

"He never forgot the people that were really friendly with him in Champaign," said Andy's youngest brother Robert Phillip. "He never forgot the fans, the sportscasters, and all of the people who were behind him at Illinois."

It's safe to say that those same fans will never forget him either.

DIKE EDDLEMAN
FORWARD: 1946-47—1948-49

To anybody growing up in the state of Illinois in the early 1940s, Dwight "Dike" Eddleman was a mythical figure—a legend whose athletic exploits spread from Southern Illinois all the way up to Chicago like a wildfire.

"Growing up you heard stories of how Dike could throw a football 100 yards, punt one 120 yards and so high that they would have to call a delay of game penalty on him, and shoot a basketball from half court," recalled former Illinois center Johnny Kerr.

Dike's tale began at Centralia High School where he was a three-time *News-Gazette* all-state player and one of the best high school basketball players ever to play in the state of Illinois. He reached the state tournament three times in his four years at Centralia and captured the elusive title his senior season in truly remarkable fashion. Trailing 25-16 to Paris heading into the fourth period, Eddleman almost single-handedly won the game. He netted 12 points in the final period—including the game-winning basket just before the horn—to bring home the title. By that time, Eddlemania had taken over the state of Illinois.

"Jack Prowell was a friend of mine and the sports editor of *The News-Gazette,*" said Bob Novak, the former Illinois student and current CNN political commentator. "He had to send a letter to Dike, and he sent it to Eddleman, Illinois and it got to Centralia. That is how big Dike Eddleman was out of high school."

As a basketball player, Eddleman perfected the kiss shot taught by his legendary high school coach, Arthur Trout.

"He would stand out there on the perimeter, hold the ball in front of his face like he was giving it a kiss, and off it would go," remembered teammate Robert Rowe.

"He could shoot that kiss shot from anywhere around the court," said guard Jack Burmaster. "Dike was a bomber. When he got the ball in his hands, you never knew if he was going to take that shot."

After sitting out his first year due to freshman eligibility, Eddleman took a three-year hiatus due to World War II. Upon coming back to campus in 1946, he sat behind the Whiz Kids, who had returned for their senior season, and scored only 12 points in limited action. It wasn't until the 1947-48 season, his junior campaign, that Eddleman started to show his prowess on the basketball court. He scored 20 points in a double-digit win over Washington, 16 in a huge win against Wisconsin, and 26 against Michigan followed by a 24-point effort against the Hawkeyes. For the season, Eddleman averaged 13.9 points a game and led the team to a 15-5 record in Harry Combes' first season at the helm.

While he was coming into his own on the court, Eddleman always possessed incredible stature off of it.

"He was as handsome an athlete as anybody has ever seen," said one-time teammate Gordon Gillespie. "Dike was 6-3, had wavy dark hair, and there wasn't a girl on campus who wasn't in love with him."

With his good looks, his incredible athletic ability, and his remarkable achievements it would have been easy for Dike to have a big head, but that was never the case.

"There was never anybody too small for Dike," said Illinois center Fred Green. "He always had the time in his day to visit with someone, talk to them and joke back and forth. He would have been a great politician because he was always on the upbeat and everybody was his friend."

Perhaps Eddleman's greatest asset in his athletic career was his confidence. His friend and fellow member of the Class of 1942, Walt Kirk, remembered Dike exuding confidence even as a young freshman.

"We were getting ready to play the varsity in the annual freshman-varsity game and the Varsity was the great Whiz Kids team that end up going 17-1 that season," recalled Kirk. "Dike goes in to see Doug Mills and with all sincerity he says, 'Doug, are you going to allow us to win this ball game?' Dike was so darn confident that he believed we were going to beat the Whiz Kids."

Dike was named captain of the 1948-49 Illini and led the team to the first Big Ten Championship of the Harry Combes era. In an early season loss to DePaul in Chicago Stadium, Eddleman struggled, shooting three of 14 from the field and scoring only nine points. A few weeks later Eddleman got his revenge against the Blue Demons in a game at Huff Gym.

"I was guarding Dike and I held him under double digits in Chicago," recalled Blue Demon forward Gordon Gillespie, who had played one year at Illinois before transferring to DePaul. "About two weeks later, I was guarding him again in Champaign and I distinctly remember he missed his first shot that day. After that, the next six times he touched the ball he knocked down what today would be six threes. They might have even been six fours—they were so far out. They all went in and Coach Meyer had to take me out, because Dike was lighting me up."

Eddleman scored 20 points in the blowout win against DePaul and went on to have a huge season. He poured in 20 against Northwestern, 19 against Iowa and 23 in the Big Ten-clinching win over Indiana on senior day. For the season, he averaged 13.1 points a game on his way to earning second-team All-Big Ten honors.

▲ Dwight "Dike" Eddleman was a sensational athlete that perfected the "kiss shot." He led the 1948-49 Illini to a Big Ten championship under Coach Harry Combes.

The win on senior day put an end to a marvelous amateur career that began in the 1939 state championship in that very same gym. Huff had been Eddleman's playground for over a decade, and he said goodbye to the gym in special fashion, as only a great athlete like Eddleman could. With six seconds left to go in his final home game, Eddleman dribbled down the floor, leaped in the air and threw the ball at the Illinois basket from a few steps passed half court. To no one's surprise, it went in. It was one more moment of greatness for the Illinois star and the perfect way to end a storybook career.

JOHNNY "RED" KERR
CENTER: 1951–52—1953–54

For three years at Chicago Tilden Tech High School, Johnny "Red" Kerr spent his time on the soccer field. That all changed the day the head basketball coach, Bill Postl, saw him in the locker room.

"Coach came up to me and said, 'Geez, why aren't you playing basketball,'" remembered Kerr. "The next thing I know I went and worked with him in the gym a few times and he said, 'One day you are going to thank me for this.'"

Coach Postl couldn't have been more right.

By the time Kerr graduated high school mid-year in January of 1950, he was all set to go and play basketball at Bradley. But Illinois head coach Harry Combes wasn't going to let him go there without a fight.

"It was my freshman year in school and Harry told me there was a kid up in Chicago who was going to Bradley and that I should give him a call to see what was going on," remembered Illinois forward Irv Bemoras. "I called John up, went to his house on the South Side of Chicago and told him all the reasons he should come down to Illinois. The next day we took the train down to Champaign and we went straight to Coach Combes' office. He was so surprised to see him there his eyeballs nearly fell out."

For Kerr it was a trip he is glad he made.

"I looked at that campus, walked down to the quad and immediately fell in love with the place," said Kerr.

▲ Johnny "Red" Kerr led the Illini to a 57-13 record during his three seasons, including a Big Ten banner in 1951-52. Teammates remembered Kerr, who broke just about every Illini scoring record, as "a real comedian."

"They took me over to the Phi Psi house, everybody welcomed me and from that point on I knew this is where I was going to go."

Coach Combes had Kerr on campus, but wasn't out of the woods yet.

"I remember staying around him the first few days on campus, because we heard that Bradley had sent a few guys down to hijack him," remembered Bemoras.

"Bradley recruited two of my high school teammates the year before and they had sent those guys down to Champaign to bring me back," recalled Kerr. "I remember we were at the movies one night and there were Phi

Psi's sitting two rows in front of me, two rows behind me and two to the side of me. They didn't let my buddies from Bradley anywhere near me."

Finally registered and officially on campus, Kerr waited a year and a half before he took the floor for the varsity. Coach Combes tinkered with the idea of playing him in the second half of the 1950-51 season, but decided he didn't want to lose Kerr midway through his senior season.

Once on the court, Kerr paid dividends immediately. As the sixth man in 1951-52, he led the Big Ten champions in scoring with an average of 13.7 points a game, including a 34-point effort on senior day against Northwestern and a 26-point game in the NCAA Tournament's third place game against Santa Clara.

In the year and a half he sat out when he first got down to Illinois, Kerr developed the shot he would become famous for.

"Every single day in practice, Howie Braun would take John to the corner and work with him for an hour on a hook shot," remembered Illinois guard Bill Ridley. "He would cut across the lane, you would pass it to him and in one fluid motion he would get that big right arm out there and bank it off the backboard from a side angle. He had that shot down to perfection."

"John Kerr had the best hook shot I ever saw before Abdul-Jabbar came along with the sky hook," recalled Bill Lyon, who covered Illinois for the Urbana Courier. "He wasn't jumping when he shot it and it was like a man doing the waltz to the "Blue Danube." It was very graceful and flowing and when he threw up that hook shot coming across the middle it was just beautiful to watch."

The hook shot wasn't the only thing that separated Kerr from other typical big man of his era.

"There were a few big men around at the time, but he could run faster than any of them," said teammate Mack Follmer. "He was one of the first big men to be very agile and fast."

"He had a tremendous ability to pass the ball," remembered Jim Wright, who was a fellow member of the Class of 1951. "John could take the ball, pass it through his legs to guys cutting in the post and get it right to them."

Kerr opened his junior season by scoring 34 points against Loyola in just 36 minutes. The scoring barrage

continued throughout the year as Kerr established himself as one of the best players in the Big Ten by averaging 17.5 points a game and earning second-team All-Big Ten honors for the 18-4 Illini of 1953.

Off the court, Kerr was one of a kind.

"He was a fun loving guy and always did different things," said Wright. "With John there was a lot of agitating and a lot of pranks on people. He was a real comedian."

Kerr was eager to pull pranks on teammates—especially the younger ones.

"I remember when my brother and I made one of our first trips with the varsity, John slipped some silverware into our jackets at the dinner place," laughed Illinois guard Paul Judson. "We were going past the person who collects the bill and John starts rattling our jackets saying, 'Hey, what are you guys doing?' as he reached and pulled the silverware out of our jackets. That was typical John Kerr."

In his senior campaign, Kerr shattered just about every Illinois scoring record. Three games into the season he put up 31 points against Loyola to pass Irv Bemoras' career scoring record of 822 points. He set the record for single-season scoring average at 25.3 points a game, which remains the second-best single scoring season in Illinois basketball history.

After scoring 20 points in a heartbreaking loss to the Hoosiers in his last collegiate game, Kerr wrapped up his Illinois career with 1,299 points scored, which today ranks 17th on the all-time scoring list.

Kerr was drafted by Syracuse in 1954 and played nine seasons with the Nationals. In those years he was a part of the 1955 NBA Championship squad and a three-time all-star. He moved to Philadelphia for two seasons and finished his professional career in the ABA with the Baltimore Bullets. He averaged double figures every year of his pro career and remarkably played in a then-NBA record of 844 consecutive games.

After retiring from professional ball, Kerr became the coach of the expansion Chicago Bulls and promptly took them to the playoffs in their first year, earning him Coach of the Year honors at the age of 34. After coaching the Bulls, Kerr bounced around the league and different businesses before becoming a broadcaster with the Bulls in 1974, where he still remains today.

Kerr credits his decision to attend Illinois as the move that shaped his life forever.

"Illinois was a great stepping stone for me," said Kerr, reflecting back over 50 years. "A lot of the great experiences I had in my life came down there at Illinois. I loved playing basketball for the Illini, loved the fraternity I was in and living in the house with my fraternity brothers, and I met and married my wife down there. In the end I know I made the right decision, because Illinois was the perfect place for me."

DAVE
DOWNEY
FORWARD: 1959-60—1962-63

By the time Dave Downey arrived on the University of Illinois campus, he was a well-known commodity in Illinois basketball circles. A two-time *News-Gazette* and *Chicago Daily News* all-state selection out of Canton, Illinois, Downey was part of the prized freshman class of 1959, which also brought Bill Small from West Aurora, Bill Burwell from New York, and Jay Lovelace via transfer from the University of Florida. Together that class was going to put Illinois basketball back on the map and Downey was its centerpiece.

Downey came to Illinois with the reputation of being an offensive force with the uncanny ability to create his own shot and score in bunches.

"He was an exceptional offensive player," remembered Downey's freshman coach Jim Wright. "He never really had a bad game and when he stepped on the floor you could always count on him having about 20 points and 10 rebounds."

In his freshman year, Downey proved each and every day in practice that he was the real deal.

"Dave had the unique ability to separate himself from his defender and he was one of the more difficult guys I ever had to guard," remembered then senior Mannie Jackson. "I usually could take space away from a player with my quickness and affect them with my jumping ability, but I just couldn't shut him down. He always found a way to get space from me."

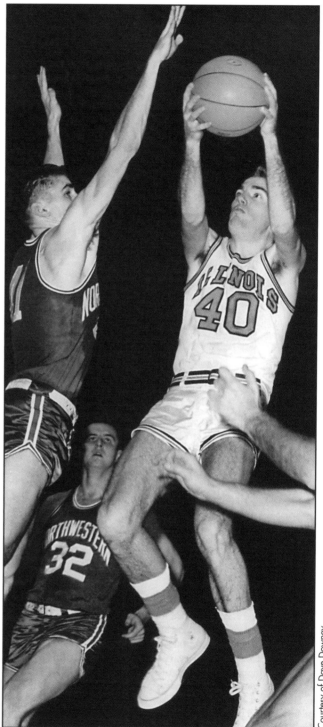

▲ *Dave Downey was a scoring machine with a bag full of offensive tricks. According to freshman coach Jim Wright, when Downey stepped onto the court "you could always count on him having about 20 points and 10 rebounds." His 53 points against Indiana in 1963 still stands as a school record.*

Standing 6-4 and weighing about 200 pounds, Downey wasn't the fastest guy on the court and he certainly wasn't the tallest. His body was not awe-inspiring, and he didn't have the skills that immediately grabbed people's attention.

What he did have was the rare ability to get his shot off in many different ways.

"Dave was one of the first white guys I ever saw that could do some of the things he could do," recalled Don Freeman, who practiced every day against Downey in his freshman year. "He could hang in the air to get off his shot and he had a bag of tricks."

In his sophomore season, he led the varsity team in scoring, averaging 16.8 points a game including 19 a clip in Big Ten play. Amazingly, for a guy his size, he also led the team in rebounding at 11.1 a game.

"People don't realize that Dave was a really good rebounder," recalled teammate Bill Small. "He was especially great on the offensive glass because he followed his shots and had a knack for where the ball was."

During his junior campaign, Downey continued to show why he was one of the best players in the Big Ten. He averaged 20.2 points and grabbed 12.2 rebounds a game for a team that started out 14-3 before losing five out of their last six games to finish in fourth place in the Big Ten.

On the court, Downey was a leader and someone that guys both older and younger looked up to.

"He was the guy we would come and talk to whenever something was going on," said point guard Tal Brody. "Dave was the guy who knew a lot about the other teams during our scouting reports and he was the guy on our team that everyone looked up to."

Perhaps Downey's greatest attribute on and off the court was his intelligence.

"What made him great was that he had a good sense of where everyone was on the court and a good sense of how to get open," recalled teammate Skip Thoren. "He was a very intelligent player and he never did anything with brute force. He was very thoughtful on the court and a lot like Bill Bradley."

Off the court, his photographic memory and success in the classroom are legendary.

"Dave remembers everything about everybody and I was always in awe of that," recalled teammate John Love, who credits Downey and his charisma as one of the main reasons he chose Illinois. "His idea of studying was just to flip through a book real quickly. While I would have to read every word and paragraph, Dave would just flip through the pages, go and take the test, and get the highest grades in the class."

Among his many other academic awards from his time at Illinois, Downey was presented the George Huff award for lettermen achieving above a four-point grade average and the 1963 Big Ten Conference Medal of Honor, which recognized proficiency in scholarship and athletics.

Downey spearheaded the way in his senior year, averaging 19.7 points and 9.8 rebounds a game as the Illini reached the NCAA Tournament for the first time in 11 years. On an early February night in Indiana, Downey scored 53 points on 22 of 34 shooting to break the Illinois single-game scoring record, which 41 years later still stands today.

After graduating from Illinois, Downey put basketball on hold. He stayed at Illinois to get his law degree and worked with Harry Combes as a freshman coach. After finishing law school in 1966, Downey entered the insurance business where he remains today. He is currently the President of the Downey Group in Champaign and a member of the Board of Directors for the News-Gazette and Bank Illinois, among many others.

Downey was a major success both on and off the court. Four decades later, Illinois fans still remember the number 40 jumping up, hanging in the air, and shooting that sweet little fade away jump shot that more times than not splashed through the hoop.

SKIP THOREN

CENTER: 1962–63—1964–65

When Illinois fans talk about the great star players who have manned the middle in Champaign, names like Johnny Kerr, George BonSalle and Deon Thomas often come up. But rarely is the name Duane "Skip" Thoren mentioned. Fans are remiss to leave Thoren out, though, because few Illini players have had the impact on their team that he did or are as prominent in the record books.

A first-team *News-Gazette* all-state player in 1961, Thoren had his choice of colleges. But nights growing up in his house in Rockford became the deciding factor when it came time to select the right one.

"I went around to several other colleges as part of the recruitment process with my Mom and Dad, but the pressure of the whole thing was getting very old," remembered Thoren. "I had an allegiance to Illinois from the days when my father and I used to sit around and listen to Illinois games on the radio. I grew up listening to Johnny Kerr and George BonSalle, so instead of flying around to a bunch of other places, I just decided to go to Illinois."

After sitting out the 1961-62 season as a freshman, Thoren's Illinois career began as a reserve on the Big Ten Championship squad of 1962-63. Thoren struggled to find playing time behind center Bill Burwell. As the season progressed, however, so did Thoren. Soon, Coach Combes began to go more and more to a twin tower look with Burwell and Thoren inside.

"He was a selfless player in a sense that he wasn't concerned about points and was more concerned about winning," said Burwell. "With Skip it was whatever it took to work with the team—it was never what was best for him."

Thoren's coming-out party came that year in the NCAA Tournament when he scored 10 points and grabbed 12 rebounds in battling with Bowling Green's 6-11 Nate Thurmond during the Illini's first round win. On the season, Skip averaged 5.5 points and 5.8 rebounds a game.

Standing 6-9 and weighing 200 pounds when he first arrived at Illinois, Thoren was one of the Big Ten's largest guys. But he wasn't a smooth offensive player at the start.

"He was a gangly, skinny kid who didn't seem all that graceful," recalled teammate Dave Downey. "As he matured though, he became a very effective player."

"He worked so hard at his game and I distinctly remember Howie Braun taking him in the corner of Huff Gym every day at practice," said teammate Larry Hinton. "He would work for hours with him on maneuvering, that soft little hook shot and all the stuff he should be doing under the basket."

Thoren was known for his little baby hook that he began to shoot at East Rockford, but refined at Illinois under the guidance of Braun.

"You weren't going to stop him when he got the ball down low and could shoot that little right handed hook," remembered Ron Dunlap, who faced Thoren in his senior year every day in practice when Dunlap was a freshman. "Once he got into the lane and set up for it that was it. He would put that elbow on you and all you could do was watch it drop through the net."

With the departure of Burwell, Downey, Starnes and Small, Thoren was challenged by the coaching staff to take his game to the next level.

"It was clear after they left that someone had to step up and take the leadership role," recalled Thoren. "Howie really laid that out to me and I worked very hard in the summer of my sophomore and junior year at trying to be able to improve my game and be the player they expected me to be."

The hard work paid off and Thoren immediately answered the challenge. In the second game of the season against St. Louis, Thoren poured in 25 points and grabbed 20 rebounds in a performance that was just the precursor of what was to come. A few games later he got 20 points and 18 rebounds against Notre Dame and 20 and 15 in the second round game of the Los Angeles Classic against Pittsburgh.

It was in the Championship game against UCLA that Thoren put in one of the greatest performances in the history of the program.

Thoren netted 24 points and grabbed an Illinois-record 24 rebounds despite fouling out with about seven minutes left in a 83-79 loss.

"UCLA had guys like Gail Goodrich, Keith Erickson and Walt Hazzard but I was told Skip was the best player on the court that day," said Jim Dawson, who was a freshman and ineligible to take trips with the team. "To score that many points and grab that many rebounds against an eventual undefeated national championship team is unbelievable."

For the season, Thoren averaged 20.3 points and 13.8 rebounds a game. In that season, he established himself as one of the best rebounders in the country. To this day, Thoren is in an elite class in the history of the Illinois basketball program when it comes to the boards.

"He wasn't the biggest guy in terms of bulk, but he knew a lot about positioning," said Illinois forward Mel Blackwell, who played with Skip in that 1963-64 season. "He just knew where the ball was going to come off, he knew how to box out and while not a great leaper he could definitely jump a little bit."

Forty years later, Thoren's 24 rebounds against UCLA still is the greatest single-game rebounding total in Illinois history. His 830 career rebounds in only three seasons ranks him fourth all-time. His average of 11.2 rebounds a season for his career ranks him second behind Nick Weatherspoon at 11.4. Thoren also holds the mark for highest rebounding average per game for a single season at 14.5 per game, over two rebounds better than Weatherspoon's 12.3 mark from 1973. Skip Thoren was the chairman of the boards in the mid 1960s.

Off the court, Skip Thoren was a very reserved and quiet guy who just went about his everyday business.

"He was like a big puppy dog," remembered teammate Jim Vopicka. "He was very low key and you knew there was a burning desire and competitive spirit within him, but most of the times he didn't show a lot of emotions."

"He was very easy to get along with and he made friends easily," said Bobby Meadows, who along with Bogie Redmon roomed with Thoren in the Beta house. "Skip joked around a bit, was never moody, and even though he was on the basketball team and very prominent he didn't demand more or less than anyone else did."

In his last season at Illinois, Thoren was named captain of the squad and took his game to a whole new level. It began with a 20-point effort in a blow out of UCLA at

▲ Skip Thoren was known for his hook shot, which helped him average over 20 points per game during his junior and senior seasons. But he was also an incredibly smart rebounder that holds the Illini mark for best season average at 14.5 rebounds per game.

the Assembly Hall and it carried over into the Kentucky Invitational.

In the first round of the invitational, Thoren faced off against 6-11 Henry Finkel of Dayton and did more than hold his own in scoring 23 points and grabbing 10 rebounds. The next day Thoren dominated the Kentucky Wildcats, accumulating 27 points and seizing 22 rebounds to give Harry Combes his first win over Adolph Rupp and the Wildcats.

"In that tournament he was intimidating, powerful and he just did everything great. To win the Kentucky Tournament in those days was amazing," remembered Downey.

But that was only the beginning. Thoren scored 37 points and grabbed 18 rebounds in only 32 minutes against Purdue, then tallied 32 points and 18 rebounds against Northwestern. On the season, he averaged 22.2 points and an incredible 14.5 rebounds a game. For those accomplishments he was named first team All-Big Ten and second-team All-America.

He finished his Illinois career with 1,164 points, which ranks 25th all time at Illinois. After completing his senior season, Thoren was drafted by the Baltimore Bullets in the fourth round of the 1965 NBA draft, but instead chose to play overseas for Olympia Milan where his team won the highly regarded Cup of Champions.

After a year overseas, Thoren returned to the states thinking his basketball career was over. But a phone call from ABA Commissioner George Mikan abruptly changed that status, as Thoren was drafted by the Minnesota Muskies. He played one year in Minnesota and then moved with the franchise to Miami for two more seasons, each year playing alongside his former Illinois teammate, Don Freeman. For his ABA career, Thoren averaged 13 points and 11 rebounds a game, finishing second in the league in rebounding in 1969.

After hurting his knee, Thoren retired and after a brief stint coaching semi-pro teams he moved to the business world and today works in Kentucky as the area general manager for SmurfIt.

In the end, his decision to come to Illinois couldn't have turned out better.

"It means an awful lot that I was able to come play for the Illini," reflected Thoren from his office in Louisville. "Growing up as a child listening to the games on the radio, I dreamed of being a part of Illinois basketball and being able to participate in it was just incredible. I was living out a dream and it was an experience I will never forget."

So the next time Illinois fans start listing the great stars in the history of Illinois basketball, please don't forget one of the brightest stars out there. In 100 years, very few have shined brighter than the Big Skipper.

DON FREEMAN
FORWARD: 1963–64—1965–66

Don Freeman first stepped foot on the Illinois campus in the fall of 1962 from the small southern town of Madison, Ill., as a raw, unrefined boy completely awed by the sight of such a large University. Four years later, he left school as a polished and confident young man that was one of the best basketball players ever to put on an Illinois uniform.

His freshman coach Jim Wright was there to see the entire transformation.

"In all of my years of being around Illinois basketball, I think Freeman grew as a player and a person more than anyone we ever had come in here," said Wright.

Standing 6-3 and rail thin, Freeman certainly didn't look the part of a great basketball player.

"He was kind of knock-kneed and pigeon-toed," remembered then-senior Dave Downey. "You looked at him and thought, 'What is this guy going to do?'"

Freeman exploded onto the scene immediately in his sophomore year. Just a month into the season, he scored 23 points in a win against West Virginia in the Los Angeles Classic and a few weeks later he scored 13 points and grabbed 19 rebounds in a victory over Notre Dame in Chicago Stadium.

Freeman gave Illinois fans and the rest of the Big Ten a taste of what was to come with a 27-point effort against Michigan State in the middle of February. The baskets kept coming, as Freeman ended his debut season averaging 14.2 points and an incredible 9.6 rebounds a contest.

By the end of his junior season, the 1964-65 campaign, Freeman had established himself as an offensive force in the Big Ten. He scored 27 points against Cazzie Russell and the Michigan Wolverines, 28 against Notre Dame in Chicago, and 26 against Ohio State. But, it was on a late February night when he proved just how tough and special he was. Playing one night after his father passed away, Freeman poured in 33 points and grabbed eight rebounds in a thrashing of the Hawkeyes. It was a performance no one will ever forget.

"He manhandled Iowa in that game and it was a very emotional one for him," recalled reserve guard Bob Brown. "I remember telling him in the locker room that your Dad must be proud of you, because there is no doubt he watched that game."

For the season, Freeman averaged 18.3 points a game and 9.4 rebounds on his way to earning third-team All-Big Ten honors. Smaller than most forwards, Freeman's ability to leap made him an outstanding rebounder. He was one of those guys that modern commentators would say could jump out of the gym.

"He jumped so darn high," remembered Love. "You didn't think he was getting up that high until you were jumping next to him and all of the sudden his hands were a foot ahead of yours."

He was also deceptively quick and lightning fast with his first step.

"He was the type of guy who could tell you 'I am going to go by you right there,' and then do it even if you knew where he was going," recalled Downey.

Off the court, Freeman was affectionately called "El Danto", which was a nickname given to him by childhood buddy and teammate Mike Graville.

"When you watched Don he was like a bullfighter in the lane and around the court," said Brown, explaining where the nickname originated. "He was just fearless and always whipping on people."

Even with his small frame, Freeman was never scared to attack the basket or mix it up with the bigger guys on the court.

"Don had no fear and he would go into the lane and battle with a guy seven feet tall," recalled Rich Jones, who was very close to Freeman and called him "Rim," which was short for roommate. "He was a thin guy and wasn't very big, but he just had so much heart. I learned from Donnie that you have to battle all the time."

▲ Don Freeman stood a rail-thin six foot three and according to teammate Dave Downey was "knock-kneed and pigeon-toed." But looks were deceiving, as Freeman was a force on the basketball court. His senior season, in which he averaged 27.8 points and 11.9 rebounds per game, stands as one of the best in the history of Illinois basketball.

Freeman, a self-proclaimed shy guy, was very reserved in public, even at times turning down the chance to accept awards.

"I remember Don was supposed to get an MVP award at the end of the year banquet, but called me up to go and accept it for him," recalled Graville. "He said he was sick, but I knew he wasn't. Donnie was too shy to get up in front of people and he never really wanted those personal accolades."

Even though some perceived him as quiet, Freeman had that certain something that attracted people to him—especially the younger guys on the team.

"Don Freeman was my idol," recalled teammate Preston Pearson. "I looked up to him on and off the court. I even idolized him to the point that I developed his pigeon-toed walk."

"Here was a guy who was an absolute star when I got onto campus, but he was always encouraging to the young players," remembered guard Steve Spanich.

Indeed, Freeman was a basketball player a younger teammate could learn plenty by watching. Freeman's senior campaign is one the greatest single seasons in the history of Illinois basketball. He scored a total of 668 points, averaged 27.8 points a game, grabbed 11.9 rebounds a contest and put together some of the greatest performances that Illinois fans have ever seen.

In an early February victory over Michigan, Freeman scored 33 points and matched Cazzie Russell shot for shot in an epic showdown at Ann Arbor. With four games remaining in the season, Freeman scored 35 points against Minnesota to surpass Downey on the all-time scoring list. He scored 1,449 points for his career, which now ranks 11th on the all-time list.

On March 5, 1966, the Illini celebrated "Don Freeman Day" in Champaign as 10,000 people, including over 250 from Madison, Illinois, came to the Assembly Hall to watch Freeman play in his last home game. To no one's surprise he didn't disappoint, scoring 32 points and grabbing 13 rebounds to send the entire arena home with one more lasting impression.

It was a special occasion for Freeman.

"It was such an emotional day for me and I will never forget the applause and ovation I got from the crowd," said Freeman almost 40 years later. "There is a picture of me with my head down at center court,

because the whole thing—'Don Freeman Day,' my last game, and the crowd—was just unbelievable. It is something I will always remember."

After graduating from Illinois, Freeman went on to play nine seasons in the ABA, finishing as the league's seventh all-time leading scorer. After playing two seasons with the L.A. Lakers to finish his career, Freeman was brought back to Champaign by two former Illinois basketball players, Dave Downey and Sam Leeper, to work at Champaign National Bank.

Freeman has been in the banking business ever since, leaving Champaign in 1987 for Texas. He is currently working at the Federal Reserve Bank in Omaha, Nebraska.

For Freeman, wearing the orange and blue uniform was a dream come true.

"As a kid I used to walk six or seven miles in freezing cold weather from the YMCA in my town to my house just so I could get in front of the TV and watch Mannie Jackson and Govoner Vaughn play," remembered Freeman. "During my recruitment all these other schools tried to convince me to come there, but what they didn't know was that when I watched these old games I used to dream about playing at Illinois."

Thankfully for the University of Illinois basketball program and Illini fans, those dreams became a reality.

NICK WEATHERSPOON

FORWARD: 1970-71—1972-73

The art of recruiting has always involved a lot of luck, and the Illini definitely had Lady Luck on their side when they connected with the milkman of a young kid named Nick Weatherspoon—"Spoon" to his friends.

It all began when team manager George Andrews attended his cousins wedding in Nick's hometown of Canton, Ohio.

"It was a big wedding and supposedly one of the biggest in the history of Canton," remembered Andrews, who later went on to represent Spoon as his agent during his NBA career. "One of my uncles bumped into a gentleman named Jim Pimpas, who was the Weatherspoon family's milkman and juice guy and had helped them out ever since they came up from Mississippi. I was introduced to the man and when I got back to campus I told Harv and Coach Campbell who were already well aware of Nick because he was a very high-profile player."

Pimpas suggested that Nick should visit Illinois, but it was the University itself that lured him to Champaign.

"My visit to Illinois sold me on the school," remembered Weatherspoon. "It's a beautiful campus with beautiful people and after talking to Harv Schmidt and seeing he was on the same page as I was, I knew I wanted to go to Illinois."

In 1969 freshman were still ineligible, but it didn't take long for Nick to prove himself as a player.

"We would battle all the time, and he was much stronger than the skinny little kid he looked like," remembered then-senior Randy Crews. "I was four years older than him, and at that age that is a big difference, but he was just so strong and a really good offensive player."

Standing 6-6 and 195 pounds, Weatherspoon was rail thin. He was long, wiry and was known for his razor sharp elbows and the long white knee brace he wore on his right leg. He might not have looked imposing, but that build was very deceiving.

"He was the strongest person I have ever seen," said teammate Rick Schmidt. "He wasn't very big and he was so wiry, but he could move you anywhere he wanted to."

"I was down on campus for the first time and we were playing in a pickup game at IMPE before the season started," recalled Bill Rucks, who stood seven-foot tall and weighed 250 pounds at the time. "I was guarding Spoon down low and he put his left hand on me, hooked me, tossed me aside and went right in for the lay-up. I couldn't believe how he did that and I realized quickly that [playing in college] was a whole new level."

In his first year on the court for the Illini it didn't take long for Spoon to make his impact. In his first ever collegiate game against Butler, he scored 19 points and grabbed seven rebounds to lead Illinois to a double-digit victory. If there was any doubt as to how great he was going to be they were answered in the final game

▲ Nick Weatherspoon stood six foot six and weighed just 195 pounds, but teammate Rick Schmidt claimed he was "the strongest person I've ever seen." Spoon's career scoring average of 20.9 points per game and career rebound average of 11.4 boards per game are both tops in school history.

of that season when he matched up against fellow sophomore George McGinnis and the Indiana Hoosiers in Bloomington.

"He dominated McGinnis in that game," remembered Andrews. "McGinnis broke the Big Ten's sophomore scoring record that day, but Spoon just took over the game. Whenever the variables were really close he was very, very dominant."

In that contest he scored 32 points on 10 of 13 shooting from the field and grabbed 15 rebounds while holding McGinnis to 17 points. Weatherspoon finished his sophomore season averaging 16.5 points and 10.7 rebounds a game. Pound for pound, Weatherspoon is no doubt the best rebounder in the history of Illinois basketball.

"A lot of people think Spoon was a great rebounder because of his leaping ability," said teammate Jeff Dawson. "It wasn't just that he could jump really high, because he was very quick in his leaping ability. He was hungry in that he wanted the ball off the boards and when it went up he would usually go get it."

In his junior campaign, the 1971-72 season, Weatherspoon established himself as one of the best players in the Big Ten as well as the country. He averaged 20.8 points and 10.9 rebounds a game, including a 37-point, 16-rebound effort in a late season win against Iowa in which he shot 16 of 23 from the field.

When Weatherspoon was hitting his jump shot he was virtually unstoppable.

"He could always hit the 15-18 foot jumper," said teammate and friend Garvin Roberson. "Spoon could knock it down off the dribble or off the catch and he would get that elbow right in front of your face when he was shooting it."

"There were a lot of times I got hit in the head with his elbows as he took that shot," recalled guard Rick Howat. "He had this fade away jump shot where you think you would be right on him and then by the time he shot it you were nowhere near him."

"He shot the ball from way behind his head so as a defender you never had a chance to block his shot," recalled Schmidt.

Weatherspoon was a guy who loved to play basketball. If he wasn't at practice he was probably at IMPE or on other courts around campus playing in pick-up

games. Wherever he was you can bet he was playing extremely hard.

"Nick Weatherspoon was the hardest working player we ever had," said Jim Wright, who coached him as a freshman. "He was a ferocious practice player and every minute on the floor he was giving 100 percent."

"When Spoon stepped on the court he meant business," recalled Jim Krelle. "He would never take a day off or a practice off."

"There is no one that practiced harder than him," remembered Otho Tucker, who was around Illinois basketball for five seasons and never witnessed anyone like Weatherspoon. "Now Nick didn't like to run sprints or drills, but if you put him out there in a full court or half court situation he would be playing the same speed he would in a game."

Off the court, Weatherspoon kept to himself and hung out with only a few guys on the team like fellow Ohioan Nick Conner and guard Garvin Roberson.

Weatherspoon was named captain of the 1972-73 Illini and had one of the greatest single-seasons in Illinois basketball history. He scored 37 points and grabbed 22 rebounds in the opener against DePauw and never looked back. On March 5, 1973, Nick needed 26 points to break Dave Scholz's career scoring record and with 10 minutes remaining in the game he surpassed the mark by knocking down a 10-foot jumper on the baseline. He scored 30 points that night and for the season averaged 25 points and 12.3 rebounds a game on his way to earning first-team All-Big Ten honors.

"He was a great player at Illinois," recalled his former coach Harv Schmidt. "There were games like the one his senior year at Michigan when he scored 27 points in the first half that we won because he was phenomenal."

Weatherspoon finished his Illinois career 1,481 points, which today ranks ninth on the all-time list. Nobody in the history of Illinois basketball has ever finished with a higher scoring average for their career than Spoon's 20.9. His 806 career rebounds in three seasons ranks sixth on the all-time list. And again, no other Illini has a higher career rebound average than Spoon's 11.4 per game.

Weatherspoon was drafted 13th overall by Washington in the 1973 NBA Draft and enjoyed a productive seven-year NBA career with Washington, Seattle, Chicago and San Diego. His finest moment as a professional came in the 1975 NBA playoffs where he averaged just over 10 points a game and dominated defensively to help Washington get all the way to the NBA finals before losing to Golden State.

It's been 31 years since Spoon last took the court for the Illini, but the faint echoes of the crowd chanting "Spoooooon" still reverberate off the Assembly Hall walls. For Weatherspoon his time at Illinois was the best experience in his life.

"I absolutely loved my time at Illinois," reflected Weatherspoon from his home in Canton, Ohio. "One of the biggest reasons I came there was to rekindle the great history of Illinois basketball and I am so proud of all the guys who came after me who have carried on the tradition. Whenever I see Illinois on television and I see Chief Illiniwek do his dance, the juices get flowing and I think I can play again."

And we all wish we could see him play just one more time, because few have brought more excitement to the Assembly Hall than Spoon.

EDDIE
JOHNSON
FORWARD: 1977–78—1980–81

During his senior year at Westinghouse Vocational High School in Chicago, Eddie Johnson enjoyed his pick of schools. The Illini, still trying to reconnect with the Chicago Public League, targeted Johnson early and wanted him bad. Johnson was the main recruiting target of assistant coach Tony Yates.

By the time Johnson traveled to Champaign for his official visit, he still had no idea where he was going to go to school, but one event on that fateful trip soon changed that.

"I went to a party at the Union with Levi Cobb and Ken Ferdinand and I wasn't a party guy at all," remembered Johnson. "I guess the two of those guys got their signals crossed on who was going to take me home, and when the lights turned on and the party was over, I couldn't find them."

A young city kid from Chicago down in Champaign for the first time was forced to walk back to his hotel on Neil Street all by himself.

"It was a cold Saturday night and it was an intimidating trip because we all know how coeds act on weekends. The walk was probably over a mile, and I was mad as you know what during it. You know what, though, it was the best walk I ever had."

Furious that two guys who played his position left him behind with no way home, Johnson made up his mind.

"I give those guys a hard time today about it [today] and I don't know if they did it on purpose, but I took it that way," reflected Johnson. "After I got back to the hotel, I called my mother and told her I was going to Illinois. The challenge had been laid down, and I always wanted to answer the challenge."

▲ *Eddie Johnson captured the Illini career scoring record with 1,692 points, an average of 15.2 points per game. During his junior and senior seasons, fans could pencil in Johnson for 17 points and nine rebounds per game.*

As a heralded freshman, Johnson struggled early to adjust to the physical play of the Big Ten. Coming off the bench, he averaged 8.1 points a game and at times found the lack of playing time to be extremely frustrating.

"It was tough and I didn't like it, but I understood the reasons for it," recalled Johnson. "Coach Henson could have played me a lot that first year and gotten other guys from Chicago like Mark Aguirre to come to Illinois. He never gave in, though, and I respected him for that. My first year there humbled me, made me work even harder on my game and in the end it was the best thing for me."

Johnson's older teammates could tell he was going to be special.

"We were down a few points in a tight Big Ten game his freshman year, and all of the sudden Eddie came down and hit three or four jumpers in a row," remembered Illinois forward Rich Adams. "I was like, 'Whoa, this guy can really shoot and is definitely not afraid to put it up.'"

Johnson was never afraid to throw up a shot.

"Eddie could flat out shoot the ball," recalled Steve Lanter, who racked up a lot of assists dishing the ball off to Johnson. "When the game was on the line he always wanted to take that last shot and more times than not he would hit it. Just from a pure shooter's standpoint, Eddie was one of the best I have ever seen."

Johnson, alongside his best friend and fellow sophomore Mark Smith, began to blossom in his sophomore year. His scoring and rebounding catapulted the Illini to a 15-0 start, which culminated with a thrilling victory over Michigan State. In that game, Johnson drilled a game-winning jump shot from the corner with three seconds left to play.

In that one moment, he had arrived. Johnson finished that year averaging 12.1 points and 5.7 rebounds a game, but the best of Eddie Johnson was yet to come.

On and off the court, Johnson exuded a great deal of confidence and always had something to say.

"On the court he was always talking and probably was one of the early trash talkers in the Big Ten," recalled teammate Rob Judson. "He always had an opinion on everything."

"We had just won the championship game of the Kentucky Tournament in his sophomore year and Eddie steps out of the locker room wearing a cream-colored suit looking like he just stepped out of *GQ Magazine*," laughed former assistant coach Les Wothke. "I made a comment to him that he looked sharp and he looked at me, spread his arms, flashed that million-dollar smile and said, 'Coach, you got to give the people what they want.' That was Eddie Johnson."

His game took off in his junior season as he averaged 17.4 points and 8.9 rebounds a game on his way to earning second-team All-Big Ten honors. More important, he led the Illini to a third place finish in the NIT, which was the team's first postseason appearance since 1963. By the time that season finished, Johnson had established himself as one of the best players in the Big Ten.

At 6-8, 185 when he first arrived on campus, Johnson wasn't the quickest, tallest, or strongest guy on the court. Perhaps his greatest quality and what separated him from the rest of the pack was his desire to get better and his doggedness in attacking challenges.

"Eddie was very focused on one thing and that was improving his game so he could play on the next level in the NBA," said teammate Bryan Leonard. "He didn't let anything distract him from that."

"When I look back at him I have to start with his character," said Coach Henson. "There were a lot of players who had things that Eddie didn't have, but no player had the combination of character, intelligence, and a burning desire to excel like he did. I can't say enough about him and he is one of the outstanding young men I have ever had the privilege to coach."

Joined by heralded guard Derek Harper, Johnson's senior year was a great one personally and for the team. He averaged 17.2 points and 9.2 rebounds a contest, earning first-team All-Big Ten honors. This time, he led the team to their first NCAA Tournament appearance in 18 years.

Midway through the Big Ten season, both Johnson and Smith passed Nick Weatherspoon on the career-scoring list. By the time the season ended, Johnson surpassed Smith to become the all-time leading scorer in Illinois basketball history. He finished his career with 1,692 points, which today ranks fifth on the all-time list.

After graduating from Illinois, Johnson was selected in the second round by the Kansas City Kings of the NBA. He went on to play 17 years in the NBA, playing for seven different teams and amassing 19,202 points, which today ranks in the top 50 all-time on the NBA career-scoring list.

After retiring from professional basketball in 1998, Johnson began a career in broadcasting and today is the color analyst on television and radio broadcasts for the Phoenix Suns. True to his old form, he also runs jump shot camps out of the Phoenix area.

Fans will always remember Johnson for his sweet stroke and for the night he drilled that shot against State. His teammates will remember him for his confidence, hard work, and determination. Most importantly, history will remember him as one of the main catalysts in putting Illinois basketball back on the map.

DEREK HARPER
GUARD: 1980-81—1982-83

There aren't many players who graduate high school with a resume as impressive as Derek Harper's. He was a 1980 Parade All-American, McDonald's All-American and was widely regarded as not only the best player in the state of Florida, but the best high school point guard in the country. There were some recruiting services that ranked him as high as the fourth best recruit in the entire nation.

He averaged 26 points a game his senior year for West Palm Beach North Shore and led them to the Class AAA State Championship. In that championship game he scored 26 points, grabbed 14 rebounds, dished out eight assists and came away with seven steals.

Derek Harper was a stud and Illinois assistant coach Tony Yates spent a whole lot of time recruiting him.

"On 21 straight Tuesdays I flew out of Champaign, Illinois on the same flight and made the same connection out of Chicago to West Palm Beach, Florida," remembered Yates. "I got to know all the flight atten-

dants, and they all knew me. All I had to do was sit down and they would bring me my ginger ale."

Harper was looking to play outside of his home state and was especially fond of the competition in the Big Ten Conference. Early reports had him leaning to Michigan, but when Johnny Orr, a former Illinois basketball player and the Wolverines head coach, left to go to Iowa State, Illinois and Coach Yates got the break they needed.

In addition to Orr leaving, Illinois was also offering something that Michigan couldn't.

"I thought Illinois gave me the best chance to play right away," recalled Harper. "Michigan had guys like Mike McGee and the Bonner twins in the backcourt, so I didn't see myself playing there right away like I would at Illinois."

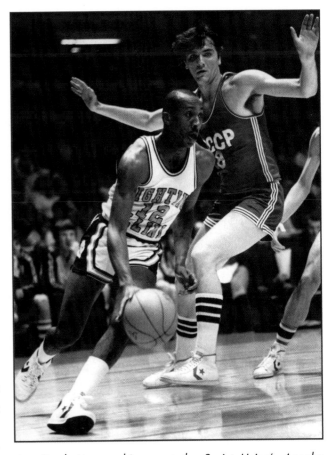

▲ *Derek Harper drives past the Soviet Union's Arvydas Sabonis in an exhibition game. After steadily improving his game and turning his immense potential into reality, Harper left for the NBA Draft after his junior season and went on to enjoy 17 successful seasons in the NBA.*

On April 16, 1980, Illinois completed its recruiting coup when Harper announced he was coming to Illinois.

"We never recruited anyone out-of-state in my time at Illinois as highly regarded as Derek was," said Illinois head coach Lou Henson. "Bringing him in was huge for the program."

As a freshman, Harper joined Mark Smith and Eddie Johnson in the starting line-up and his presence paid dividends right away. He came into town with a great deal of accolades, but without the big head that often accompanies such recognition.

"Derek was always very respectful to the older guys on the team," remembered Eddie Johnson. "He didn't come in thinking that he was this big time player and highly rated recruit. Instead, he worked on his game, made sure the older guys got their touches and I wish

he would have been a junior when I was a senior because I think we would have had a real opportunity to go to the Final Four."

In his freshman year, Harper struggled early on to score but had a breakout game against Marquette in mid-December when he scored 18 points and propelled Illinois to a one-point victory. For the season he averaged 8.3 points and 5.4 assists a game in helping to guide Illinois to its first NCAA Tournament appearance in 18 years.

While his offensive skills took time to develop in college, Harper was outstanding on defense from day one.

"He was an unbelievable defender," remembered Craig Tucker. "He was 6-4, had long arms and was lightning quick with his hands and feet. Playing against him every day in practice really helped my game, because

▲ *Derek Harper worked incredibly hard in the off-seasons to improve his strength as well as his jump shot. "He would eat, sleep, and breath basketball," remembered assistant coach Bob Hull. Coach Bill Kroll (above) oversees Harper's workout.*

you couldn't play around with the basketball. If you played around with it while Derek was guarding you he would be going the other way shooting a lay-up."

"He is probably the toughest guard I have ever seen play," said Illinois forward Anthony Welch. "Harper was one of the few guys who could just dominate a game defensively."

"He was cat quick on defense and often times we would put him on our opponent's best guards," remembered assistant coach Dick Nagy. "When that happened, the other teams wouldn't want that guy bringing up the ball so they would change their entire offensive scheme to have someone else bring the ball up. They had to at times, because Derek could just dismantle you on defense."

After the graduation of Johnson and Smith, many thought Harper would drastically pick up his scoring in 1981-82, but it wouldn't be the case. He averaged just 8.4 points a game and struggled with the consistency of his jump shot. In guiding the team to an appearance in the NIT, he picked up the pace in other areas of his game, however, by averaging five assists, 4.6 rebounds, and 2.3 steals per game.

From the first day he arrived on campus, Harper was very focused on his long-term goals—improving his game and preparing himself for a career in the NBA.

"Derek was very focused on what he wanted to do, who he wanted to become and where he was going," remembered Scott Meents.

"His work ethic was phenomenal," said teammate and friend Quinn Richardson. "We worked out together, ran a lot, and he shot 200-300 jumpers [per day] during the summer to try and get better."

Off the court, Harper was very unassuming.

"He was very opinionated about how he felt about things, but I think he was always on the quiet side," said Bruce Douglas, who became very close to Harper in the year they played together. "He was very friendly, someone you could count on, and a guy who taught you what he knew."

The hard work on his jump shot during that summer between his sophomore and junior year paid off. By the time the Big Ten season rolled around, Harper's scoring was up and he was clearly the leader of the team. After a 26-point loss to Minnesota in the Big Ten

opener, Harper called an emotional team meeting that consequently turned things around.

By the middle of the Big Ten season, an already confident Harper became red hot. In a 25-point effort against Michigan he nailed his last seven shots of the game. Two days later, he scored 27 points against Michigan State and shot a perfect 11 of 11 from the field. Harper hit his first shot in the next game at Purdue before missing a contested lay-up to finish with 19 consecutive baskets, falling just six shots short of tying the NCAA record.

He remained hot for the entire remainder of the season and capped it off by drilling a 25-foot three-pointer from the top of the key in double overtime to beat Minnesota and send Illinois back into the NCAA Tournament.

On the season he averaged 15.4 points, 3.7 assists, 3.5 rebounds, and shot an incredible 57 percent from the field in conference play on his way to first-team All-Big Ten and second team All-America honors.

The days of Harper being an inconsistent shooter were over.

"His first year he was around 36 percent, the next year he went up to about 40, and in the final year he shot an unbelievable percentage from the field," said Lou Henson. "It just shows how great a work ethic he had and how badly he wanted to get better and win."

After a wild and confusing week of going back and forth with his decision to leave for the NBA or stay in school, Harper's decision became official when he didn't travel with the team on their overseas trip to Yugoslavia.

"We were packing up, getting ready to go on a tour of Yugoslavia, and it was right around when Derek was making his decision," recalled reserve forward Dee Maras. "I remember seeing him as the bus was pulling away and that was a sad moment for a lot of the guys on the team, because we knew he was going pro."

Shortly after, Harper officially announced that he was forgoing his senior year of eligibility to enter the NBA Draft. It was a very difficult decision.

"I thought about how good the team could be in 1983-84 before I left," recalled Harper. "More than anything, I thought about how good the backcourt could have been with Bruce and me. It was disappointing leaving him, because we had a brother-like relationship and I thought I could have had a bigger impact on his career."

In the 1983 NBA draft, Harper was selected 11th by Dallas, thus becoming the first ever draft choice of the Mavericks. He played his first 11 seasons with the Mavericks and 17 seasons in all, averaging 13.3 points a game over his career while amassing 15,997 points and 6,571 assists. He retired from the NBA in 1999 and currently is the color man on the Dallas Mavericks television broadcasts.

Almost 25 years ago Derek Harper made the tough decision to leave his mother in Florida to head north to play college basketball. He came to Champaign with hopes that it would help him get to the NBA, but along the way he realized it was the best decision he ever made.

"I wouldn't change that experience for anything in the world and it was the best three years of my life," reflected Harper from his home in Dallas. "That was the first stepping stone for me growing up and becoming a man. Going through Illinois, playing basketball there, and growing up there as a person was awesome."

It was just as great for Illinois fans that had the pleasure of watching Harper for three great seasons.

BRUCE DOUGLAS
GUARD: 1982–83—1985–86

In the early 1980s one didn't have to look too hard to find college coaches in the stands of Quincy High School basketball games. Coaches regularly flocked to the western part of the state to see Bruce Douglas.

He was the best player on the best team in the state and in his four years at Quincy his teams went 123-5, including a 64-game winning streak and one state championship. He was named Mr. Basketball in Illinois in 1982 and selected to the McDonald's All-American game. By the time he was a senior it was clear that Douglas was one of University of Illinois' top priorities and that they were going to cover every angle in recruiting him.

"His current wife, Madge, was a cheerleader at Quincy High School when he was there and one of the ways we recruited Bruce is we recruited her," laughed Illinois assistant coach Dick Nagy, who was one of the lead assistants in the Douglas recruitment. "We figured if we recruited her we would get Bruce too. She was definitely part of the package."

For Bruce the decision to come to Champaign just made sense.

"It was a place and a gym that I became comfortable playing in, but more than that it had everything I was looking for," recalled Douglas. "It was close to home, it was a good program that had the potential to become great and it had fantastic coaches."

In Douglas' first year he joined junior guard Derek Harper in the backcourt and together they formed the best defensive backcourt in the history of Illinois basketball and one of the best in the annals of college basketball.

His job during the season was to run the offense and get the ball to Harper, but Douglas contributed in a number of ways. He averaged 9.4 points a game, which included an 18-point night at Wisconsin and a 22-point showing at Ohio State, and he dished out six assists a game, including a 12-assist night against the Badgers. On the defensive side of the court, his 78 steals (2.44 per game) topped Harper's 72 (2.25 per game).

It was clear the young Douglas felt comfortable on the court and from the start there was never a doubt that he would be ready for the challenge mentally.

"He was as fundamentally sound a basketball player as any player I have ever seen coming out of high school," recalled Nagy. "He was so smart on the court."

"He probably had the best instincts I have ever seen in a basketball player," said Tony Wysinger, who had a chance to play with Douglas for three years at Illinois and marveled at his basketball savvy. "He was reading the play as or before it happened and at the same time was thinking a play ahead."

His head coach, Lou Henson, still has never seen anything like him again.

"I have never had a player who understood the game and knew the game better than Bruce Douglas," said Henson. "He was an ideal point guard, because he always knew what to do with the ball."

When Harper departed for the NBA, Douglas became the team leader in 1983-84 and certainly picked up his play. Early in the season, in an overtime road loss to Indiana, the Illini backcourt was torched by the Hoosiers. Freshman Steve Alford poured in 29 points and senior guard Chuck Franz added 20. Douglas was absolutely furious.

"After that game Bruce said when we play these guys again, I am going to dominate both of those guys," recalled Wysinger. "When we played Indiana at home, he probably put up his best game ever at Illinois, scoring 28 points. We thoroughly dominated them and that's exactly what Bruce said he was going to do. He was a man of his word."

That year, he played all 60 minutes of a four-overtime victory against Michigan in late January, which remains a single-game record for minutes played. That game wasn't an aberration, because he was very rarely taken out of games.

"I don't know if he ever got tired," said assistant coach Bob Hull. "Some people just have a bigger heart and better lungs. Bruce never wanted to come out of a game and if he did he wanted to go right back in."

He also set an Illinois single-game record with eight steals against Purdue in February of his sophomore season. He finished the season averaging 12.9 points, 5.7 assists, 4.4 rebounds, and 2.35 steals a game on his way to leading the team to a 26-5 record and a Big Ten Championship. Individually, he earned first-team All-Big Ten honors and was the Big Ten Co-Player of the Year. In accumulating 73 total steals on the season, Douglas proved he was one of the premier defenders in the country.

"As far as guarding the ball, he is the best defender I have seen at any level," said Ken Norman. "I am talking about high school, college, and the pros. No one has ever guarded the ball as well as Bruce, because he had quick hands and great anticipation."

Standing 6-3 with long arms, Douglas could wreak havoc on opposing guards.

"He had a knack for getting his hands on the ball and tipping passes away," remembered backcourt mate Quinn Richardson. "With those long arms, fast hands and quick feet it really made it tough on the guys he was guarding."

▲ Bruce Douglas was a phenomenal point guard. His 765 career assists is easily the school's benchmark. Coach Henson said Douglas "always knew what to do with the ball."

Perhaps what separated Bruce from other great defenders was his ability to anticipate.

"He wasn't the best at stealing the ball from you like he was picking your pocket, but when you made a pass to the post or the wing he was good at anticipating when that pass was coming," said Wysinger. "It's like he always knew where and when the pass would be made or he studied the play call. His anticipation ability was incredible."

Expectations were sky high for the 1984-85 team and for Douglas going into his junior year, but with the loss of his backcourt partner, Quinn Richardson, and new additions to the line-up, Douglas struggled to pick up his scoring. But while his scoring output dropped, he continued to dominate in other areas. He nabbed seven steals in a February game against Northwestern on his way to averaging over 2.43 a game and he dished out 13 assists in a 26-point thrashing of Minnesota in March. He led the team to a 26-9 record, a trip to the Sweet Sixteen and won the Big Ten Defensive Player of the Year Award.

Off the court, Douglas wasn't a very vocal guy, but he was highly regarded by his fellow teammates.

"He was down to earth, really easy to talk to, and he wasn't very emotional," recalled Richardson. "He never got too upset about anything on the court and brought a maturity level that was way beyond his years."

His teammates weren't the only ones who loved him.

"He was one of the best we ever had with the media," recalled Henson. "They just loved to interview him and chat with him after the games."

If the media ever needed to ask a random question about the game they knew Douglas was their guy.

"He had total recall on basketball games and I would just sit there in awe while he was being interviewed," said Hull. "Someone would ask him a question about a situation and he would tell him exactly who had the ball, what the score was, where they were on the court, and exactly what happened. He could go through the whole game and tell you about it like he had a play-by-play sheet in his hand."

Douglas was named captain, alongside Efrem Winters, for the 1985-86 basketball season. He led the team to a 22-10 record while averaging 8.8 points, 6.2 assists, and 2.8 rebounds a game. His average of 2.75 steals a game is still an Illinois record and it helped him win his second straight Big Ten Defensive Player of the Year Award.

For his career, Bruce Douglas is all over the Illinois record books. His 765 career assists is 263 more than anyone else. His 324 career steals is 106 more than his closest competitor. And nobody has played more career minutes than Bruce Douglas.

The Sacramento Kings selected him in the third round of the 1986 NBA Draft. Douglas enjoyed a brief NBA career before playing some in the CBA and moving on to a career in business. He is currently the Southern Region Operations Supervisor at Exelon and

was just recently ordained as a minister at the Broadview Missionary Baptist Church.

He wasn't the best shooter, he wasn't the quickest guard, and he definitely wasn't the strongest player in the history of the program. But all Douglas did in Champaign was win basketball games. In the 100-year history of the Illinois basketball program, few match up to Bruce Douglas in terms of being an all-around basketball player.

KEN
NORMAN
FORWARD: 1984-85—1986-87

From the very early stages of his life, Ken "Snake" Norman set clear goals and was determined to succeed. He wanted to get to the NBA so that he could provide for his family—and nothing was going to stop him from accomplishing that.

Not everyone believed in Norman's ability to reach his goals. As a high school basketball player at Crane High School, there were more than a few people who thought he wasn't going to thrive at the next level.

"A lot of people didn't think he was going to be able to play college basketball," remembered Illinois head coach Lou Henson. "We always thought he was going to be a good one."

In his senior year at Crane he averaged 23 points and 10 rebounds to lead them to the Public League Championship game. He originally committed verbally to Wisconsin, but when Badger head coach Bill Cofield was fired, he backed out of that commitment and became a part of the Illinois Class of 1982.

Before he could enroll at Illinois, Norman was forced to head to Wabash Junior College because he didn't have the grades to qualify for a scholarship. Norman wasn't going to give up, but when he first got to Wabash things weren't going well.

"He was [having a] very difficult [time] in the first semester of his freshman year and towards the end of the semester I went to see him in the locker room," remembered then-Wabash head coach and future

Illinois assistant Mark Coomes. "I gave him the Junior College Directory and I said, 'Snake, I have five junior colleges I want you to call. I can't coach you anymore, because you don't listen to me and you don't want to get better.' I told him he needed to transfer, because if he stayed it was going to be frustrating for both of us."

The incident surprised a young Norman.

"I was immature, as a lot of college kids are, and it shocked me when he did that," recalled Norman. "I wouldn't say it was a turning point, but it definitely woke me up. I liked it at Wabash and I didn't want to transfer."

From that point on Norman was a different player.

"He averaged 25 points and 17 rebounds a game after that talk," recalled Coomes. "That was a turning point in my relationship with him, but also with him understanding where the line needs to be drawn. Before that he was silly but after that he got very serious."

After having a big year at Wabash, Norman decided to transfer to Illinois and sat out the 1983-84 season.

"I felt at the time my skills were a little advanced for the junior college level, and that I would do better sitting out the year at Illinois," recalled Norman. "It would give me a chance to get acclimated academically, to mature as a person and to get in the weight room to get physically stronger."

There was little doubt that Norman would be spending a lot of time in the weight room throughout his Illinois career.

"He worked so hard and he had the body of Atlas," recalled Kendall Gill, who was a freshman when Norman was a senior. "He was rock solid and able to overpower a lot of people at his position."

When he finally took the court at the beginning of the 1984-85 season things certainly didn't go smoothly. After playing in the opener against Oklahoma, Norman was suspended for three games for playing in a Church-organized league the previous summer. When he returned from the suspension, he had a break-out game with 15 points against American University in the Illini Classic. But he continued to struggle all year long to adjust to the college game and find playing time behind a crowded Illinois frontline. For the season he averaged 7.8 points a game and shot 63 percent from the field.

After his initial season at Illinois, Norman knew

Forward Ken Norman led the 1986 and '87 Illini squads that won a combined 45 games. Norman earned first-team All-Big Ten honors both seasons. His senior season was his best, as he averaged 20.7 points and 9.8 rebounds per game.

there were things he had to improve and he wouldn't stop working the entire off season.

"He had an unrelenting work ethic and when he first arrived at Illinois he couldn't even make a six to ten foot jump shot. But he knew to be a great college player and play in the NBA he would have to be able to knock the 10-to-15-foot shot down," recalled Tony Wysinger. "In the summer, I would go with Ken and he would shoot 300 jump shots a day. He would always call me and say 'lets get to the gym early,' and, in fact, he would call anyone who could help him out. By the time his senior year rolled around he could get the ball on the wing and knock down that shot."

"Snake's biggest [asset] was his drive," remembered reserve forward Dee Maras. "He had such an internal drive—more than I had ever seen before from a player's standpoint. He worked hard in practice, he lifted weights and everything he did was to the best of his ability."

Whenever he was tired or didn't want to put in the necessary work, Norman just remembered where he came from and what he was working toward.

"I came from a very poor family and my whole goal in life was to be able to buy my mother a house and not have her struggle the way she struggled to raise us," said Norman. "That always motivated me and whenever I got tired of lifting weights or didn't want to go to class, I thought about my mother."

When he returned for his junior season he looked like a different player. With the departure of George Montgomery, Norman was inserted into the starting line-up and it paid dividends immediately. He led the Illini with 16 points in an opening game win against Loyola, scored 24 in a big win over Houston in the Assembly Hall a few weeks later, scored 27 against Ohio State, and hit the Indiana Hoosiers up for 24 points.

On the season, he led the team in scoring with 16.4 points a game and contributed 7.1 rebounds a contest. He earned first-team All-Big Ten honors and shot a remarkable 64 percent from the field, which almost 20 years later is still an Illini single-season field goal percentage record.

Off the court, Norman was a unique individual. He was never the type of guy to follow with the crowd.

"I was always the type of person that hung out alone," said Norman. "My mother always told me if you are going to get into some trouble get into it by yourself."

But when he was around the guys at practice you can bet that Snake was having a good time.

"He loved playing tricks and loved doing things to get people to laugh," recalled Wysinger. "I would think of different ways to mess with guys and so would he, but he would always do it."

After flirting with leaving for the NBA following his junior season, Norman decided to come back for his senior year. By the time that season began he was a force in the Big Ten.

"If you look up warrior in the dictionary it would describe Ken Norman," said Nagy. "He was never intimidated because he was the intimidator."

"He would always battle and it didn't matter if the guy in his way was seven feet tall," recalled Henson. "Snake was going to take it at him, because he wasn't scared of anybody or anything."

Norman began the season scoring 26 points in a win over New Mexico State in Hawaii and never looked back. He poured in 24 against Missouri, 29 in the Big Ten opener against Michigan, 27 against Minnesota, 26 against Ohio State, and finished his career in the Assembly Hall with a 24-point effort in a huge win over Indiana.

For the year, he averaged 20.7 points a game, shot 58 percent from the field and grabbed 9.8 rebounds a game to lead the Big Ten. Norman was named a second-team All-American, first-team All-Big Ten and in his three seasons on the court he racked up 1,393 points, which ranks 15th on the all-time list. He also finished his career shooting 61 percent from the field, which is the best percentage in the history of the program.

In the 1987 draft, his lifelong dream came true when the Los Angeles Clippers selected him 19th overall in the first round. He played six seasons with the Clippers before being traded to Milwaukee and then finishing his career in Atlanta. Overall, he played 10 years in the NBA, amassed 8,717 points and averaged 13.5 points a game. He retired at the end of the 1996-97 season and currently is working in the real estate business in the Chicago area.

Illinois was the ideal step to Norman's ultimate goal.

"It meant a lot to be from Illinois and go to the most prestigious school in the state," reflected Norman. "I don't feel I could have learned what I did there at any other university in the country and it has afforded me a great lifestyle on and off the court. In my eyes Illinois is the best school in the entire country."

All those days shooting jump shots, lifting weights, grinding it out at practice and working on his game finally paid off for Norman shortly after he got his first NBA contract in the NBA. Almost immediately after signing on the dotted line he was able to do what he had always dreamed of: he bought his mother a house.

NICK ANDERSON

GUARD: 1987-88—1988-89

When assistant coach Jimmy Collins walked into his office on his first day on the job at Illinois, Lou Henson dropped three recruiting files on his desk. One was Lowell Hamilton, a kid from Providence St. Mel, one was Simeon High School's Ben Wilson, and the other was a younger kid out of Prosser High School named Nick Anderson.

"I had never really seen him play when I first got to Illinois so I decided to go up there and see him in a game," recalled Jimmy Collins. "When I got up to the place where they practiced, I walked into the training room and there was this guy on the bicycle riding it really hard. He was a big, big guy and I said, 'Do you know where I can find Nick Anderson?' He looked at me, smiled and said, 'Right here on this bicycle.'"

"I was only a sophomore in high school riding the bicycle in the training room when this clean-cut guy with a sharp smile asked me if I could help him find Nick Anderson," said Anderson, reflecting on his first meeting with Collins. "I'll never forget the look on Jimmy's face when I told him it was me. He said, 'What!' with a shocked look because he couldn't believe how big I was as a sophomore."

For Coach Collins it wasn't just the physical maturity that amazed him with Anderson.

"In that particular game that night he scored something like 25 points and grabbed 25 rebounds," remembered Collins. "I went back to Champaign and told Coach Henson that we had to have this guy."

By the time he was a senior, about 200 schools recruited Anderson but he never forgot that Collins was the first person to come and see him. In mid-April of 1986, he made it official by announcing that he would be attending the University of Illinois. Illinois fans, the coaching staff and the guys on the team couldn't wait to see him on the floor, but they would have to be patient as Anderson's first year was wiped away by Proposition 48, which toughened the NCAA's academic requirements for athletes.

"It was real hard to sit out that year. I couldn't go to practice, I wasn't allowed to travel with the team, and I couldn't even eat with the team," said Anderson. "They took a lot of things away from me, but that didn't stop me. I did my work in the classroom and I played basketball every day at IMPE."

It was in those early pick-up games at IMPE and Huff Gym that the Nick Anderson legend began.

"I never played against him before, but I remember the first day he walked in the door when we were playing a game over at Huff," remembered Ken Norman. "I couldn't guard the man. He is fresh out of high school and I am going into my senior year and I couldn't do anything to stop him. It didn't matter if he posted me

The Champaign-Urbana News-Gazette

▲ *Nick Anderson led the Illini in scoring two consecutive seasons before entering the NBA Draft after Illinois' spectacular 1989 season. "There were things he did on the court that just made your jaw drop," recalled teammate Lowell Hamilton.*

up or took me on the perimeter. He was just unbelievable."

"Nick and Lowell [Hamilton] were checking each other [during a game] and Lowell made an awesome move to dunk over Nick," recalled Illinois forward Glynn Blackwell. "Lowell had those long arms and he elbowed Nick in the face when he threw it down. Nick screamed back at Lowell to watch his elbows and then Lowell yelled back, 'Little fella, just check up.'

"They threw the ball into Nick, he dribbled down the entire floor with guys all over him, and the next thing I knew he jumped over everybody and dunks the ball. Hard. Boom! Everyone stopped playing, that game was over, and right then we all knew how special he was."

Standing 6-5 with a rock-solid build, Anderson was tough to miss when he walked into a gym.

"He was a man among boys in college," said teammate Kendall Gill.

"He was just a naturally strong kid that had a physique that you can't even imagine."

More than anything else, Anderson was blessed with God-given ability.

"Nick is still one of the purest basketball players I have ever seen," recalled Hamilton. "He had so much talent and I was so amazed with Nick that sometimes I would catch myself watching him play, just in awe of his athletic ability. I would have to snap out of it and get back to work, because there were things he did on the court that just made your jaw drop."

Finally in uniform at the start of the 1987-88 season, Anderson didn't disappoint. After getting off to a slow start by his standards, he finished the season averaging 15.9 points and 6.6 rebounds a game while shooting better than 57 percent from the floor.

Growing up in a tough neighborhood in Chicago, Anderson became a fierce competitor. That competitiveness was both his greatest asset and his worst enemy.

"When we would lose a game, Nick would actually cry," recalled Collins, who became very close to Anderson in his time at Illinois. "I would have to stay with him for a while to console him, because losses just didn't sit well with him. He would mope around for two or three days, but that is also the reason he played and worked so hard to win."

Away from the court, Nick was a very sensitive kid.

"He was a great guy who loved everyone. He wanted everybody to be like a family," said Gill.

"Nick was the hardest of all of the guys to analyze, because you never knew what was going on in his head," remembered Illinois assistant coach Mark Coomes. "Yelling at Nick was not productive and you had to know that the best thing to do to make him play good was to put your arm around him."

Perhaps no one saw the dynamics of his personality more than manager Ryan Baker.

"Nick needed to know that you needed him, you wanted him and that you loved him. He needed that emotional reinforcement to get out there," said Baker. "There were more than a few times during his sophomore year that he said that he was leaving and going back to Chicago, but then we would pump him up, he would have a big game and be back on cloud nine."

In fact, Anderson did head back home to Chicago with thoughts of transferring numerous times throughout his Illinois career. Each time he got home the exact same thing happened.

"Every time I got through the door, Coach Collins would call me and ask me what I was doing," said Anderson. "I would say that I wasn't coming back to school and that I was staying home. He would say, 'No, you are not,' and he would come up to Chicago to get me. He wouldn't let me stay, he wouldn't let me quit and that is what I love about him."

By the time his junior year arrived, everybody expected big things out of Anderson and he delivered. He averaged 18 points and 7.9 rebounds a game in a season that would be an emotional roller coaster for Anderson.

After the team lost their first game of the year at Minnesota, Anderson almost suffered a much bigger loss.

"I got a call at four in the morning from my sister saying that my mother was in a real serious car accident," recalled Anderson. "I rushed to Chicago and when I got there my mother was in a full body cast. I will never forget that sight."

Anderson scored 21 points on no sleep in the first game after his mom's accident and went on to have a magical season. His game-winning shot at the buzzer against Indiana is etched into Illinois lore. So is his 24-point, 16-rebound game against Syracuse—one of the single-best performances in school history—that propelled Illinois into the Final Four.

With one more year of eligibility left and Anderson telling everyone he was coming back it seemed that the best was yet to come. But he would never wear the Orange and Blue again as Anderson changed his mind right before the entry deadline for the NBA Draft.

"The decision to leave was really hard, but it was something I had to do," said Anderson, reflecting back on the events after the 1989 season ended. "With my mom's terrible accident during the season she was not in position to take care of my sisters and me. I had to be the breadwinner of the family."

Nick was drafted 11th overall in the 1989 draft, becoming the first ever pick of the expansion Orlando Magic. He went on to have a 13-year NBA career in which he scored 11,529 points and averaged 14.4 points and 5.1 rebounds per game. He retired in 2002.

People in Champaign will always remember the thunderous dunks, the 40-inch vertical leap and the many great moments he was a part of in his two years on the floor. Nick won't soon forget his time in Champaign either.

"I am proud to say I went to Illinois and am proud that I made the University of Illinois my final choice out of high school," reflected Anderson from his home in Atlanta. "I loved my time there and I have absolutely no regrets in choosing to be a Fighting Illini."

KENNY BATTLE
FORWARD: 1987-88—1988-89

In the spring of 1986, Northern Illinois University made a decision that would forever impact the history of Fighting Illini basketball. After deciding to pull out of the Mid-American Conference, they fired head coach John McDougal, who had an extremely close relationship with star player Kenny Battle.

"I felt Coach McDougal was fired for no reason and I didn't like the direction the school was going," reflected Battle. "At the time I felt it was in my best interests

to go another direction as well so I transferred to Illinois."

Battle was the leading scorer at Northern in his first two seasons, finishing his sophomore campaign averaging just less than 20 points a game. He would have to sit out the 1986-1987 season, but he spent the whole year proving to everyone that he could make the big jump to the Big Ten.

"He would go up against Ken Norman every day in practice the year he sat out and one day Coach Henson tried to run a play for Snake to get a last shot," recalled Illinois assistant coach Jimmy Collins. "Norman was bigger and stronger than [Battle]—the weight difference had to be at least 100 pounds. Kenny was such a battler that he wouldn't let Ken get the ball. Eventually Norman just said, 'Go to someone else because he is not going to let me get it.'"

When Battle walked into the gym each and every day you knew exactly what you were going to get.

"It didn't matter what time we practiced, because Kenny would play the same way," remembered teammate Marcus Liberty. "If we practiced at eight in the morning or late at night, he was going to be running around, doing his 360 dunks and stealing the basketball."

Standing 6-5 with a slender build, Battle was an astonishing athlete who was able to run and jump with just about everyone.

"I don't think there was a better 6-5 player in the entire country," said head coach Lou Henson. "He could post up bigger guys in the lane, he could shoot the 15-18 foot jumper and he was one of those players who had a knack for scoring."

It didn't take long for Battle to make an impact on the court. In only his second game in an Illinois uniform, he scored 28 points and grabbed six rebounds against the Villanova Wildcats in Maui. He finished his first season averaging 15.6 points and 5.5 rebounds a game, but his impact stretched far beyond the statistical numbers he put up.

The Illinois players and fans were feeding off of Battle's infectious energy.

"He was the emotional soul of [the Flying Illini team]," recalled assistant coach Mark Coomes. "He was like a magnet and [the other players] surrounded him like a nucleus. They fed off of his energy and his play, especially when he put down one of his incredible dunks. There is nothing like a Kenny Battle dunk."

Fifteen years later fans and teammates talk about his dunks with amazement. They couldn't believe his dunks then, and some are still trying to figure out how he did it.

"We were involved in a tough, close game against Northwestern. Kenny got a break away towards the end of the game and did a ridiculous 360 dunk," remembered manager Ryan Baker. "It was one of those dunks where everybody in the place looks at each other and says, 'Did you see what he just did?'"

Perhaps no one personified the name "Flying Illini" and gave that team its identity more than Flight number 33, Kenny Battle.

Mark Jones

▲ *Kenny Battle kept the Flying Illini's motor running with his superb defense and array of dunks. "He was the emotional soul of [the Flying Illini team]," recalled assistant coach Mark Coomes.*

"We were playing against Ohio State and they had a big seven-footer named Grady Matteen," said Coomes. "Kenny gets an offensive rebound, lifts up on his two feet and got so high he dunked it over Matteen behind his head. I couldn't believe it."

His passion made practices intense and his mouth would be running up and down the court just as much as the rest of his body.

"He was a trash talker and when you came to practice each day you had better come with it," remembered Lowell Hamilton. "If you were on his team he would talk you up, but if you weren't on his team you better make sure he didn't get the best of you. If he did you were going to hear about it all practice long."

"I was the type of person who angered a lot of my teammates," said Battle, looking back on those heated practice sessions. "I frustrated each and every one of them."

On and off the court, Battle was the life of the party.

"I don't know of a day where he wasn't laughing or having fun with what he was doing," remembered Tony Wysinger. "He just seemed to be having more fun than everyone else."

"No matter what the situation he was out there having a good time," recalled assistant coach Dick Nagy. "It just wasn't work for him and for a lot of players basketball seems like hard work, especially on the defensive end. Defense wasn't work for Kenny, because he loved it."

Defensively, Battle seemed like he was all over the court.

"When he stepped on the court he was guarding his man, my man and everybody else's too," said Anderson.

With his speed and quickness he became the central figure in many of Illinois' defensive schemes.

"He was a frontline player, but we would put him on the point in our press," said Henson. "He was so good defensively at knocking down passes, picking off balls, and if they ever got past the press he would just sprint back to cover his big man inside."

Battle was co-captain alongside Hamilton in the Final Four year of 1989. For the season he averaged 16.6 points, 2.5 steals and 4.8 rebounds a game on his way to earning second-team All-Big Ten honors. His last game in an Illinois uniform was one of his best as he scored 29 points in a losing effort to Michigan in Seattle. Battle finished his two-year Illini career with 1,112 points, which currently ranks 31st on the all-time list.

Battle was drafted 27th in the first round of the 1989 NBA draft by the Detroit Pistons, who traded his rights to the Phoenix Suns. He spent four years in the NBA before retiring to pursue other ventures, including a stint as an assistant coach for the Harlem Globetrotters. He currently is the head basketball coach at the Illinois Institute of Technology in Chicago.

There were certainly some rocky times in the spring of 1986, but for Battle it all worked out in the end.

"Being able to play for the biggest school in the state that was recognized for not only Coach Henson, but for all of the outstanding players who had played there before me was an honor," reflected Battle. "When you have the opportunity to have your name mentioned with those great players it certainly makes you feel good."

His name is more than mentioned. Each year an Illinois player receives the Kenny Battle Award at the end of the year banquet for hustle, energy and dedication. Those three words personify the man whose smile, ability, and energy lit up the Assembly Hall in the late 1980s.

KENDALL GILL
GUARD: 1986-87—1989-90

For Illinois basketball fans, Michael Christian might not be a household name. If they only knew more about him he might still be on their holiday card list. If Christian, a 6-3 point guard out of Denver who was ranked in the top five nationally, committed to Illinois instead of Georgia Tech in the recruiting class of 1986 there would have never been a Kendall Gill wearing Orange and Blue.

Shortly after being hired in 1984, Illinois assistant coach Jimmy Collins first met Gill.

"I was visiting a friend in Chicago and Kendall happened to be a friend of this guy's son," remembered Collins. "Kendall was in the 10th grade at the time, and he saw that I had Illinois posters in the back of my car. He turned to me and said, 'I want to play for Illinois someday,' and I just kind of joked with him, but I never thought a tall, skinny kid like that could ever play Division One college basketball."

Two years later, Gill, now physically mature, had turned into an all-state high school basketball player for Rich Central High School. Collins happened to be at one of his games that year and noticed this skinny kid had grown some, but it wasn't until Collins paid a recruiting visit to Gill's house that he convinced himself that Gill could play at Illinois.

"I was at Kendall's house for a visit and he and his brother, Keith, got into a big fistfight," said Collins. "I realized right then how competitive Kendall was because Keith really handled him that day and was really the tougher of the two. That day I saw that Kendall was a fighter and it showed me that he would never stop and never quit."

Shortly after Christian chose Georgia Tech, Collins lobbied for Gill.

"We really put a lot of cards on the table for Michael Christian and were in a tough spot, but I told Coach that I have always liked Kendall and I think he could really help us," recalled Collins. "Coach Henson turned to me and said, 'I am going to give you one recruit this year, so if you want him go and take him.' The next day I offered Kendall a scholarship and he was coming to Illinois."

"Kendall and Michael Christian came on their official visits at the same time, so I think Kendall was well aware that he wasn't their main guy," remembered Illinois guard Glynn Blackwell. "I think what drove him was the fact that no one believed in him. Whenever someone tells you that you can't do something you are going to do everything in the world to show them you can."

Arriving on campus in the fall of 1986, Kendall wasn't comfortable right away in his new surroundings.

"I think Kendall was scared when he first got down to campus wondering if he was going to fit in or not," said Tony Wysinger, who was a senior guard at the time. "We would always get on him, because his arms were so long that none of his clothes fit, but we knew he was going to be a good player. It was only a matter of when."

Gill's first year on the court at Illinois wasn't a banner one. He struggled to get acclimated to the Big Ten and struggled to find playing time on a good Illinois team. He finished the year averaging 3.7 points a game without really discovering any consistency with his game. But he started to blossom during his sophomore campaign as his minutes increased. Still, Gill struggled to find any consistency with his jump shot. The frustration boiled over in a Big Ten game at Carver Hawkeye Arena.

"I won't ever forget that game, because I missed a ton of jump shots," said Gill, reflecting on a game where he shot two of 10 from the floor and one of seven from the three-point line. "The Iowa fans were ripping me, making fun of my shot, and I vowed the next year I would come back as one of the best shooters in the league."

He finished the year averaging 10.4 points a game and seemed to prove he could play at the Big Ten level, but Gill still had questions.

"Going into that summer, I still had some doubts in my ability," remembered Gill. "I knew that All-American Marcus Liberty was coming in the next year and it made me think that if Marcus comes in where is my spot?"

The Champaign-Urbana News-Gazette

▲ *Kendall Gill worked tirelessly to improve his game throughout his Illini career. Coach Henson remembered that Gill was "obsessed with being the best he could be." The results were a fabulous senior season in which he averaged 20.0 points per game and a ticket to the NBA.*

Gill only told two people about his thoughts of transferring, but they were certainly the right people to talk to.

"I never told the coaches about what I was thinking and I only told my parents," remembered Gill. "They talked to me about it and they said winners never quit. They weren't going to let me leave and quit. I decided then that I had to make my own spot and that's exactly what I did."

After quickly deciding to stay, it was time to go to work and work hard. Perhaps no one in the history of Illinois basketball has improved more in one summer than Kendall did between his sophomore and junior seasons.

"That summer, he just dedicated himself to becoming a better player," remembered friend and team manager Ryan Baker. "He shot between 500 and 1,000 jumpers a day—all he did was work on his basketball game."

Kendall's transformation didn't just happen on the court.

"He got into the weight room and he worked so hard in there," said Illinois assistant coach Dick Nagy, who couldn't believe what he saw. "By the time he left school in May and returned in August he didn't even look like the same kid. If you didn't know him real well you wouldn't have even recognized him."

Armed with a much more consistent jump shot and 10 pounds of bulk, Gill was ready to take his game to the next level.

"In all of my years of coaching, I have never seen anyone train as hard as Kendall Gill," said Coach Henson. "I have also never seen anyone take care of himself the way he did. He was just obsessed with being the best he could be."

In his junior year, the magical season of 1988-89, Gill's improved play was evident right away. Seventeen games into the season he was shooting over 50 percent from the field, averaging 15.5 points a game and often dominating other teams. Against LSU in late December he scored 27 points on 11 of 14 shooting.

Exactly one month later, on Super Bowl Sunday with the team 16-0, he suffered a broken left foot while going for a rebound and missed 12 games before returning with two games left in the regular season. During that stretch, Gill was with the team every step of the way.

"What impressed me the most about him was that when he got hurt he was always on the sideline with a cast on his foot," remembered Nick Anderson. "He was at every practice, every game and was always encouraging everybody. Some guys when they go down with injuries, you don't see them until they are healed, but that wasn't the way Kendall was. I always respected him for that."

Off the court, Gill was a guy who kept to himself.

"Kendall is his own guy and is not the type of individual who would be one of the guys in a group," said Baker. "He might end up in the same place as everybody else, but nine times out of 10 he is rolling solo."

With the departure of Battle and Anderson to the NBA following the 1989 season, Gill became the go-to guy in his senior year and did not disappoint. He averaged 20 points a game for the season while shooting 50 percent from the field. In his last game at the Assembly Hall, Gill racked up 25 points in a trouncing of the Iowa Hawkeyes. He garnered first-team All-Big Ten honors, consensus All-America honors and became the only Lou Henson player to lead the Big Ten in scoring.

After graduating, Gill realized his dream when he was selected fifth overall by Charlotte in the 1990 NBA draft. Gill has enjoyed a prosperous 14-year NBA career spanning six different teams. Currently he is back in Chicago playing for his hometown Bulls.

It seems like the perfect ending for a guy who always knew he wanted to stay in his home state. For Gill, his time at Illinois is something he will never forget.

"It doesn't matter what team I play for in the NBA, because I am always an Illini," reflected Gill from his home in the south Chicago suburbs. "That is where I got my start, that is where my loyalty is and I knew the day I heard Coach Henson's voice on the other end of the phone that I was going there."

Recruiting is certainly an inexact science, but in a simple twist of recruiting fate Illinois hit the jackpot. While he wasn't initially the guy they wanted to get, Gill became the guy they needed to have.

Its hard to imagine the Flyin' Illini without Flight number 13 and Illinois fans everywhere are thankful they had the chance to watch him play.

DEON
THOMAS
CENTER: 1990–91—1993–94

Todd Rosenberg/Getty Images

▲ *Deon Thomas, the Illini's career scoring leader with 2,129 points, is proof that hard work and determination pay off. "Illinois basketball was something that I fought for," said Thomas, speaking of the off-the-court adversity he overcame during his Illini career.*

In the fall of 1989, Deon Thomas was living the high life for a high school basketball player. He was one of the best players in the nation out of Simeon High School in Chicago and colleges from all over the country were sending him letters and placing phone calls to his house trying to lure him to their school. He was big time and life couldn't be better.

Thomas eventually decided to follow in the tradition of fellow Simeon stars Nick Anderson and Ervin Small, and announced he was going to Champaign to play for the Illini. Shortly thereafter, his world changed forever.

The University of Iowa coaching staff, led by assistant Bruce Pearl, alleged recruiting violations by the Illinois staff and Pearl taped a conversation between the two where Thomas said Illinois had given him money to attend school.

Even 15 years later the subject is difficult for Thomas to talk about.

"I said it then and I will say it now," said Thomas. "None of that was true and that was the most difficult thing. My biggest regret is not being able to read someone's character and allowing myself to be wooed by Coach Pearl. He wasn't what he made himself out to be and I should have known that."

In Thomas' first year on campus at Illinois, he barely touched a basketball. While most freshman spend their time getting acclimated to school and their new teammates, Thomas spent it familiarizing himself with the NCAA and his attorney, Steve Beckett. It was an extremely difficult year for Thomas.

"There was a cloud over me and the program and people were thinking about all types of things," recalled Thomas. "It actually hurt to be around the team because I was looking forward to playing with the remaining guys from the Flying Illini team. To have that taken away, especially when you didn't do anything wrong, was extremely hard for me."

After persevering through his initial season in 1989-90, Thomas finally took the court for the Illini on Nov.

23, 1990 and scored a team-high 21 points in propelling Illinois to a 19-point victory over American University. It was only a warm-up. During a trip south a few weeks later, Thomas showed everyone how dominating he could be.

"He scored 28 points and grabbed 16 rebounds in a game down at Memphis," recalled Illinois assistant coach Mark Coomes. "I remember thinking, 'Boy this kid is going to be something,' and he sure was."

Thomas completed his freshman season averaging 15.1 points and 6.8 rebounds a game, earning third-team All-Big Ten honors. He was a wizard with his back to the basket and when he got the ball down low the other team was in deep trouble.

"Deon had all the tools, and for a post player his size, he was incredible," said teammate Richard Keene. "He could handle the ball, he had a very soft touch on his shot and he would just dominate people down low."

In his sophomore season, Thomas continued to improve on the floor. His dominating performances offensively were becoming a common occurrence—against Illinois-Chicago he poured in 39 points and grabbed 16 rebounds in what is one of the greatest single-game performances in the history of Illinois basketball. He was named second-team All-Big Ten and finished the season averaging 19.4 points and 6.9 rebounds a game.

Off the court, the 6-9, 255-pound Thomas was very reserved and quiet, but was also loved by his teammates.

"He's a fun-loving guy and great to be around," said reserve guard Gene Cross. "Everybody likes Deon. You look at him and he is this big menacing guy but then he comes up with this soft little voice. We used to call him Sweet D, because of that voice."

Thomas continued to lead the Illini in scoring during his junior season, averaging 18.3 points a game and 8 rebounds. His consistency game in and game out—due in part to a superior 60 percent field goal percentage—was incredible.

His teammates remember Thomas as a guy they could turn to when things weren't going well.

"I always felt like I could talk to Deon about my struggles with the transition to the college game," recalled Brooks Taylor, who came in with Thomas in 1989. "I would talk to him about my frustration and he was always very positive. He kept telling me to stick it

out and it's amazing that he had such a level head at that age."

Going into his senior season there was no question that Thomas was going to break Eddie Johnson's career scoring record—it was only a matter of when. He entered the year with 1,581 career points, just 111 shy of Johnson, and, five games into the season he was 20 points away.

Thomas started the game against American University on December 11, 1994, on fire and with 5:28 remaining in the first half, Thomas got a feed in the post on the right baseline from Jerry Hester. He paused and then turned around for a short four-foot baby hook shot that rolled around the rim and dropped in.

"It was one of the greatest times as an individual player I have ever had," said Thomas from his home in Israel. "That feeling is something that stands by itself, but I have to say that my teammates were the ones to get me there and without them I wouldn't have been able to do it."

Thomas was now all by his lonesome on the top of the Illinois all-time scoring list. The game was stopped for about three minutes as Thomas was presented with the game ball in a ceremony at half court.

"It was great to see him break the record, but what made it more special was to see the enjoyment in Deon's eyes when his Grandma Bernice walked out on the floor with Coach Collins," remembered Wheeler. "You think about what Deon and Coach Collins had to go through together and here they were four years later still very close. It just seemed that finally everything was behind him and the weight was off from the investigation."

"The biggest moment for me was not making the basket, but having my grandmother out on the floor to celebrate with me," reflected Thomas, who was also joined on the court by his young son. "She was always my biggest supporter and she always stuck behind me."

Thomas finished the game shooting 14 of 17 from the field on his way to 31 points in 24 minutes. For the season he averaged 19.6 points a game and 6.9 rebounds to finish his Illinois career with 2,129 points and 846 rebounds. In 10 years since his career ended only one person, Kiwane Garris, has even gotten within 200 points of Thomas' record. In this day and age of college basketball, Thomas could very well hold that record forever.

Even after his career was over, the allegations left an indelible mark on Thomas.

"It's almost impossible even after all this time to explain things clearly about how I felt through the whole thing," said Thomas. "Although Coach Collins and I were not guilty of anything, the school was still punished. They never came out and said, 'These guys didn't do anything wrong,' so there was still a cloud hanging over me, which should have been lifted because nothing happened. It was like a big huge chunk of me was taken away and never given back."

Yet through all the pressure, all the questions and all the allegations, Thomas persevered. While the whole world was swirling around him, he never let it affect his play on the basketball court.

Fifteen years ago, Thomas didn't know if he would ever suit up in the Orange and Blue. When he finally did, he had a different perspective on how much basketball and especially Illinois meant to him.

"Illinois basketball was something that I fought for and it was something that was a part of me then and will always be a part of me," reflected Thomas. "To this day, I look back with great pride in the coaches I had, my teammates, and the career I was able to have at Illinois. It's not just the records or things like that, because to be able to play at such a great university and be part of the legacy of players who came through there is awesome. It's one of the most important things in my life."

FRANK WILLIAMS
GUARD: 1998-99—2001-02

He came to Illinois after winning three state championships at Peoria Manual High School with the reputation of being an incredible talent and a clutch player. He was a McDonald's All-American and, along with his high school teammates, Sergio McClain and Marcus Griffin, he was supposed to be the one who would put Illinois basketball back on top.

Frank Williams' career at Illinois would go through the lowest of lows and the highest of highs, but when he departed Champaign four years later he would leave

his mark on Illinois basketball as possibly the greatest clutch performer the program has ever seen.

Right off the bat things didn't go according to plan for Williams.

"He barely missed getting the necessary test score on the ACT, so he was a partial scholarship player, which meant he could practice but not travel or play with the team," said assistant coach Rob Judson, who was instrumental in bringing the Manual trio to Illinois. "It was the first time in his life he was without basketball so he certainly went through his ups and downs and his struggles."

After getting through that initial 1998-99 season, everyone in Champaign was anticipating his debut on the court as expectations soared. But at the start, things didn't come easy for Williams as he struggled to meet those lofty expectations and adapt to the college game.

In his third ever collegiate game, he shot four of 17 from the field in a nationally televised game against Duke. His struggles came to a head four games into the Big Ten season when he scored three points, committed six turnovers and played only 15 minutes against Michigan in Ann Arbor.

"Frank learned during that season that you couldn't have successes on the court without having victories off the court," said Judson. "When he finally figured that out and realized he needed to meet his commitments his game took off."

As his maturity grew, his game improved and Williams finished that season playing much better. He scored 21 points against Pennsylvania in the first round of the NCAA Tournament and for the year averaged 11.4 points and 4.1 assists a game.

His reputation as a great passer started in his days at Peoria, but in Champaign he became known as a magician with the basketball.

"With Frank I always had to have my hands ready for a pass," said teammate Brian Cook. "It would come from behind his head, behind his back, or between the legs and he was just so creative with the ball."

There was an unwritten code between the big men on the team that developed from being on the court with Williams. They always knew they had to be paying attention.

"All of the big men who played with him can tell you about the time he almost broke their nose with a pass," said forward Damir Krupalija. "If you didn't have your hands up you were going to get hit in the face, because he saw things that no one else did."

Williams' game improved dramatically during his sophomore season as he became more consistent. In a December game against Seton Hall, he ignited a 21-point come-from-behind victory, scoring 17 of his 21 points in the second half. But, the heroics wouldn't stop there. Just a few weeks later against Missouri in the annual Braggin' Rights Game, Williams took over late in the game by scoring the last four points in regulation and seven of the Illini's 14 in overtime to give Illinois the victory. He also poured in a then-Illinois record for the NCAA Tournament by scoring 30 points in a dominating performance against Kansas in the NCAA Sweet Sixteen. For the season, he averaged 14.9 points and 4.4 assists a game on his way to being named the Big Ten Player of the Year.

Yet for all his accomplishments on the court, Williams wasn't a very vocal guy. He was reserved in his public persona, but well liked by his teammates.

"He just had the characteristics of a leader," said teammate Sean Harrington. "Frank could step in a room and get everybody excited. When he had a good day the rest of the team had a good day, because we all fed off of him."

Behind closed doors and around his teammates, Williams was very different from what most people think.

"Frank was so cool and the personality he portrayed to everyone else was all by design," said his former head coach Bill Self. "All the guys loved him, and if I was a younger guy, he would be the type of guy I would gravitate to."

Williams rarely showed emotion on the court and was so immensely talented that at times it didn't seem like he was always playing at full speed.

"The game was in slow motion to him," said Self. "He was never in a hurry and he saw things so well. He was also extremely bright and I was always amazed at his basketball IQ. Frank could pick up things real quick in the scouting report and you only had to tell him something once."

On the court Williams didn't look real quick—but looks could be very deceiving.

Mark Cowan/Icon SMI

▲ *The game was in slow motion for Frank Williams, who made his mark as a clutch player and an exciting passer. "He would think of the pass that no one else could or would think of," remembered teammate Lucas Johnson.*

"You would watch him and say, 'He isn't that fast,'" remembered Krupalija. "But ask anybody who ever guarded him in practice what happened when he took that first step. Most of the time he was four feet ahead of you and all you could do was yell for help."

He was never known for his hard work or for being a gym rat, but Williams played more basketball than most realized.

"I remember chewing Frank out because he wasn't playing enough. I told him that we saw him coming late and leaving early from pick-up games," recalled Self. "I would yell at him and tell him he doesn't care about basketball and being a player, but he would never say a word. Afterwards the guys came up to me and told me, 'Coach, you may not know this but as soon as Frank leaves here he goes and plays three hours in the park.'"

Many thought Williams would turn pro after his sophomore season, but the Champaign-Urbana community rallied around him that spring as billboards of "Stay

Frank Stay" popped up all around Champaign-Urbana. In a dramatic announcement at the end-of-the-year awards banquet, Williams told everyone he was spending one more year with the Illini.

Entering the 2001-02 season, expectations were sky high for the Illini and even higher for Williams, but his final season in an Illinois uniform was a trying one. With Williams struggling from the field and the team struggling to win a game on the road, all of the criticism turned to the All-American point guard.

It all came to a head on Super Bowl Sunday when Williams and the team seemed lackluster in a home loss to the Michigan State Spartans. During the national television broadcast, Williams was personally called out by CBS commentator Billy Packer. The firestorm began and for weeks Williams was cited as the reason that Illinois was struggling. Yet through the entire controversy, he proved why he was a leader.

"He is one of the few players I have ever been around that never makes an excuse," said assistant coach Norm Roberts. "Frank knew all the pressure for the team winning and losing was on him and he took it for everybody. He shielded it away from Cook, he shielded it away from all the other guys, and it showed how tough he was."

Just over a week later, the Illini traveled to the Breslin Center where the Spartans had only lost once to a Big Ten team in the past 54 games. It was a night where Williams reminded everybody how great he was.

"That was the most hyped up I have ever seen him in an Illinois uniform," recalled Roberts. "He was raring to go."

Williams didn't disappoint, dominating in all facets of the game. He smothered Marcus Taylor on defense, holding him to four of 15 from the field, while controlling the game on offense. With just over a minute left in the game and the shot clock running down, Williams launched a three-point attempt from NBA range at the top of the key that dropped in and put a dagger in the hearts of the Spartans. In a rare showing of emotion, Williams pumped his fist and yelled out into the crowd as the Spartans called for a time-out.

"That was just awesome and it was even greater because it came at a time where everybody was criticizing how hard he plays and how much it means to him,"

said Johnson. "He stepped up to take control of the game and without that we don't win the Big Ten title that year. I have watched that game since and it literally gives me goose bumps to see Frank's emotion after hitting that shot."

Three weeks later, the Illini looked to clinch a share of the Big Ten title at Minneapolis against the Gophers. With 6.9 seconds remaining and the Illini down one, Williams took the ball, drove through the lane and put in a bank shot over Travarus Bennett to give the Illini the lead and a share of their second-straight Big Ten Championship.

In a season that looked to be lost, Williams led the Illini to an incredible stretch run of seven straight Big Ten wins.

"I give Frank so much credit for that entire season because he basically said, 'Alright guys when we lose it's my fault and when we win it's a team win,'" said Johnson. "It showed that it was his team, he was the leader of the group and he was going to get the job done."

For the season, he averaged 16.2 points, 4.4 assists, 4.7 rebounds and 2.01 steals a game on his way to being named a first-team All-Big Ten selection and an honorable-mention All-American.

In his three seasons as an Illini, he scored 1,440 points, which today ranks 12th on the all-time list. Williams was drafted 25th overall in the 2002 NBA Draft by the Denver Nuggets and was then traded on draft day to the New York Knicks. Last year, in his second NBA season, he averaged 3.9 points a game as a backup point guard.

While his career at Illinois seemed like a rollercoaster ride, his performances over the years are some of the greatest in the history of the program. In 100 years of Illinois basketball, with the game on the line there has been nobody better with the ball in his hands than Frank Williams.

BRIAN COOK

FORWARD: 1999–2000—2002–03

As Brian Cook entered Lincoln High School in 1995, he had already earned the attention of many college coaches across Illinois. By the time Lon Kruger came into the picture, the Illini and their top assistant, Rob Judson, were well aware of his background and his potential.

"I knew the history of Brian's father and what a great player he was, and I also knew that his mom played on a team that was runner-up in the girls state championship," remembered Judson. "Brian had a top-notch coach in Neil Alexander and he brought Brian and Joyce over to a lot of games when he was a freshman and sophomore [in high school]."

By the time he reached his junior year in high school, Cook was ready to make his decision.

"For me it was pretty much an easy choice," said Cook. "I am kind of a homebody who likes to be close to home and my friends and family were all in the area. I also grew up watching Illinois basketball so it was an honor that they wanted me."

Cook committed to Illinois during his junior season, prior to an outstanding senior year in which he was named Mr. Basketball in Illinois.

"It was big for us to land him," remembered Judson. "We had Mr. Basketball with Sergio and Frank and now got a third one in the fold with Brian Cook. It definitely elevated the program."

Things started very slowly for Cook as a freshman as he struggled to get playing time and adjust to the physical nature of college basketball. He first showed his ability to score in a late non-conference game against Bethune-Cookman when he poured in 18 points in just 23 minutes. But it wasn't until Marcus Griffin tore his lateral meniscus in a mid-season practice that Cook took off. In the first game after Griffin's injury, Cook was inserted into the starting line-up and scored 20 points against Penn State. He followed that with a 19-point effort against Iowa.

Cook was quickly becoming an impact freshman. For the season, he averaged nine points and 4.5 rebounds a game on his way to becoming Co-Big Ten

Rookie of the Year. It was no surprise to anyone that Brian could make an impact right away.

"When you combine his size with his skill level there was no doubt he was going to be very good," recalled his former head coach Lon Kruger. "He wanted to be a good player, he had very good passing abilities, and at 6-11 he had a very nice touch."

When Bill Self came on board in 2000, Cook was inserted into the starting line-up for good. After going through an early season slump, he broke out with 17 points against Wisconsin-Milwaukee and then had the best game of his young career two weeks later as he helped the Illini win the annual Border War game against Missouri by scoring 25 points and grabbing 11 rebounds. Over the course of the year Cook began to come into his own, averaging 11.2 points and 6.1 rebounds a game.

He was a timid and shy freshman when he came on board, which earned him the 'soft' label from many of his critics. His teammates pushed him around in practice all the time, but during that sophomore campaign he started to fight back.

"I remember pushing him around so easily in his freshman year, because he was easily moved and not every tough," remembered forward Lucas Johnson. "I would give him a little shiver or bump coming down the court and he would either go flying into the mat or just take it as he ran down the court. Starting in his sophomore year he began to give it back and you could tell he wasn't going to be pushed around anymore."

Bradford saw Cook's competitive spirit a little earlier than others during the next to last home game of Cook's freshman year.

"We were playing against Indiana. Cook got a rebound in the middle of the lane, and threw it up there as he got hammered," recalled Bradford. "He got it back and just did this gorilla wild dunk that cleared everybody out of the middle of the lane. He was hopping up and down screaming, 'Give me the damn ball! Give me the damn ball!' It showed he could be real aggressive."

In his junior season, Cook took another step towards being a star player. With the team reeling on a three-game losing streak, he put on an inspired 19-point, nine-rebound performance in helping the team come back from a 13-point deficit to beat Michigan at Ann Arbor. Early in the second half, Cook made a play that defined how hard the Illini were going to fight during that season.

"We both dove after a loose ball and collided heads," recalled Johnson. "Both of us were basically knocked out, and earlier in his career, I would have thought Brian would be out for a week or two. He got up, played great the rest of the game, and we got a huge victory. It showed me that Brian was going to fight for you and he would be there when we needed him in the clutch."

During that same week a story was written in *Sports Illustrated* about Cook's childhood growing up in Lincoln with his mother, and his relationship with his father.

"For Brian to overcome all of that and talk about it was very important," said Judson, who was extremely close to both Cook and his mother. "His freshman and sophomore years when we played Kansas he didn't want to talk about his dad, but I think as he went on and was able to deal with those feelings it helped him mature and assume a leadership role on the court. I noticed a big difference in him after that article came out."

In the first game after the article, Cook scored 10 points and grabbed seven rebounds, but more importantly sank two crucial free throws late in the game to give Illinois a huge victory over the Spartans in the Breslin Center. For his junior season, he averaged 13.5 points and 6.7 rebounds a game on his way to earning second-team All-Big Ten honors.

By the time his junior year ended, the improvement both physically and mentally in Cook's game was astonishing.

"Of all the athletes I have watched in my 13 years as athletics director, Brian Cook grew as much as anyone," said Ron Guenther. "He grew as an individual and as a basketball player. He is a guy that took full advantage of the University experience."

Cook's growth as a player didn't happen overnight; it took years of working hard on his game.

Jonathan Daniel/Getty Images

▲ By the time Brian Cook was a senior averaging 20.0 points per game, no one was left questioning his aggressiveness. "He was the man and everybody knew it," said teammate Dee Brown.

"His work ethic was incredible and he worked hard every single day no matter what," remembered assistant coach Norm Roberts. "He is one of the hardest-working practice players I have ever been around. He would dive on the floor, he would take charges, he would run, and I mean he would do whatever it took in practice."

As a person, Cook was as nice as they come. You could talk to people all day long and still not find anyone who had something negative to say about him.

"He is as good a young man as you will ever coach," said Self. "He is a stud all-around, and it bothered me so much when people didn't say Brian played tough. If you were at practices you would see he was physical, he liked contact, and the best thing about him is that you could run a bad offense and still come away with two points when he was on the floor. He is definitely one of my all-time favorites."

"Brian was a great teammate and he was a guy who almost hurt himself because he was so respectful of the older guys on the team," recalled Robert Archibald. "We would have to tell him to shoot more."

The departure of five seniors to graduation and the NBA in 2002 meant that the 2002-03 squad would be Cook's team.

"You could tell during the summer going into our senior year that there was a different feel to him," said Sean Harrington, a fellow member of the recruiting class of 1999. "It was his last year and he wanted to go out with a bang. He worked really hard on his game that summer, hit the weights hard, and tried to teach the younger guys as much as he could."

The whole team looked up to Cook, especially the young freshmen.

"He was the man and everybody knew it coming into the season," recalled teammate Dee Brown. "He didn't show it that much because he is always a laid-back, humble guy, but when it came down to the games he always wanted the ball."

He wanted it and he got it. He hit for 22 points against North Carolina, 25 against Temple, 22 against Oakland, and by the time Big Ten play came around it was clear that Cook was a dominant player. More importantly, he led a very young team to a 10-1 record heading into the conference season.

"I think he is one of the best leaders I have ever been around," said James Augustine, who credits Cook for helping his development.

Against Minnesota in the Big Ten opener, Cook poured in 25 points and in the following game against Wisconsin he exploded for 31 in a win over the Badgers. He carried the team on his back throughout the season, which was never more evident than in a late January home game against Michigan. After a lackluster first half, Cook single-handedly willed the Illini to victory by scoring 26 of his 30 points in the second half.

Cook graduated as a senior after averaging 20 points a game and becoming the first Illini player to lead the Big Ten in scoring since Kendall Gill in 1990. He finished his Illinois career with 1,748 points, which ranks third on the all-time scoring list.

That success translated into a job in the NBA. Cook was selected 24th overall by the Los Angeles Lakers in the 2003 NBA Draft. He averaged 4.4 points a game in his rookie season and had the opportunity to play in the NBA Finals.

His years in Champaign were a long journey of maturity for Cook. He transformed from a shy and timid freshman to a confident leader able to carry a team by his senior year.

"Being a part of Illinois [basketball] was real special," reflected Cook from his home in Los Angeles. "There is so much tradition there and you have the screaming fans, the Assembly Hall, and all the guys who played there before me. It was a family atmosphere, it was a very comfortable place for me, and I wish I could go back and play six more years."

The Illinois fans wish he could too. In the 100 years of Illinois basketball, there have been few players, if any, who were more beloved than Brian Cook.

CHAPTER TWENTY

"WHAT ILLINI BASKETBALL MEANS TO ME"
REFLECTIONS FROM FORMER ILLINOIS PLAYERS AND COACHES

LEVI COBB
ILLINOIS FORWARD: 1977-1980

"What meant more to me than anything from my time at Illinois was how I was received. One of the lowest points of my playing career came as a senior, because I wasn't playing as much as I wanted to. It was late in one of the last home games I would play and the crowd just started chanting, 'Levi, Levi, Levi' because they wanted Coach to put me in. I remember thinking to myself, 'Here I am at one of the lowest moments of my playing career but the fans still respect me enough to want me to be out there.' The fans of Illinois basketball and the people of Champaign-Urbana are what made Illinois basketball special and are the reason I made the right decision to go there."

MARCUS LIBERTY
ILLINOIS FORWARD: 1989-1990

"My time playing Illinois basketball was a great experience. What made it even more special was here I was as one of the top players in the state and country during my senior year of high school and I still played my college ball in that same state. The same fans who were able to watch me and were behind me in high school got a chance to see me play a lot more than if I would have gone somewhere else. I think that showed everyone that I cared about basketball in Illinois and following the guys from Chicago who were Illini before me was really special."

MIKE WASHINGTON
ILLINOIS FORWARD: 1975-1976

"Illinois basketball was a big family. It was such a big school and had such a big following that you felt like somebody special when you were out in Champaign-Urbana. You had big people in business knowing you on a first-name basis. You could be walking out at the mall and see some president of a bank and, because he was a follower of the team, he would say 'hi' to you and ask you how you were doing. For somebody young that was very impressive and it left a lasting impression."

DON KLUSENDORF
ILLINOIS GUARD: 1984

"It means the world to me to be a part of the tradition and heritage of Illinois basketball. I've talked to people who have said, 'Didn't you want to transfer to a school where you could play more?' But I wouldn't have traded my experience at the University of Illinois for anything. It's not only the friendship of my teammates, but also the support of the fans and the community, which is something I take with me forever. As I get older and go on it means more and more to me."

JENS KUJAWA
ILLINOIS CENTER: 1986-1988

"Illinois basketball was the 'toughening up' part of my career. I never had to work—before and after my time in Champaign-Urbana—so hard in my life to reach a goal. The mental and physical stress was enormous and it prepared me very well for a 13-year professional basketball career in Germany. After surviving four-hour Illinois practices of endless suicides with only a small cup of Gatorade, practices in Germany could never measure up."

JACK BURMASTER
ILLINOIS GUARD: 1945-1948

"Everything that happened to me in my life I owe to Illinois, and, Illinois basketball in particular. I was able to have a brief fling in the NBA and then went into coaching, having a 20-year career with Evanston High School. I met so many friends down there on and off the basketball court that have been a big part of my life and I will always be a member of the Fighting Illini."

ROBERT 'CHICK' DOSTER
ILLINOIS FORWARD: 1946-1947

"I really can't put into words what Illinois basketball meant to me. It opened so many doors throughout my life. First of all, it allowed me to get an exceedingly good business education from the College of Commerce from which I am pleased to say I graduated with honors.

"Even now, more than 50 years later, I will be at an athletic event and someone will want to come over to shake my hand and talk about the good old days. I know a lot of kids don't realize this, but it is such an honor to play for your state school and that opportunity follows through for the rest of your life and opens doors you could never imagine would have opened."

PAUL NITZ
ILLINOIS FORWARD: 1964-1968

"Illinois basketball was much more than a sport to me. It was a way to see the different parts of the country. I had come from a very modest background, really hadn't traveled much, and even though I was a very good student, I wasn't a sophisticated person by any means. Without Illinois basketball, there are places throughout the United States I still wouldn't have seen today.

"Maybe more importantly, my time at Illinois taught me determination, focus, and hard work. Without it there is a very good chance I wouldn't have the education I have today, so it meant everything to me."

MARSH STONER
ILLINOIS ASSISTANT COACH: 1972-1974

"One of the greatest thrills of my life happened on my first day on the job at Illinois. My wife and family dropped me off at the Assembly Hall. Walking up to that magnificent building, knowing that I was truly a coach there, was a feeling that I still get goose bumps over. I had to pinch myself."

DEREK HARPER
ILLINOIS GUARD: 1981-1983

"Illinois basketball meant the world to me. First off, basketball and the University of Illinois gave me an education and the opportunity to better myself as person. My time there was the stepping-stone to becoming a man.

"I remember being a freshman who had come to Champaign from South Florida and having my phone cut off because I was so home sick and missed my mother. But as time went on, being on my own really made me grow up and when I look back on it I wouldn't trade my time there for anything in the world because it was the best three years of my life."

RICH ADAMS
ILLINOIS FORWARD: 1975-1978

"I was just so fortunate to be able to attend a university where I could excel at a high level not only with athletics, but on the academic side as well. It's been 30 years since I played Illinois basketball and it seems like yesterday. I really take pride in the fact that the guys in the mid to late-1970s were part of the rebuilding of Illinois basketball and that is what I always remember about my few years there.

"I am a proud alum of the University of Illinois and I take great pride, no matter where I am, in saying that I am a Fighting Illini. No one can ever take that away from me."

LARRY BAUER
ILLINOIS FORWARD: 1964

"I grew up in Springfield, Illinois watching Johnny Kerr, Bill Ridley, and those great Illinois teams in the 1950s. No one in my family or really anyone I knew in my town had gotten a college education, but I kept

telling everyone that I was going to get a scholarship to Illinois and eventually be a teacher. When I said this to people they would laugh at me.

"When I graduated high school, I had over 100 scholarship offers but there was no doubt where I wanted to go. I grew up on Illinois, grew up getting chills watching Chief Illiniwek go endzone to endzone at the football games and it means a lot to me to have been apart of that university and the basketball program."

JIM VOPICKA
ILLINOIS GUARD: 1964-1965, AND THE SON OF JAMES VOPICKA, WHO LETTERED FOR ILLINOIS FROM 1936-1937

"Illinois basketball probably means more now than it did at the time I was a player. I have lived all over the country and have been primarily on the West Coast over the last 20-30 years. But when you talk to people around the country, Illinois basketball is highly, highly regarded. So, to look back and think that I was able to be a part of that rich history is incredible I'm very proud of my time playing basketball at Illinois."

PHIL JUDSON
ILLINOIS GUARD: 1955-1956

"The Orange and Blue meant everything to me. With my brother Howie going there, my brother and I grew up around Illinois basketball and there had been so many great players who had already come out of there.

"When we were growing up in Hebron, we would play with the neighborhood kids pretending it was the state tournament. My dad was a trap shooter and he had won a trophy so that was the trophy we were playing for. One spot would be the district, then we would move to another hoop for the regional, our driveway would be the sectionals, and then this barn across the street would signify the finals in Huff Gym. We all would pick out a player we wanted to be. I was Jessie Clements, Paul was Dike Eddleman, and another would be Max Hooper. Illinois basketball was always on our mind."

STEVE LANTER
ILLINOIS GUARD: 1977, 1979

"Illinois basketball was the most enjoyable stage of my life. When I think back to a stretch that was pure enjoyment, that four years in Champaign was it. It was a period where life-long memories were made and life-long friendships were formed.

"It was also a time that prepared me for my business career. My dad always told me that if I could transfer my work ethic from athletics to the business world I would be successful, and I think at Illinois, learning how to deal with injuries and how to cope with victory and defeat, laid a great foundation."

ED PERRY
ILLINOIS FORWARD: 1958-1960

"I lived to play basketball at Illinois ever since I was in grade school. My family didn't have enough money for me to go to a large school if I didn't have a scholarship. If I wouldn't have played basketball at Illinois, I probably wouldn't be in the profession I am in today or had the experiences that I have had.

"Before I played at Illinois, I never was really far away from home and with Illinois basketball I got to go all over the country. It was just a wonderful experience for me."

PAUL JUDSON
ILLINOIS GUARD: 1954-1956

"Every time I put on the Illinois uniform I felt a thrill. It was just incredible for a young kid from Hebron like myself to be able to play for his state school as a sophomore and do well my junior and senior years. I enjoyed playing for Illinois, representing Illinois, and whenever people ask me why I went there I said, 'You play with the best at Illinois and you play against the best in the Big Ten.' I still look back at being a part of Illinois basketball as a big thrill."

T.J. WHEELER
ILLINOIS GUARD: 1992-1994

"Playing for Illinois was probably a lot different for me than for some of the guys who came from Chicago. I grew up in a town of 400 people and my whole town was Illini fans. I can still go back there today and see little kids in number 44 shirts. I guess now that I sit back and see what I did 12-13 years ago, I understand a lot more about how special Illinois basketball is.

"It also is special now to bring my son, who is four years old, into the Assembly Hall and say this is where Daddy played. I will always be able to say I had the best four years of my life, and it was because Lou Henson gave me a chance to play Fighting Illini basketball."

JAKE STAAB
ILLINOIS FORWARD: 1944-1945

"I was so thrilled and awe-struck to be able to play basketball at the University of Illinois. I couldn't have even dreamed about being able to do something like that and it was such a wonderful experience. I always felt my time playing basketball at Illinois taught me a lot about teamwork, but even more importantly, it gave me confidence and an attitude that I could do big things in life."

RICK HOWAT
ILLINOIS GUARD: 1969-1971

"I grew up around Illinois and Illinois basketball. My two oldest brothers went to Illinois and ever since I was eight years old, I had Jim Dutcher, a neighbor who played Illinois basketball in the early 1950s, bloodying me in the drive way.

"It felt great to play at Illinois and to put on that uniform each and every time. I used to love playing in the Assembly Hall and this past year I took my seven-year-old son, who loves basketball, to a few games and we even got to run around on the floor after the game. Illinois has established quite a program and I am still watching every game they play. Being a part of Illinois and Illinois basketball is something that will never leave me."

JIM DUTCHER
ILLINOIS FORWARD: 1954-1955

"It meant a great deal of pride to play basketball for Illinois. I was fortunate to be on teams that [were real good] in my time there and the worst finish we had was about 19th in the nation. We did it with all Illinois kids and when a player was invited by Harry Combes to come play basketball it was a big deal. Illinois was and is a great basketball school and I feel honored to have been a part of that."

ROGER TAYLOR
ILLINOIS GUARD: 1956-1959

"I feel very fortunate to have been able to be a part of Illinois basketball. It is a special university, and to play basketball at that level is something I will never forget. Just the other day I received the ballot for Illinois's All-Century Team and I was extremely honored to be listed on that ballot. To be there among all the great players who came before and after me was a tremendous honor."

DAVE ROBERTS
ILLINOIS FORWARD: 1973-1975

"Being part of the Illinois basketball program was a tremendous honor for me and, in spite of the fact that our team's record was less than impressive during my junior and senior years, I have many fond memories of my days as a Fighting Illini.

"Clearly some of the highlights that come to mind are the games where we competed against the finest teams of that era such as the Bill Walton-led UCLA squad in 1973 and the great Indiana teams of the mid-1970s. But my fondest memories revolve around my coaches and fellow players. We shared the joy of many victories together, but also pulled together to persevere though some difficult times. Some of the lessons that I learned during those years about dealing with adversity and pulling together as a team when things aren't going well—things that Harv Schmidt often spoke to us about—have helped me tremendously throughout my business career."

EFREM WINTERS
ILLINOIS FORWARD: 1983-1986

"I remember growing up as a kid and all we used to watch was Illinois basketball. All I wanted to do when I grew up was to be a part of the University of Illinois and their basketball program. Looking back on my time there, it meant a great deal to me to go to Illinois and to play basketball, and if I had the chance to do it all over again, I would."

CLIVE FOLLMER
ILLINOIS FORWARD/CENTER: 1951-1953

"I started out as a young kid listening to state tournaments and then as I grew up I came down to a lot of the tournaments. I don't think I ever thought seriously about going anywhere but Illinois, and it has meant a great deal to me.

"The history and the traditions are outstanding. There are very few times that I haven't watched the Chief, sung the Illinois loyalty, or been at a game that doesn't choke me up a little bit. I am very proud that I was a part of Illinois basketball."

BILL MOHLENBROCK
ILLINOIS GUARD: 1957-1961

"I was the only freshman in my class to play all four years and I think Illinois basketball taught me a lot about persistence. The best teacher I ever had in college—bar none—was my freshman coach Jim Bredar, because he taught me discipline on and off the court. I was able to translate what he taught me in practice to my studies and I think my success in getting into medical school was due to Jim Bredar's teaching.

"During my interview for medical school, I remember being terrified as the dean asked me chemistry questions. But finally he turned to me and said, 'I want to know how good those Ohio State teams really were.' So playing basketball at Illinois directly helped me get into medical school as well.

"It was a great experience, I made great friends who I am still very close to today, and I really believe I wouldn't be where I am today without Illinois basketball.'

BILL RIDLEY
ILLINOIS GUARD: 1954-1956

"Being a part of Illinois basketball meant everything to me back then and I didn't even realize at the time how big it really was. After you play at Illinois and you travel around the state, it's amazing how many people remember you.

"Now my wife and I have become super fans of the program. She really knows the game, the team, and we watch every game together. She puts on her orange and blue, I sit down in my chair, and that is a night when everyone knows not to call us.

"It was an honor to play at Illinois, and I realize that today more than ever."

CHAPTER TWENTY ONE

FAVORITE ILLINI MEMORIES
FROM UI'S CELEBRITY ALUMNI
AND FAMOUS ILLINOIS RESIDENTS

GENE SHALIT
(ILLINOIS STUDENT FROM 1943-1949 AND CURRENT NBC TODAY SHOW CRITIC)

"The huge cage rivalry at the time was Illinois-Iowa because the Hawkeyes had brothers named Clayton and Herb Wilkinson who were a fabulous pair. I remember collapsing from excitement in the press box during an Illinois-Iowa game and (former sports information director) Chuck Flynn rushing to my rescue thinking I had had a heart attack. It was actually a Hawkeye Attack! I was embarrassed; after all, I was supposed to be a professional sports writer."

GEORGE M.C. FISHER
(ILLINOIS STUDENT FROM 1958-1962 AND RETIRED CHAIRMAN AND CEO OF EASTMAN KODAK CO.)

"One of the things I remember most about Illinois basketball was Huff Gymnasium. The noise level in that place was incredible. You couldn't help but get into the game as a fan, and I am sure the players felt that way too. It didn't hold that many people, but that gym just reverberated with energy."

ROGER EBERT
(ILLINOIS STUDENT FROM 1960-1964, 1966 AND CURRENT PULITZER PRIZE-WINNING FILM CRITIC FOR THE CHICAGO SUN-TIMES AND THE TELEVISION SHOW EBERT & ROEPER)

"What I remember most vividly is attending Illini home games in Huff Gymnasium, which when it was packed with supporters generated an unbelievable noise volume. It was in the early to mid-1950s and my dad would take me. Sitting there next to my dad during those games is one of the most precious memories of my life.

"The coach was Harry Combes, a true legend. My heroes were Johnny Kerr and the Judson twins. When I met Kerr in person, years later when he was a Bulls announcer, I was amazed at the hero worship I felt."

BILL GEIST
(ILLINOIS STUDENT FROM 1964-1968 AND CURRENT CBS NEWS CORRESPONDENT AND AUTHOR)

"I loved Huff Gym. It was a real home-court advantage because it was so noisy, and I mean there would be a horrifying racket in that building during the games.

"Sometimes it wasn't that easy to get into a game in Huff, because it was a tough ticket. I remember sneaking into Huff with some friends the night before the state tournaments and sleeping in a closet just so we could be in the building and watch guys like Govoner Vaughn and Mannie Jackson."

SCOTT ALTMAN
(ILLINOIS STUDENT FROM 1977-1981 AND CURRENT NASA ASTRONAUT)

"I remember being in the first ever Orange Krush section in 1979 and I will never forget being in the building when the Illini took on Magic Johnson's top-ranked Michigan State Spartans during Christmas break of the 1978-79 basketball season. The game was an emotional rush, and the Assembly Hall was just crazy that day. I vividly recall Eddie Johnson drilling the jumper from the corner to cap off one of those fall-down-on-the-ground, emotional-rollercoaster-type games.

"A guy I was a friend with in Naval graduate school was a huge Indiana basketball fan and I remember going over to his place to watch the 1989 game in Bloomington. It didn't look good, but when Nick Anderson buried that shot to win the game it was a great thrill and it gave me bragging rights for a little while."

DICK MURPHY
(ILLINOIS STUDENT FROM 1961-1965 AND CURRENT MAYOR OF SAN DIEGO)

"My Illinois basketball memories pre-date the time I came down to Illinois as a student. I remember as a little kid sitting with my father and listening to Illinois basketball games when they had Bruce Brothers, Bill Ridley and guys like that. Both my parents graduated from Illinois, so from a very early age Illinois basketball was a part of my life.

"At school, my favorite Illinois basketball memory was the 1964 opening game against UCLA. The Bruins were the unbeatable team at the time with John Wooden and Gail Goodrich at guard, but the Illini really handled them that day in the Assembly Hall."

JOE TANNER
(ILLINOIS STUDENT FROM 1968-1973 AND CURRENT NASA ASTRONAUT)

"I didn't get a chance to attend too many basketball games while I was at Illinois, because I was on the swim team and we were either at a practice, away at a meet, or too tired to do anything else. But I have become a much bigger Illinois basketball fan since I graduated and follow them as much as I can down here in Texas.

"There are a lot of friendly bragging rights down here in the NASA program. Just before the big Sweet 16 game against Duke in 2004, I heard a fellow Illini graduate and astronaut, Lee Archambault, over the radio and I said, 'ILL' into the radio and got an 'INI' from Lee right back at me."

GEORGE WILL
(FORMER CHAMPAIGN RESIDENT FROM 1941-1958 AND CURRENT PULITZER PRIZE-WINNING WRITER, AUTHOR, AND SYNDICATED COLUMNIST)

"My first memories of Illinois basketball come in Huff Gym and are more specifically memories of the state tournament. To be a basketball fan in Illinois at the time was to be mesmerized by the tournament, and one of my earliest state tournament memories was watching Hebron High School and the Judson brothers win the title in 1952. It was a time in Champaign where Harry Combes was a celebrity and people still talked all the time about the Whiz Kids.

"I remember watching the Judsons when they came down to Illinois along with guys like George BonSalle and Bill Ridley. Ridley was my favorite player, because, like me, he wasn't very tall and wore glasses. One major difference is that he was a great basketball player and I wasn't."

ANG LEE
(ILLINOIS STUDENT FROM 1978-1980 AND CURRENT AWARD-WINNING FILM DIRECTOR)

"Coming from Taiwan, I loved to watch basketball and I can vividly remember my first Illinois basketball memory. I went over to the Student Center in the Union to buy a ticket to an exhibition game against the Russian National Team over at the Assembly Hall. Walking up to that 'UFO-like' building that night was impressive. It is such a gorgeous arena. That night, the height of the players, the skill, and the dunks were just amazing. It was jaw-dropping.

"What I will never forget from my time at Illinois was being in the stands to see the Illini play Michigan State and Magic Johnson in 1979. The building was crazy that night, and it was an atmosphere I had never seen before. I can remember Eddie Johnson hitting that last shot. We all went nuts and the Assembly Hall was shaking. Everybody was thumping, yelling, and when we got outside of the stadium the whole town was honking their cars. Walking out of the stadium that night everyone was chanting, 'Who believes in Magic—not the Fighting Illini!'"

BILL LYON
(ILLINOIS STUDENT FROM 1952-1956 AND CURRENT SPORTS COLUMNIST FOR THE PHILADELPHIA ENQUIRER)

"Growing up, my first real memories of Illinois basketball centered around Dike Eddleman. He was probably about 6-5, but to a young kid he might as well had been over seven feet tall.

"After finishing school, I went to work for the *News-Gazette* and I was always assigned to the opposing lock-er room in Huff Gym. I remember watching those great Ohio State teams with Lucas and Havlicek. Every year their coach, Fred Taylor, would meet with the press out near the floor, look around Huff, and say, 'You know this is the first time we have won here since the Civil War.' I guess he had forgotten they won something like eight in a row.

"I'll never forget when the Assembly Hall opened and we called it the 'Mushroom on the Meadow' because it looked like someone dropped a flying saucer in the middle of the agricultural test fields."

JEAN DRISCOLL
(ILLINOIS STUDENT FROM 1987-1991 AND CURRENT CHAMPION WHEELCHAIR ATHLETE)

"I was new to the orange and blue culture of Illinois in 1987. I grew up in Wisconsin and was accustomed to red and white. I'll never forget looking out my window at Garner Hall during my first couple of weeks in Champaign and gasping at the sea of orange and blue everywhere. It felt like culture shock!

"As I began to follow the sports teams, however, I became accustomed to the colors. When I started competing, I was very proud to wear them. During my second year at Illinois, the men's basketball team went to the Final Four. One of the celebrity athletes on that team, Kendall Gill, was in one of my speech communication classes and there was a lot of talk about his NBA prospects. I bought a "Battle to Seattle" t-shirt that year and it was my favorite t-shirt for at least five years. The electricity in Champaign-Urbana was contagious and exciting. It still is one of my fondest Illinois sports memories, despite the outcome of the national championship semifinal game."

SAM SKINNER
(ILLINOIS STUDENT FROM 1956-1960 AND SECRETARY OF TRANSPORTATION/CHIEF OF STAFF DURING THE FIRST GEORGE BUSH ADMINISTRATION)

"I first became interested in Illinois basketball from watching Hebron High School win the state championship. After that, the Judson twins went down to

Illinois, and I just kept following their careers, because we all felt like we knew those guys so well.

"My fondest Illinois basketball memory since I graduated was being able to see Lou Henson coach in his final season at Indiana against Bobby Knight. I was a professor at Indiana at the time and, of course, I had watched Lou for so many years and it was kind of an emotional thing to be a part of his last game in Bloomington."

ROBERT NOVAK
(ILLINOIS STUDENT FROM 1948-1952 AND CURRENT CNN POLITICAL COMMENTATOR)

"I was 11 years old when my father took me to Chicago Stadium to watch the Whiz Kids play Northwestern (February 27, 1943). There was a sellout crowd of about 20,000 people there to watch the Whiz Kids play against a pretty good Northwestern team that had Otto Graham. The Whiz Kids won that game 86-44, and 86 points at the time was an incredible number of points to score.

"When I first got down to school, I asked around about how to get tickets to the basketball games. In the student plan, because the gym was so small, you only got about a third of the games in the season. Well, I couldn't deal with that, so I found out the only way to guarantee you to get into Huff for every game was to be an usher. To get an usher position with basketball you first had to be a football usher and then get randomly selected. So I joined up to be a football usher and guess what, I was selected to be a basketball usher, so I never missed a game in that great 1948-49 season."

BONNIE BLAIR
(FORMER CHAMPAIGN RESIDENT AND WORLD FAMOUS OLYMPIC SPEED SKATER)

"I always thought the basketball program had a really cool facility in the Assembly Hall. It is unique in structure and as far as basketball arenas go what better place is there to play college basketball games? On game days in Champaign there would always be a buzz and people were always talking about the Illini.

"Around 1994, I had the chance to sit front row at Madison Square Garden at a New York Knicks game and I remember thinking that these guys were bigger than life. After the game, I had the chance to go backstage and Derek Harper picked me out and came over to shake my hand. He said, 'I went to the University of Illinois,' and we talked about Champaign for a little bit. To me it was impressive that someone of his stature knew who I was, but it shows how connected the community and Illinois basketball is.

"Today I am living in Wisconsin, but I still feel connected to the Illinois basketball team. I always look to see how they are doing and where they are in the standings. Even when they are playing Wisconsin, I am still rooting for the Illini."

RICH FRANK
(ILLINOIS STUDENT FROM 1960-1965 AND FORMER PRESIDENT OF DISNEY STUDIOS, CURRENT PRESIDENT OF FIRM ENTERTAINMENT)

"I was from Brooklyn, N.Y. so my first real Illinois basketball memories came on campus. I remember playing in Huff Gym myself during physical education classes, but I will never forget going to basketball games there. It sat about 6,000 people, but it was so packed that it seemed like there were 100,000 people in the gym.

"It seemed like everybody was one step off the court and it was really tough to play there. It was very intimidating, because if you took a shot from the baseline or near the out-of-bounds-line, the student body was basically on top of you, and they were always getting on the opposing teams.

"I have had a chance to follow Illinois since I graduated and my biggest disappointment was seeing them lose in person in Seattle. I couldn't even stick around after that loss, it was so hard to take. The program is in great shape now and I look forward to great things in the future."

EPILOGUE

BY BRIAN COOK

There are many things that I treasure in life such as God, family, basketball and friendships. But one of my favorite treasures is the time that I spent in Champaign-Urbana. The four years I spent at Illinois were some of the best years of my young life and something I will never, ever forget.

I grew up in the small central Illinois town of Lincoln with my mother and two sisters. I was so attached to them growing up that I felt like I was the man of the house. The proximity of the University of Illinois to my hometown afforded me the opportunity to check up on my family and really pay attention to how they were doing. So, when Illinois started recruiting me, there wasn't any doubt in my mind—it was the school for me.

I can remember going to Illini games in high school and feeling really comfortable with the fans, the people in the community, the institution and the teammates that I would have at Illinois. It felt like home, and it felt like a place where I could be secure. I also believed that the University of Illinois would give me the best guidance in terms of becoming a better person and finding success in my career after college.

Throughout high school, I played in a number of local tournaments where I first watched and then played against guys like Sergio McClain, Marcus Griffin, Frank Williams, Lucas Johnson, Damir Krupalija and Jerrance Howard. Those guys—along with Cory Bradford, Nate Mast, Sean Harrington, Robert Archibald, Joe Cross, Dee Brown, Deron Williams, James Augustine, and many others—became my teammates. These were the guys I battled with and laughed with, and we all shared countless memorable experiences together.

▲ *Brian Cook, one of 20 members of Illinois' All-Century Team, is surrounded by adoring Orange Krush fans.*

Each of them brought something unique to the table. Every single one of them was competitive. Sergio, Marcus and Frank had won the last four state championships at Peoria Manual. Lucas and Damir were the top players on their high school teams, and they brought determination and grit. Robert was a very tough big man who could really play. Cory was a great shooter and a tough individual, and Jerrance was the best point guard in the state of Illinois during our senior year in high school. Jerrance brought an incredible attitude to the team. He was a "glue guy" who promoted team unity while being a great leader on the floor. Jerrance and I became great friends and decided to attend the University of Illinois together so that we could be teammates.

I knew with the guys we had at Illinois that we were going to be a great team. We all knew that we wanted to be great, and we put a lot of sweat and tears into our time at Illinois. All of the guys I played with made my time at Illinois that much greater because I made so many friends and got to know so many different types of people. Going to a school with over 36,000 people, how could you not?

My time spent at Illinois was the best thing that happened to me. I thank God that I learned all the things I did in my time there, and I look back now and realize just how many life lessons I learned. I learned how to flip negatives into positives, and that to me is what life is all about. I learned that you have to have confidence in yourself before you start winning, both on the court and in life. I want to take this chance to thank the teachers, coaches and family that I had around me who helped me become what I always wanted to be—an NBA basketball player.

The future of Illinois basketball is in good hands with the current coaches and players who are in place. Coach Bruce Weber and his staff are very good coaches who are going to keep the winning tradition alive in Champaign-Urbana. With players like Dee Brown, Deron Williams, Roger Powell, Luther Head, James Augustine, Nick Smith, and the younger players our senior class left behind, there is a tremendous amount of potential. A trademark of Illinois basketball through the years has been older players passing down to the younger guys the meaning of competitiveness and teamwork and a will to win. This is how the teams that I was on became so good. It came from the leadership of the upperclassmen who showed the younger guys how to play as a team and win. With the group of players Illinois currently has and the momentum that the program has been building, I believe the future is very bright for the University of Illinois, the entire state of Illinois and Illini fans everywhere. The tradition of Fighting Illini basketball lives on...